NEWCASTLE AND NORTHUMBERLAND
Roman and Medieval Architecture and Art

General Editor Alixe Bovey

Professor Martin Henig addresses conference delegates at Housesteads Roman fort

NEWCASTLE AND NORTHUMBERLAND
Roman and Medieval Architecture and Art

Edited by
Jeremy Ashbee and Julian Luxford

The British Archaeological Association

Conference Transactions XXXVI

Cover illustration: The castle keep, Newcastle upon Tyne, from the south-east
Photo: Steven Brindle

The publication of colour plates in this volume has been assisted by a grant from the Marc Fitch Fund

ISBN Hardback 978 1 907975 92 9
Paperback 978 1 907975 93 6

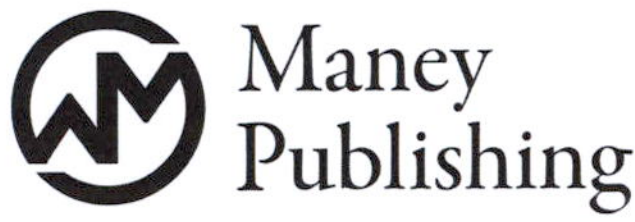

PUBLISHED FOR THE BRITISH ARCHAEOLOGICAL ASSOCIATION BY MANEY PUBLISHING
JOSEPH'S WELL, HANOVER WALK, LEEDS LS3 1AB, UK
PRINTED AND BOUND BY CHARLESWORTH PRESS, WAKEFIELD, UK

List of Abbreviations

AA	*Archaeologia Aeliana*
Antiq. J.	*Antiquaries Journal*
Archaeol. J.	*Archaeological Journal*
BAA Trans.	*British Archaeological Association Conference Transactions*
Bede, *EH*	*Bede's Ecclesiastical History of the English People*, ed. and trans. B. Colgrave and R. A. B. Mynors (Oxford 1969)
B/E Northumberland	N. Pevsner and I. Richmond, *Northumberland, the Buildings of England,* 2nd edn (New Haven, CT and London 2002)
BL	London, British Library
Carlisle and Cumbria	*Carlisle and Cumbria. Roman and Meieval Architecture, Art and Archaeology*, ed. M. McCarthy and D. Weston, *British Archaeological Association Conference Transactions* XXVII (Leeds 2004)
CSIR	*Corpus Signorum Imperii Romani* [multiple editors, multiple volumes published in fascicles]
HN	[Various authors], *A History of Northumberland*, 15 vols (Newcastle upon Tyne and London 1893–1940)
JBAA	*Journal of the British Archaeological Association*
ODNB	*Oxford Dictionary of National Biography*, 60 vols (Oxford 2004)
PL	*Patrologiæ Cursus Completus: Series Latina*, ed. J.-P. Migne, 221 vols (Paris 1844-64) plus supplements and indices (1958–74)
SS	Surtees Society
TNA	The National Archives, Kew

Contents

Preface

THE SUMMER conference of 2010 took place between Saturday 17 and Wednesday 21 July in Newcastle upon Tyne, with the theme *Newcastle and Northumberland*. The Association had not visited the region for over a century, despite several near misses, notably Durham in 1977 and Carlisle in 2001. The city and county possess, nonetheless, many features eminently worthy of a conference, and a chance conversation between the convenors in 2005 turned into a recitation of some of them, rapidly evolving over the course of an evening into a provisional conference programme. These included, in no order of significance: the Roman remains of Hadrian's Wall and military and civilian settlements associated with it, monuments and artefacts from the early period of Christianity in Northumberland, including the remains of St Paul's monastery in Jarrow and the evocative crypt and other fragments of Bishop Wilfrid's cathedral at Hexham, a number of fine and important monastic sites and parish churches of the later middle ages, and an outstanding body of castles and fortified houses, not least the surviving keep and gatehouse of 'the new castle upon the Tyne' and a pre-eminent group comprising the castles at Alnwick, Bamburgh, Dunstanburgh and Warkworth.

The study area, the county of Northumberland and the former county of Tyne and Wear, is not only rich in archaeological and architectural remains, it is also enormous. The decision was therefore taken early in planning that while presented papers and the resultant transactions should address as wide as possible a range of sites and topics, the programme of excursions would of necessity be much more restricted. For reasons as much practical as scholarly, site visits were to be concentrated in the southern part of the region around the river Tyne: to buildings in the historic centre of Newcastle, east to Jarrow and Tynemouth, and west to Bywell, Housesteads Roman fort, Hexham and Aydon. The programme presented an interesting contrast to the previous year's very successful and highly praised conference at Canterbury, at which there had been an understandable focus on one central building, the cathedral, comparatively few papers about the wider area of East Kent and no excursions outside the city. The intention behind the planning of the 2010 conference was to make a virtue of the dispersed and varied nature of the subject matter.

The conference was attended by about one hundred delegates from all parts of the United Kingdom and from the Republic of Ireland, Germany, and the United States of America. We were pleased to welcome seven student scholars, who made a valued contribution to the social life of the conference, and one of whom gave a paper. In total, twenty-four speakers presented papers in the Herschel Lecture Theatre on the campus of the University of Newcastle, and a number of site presentations were given during the excursions, several speakers coping valiantly with weather most unconducive to open-air public speaking. Site-presenters included Steven Brindle (Newcastle castle keep), Eric Cambridge (Saint Nicholas's cathedral in Newcastle and the two churches at Bywell), Rosemary Cramp (Saint Paul's monastery and church, Jarrow), John McNeill (Tynemouth priory), Philip Dixon (Bywell and Aydon castles), Martin Henig (Housesteads Roman fort), Peter Fergusson (Hexham moot hall) and Geoff Brandwood, Jenny Alexander, Charles Tracy and John Crook (all Hexham abbey). Grace McCombie, Dave Heslop and colleagues devised and led the walking tour of the centre of Newcastle on Sunday afternoon.

Following established tradition of the summer conferences, the members were entertained at evening drinks receptions and meals in fittingly historic locations. Thus the proceedings of the first evening ended with the President's Reception and supper in the magnificent surroundings of the newly re-ordered galleries of the Great North Museum (formerly Hancock Museum) adjacent to the campus, where David Breeze, President of the Society of Antiquaries of Newcastle-upon-Tyne, gave a brief introduction to the museum's re-presentation and the Society's work there. On the following evening, after a walking tour of historic buildings in the centre of Newcastle, we were received in the Neville Hall of the Mining Institute by the Leader of Newcastle City Council, Councillor Lord John Shipley OBE, who welcomed the Association and gave a short and inspiring speech on the importance of Newcastle's history to the city's strong and distinctive identity. At the end of the excursion westward along the Tyne valley and Hadrian's Wall, where members had been given lunch in the quire stalls of Hexham abbey (a strong contender for the most memorable dining location ever experienced at a conference) the Association enjoyed a drinks reception in the 13th-century Aydon castle, made possible by an admirable display by our coach-drivers of long-distance reversing along impossibly narrow lanes, followed by a most convivial dinner in the 1774 Assembly Rooms in the centre of Newcastle.

The organizers are indebted to our hosts, Newcastle University, and to a number of institutions and individuals for granting us access and a warm welcome at the historic sites visited: the staff of English Heritage at Tynemouth priory, Housesteads Roman fort and Aydon castle, the custodian of Newcastle castle keep, the Newcastle guildhall, the Master and Brethren of the Trinity House, the Dean and Chapter of Newcastle, the Vicar and verger of Saint Paul's church, Jarrow and the staff of Bede's World, the Vicar of Bywell and the Churches Conservation Trust, Lord Allendale, and the vicar and vergers of Hexham abbey. The two last-mentioned are particularly thanked for allowing us to visit Bywell castle, not normally open to members of the public, and for opening literally all parts of Hexham abbey, from below-ground archaeological remains to the triforium.

The convenors also wish to express their deep gratitude to all the speakers, session chairs and site-presenters for preparing and delivering their presentations with scholarship and aplomb. Throughout the last year before the conference was convened, two people in particular provided invaluable guidance, advice, local contact details, and negotiation: Dave Heslop, County Archaeologist for Tyne and Wear, and Grace McCombie, most recently author of the 'Pevsner City Guide', *Newcastle and Gateshead* (New Haven and London 2009). Time and again, they suggested improvements to the programme and made arrangements to implement them: that the conference could take its eventual form is very largely a testament to their commitment to showing their town and county to interested visitors. From within the membership, our thanks are due most of all to Natalie Hill, our indefatigable honorary conference secretary, and to Kate Davey, in her first year as honorary conference organizer, who ran a challenging and complex programme with patience and apparently effortless command and efficiency.

Our final thanks go to Peter Draper, for whose presidency of the association the Newcastle conference was something of a swansong. His wise leadership, instinctive capacity for finding the right remark, and kind and supportive presence to all members were abundantly in evidence throughout the conference, just as they had been since he took over the presidency in 2005.

Jeremy Ashbee and Julian Luxford
Conference convenors

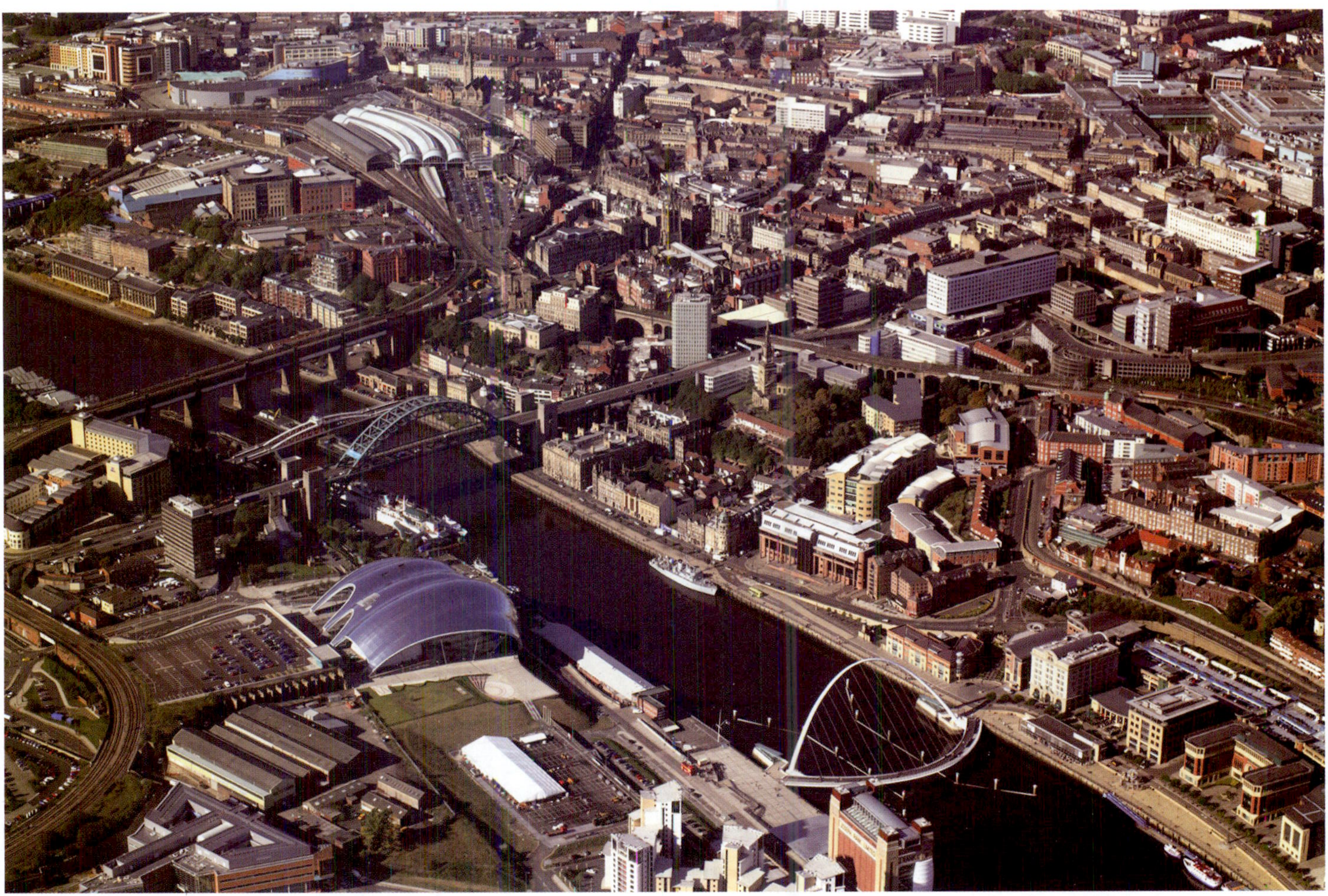

PLATE I (HESLOP AND MCCOMBIE FIG. 1). The bridging point across the Tyne between Gateshead (foreground) and Newcastle, from the south-east

Aerial photo by Steve Brock

COLOUR PLATE II

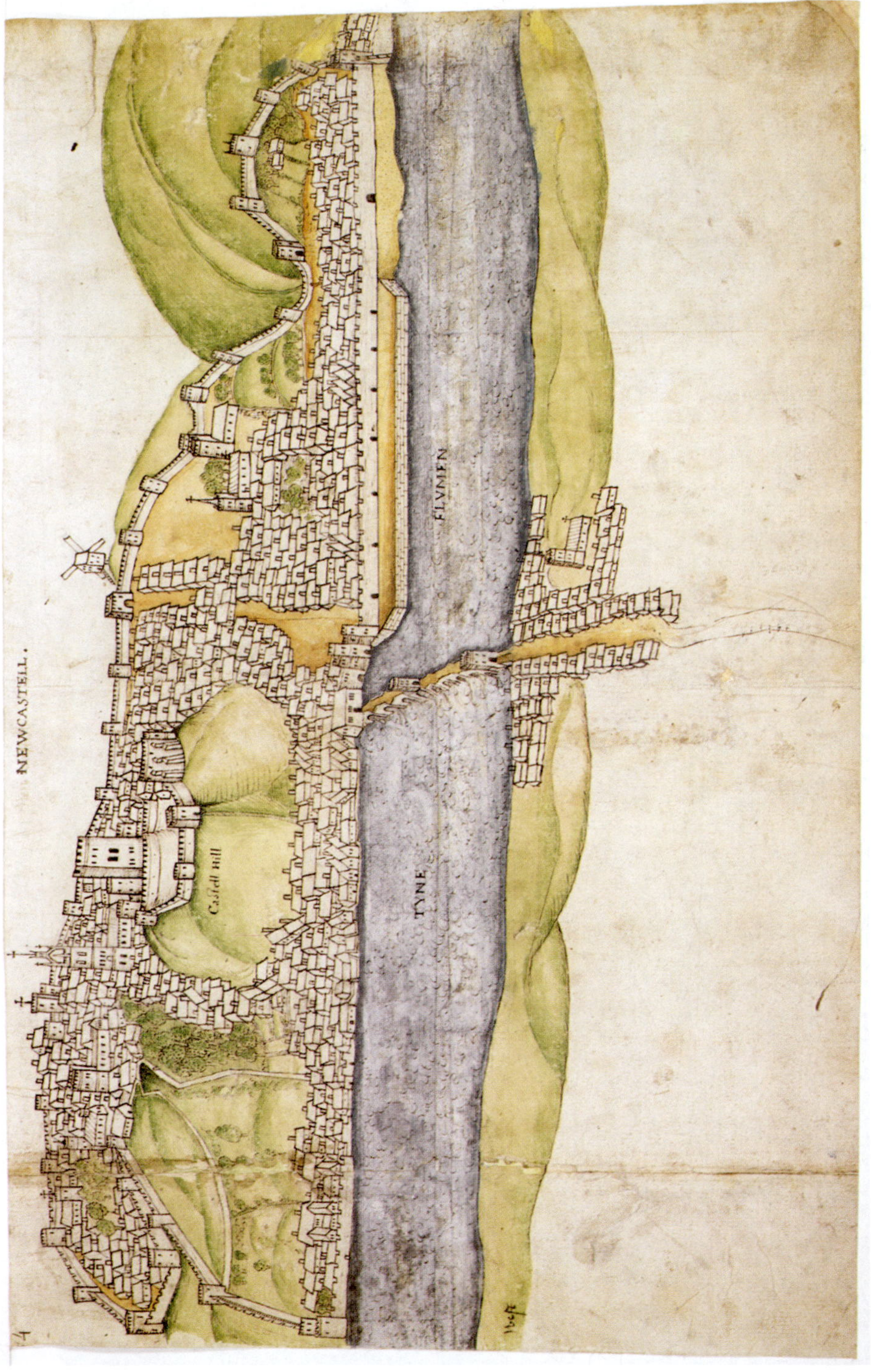

Plate II (Heslop and McCombie Fig. 4). A Tudor view of Newcastle, now BL, MS Cotton Augustus I.ii.4. This map shows the principal features of the medieval town: crowded streets encircled by the town wall, the river with shipping tied up downstream from the bridge, and overlooking the bridge, the Norman castle with its strong keep

Reproduced by permission of the British Library Board

COLOUR PLATE III

PLATE III (HESLOP AND MCCOMBIE FIG. 7). 55–57 Westgate Road; staircase plaster and Venetian window. Sophistication of early 18th-century Newcastle

By kind permission of Mike Tilley. Courtesy of English Heritage; © English Heritage and James Davies

COLOUR PLATE IV

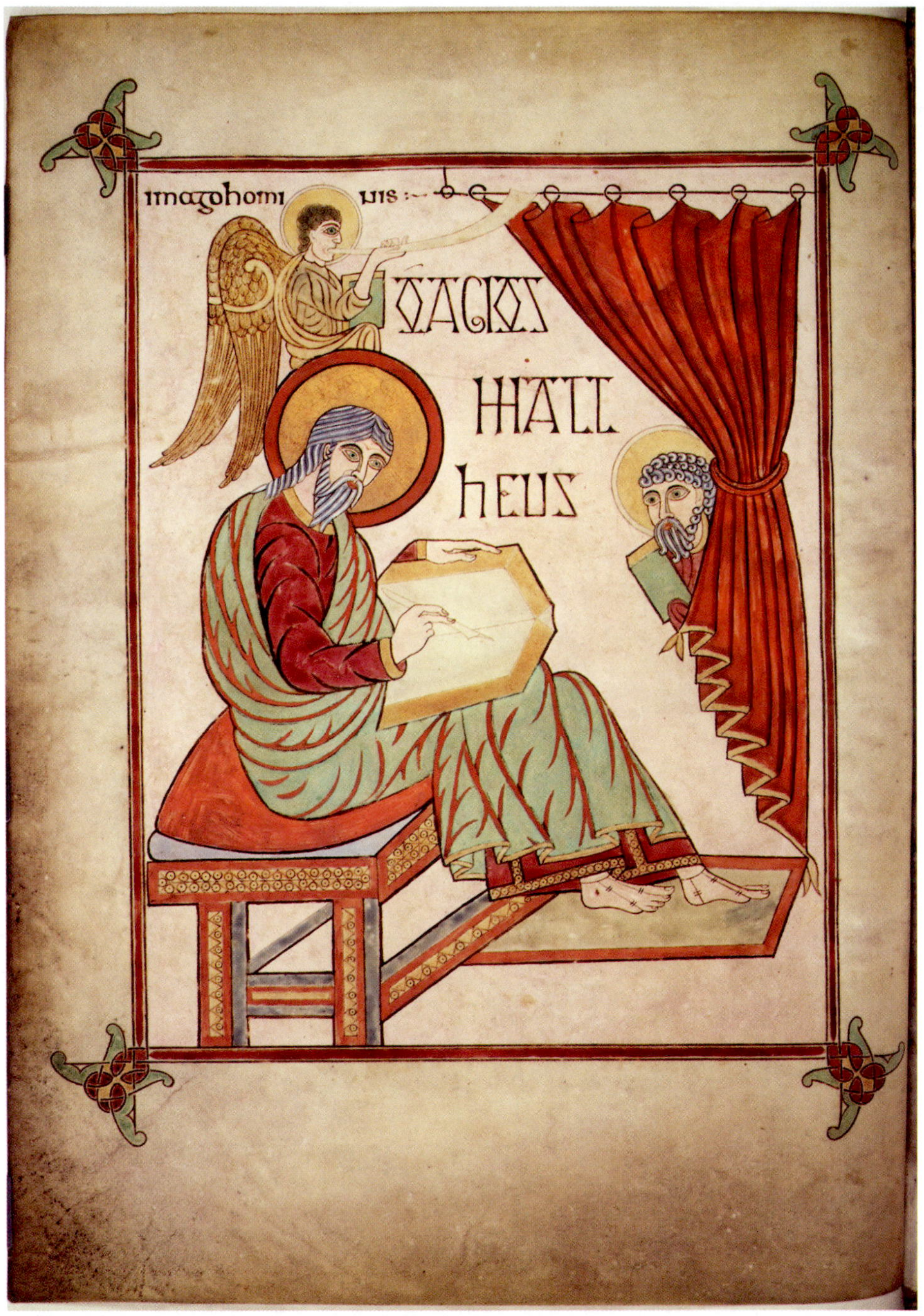

Plate IV (Pulliam Fig. 1). Lindisfarne Gospels, British Library Cotton MS Nero D.IV, Matthew Portrait page, fol. 25v

COLOUR PLATE V

Plate V (Pulliam Fig. 2). Lindisfarne Gospels British Library Cotton MS Nero D.IV, Mark Portrait page, fol. 93v

COLOUR PLATE VI

PLATE VI (PULLIAM FIG. 3). Lindisfarne Gospels, British Library Cotton MS Nero D.IV, Luke Portrait page, fol. 137v

COLOUR PLATE VII

PLATE VII (PULLIAM FIG. 4). Lindisfarne Gospels, British Library Cotton MS Nero D.IV, John Portrait page, fol. 209v

PLATE VIII (PULLIAM FIG. 5). Lindisfarne Gospels, British Library Cotton MS Nero D.IV, John carpet page, fol. 210v

Plate IX (Pulliam Fig. 6). Lindisfarne Gospels, British Library Cotton MS Nero D.IV, John carpet page, fol. 210v, detail

PLATE X (PULLIAM FIG. 7). Lindisfarne Gospels, British Library Cotton MS Nero D.IV, John Portrait page, fol. 209v, detail

PLATE XI (PULLIAM FIG. 8). Lindisfarne Gospels, British Library Cotton MS Nero D.IV, Matthew Portrait page, fol. 25v, detail

COLOUR PLATE XII

PLATE XII (PULLIAM FIG. 9). Lindisfarne Gospels British Library Cotton MS Nero D.IV, Mark Portrait page, fol. 93v, detail

PLATE XIII (PULLIAM Fig. 10). Lindisfarne Gospels, British Library Cotton MS Nero D.IV, Luke Portrait page, fol. 137v, detail

Plate XIV (Pulliam Fig. 11). Book of Durrow, Dublin, Trinity College Library, MS A. 4. 5. (57), fol. 21v

PLATE XV (PULLIAM FIG. 12). Book of Durrow, Dublin, Trinity College Library, MS A. 4. 5. (57), fol. 84v

PLATE XVI (PULLIAM FIG. 13). Durham Cathedral Library A.II.17, Crucifixion page, fol. 38v

COLOUR PLATE XVII

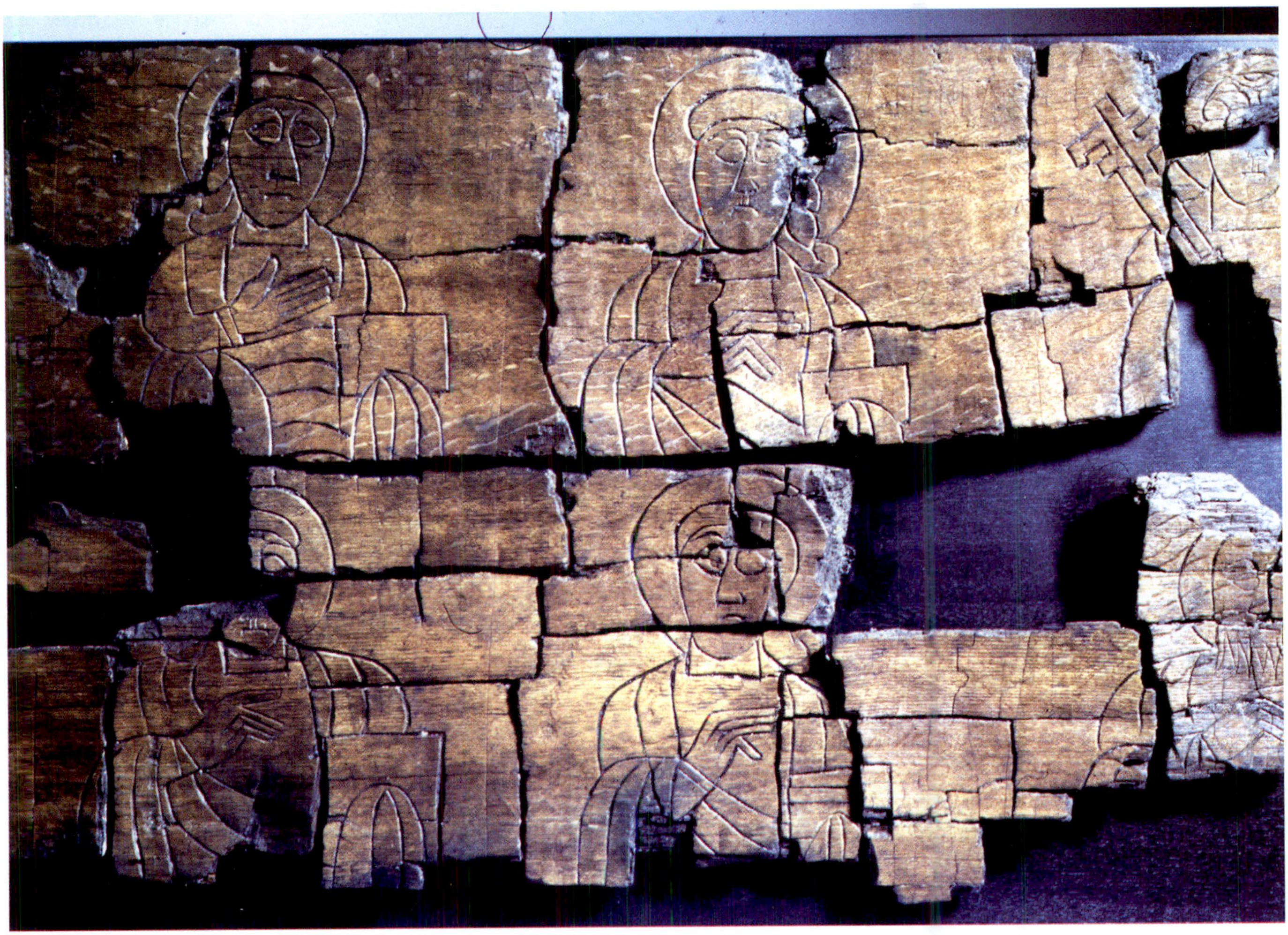

Plate XVII (Ní Ghrádaigh and Mullins Fig. 1). Detail of the apostles, John and Andrew. St Cuthbert's coffin

By kind permission of the Dean and Chapter, Durham

PLATE XVIII (BRINDLE FIG. 1). The castle keep, Newcastle upon Tyne, from the south-east

COLOUR PLATE XIX

Plate XIX (Brindle Fig. 4). A conjectural reconstruction of the south-east side of the castle keep as it was first built, showing it with higher battlements and turrets. The lost outer part of the fore-building, connecting it to the dividing wall between the two baileys, is also shown

COLOUR PLATE XX

PLATE XX (BRINDLE FIG. 5). A conjectural reconstruction of the south-east side of the castle keep, taking a section through the fore-building steps and showing the chapel beneath the steps, the putative upper chapel opening off the landing, and reconstructing the lost entrance to the doorway over the fore-building

Plate XXI (Brindle Fig. 6). A conjectural reconstruction of the original 12th-century roof over the keep, based on contemporary examples in Normandy and the evidence of the beam sockets

COLOUR PLATE XXII

PLATE XXII (ALEXANDER FIG. 16). View across the eastern side of the transepts from the south-west

COLOUR PLATE XXIII

Plate XXIII (Tracy Fig. 1). Hexham abbey: pulpitum from west

C. Tracy

COLOUR PLATE XXIV

PLATE XXIV (FAWCETT FIG. 1). Tynemouth priory, viewed from the north-west
Author

PLATE XXV (FAWCETT FIG. 7). Tynemouth priory: the internal east and south walls of the feretory and presbytery
Author

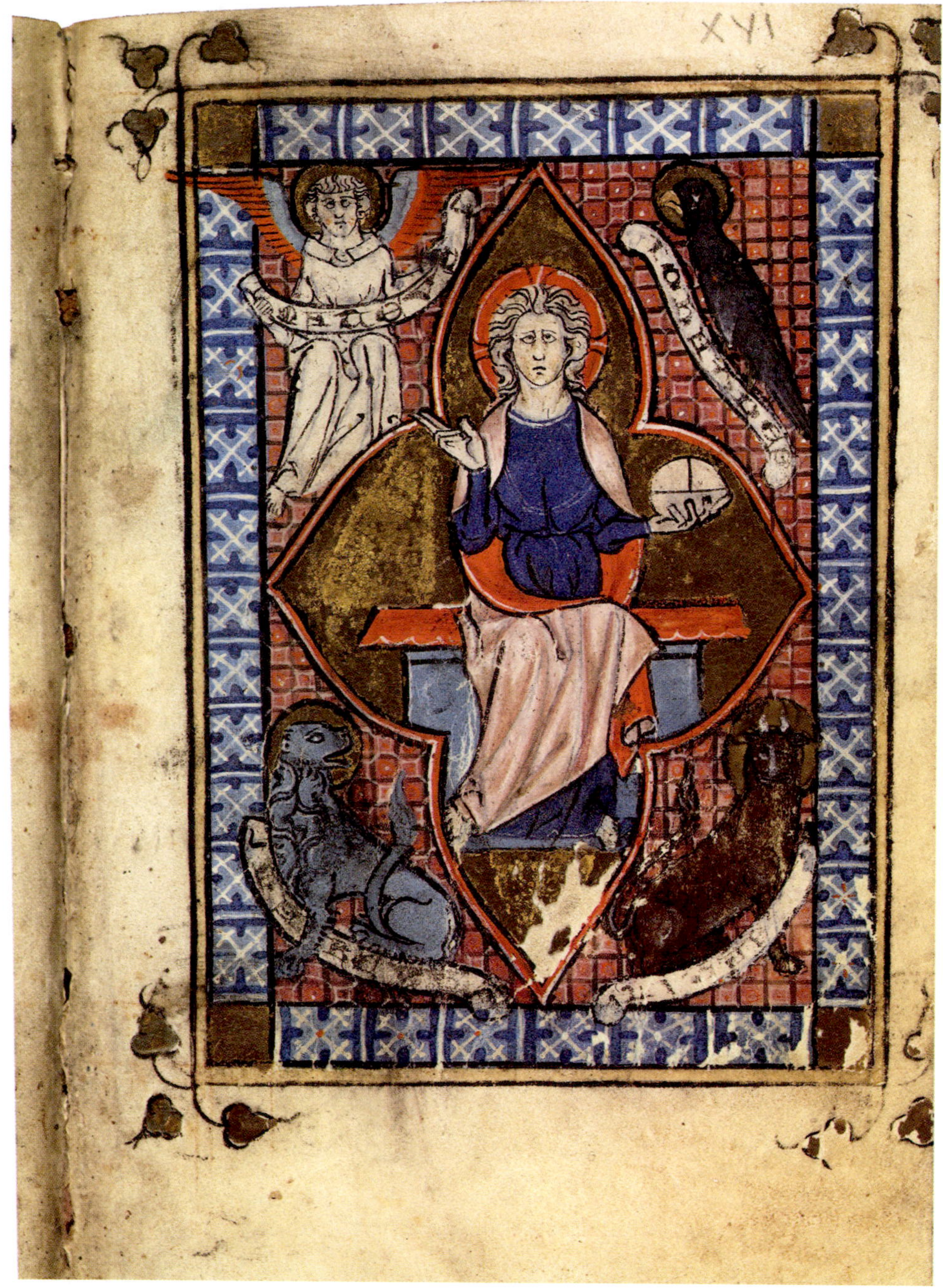

PLATE XXVI (LUXFORD FIG. 8). Oxford, Bodleian Library MS Gough lit.18, fol. xvir. This image of Christ in Majesty is one of four early 14th-century images which precede a Tynemouth/St Albans calendar added in the early 15th century

Reproduced by permission of the Bodleian Library, Oxford

COLOUR PLATE XXVII

PLATE XXVII (GOODALL FIG. 1). View of Alnwick Castle from the north-east

Paul Barker / Country Life Picture Library

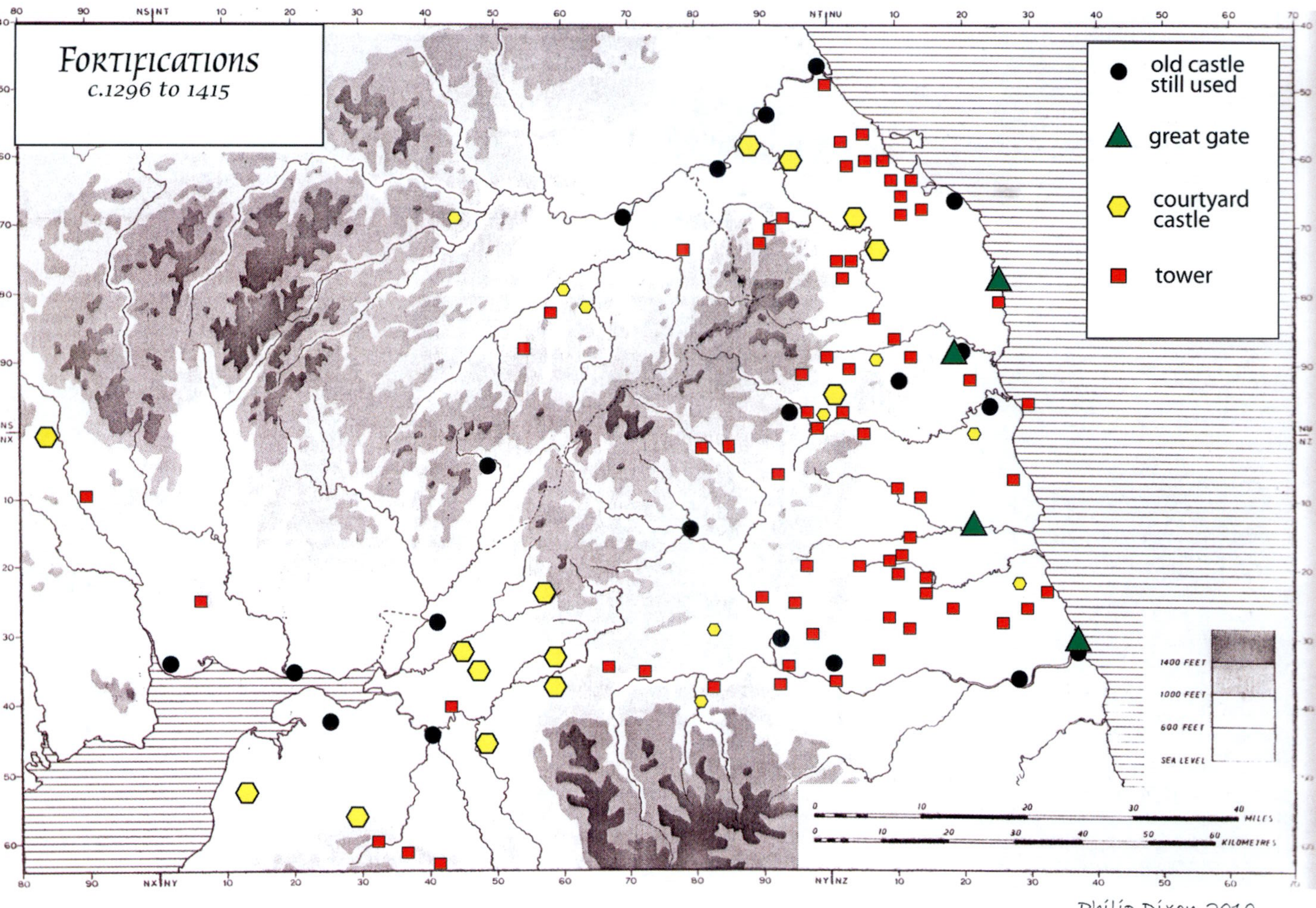

Plate XXVIII (Dixon Fig. 3). Fortifications in the region in the first stage of the Wars of Independence

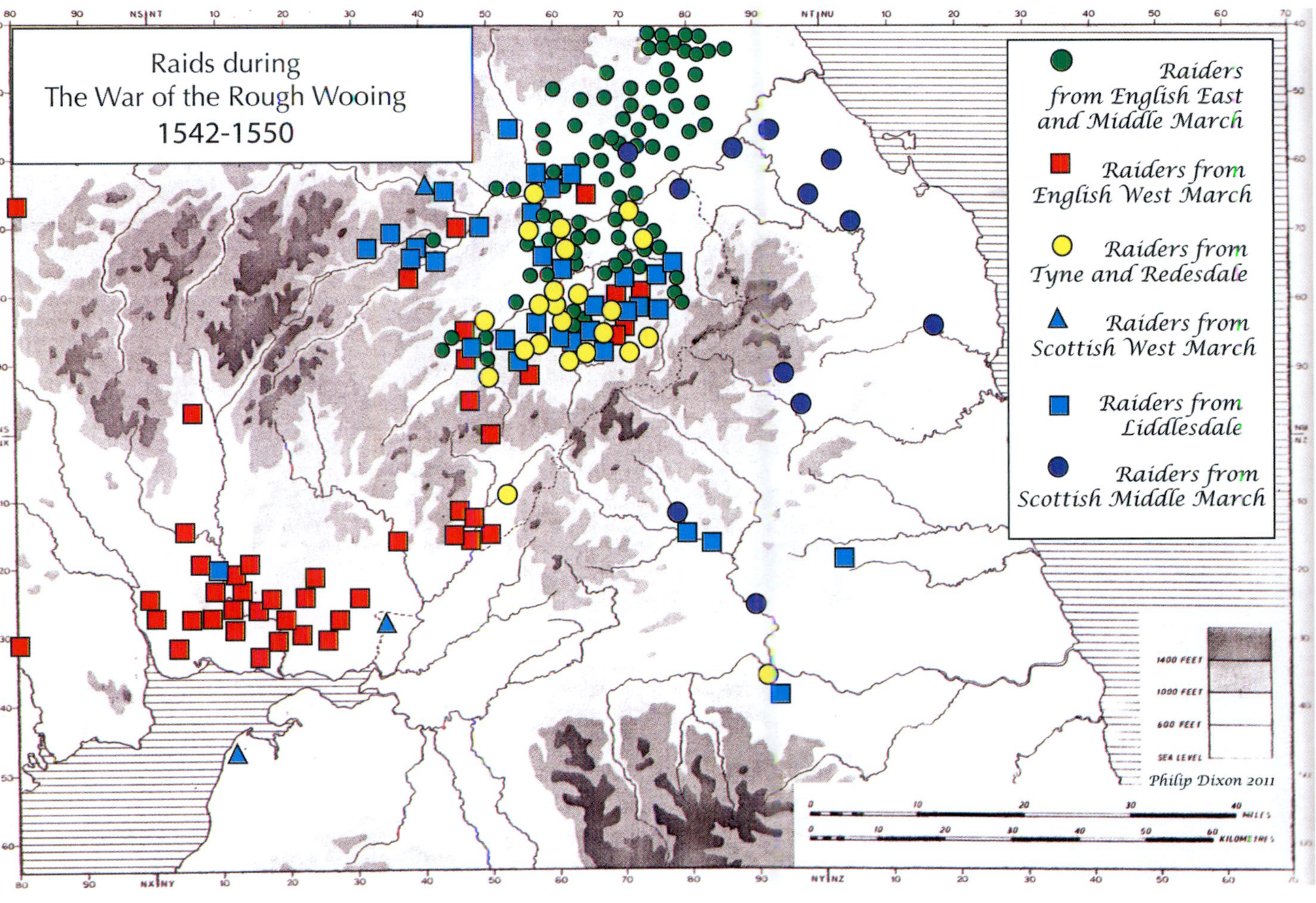

Plate XXIX (Dixon Fig. 10). The location of the recorded raids from 1542 to 1550

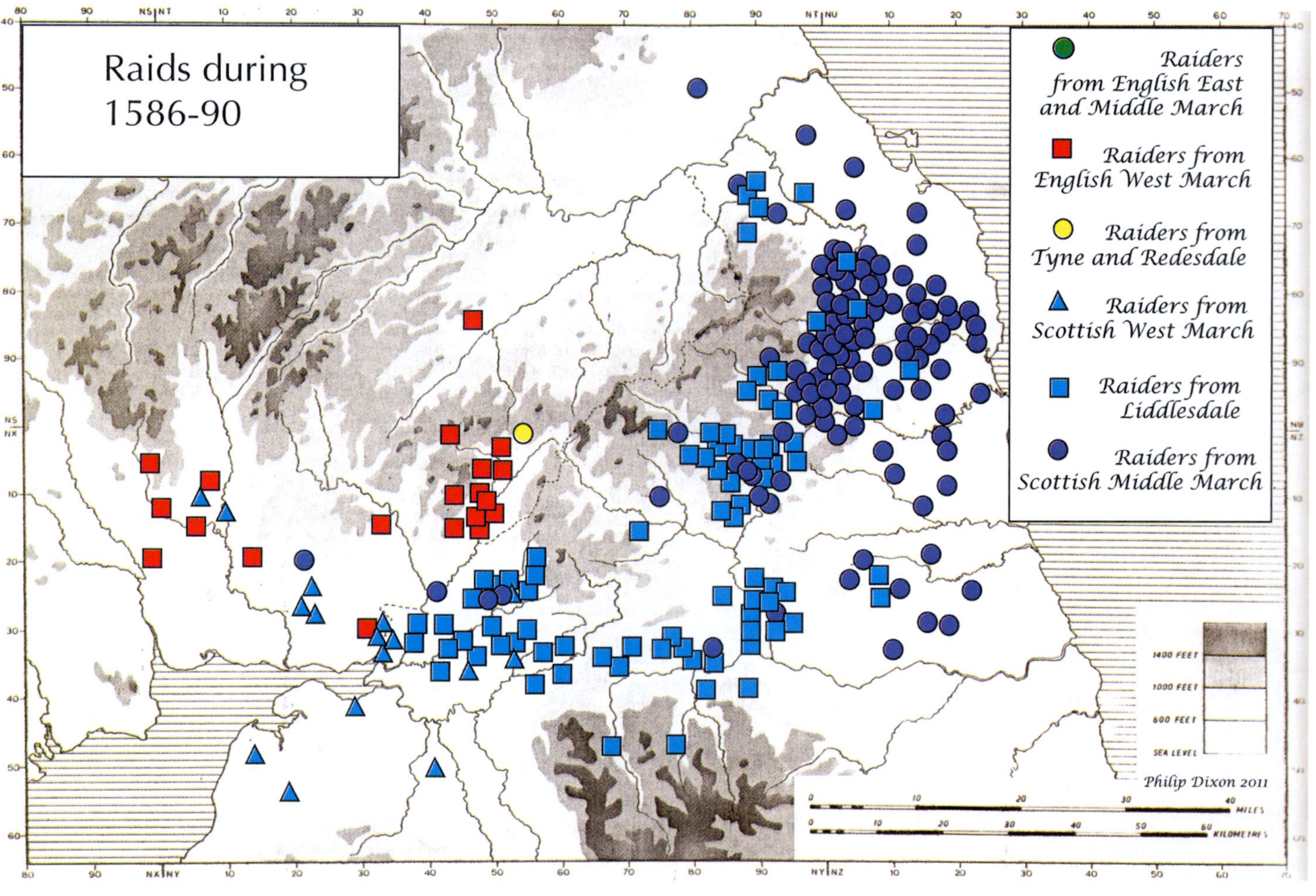

PLATE XXX (DIXON FIG. 11). The location of the recorded raids from 1586 to 1590

COLOUR PLATE XXXI

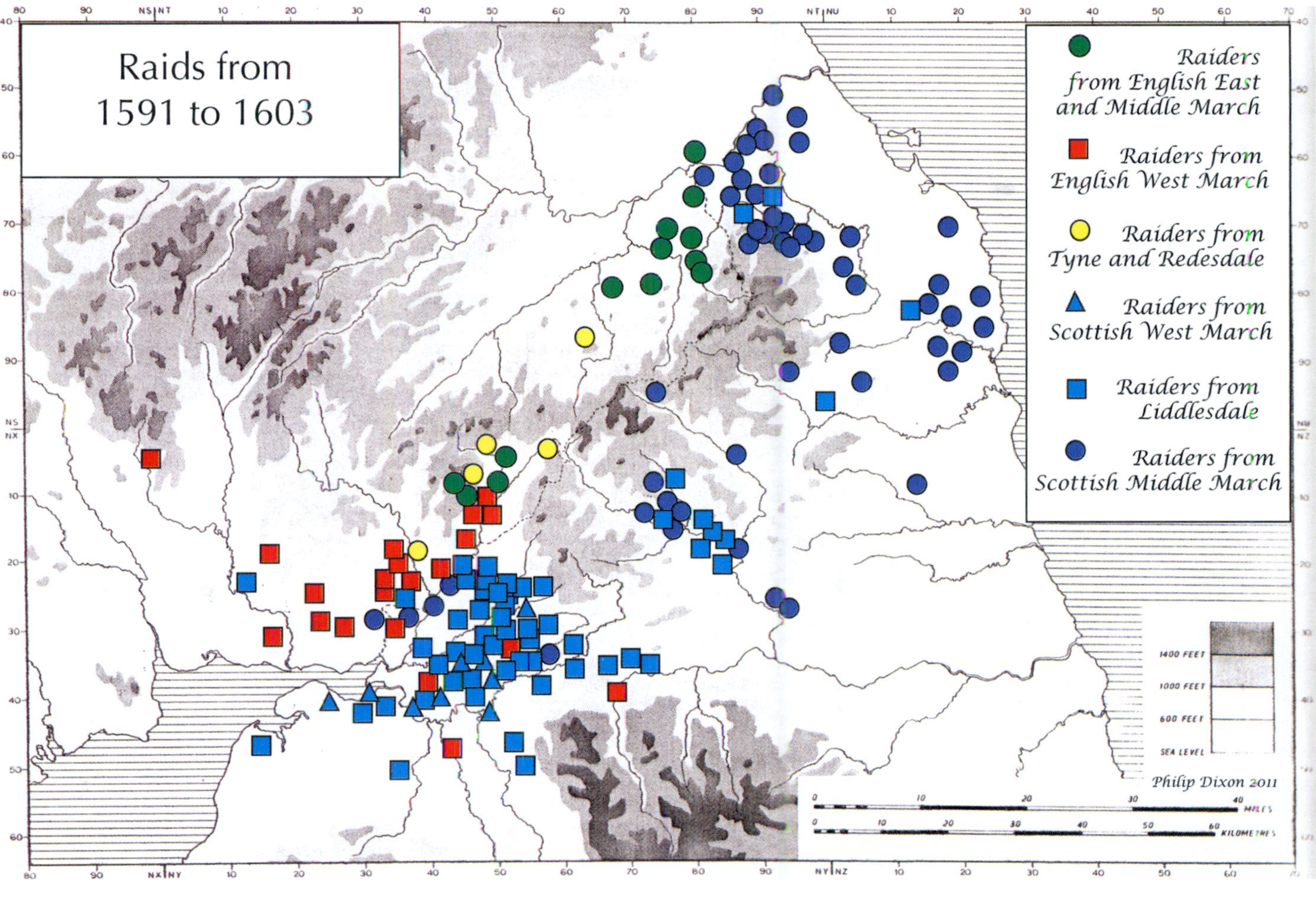

PLATE XXXI (DIXON FIG. 12). The location of the recorded raids from 1591 to 1603

COLOUR PLATE XXXII

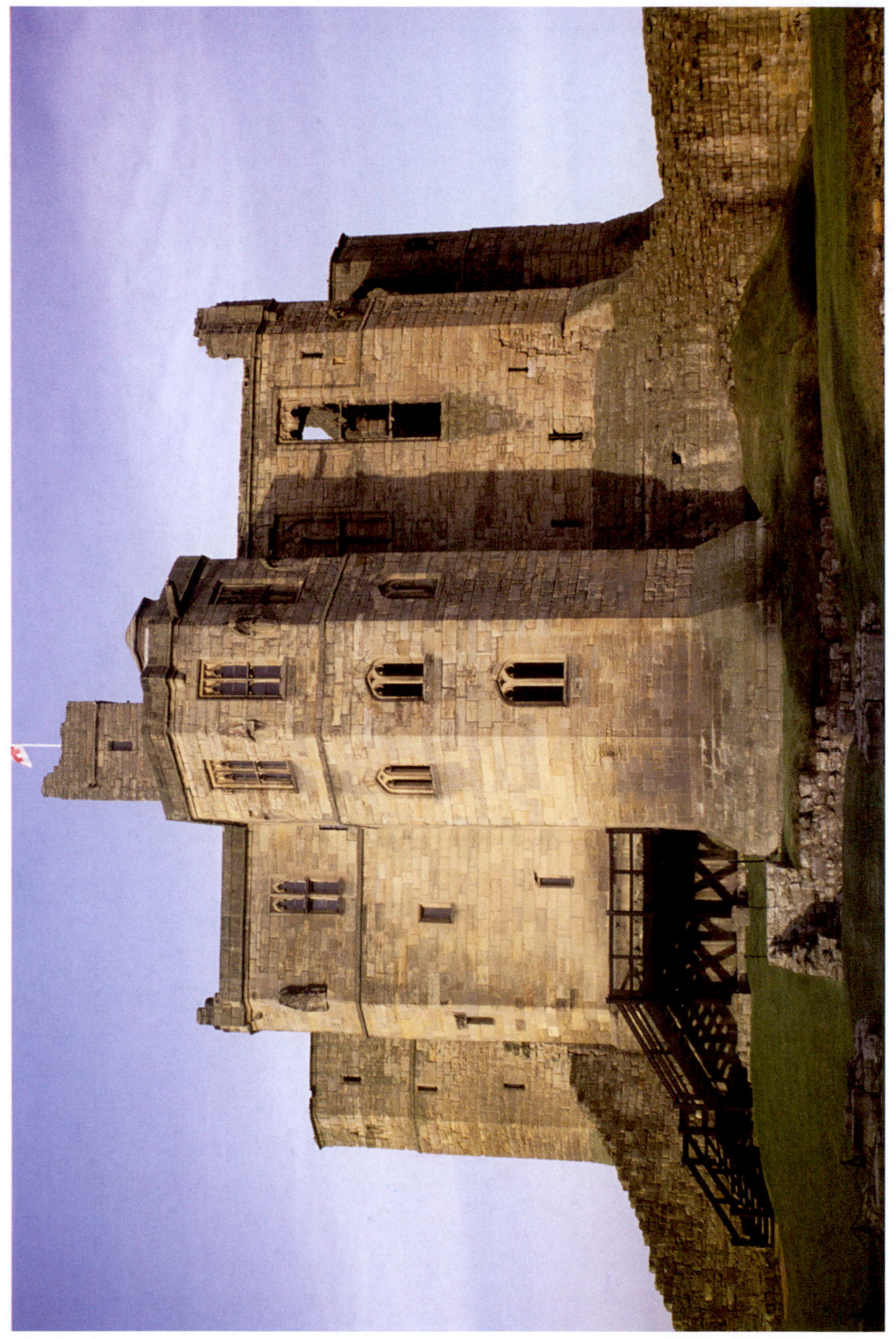

Plate XXXII (Woodman Fig. 1). Warkworth castle: tower keep

The Making of Newcastle

DAVID H. HESLOP and GRACE McCOMBIE

Tantalizing traces of prehistoric and early Roman material hint at the early importance of the river crossing that today unites Newcastle and Gateshead, but it is only from the time of Hadrian that a clear picture of the development of the river banks comes into view. The archaeological excavations triggered by several major developments have contributed to our growing understanding of the Roman geography of Pons Aelius, aided by the publication of keys sites and research reviews. In contrast, the post-Roman development continues to elude our grasp, until the construction of the castle in 1080, an event that might have concealed strands of continuity behind the apparent dislocation of the building of the king's northern fortress. The undulating surface of the ground, together with the steep cliffs which the river had gouged out of the land, were the foundations for the fortifications which defined medieval Newcastle. This tightly bound core was gradually loosened as new buildings and streets spread up to and beyond the town wall. The river and the coalfield brought increased prosperity, and the town became a major port and trading centre. Richard Grainger added fine new streets and structures to the town, engineering flourished, and the Tyne, once with a single low-arched bridge linking Newcastle and Gateshead, was crossed by several roads and rails at high and low levels.

INTRODUCTION

THE turn of the millennium and early years of the 21st century witnessed a decade-long boom in the economic fortunes of the urban centres of Newcastle and Gateshead, seeing the transformation of the river and its hinterland. Many impressive new buildings appeared amid much infrastructure and urban renewal (Fig. 1 and Col. Pl. I in print edn). A new identity for the city has been constructed, based as much on the provision of cultural services as of industrial materials and products. But as night follows day, the recent banking crisis and economic downturn have seen the pace of new building reduce dramatically, and many sites earmarked for development now lie quiet. In syncopation with the period of growth, the decade witnessed a wave of archaeological excavations, providing opportunities in a number of locations for archaeologists to examine the origins of development on Tyneside. The slow-down has provided an opportunity to review our thinking by writing up these sites and absorbing the results to formulate new research agendas for the two urban centres. This is timely, as the decade also saw the production of new research frameworks for the region and its principle monument: the imperial frontier of Hadrian's Wall.[1] We now have a much more explicit research context in which to articulate our developing understanding of the city and its surrounds. For Newcastle and Gateshead, these developments in research understanding are complemented by the publication of a group of important excavations. Some, like the area excavations on the Gateshead side at Oakwellgate and Bottle Bank, are products of the renaissance. Others relate

BAA Trans., vol. XXXVI (2013), 1–17

FIG. 1. The bridging point across the Tyne between Gateshead (foreground) and Newcastle, from the south-east

Aerial photo by Steve Brock

to major investigations conducted in previous decades, notably the major campaign between 1974 and 1992 in the castle garth.[2]

PREHISTORY

THE physical setting of Newcastle has, from the earliest times, subtly influenced the course and character of development along the river valley. Our picture of early settlement is, however, frustratingly indistinct. Certainly, the well-watered, gently rolling topography of the middle Tyne valley would have been attractive to early settlers. The palaeo-sedimentary history of the valley, one of the largest drainage catchments in the country, has been particularly well researched and published, complimenting work done elsewhere in the region.[3] Episodes of accumulation of alluvial deposits can be linked to periods of greater precipitation thought to be the product of climatic deterioration. Simultaneous forest clearance and agriculture may have contributed to this effect, but the picture is made clearer in the data provided by pollen analysis, both from these investigations, and more widely.[4]

The river banks are not well endowed with evidence of archaeological activity between Newcastle and Gateshead and the estuary at Tynemouth (a distance of eight miles as the crow flies). Upstream, beyond the reach of the activities of the Tyne Improvement Commission (active from 1854 to 1968), the hillsides overlooking the river are studded with flint sites and barrows, but below the bridging point the distribution maps show little primary evidence. When was the site of Newcastle and Gateshead first occupied? The traditional narrative recognizes nothing before the Roman occupation. Recent excavations on the Sage Music Centre revealed (within the restricted area of the dig) a pair of ditch terminals at the bottom of the stratified sequence and on a different alignment to the medieval tenement boundaries. (These were sectioned but not followed for any distance (Fig. 2).) The presence of a scrap of what may be Roman-period Samian ware led the excavator to suggest that the ditches could form part of the enclosure of the putative monastery at Gateshead alluded to by Bede.[5] In appearance, however, the ditch terminals are very like the interrupted ditched enclosures (or 'causewayed enclosures') of the early Neolithic period. Mavesyn Ridware in Staffordshire displays typical examples of this sort of enclosure, similar in size and setting, and also on the edge of a major river (the Trent). It is also typical in having the closely spaced perimeters that have been identified as being common in riverine locations.[6]

The presence of Roman pottery in the ditch fill need not categorically exclude a prehistoric origin here. It may show no more than that the ditch was still an open feature in the 1st millennium AD. The Ferrybridge henge in West Yorkshire, datable between 3000 and 2500 BC, produced fourteen Roman pottery sherds from a short section excavated in 1991, and the fact that the Iron Age and Romano-British landscapes of field boundaries and pit alignments clearly respected the henge demonstrates the degree to which the ancient monument was still prominent in later periods.[7] The phenomenon of Roman-period appropriation of ancient religious sites is destined to become an increasingly important line of enquiry in archaeology. While it is

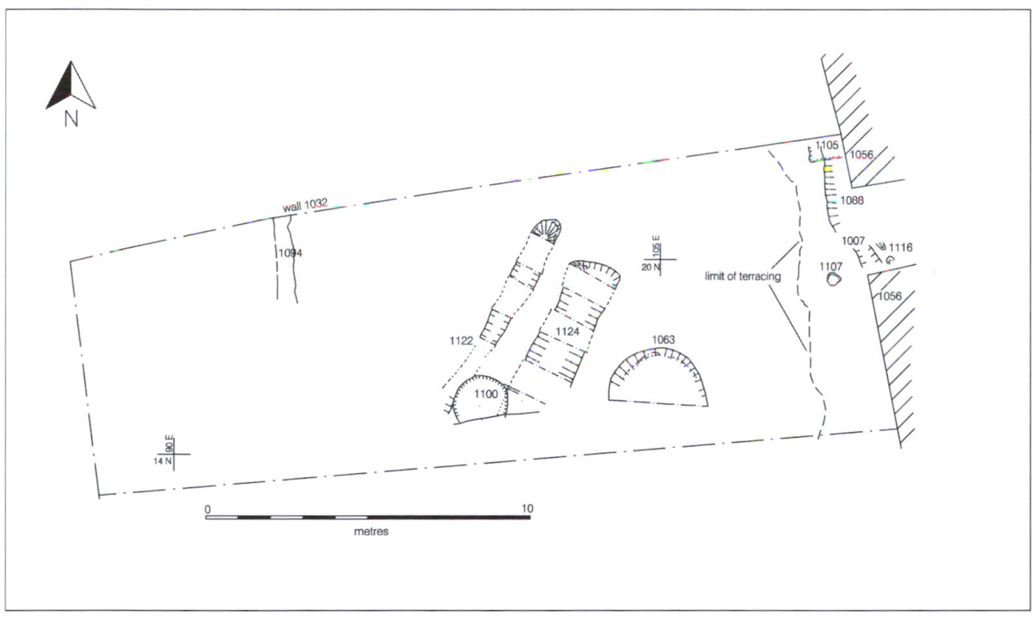

FIG. 2. Possible prehistoric site, Robson's Yard, Gateshead. Nolan and Vaughan, 'Excavations' (as n. 5), fig. 21

possible that the Music Centre enclosure is post-Roman, a Neolithic congregation site would be expected at exactly this location, where the Great North Road crosses a major east–west river.[8]

The large lowland enclosure is becoming a feature of the prehistoric archaeology of the region. Such enclosures span the date-range of early Neolithic to Iron Age, and many clearly witnessed long periods of settlement that cross our period boundaries. They are always associated with important features in the landscape or topography. Examples have been discovered through reconnaissance fieldwork in advance of redevelopment, as at Humbledon Hill and on the former Vaux brewery site in Sunderland. Others, though already known, have become better understood, as at Maiden castle in Durham.[9] Yet other sites of longer standing, like the supposed coastal promontory fort or enclosure at Tynemouth castle, remain poorly understood. (The only evidence for the existence of prehistoric settlement at Tynemouth is the discovery of a roundhouse of uncertain date and Iron Age/Romano-British finds under the priory church: otherwise the site has little to recommend it beyond a general feeling that there should be something important at this prominent location.)[10] The next twenty years may well see a reinterpretation of the settlement record, with recognition of the importance of these sites as foci of congregational activity. Such large lowland enclosures, which were religiously and ideologically significant but not necessarily the residences of high-status individuals, give physical expression to the way superficially dispersed, socially unstratified communities were interlinked.

For the later prehistoric period, the loss of evidence caused by the extent of urban sprawl has in some measure been offset by greater opportunities for site recognition offered by Planning Policy Guidance and Planning Policy Statement-triggered reconnaissance. An example of this has provided the first observation of permanent settlement within the urban core; in Newcastle, 300 metres north of the castle, and on the route of what would later be called the Great North Road. A roundhouse approximately 10 m in diameter was recorded at the bottom of a sequence of medieval urban deposits at 44–48 High Bridge, and dated by radiocarbon to the Late Bronze Age.[11] Pollen from the fill of one of the wall slots of the house derived from a scrub woodland environment dominated by hazel with a relative abundance of herbs, clearly distinguished from the urban ecological assemblage of the medieval burgage plots. That the High Bridge round house is not a small fraction of a larger settlement in this immediate location is strongly suggested by the fact that not one of more than 150 excavations within 2 km of the bridging point has produced any other pre-Roman structural remains. As has been noted by Bradley, the grey literature may contain records of features dating to early periods among the occasional undated features — pits, ditches and postholes — that represent traces of prehistoric activity at one or two excavations, but a major settlement either awaits discovery or never existed in the area covered by the modern city. Given the weight of negative evidence from such a large number of interventions, it seems reasonable to suggest that, despite the later documented religious significance of the location, there was never a large settlement in the vicinity of the river crossing before the Roman occupation.[12]

Outside the urban core, major advances have been achieved as a result of the area excavation of several Iron Age settlements. An intensity of settlement in later prehistory in the region might be expected from what is known of the palaeo-ecological record, which shows the progressive deforestation of the landscape towards the close of the 1st millennium BC, so that by the late Iron Age (i.e. well before any possible impacts of the Roman conquest and occupation), the countryside was approaching the levels of openness seen today.[13] The exemplary publication of the landscape and settlement areas at Pegswood, near Morpeth, has set a standard for subsequent work.[14] Extensive excavations have been undertaken to the north of Newcastle in advance of housing development (at East and West Bruton) and open-casting (at Fox Covert, Dinnington, and Dehli, Stannington). At Fox Covert, a substantial pit alignment has been recognized over several kilometres.

THE ROMAN PERIOD

THE relationship between the indigenous populations and the Roman authorities is a theme highlighted in the Hadrian's Wall Research Design.[15] The Iron Age sites north of Newcastle show little sign of use after the establishment of the imperial frontier by Hadrian in 122 AD, but the landscape was clearly intensively farmed throughout the period. The main problem is one of site recognition, which is as much an issue for the post-Roman period as the Roman one. If settlements were not defined by substantial enclosures and domestic buildings by pen-annular ditches, or if the standard building material was timber rather than stone, or if the occupants did not leave artefacts for modern archaeologists to collect, then sites of this period are extremely difficult to detect. In the military zone, it seems inconceivable that the majority of the population left their ancestral homes to move to the extra-mural neighbourhoods (*vici*) and small towns, and, if they did so in the 2nd century, one might ask where they lived after the *vici* were in decline and abandoned around 250–70 AD (as appears consistently to have occurred). One possibility might have been drift of occupation to new points of settlement in the landscape, perhaps along the road system, as with the newly recognized sites at Sedgefield and Gateshead, or else along the more navigable rivers and coastal littoral, the latter a landscape type that Steve Willis has observed was shunned by Iron Age communities.[16] The movement within existing territorial units to roadside or coastal locations would have allowed a local rural population to exploit new economic possibilities, as well as continuing with the traditional farming activities. To date, however, settlement sites have not been located in significant numbers.

By contrast, the early years of the 3rd millennium have seen striking advances in our understanding of the Roman geography of the military-related occupation of Newcastle and Gateshead. With the exception of the bridge, all of the major elements of the settlements have to varying degrees come into view. New work has helped define the course and character of the imperial frontier on Tyneside, although there are still areas of uncertainty in the Ouseburn valley (3 km east of the bridging point) and in the centre of Newcastle.[17] At the Ouseburn, we do not know if the Wall actually traversed the ravine (which it could have either with a bridge across the river or a culvert through the Wall). Bore-hole examination of deep deposits at one development site on the east bank (Foundry Lane) has shown stone obstructions well above the anticipated level of rock-head at four locations along the ordinance survey alignment: tantalising but inconclusive evidence.

At Newcastle, the line of the Wall has been lost to the east of the Roman fort, an area that has not only been very intensively overbuilt, but also, because of the steeply ravined nature of the riverbank, subject to massive topographic remodelling, which has filled in the Pandon Dene and the Lort Burn, and remodelled the banksides to create building platforms and achieve reduced road gradients. A targeted programme of evaluation, years ahead of its time, was devised throughout this area in 1929 and

1930 by the North of England Excavation Committee.[18] The results of this programme of trenching across the city centre might be re-examined in the light of modern discoveries, but any future research will remain heavily indebted to the exemplary pioneering work of this group. There are two possible routes of the lost section of the Wall, a southern one from Sallyport tower down the slope of the Pandon Dene and then back up to All Saints church along Silver Street, and a northern one, following the contours approximately where the railway viaduct cuts through the ground east of the castle keep. Considerable trenching for developments in the Pandon Dene has failed to reveal any evidence for the southern route, while the possible northern route is largely unavailable for examination as a result of destructive 19th- and 20th-century development. On balance, what negative evidence we have suggests that the northern route is the more probable one. A detailed review of the current state of knowledge of the line of the Wall through Newcastle has been recently compiled.[19]

The redevelopment of the south bank between the Tyne and High Level bridges to construct the Gateshead Hilton hotel triggered area excavation to the rear of the High Street (that is, along the medieval bridge approach road). Frontages here were cellared, but the back-plots revealed a landscape of Roman tenements linked by a ditch-system.[20] The whole is best interpreted as an extensive industrial settlement, possibly running along a road down to the crossing-point. Industrial activity, largely involving metalworking, was the predominant activity revealed by excavation, although residential areas may await discovery nearby or on the frontage. The general spread of pottery is late 2nd to early 3rd century, with little being recorded after the period of decline of the Wall *vici* in the mid to later 3rd century AD. The earliest material predates the fort on the Northumberland side of the river at the castle garth. Paul Bidwell and Margaret Snape argue convincingly that an early fort existed in this area, possibly comparable with the timber fort of AD 72–73 at Carlisle.[21]

The fort of *Pons Aelius* has been fully published in a recent volume of *Archaeologia Aeliana*, and needs little further discussion here.[22] Much valuable information has been gleaned, but the fundamental questions of the date of the fort's foundation, as well as the form of its plan and its layout of the interior to either side of the central zone, are still unresolved. In common with many forts in the northern military zone, its 5th-century history is very poorly understood. To the west of the fort, excavations in 2008 revealed the first clear evidence of the *vicus*, on a site to the south of the Central station, close by the steep clay-scarp down to the river. The excavated area was bisected by a Roman road with deep flanking ditches, which ran from the west gate of the fort towards the slope leading down to the bridgehead. To the west of the road was a high-status cemetery: two fine sarcophagi were excavated in 2008, to add to the similar pair discovered in front of Turnbull's warehouse in 1903. While undecorated, these were very finely sculpted, their coped lids sealed with steel pins held in lead-filled sockets. The coffins were intermittently water filled, and skeletal preservation was very poor, but preliminary analysis suggests that one held two inhumations, an infant and juvenile, and the other a female in her late teens or early adulthood accompanied by a very fine jet pin with faceted head.

To the east of the road were small tenements with insubstantial strip buildings, of post and rail construction. Pits and wells produced a small assemblage of material that confirms the wider chronology of *vicus* occupation — from the late 2nd to mid- or late 3rd century. At Newcastle, the concentration of coins from open areas in the fort suggests that the market function of the *vicus* may have been taken over by the fort between *c.* AD 270 and *c.* AD 375.[23] With its southern extent being defined by the river cliff, its eastern boundary by the fort, and its northern perimeter presumably defined by Hadrian's Wall, it is only the western edge of the civilian settlement that is completely unknown. As this part of the city becomes engulfed by development, the size and status of the settlement may come into better focus. Our rapidly expanding knowledge of the Roman settlement of Newcastle and Gateshead can be contrasted by the total lack of comparable evidence from other towns in the region, most notably, perhaps, Sunderland, which clearly never had a significant Roman presence.

MEDIEVAL NEWCASTLE

THE recognition of post-Roman occupation across Tyneside is perhaps the most challenging problem for understanding the history of the area. Even in the most promising part of the town, the castle garth, the remains are scanty and ambiguous.[24] Settlement activity did continue into and beyond the 5th century, but the evidence for this has been much disturbed by the graves of the later cemetery (in use *c.* 700 to 1100). However, it is clear that post-built structures were erected and used, and paths laid out and paved. A more permanent presence is suggested by the construction of a drain or aqueduct which was cut across the foundations of one of the Roman fort granaries. These traces may belong to the supposed monastery of 'Monkchester' (Thomas Tanner's 'Castrum, vel civitas monachorum'): if so, it was a poorly endowed and comparatively short-lived institution, being formed in the 6th century and failing before the 9th.[25] Monkchester was perhaps on the losing side of Colmán, bishop of Lindisfarne (661–64), in the dispute between the Celtic and Roman divisions of the early church over the keeping of Easter, chronicled at length by Bede.[26]

Across the Roman horizons in the castle garth and surrounding areas, a spread of dark earth is commonly encountered in areas not damaged by later development, thought to be re-worked occupation material transformed by soil-mixing agents and horticulture. Outside the castle garth, within the city centre, and on the Gateshead side, the numerous excavations triggered by development have not produced a single post-roman sherd or stratified metal find. That the cemetery was used by a considerable population from the surrounding area and was able to attract high-status inhumations (as shown by the two chest-burials) was probably an expression of the continuing spiritual importance of the location in the lives of the people of the area.

The medieval street plan

TRIBUTARIES of the Tyne had scored deep denes out of the land: the Lort and Pandon burns within the town, the Ouseburn further east. Routes developed on the ridges flanking the Lort Burn: on the west, the route to the parish church and the castle evolved into a market place where food and cloth were sold from stalls. Further out, Newgate (street) ran north and north-east from Bigg (barley) Market to the New Gate in the town wall, and continued to the countryside beyond as Sidgate (now Percy Street). On the eastern bank, All Hallows (All Saints) church stood on another promontory, and the route down that ridge became Pilgrim Street. Vehicle routes to the higher ground from the bridge on Sandhill were the Side and Butcher Bank, both steep and narrow. For pedestrians, several long flights of steps led to the waterfront.[27] A third route ran west from the castle and through the west gate. Excavation has confirmed that it followed the line of Hadrian's Wall along Westgate (later Westgate

Street, then Westgate Road). Those three routes still exist, as do the two riverside streets; and in the present city some early structures survive among later buildings.[28]

The river and the quayside

THE river itself had changed during the middle ages, gradually narrowed downstream from the bridge as jetties were constructed, and upstream as burgage plots were extended into the water. Excavations have shown that by 1400 the river jetties had become lanes (the present quayside chares), and the reclaimed land between them had been developed.[29] Speed's 1610 plan of the town shows these chares, two riverside and three radiating streets of the medieval town plan, with the castle and St Nicholas's church still prominent (Fig. 3).

A sandy hillock at the mouth of the Lort Burn became Sandhill, at various times a popular place for recreation and a market.[30] An arch of the medieval bridge survives in the cellar of Watergate Buildings at Sandhill's west end. The town house on Sandhill's south side (rebuilt in the 1650s and now called the Guildhall) was the seat of the town council until 1863. Speed in 1610 shows the street called Quayside, downstream from Sandhill, with houses on its north side and the town wall, a defence against sea-borne invasion, on its south. Ships' cargoes were unloaded onto the town quay

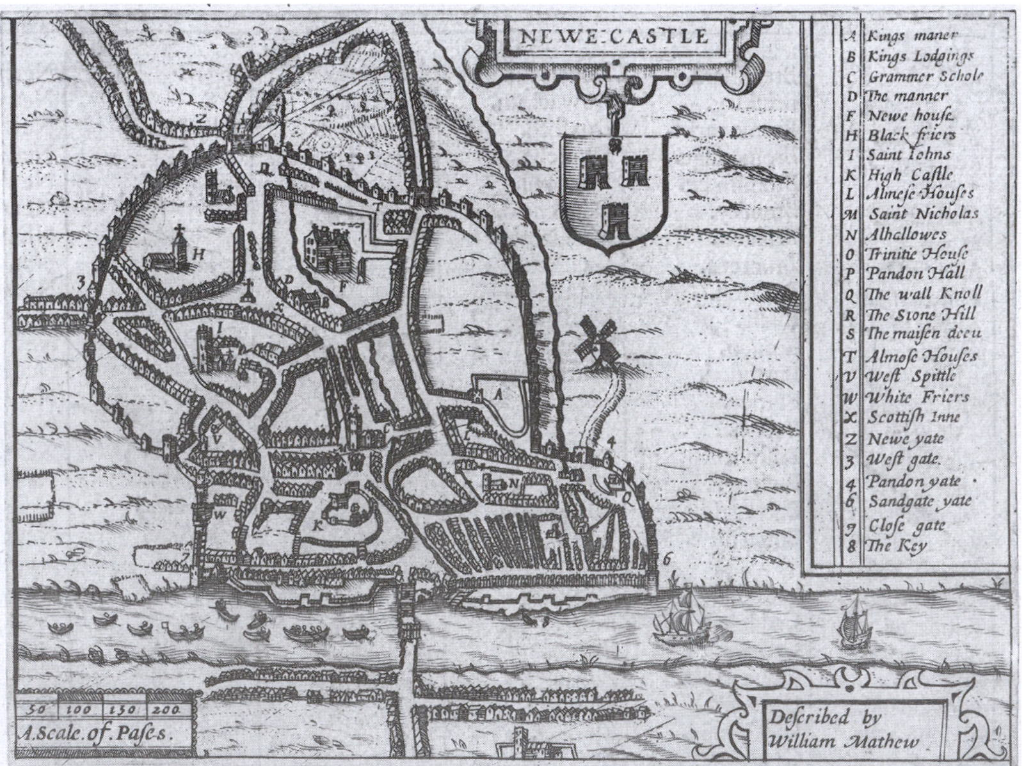

FIG. 3. John Speed's map of Newcastle (1610)

and carried through narrow gateways in the wall to cellars, shops and lofts, and to warehouses, in the chares and the town beyond. Upstream from Sandhill, properties on the south side of the street called the Close had the advantage of direct access to the river.[31] This is clearly shown on the Tudor bird's-eye view, probably drawn *c.* 1545, in BL, MS Cotton Augustus I.ii.4 (Fig. 4 and Col. Pl. II in print edn). By then the natural topography had been changed. Buildings had been constructed on new ground between the jetties which had projected into the river from its north shore; the jetties themselves had become lanes or chares between the new buildings on the raised ground; and the Lort and Pandon burns were culverted before they poured into the river. Samuel Buck's 1723 'South Prospect of Newcastle upon Tyne' shows a town still contained within its medieval wall, still served by its medieval bridge, still overlooked by the castle and St Nicholas's church (Fig. 5).[32]

The surviving medieval core

THIS layout is still the skeleton of central Newcastle. The medieval core is enclosed by the line of surviving town wall or by its site: development was limited by it, so that its ghost is sometimes there when its substance has gone. Post-medieval development has led to the demolition of most of the town wall, so that now not one of its original gates remains.[33] In the later middle ages there were still open spaces within the wall. At west, there was the Blackfriars precinct, cut in two by the wall; at east, Carliol Croft, with Pandon Burn flowing outside it and then under the wall and on through the irregular street pattern of Pandon vill (added to Newcastle in 1298) to the river; at north, the combined precincts of the former St Bartholomew's nunnery and the Franciscan friary.

Richard Grainger's new town

ON the site of the friary, Speed marks 'Newe House'. Later known as 'Anderson Place', this building and its two medieval precincts were bought by the town corporation in 1834 for Richard Grainger's spectacular urban development. Grainger demolished that mansion, filled in the Lort Dene that ran through the grounds, and built a new covered market (by John Dobson; now 'the Grainger Market') and ashlar-fronted streets. His fine classical 'new town' was thus astonishingly achieved. Thomas Oliver's survey of 1851 shows this and other significant developments. It is worth noting that Grainger made maximum use of undeveloped land. Apart from the destruction of Anderson Place itself, he generally demolished buildings only so that new streets could break into existing ones. That is why the Theatre Royal in Mosley Street was demolished: so that the junction with Grey Street could be formed.

Newcastle's medieval houses were timber-framed, or of stone, or built of a combination of these materials, both readily available near Newcastle. Surviving medieval buildings are stone: three churches, St Nicholas, St John, and St Andrew (All Saints was rebuilt in 1786–96), and the castle with its keep, Black Gate (with brick 17th-century upper floors and 19th-century rear wing), associated structures, and the remaining sections of the town wall. At the head of Broad Chare, one medieval stone house still stands. It was sold in 1505 to the company of Masters and Mariners, which had established a fellowship of the Blessed Trinity, so that it became known as Trinity House.[34] No. 35 The Close, formerly a waterfront warehouse (now a public house), has early 16th-century roof trusses (some exposed in the gable facing the High Level Bridge), and some timber framing that is now obscured.

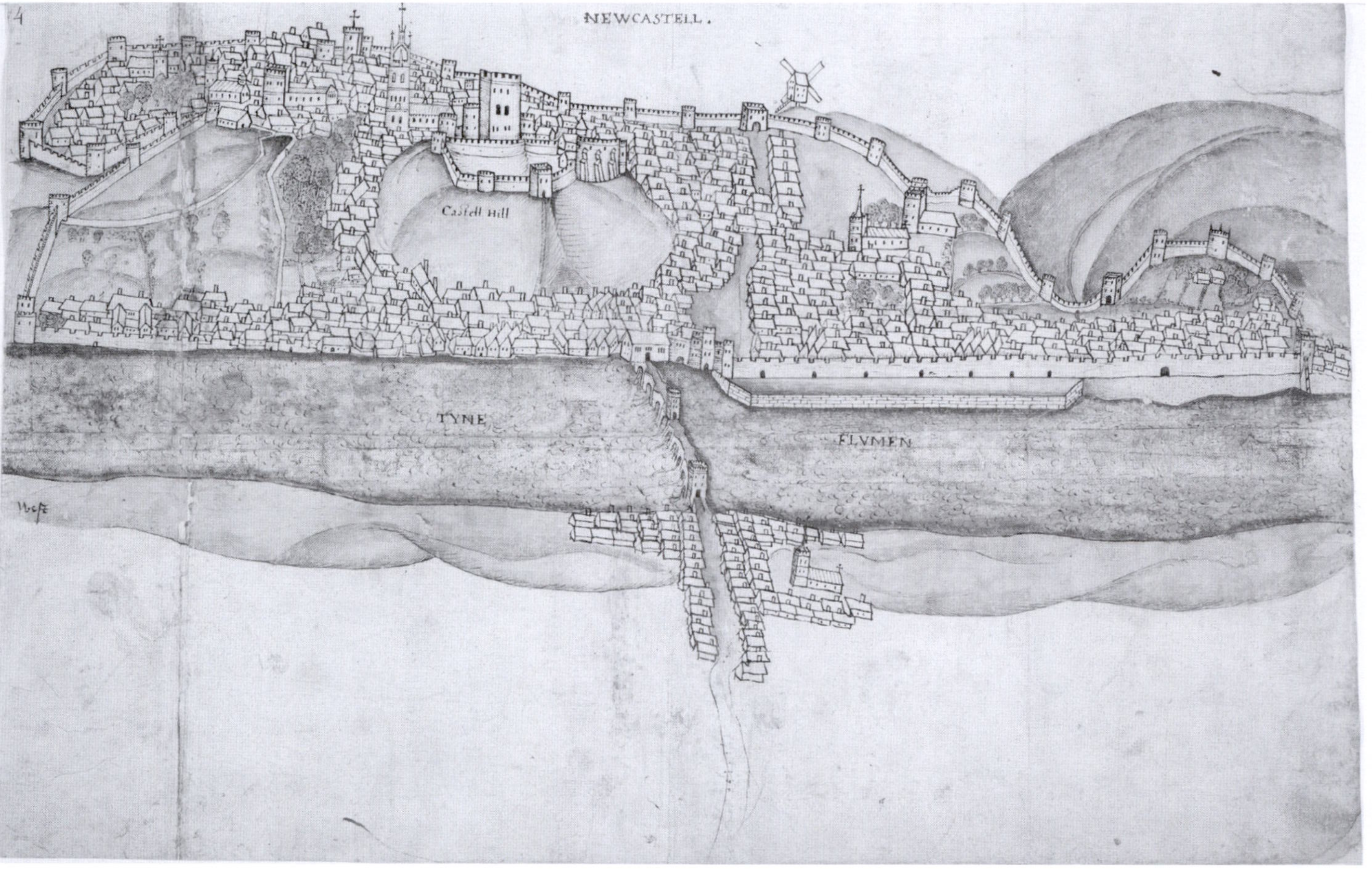

FIG. 4. A Tudor view of Newcastle, now BL, MS Cotton Augustus I.ii.4. This map shows the principal features of the medieval town: crowded streets encircled by the town wall, the river with shipping tied up downstream from the bridge, and overlooking the bridge, the Norman castle with its strong Keep

Reproduced by permission of the British Library Board

FIG. 5. Samuel Buck's 'South Prospect' of Newcastle (1723), showing the town still contained within its medieval walls

POST-MEDIEVAL DEVELOPMENT: TOPOGRAPHY AND TRADE

THE navigable river Tyne and the coalfield around it are the keys to Newcastle's medieval and post-medieval success.[35] In earlier times the river had filled the valley floor between steep cliffs. Trade grew because sea-going ships could load and unload at the town quay; they brought a variety of goods into the harbour when they came to pick up cargoes of coal, millstones, hides and wool. The river crossing carried the main road along the coastal plain, linking Newcastle and Gateshead to London and Edinburgh. Wenceslaus Hollar's 1654 map of the Tyne indicates the significance of this location (Fig. 6). Coal was first won from outcrops, and then by developing technology: bell-pits at first, later deep workings extending miles below the North Sea (and now by surface extraction through open-cast mines). Local, national, and

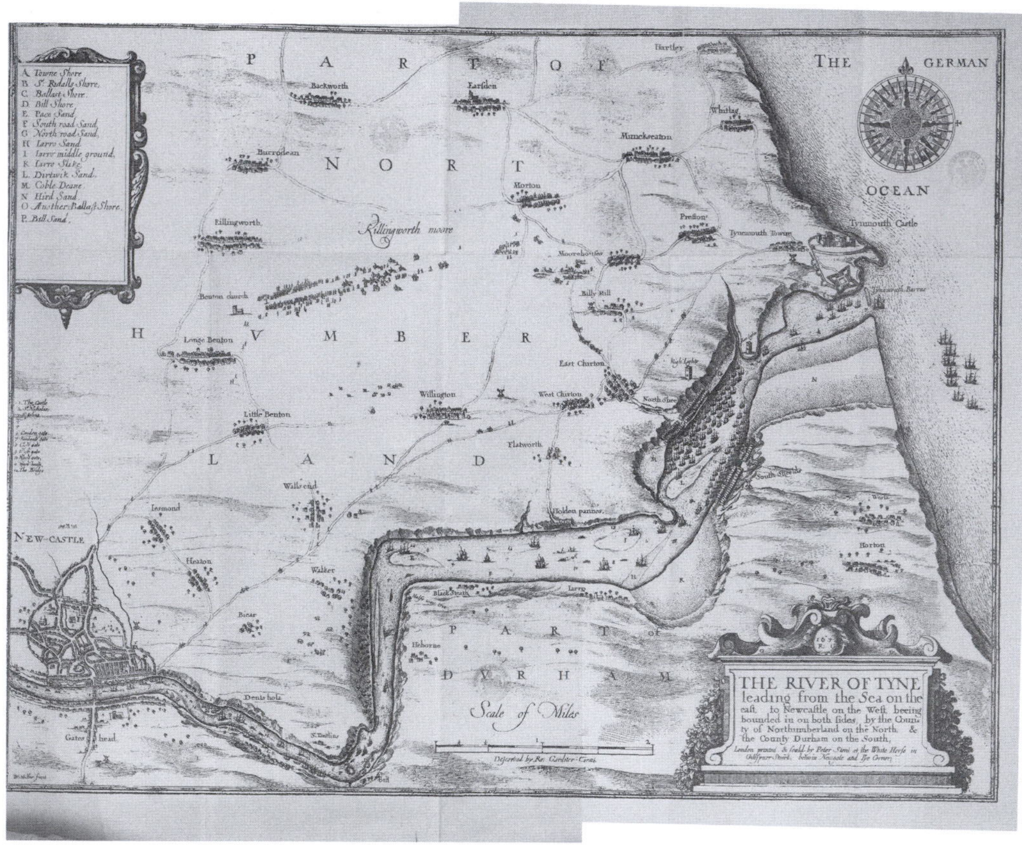

Fig. 6. Wenceslaus Hollar's map of the Tyne (1655). This was intended to show that it was not easy for ships to navigate the river, but shows much more than ships staying in the harbour at North and South Shields, or stuck on sandbanks. It shows a busy commercial town, with its quays and riverside streets, still encompassed by its town wall. The Newcastle races are shown on Killingworth Moor

Image courtesy of Newcastle City Library

overseas trade increased rapidly as improvements in mining technology and transport brought income to colliery owners, owners of land over which coal had to be transported, the labour-force in general, and also the professionals and others who served the industry: sailors, farmers, shopkeepers, craftsmen, surveyors, engineers, lawyers, and bankers. For many centuries standards were controlled by the trade and craft companies of the town.[36]

Sir William Brereton had admired Newcastle in 1635: ‘This is beyond all compare the fairest and richest towne in England, inferiour for wealth and building to noe citte save London [or] Bristow’.[37] After first being used as nogging in timber-framed buildings, by 1700 brick was the principal building material in the town (although stone was still used for churches and important civic buildings). Celia Fiennes said in 1698 that Newcastle ‘most resembles London of any place in England, its buildings lofty and large of brick mostly or stone, the streets very broad and handsome’. She described the exchange or guildhall on Sandhill (built in 1658), and the fine quay beside it, ‘full of merchants walking to and againe [. . .] it runs off a great Length w[i]th a great many steps down to ye water for the Conveniency of Landing or boateing their goods, and is full of Cellars or ware houses’.[38]

The town’s late 17th- and early 18th-century brick houses had pantiled roofs with shaped gables (concave and convex curves). Windows were at first mullioned, sometimes with transoms. The window openings of Alderman Fenwick’s House on the west side of Pilgrim Street reveal alterations made to take the narrower and fashionable vertical sliding sashes. Early 18th-century sashes are found in Trinity House and in the Plummer Tower, and slightly later sashes in the stair hall of the fine interior of 55–57 Westgate Road.[39]

As Newcastle expanded, burgage plots were filled with houses and outhouses, and open spaces were developed. On the former precinct of the Dominican friary, Newcastle’s first London-type square, Charlotte Square, was built. Near it, in 1786, the town’s first purpose-built assembly rooms were opened (both designed by William Newton). Newcastle merchants and Northumberland and Tyneside gentry with houses in the countryside had strong connections with London society. Cultural pleasures included musical concerts and recitals, theatrical events, and exchanging visits with friends in town and country. Trade and cultural interests were advanced in Newcastle, and houses were built and decorated in accordance with the best national practice. The rooms of 55–57 Westgate Road have fine plaster decoration of the most fashionable kind (Fig. 7 and Col. Pl. III in print edn).

Communications began to improve. After the medieval bridge had been destroyed by floods in 1771, Newcastle’s Corporation and the bishop of Durham built a replacement bridge. In 1784 a scheme was revived that had been laid to one side while the new bridge was planned and paid for: most of the Lort Burn (by then described as ‘nauseous’) was culverted and its Dene partly filled in, and over it a ‘T’ plan of new wide streets (Dean Street and Mosley Street) was constructed. Gateshead’s Church Street was also made then. For the first time, carts, coaches and cattle could more easily ascend the steep hills from the bridge. In 1811, with the completion of Newcastle’s first east–west route (when Collingwood Street linked Mosley Street to Westgate, later Westgate Road), the framework was available for Richard Grainger’s fine town streets of the 1830s. Grainger’s architects designed Grey Street, extending Dean Street northwards on the high ground, and around it, rows of new, ashlar-fronted shops and houses went up. There was also a new theatre and an academy of art.[40]

FIG. 7. 55–57 Westgate Road; staircase plaster and Venetian window. Sophistication of early 18th-century Newcastle

By kind permission of Mike Tilley. Courtesy of English Heritage; © English Heritage and James Davies

Alongside all these post-medieval changes, and earlier than them, the work of a major institution near the river must be mentioned, because it helped Newcastle to keep its status as a centre of trade in the modern period. Trinity House, the headquarters of the company (formerly fellowship) of Masters and Mariners of Newcastle, managed shipping on the river and promoted high standards of navigation at sea. The organization was founded before 1505: in that year, it acquired the medieval courtyard house in Broad Chare where its members still meet.[41] In 1536 Henry VIII granted them a licence to build lights (lighthouses) at Shields to guide ships through dangerous waters into the port of Newcastle; and for the Corporation, who managed the tidal stretch of the Tyne, they checked the depth of the river channels. Hollar's 1655 map (Fig. 5) shows the lights (i.e. lighthouses) and the sandbanks. Trinity House can be identified on the Tudor view (Fig. 4) because its lower or southern yard is the only open space in the crowded quayside chares. Recent examination of their company's buildings has yielded remarkable 12th-century tree-ring dates.[42] The stone building which is set into the cliff, and was used in the 18th century as a rigging loft, is clearly a medieval house: its pointed rerearches, a garderobe with shouldered lintel, and other details, all are manifestly original.

The 1723 engraving of Newcastle by Samuel Buck shows the nature of the two towns and the river at that date, with Anderson Place prominent on the skyline (Fig. 5). Newcastle's Guildhall (or Exchange) can be recognized on the south side of Sandhill, overlooking the river. St Nicholas's church displays its remarkable spire and still has the small south vestry which was replaced in 1736 by the present two-storey James Gibbs choir school and vestry.[43] Both river banks are crowded with buildings. A summary of the town's development after 1800 — something with which this essay is not concerned — would refer to the growth of industry in the 19th century, with many new streets of houses overwhelming the medieval villages. It would also refer to the 20th-century reconstruction in the medieval core and the development of prosperous suburbs. Post-World War II theories of urban planning were given substance — mostly in concrete — and have not all weathered well. (There was — is — also the brilliant, and internationally admired, housing scheme at Byker.)[44]

CONCLUSION: THE OLD TOWN IN THE NEW CITY

EVEN today, the medieval arrangement of Newcastle (if not its Roman and pre-Roman layouts) is in places still clear on the ground. This is especially the case in lower Pilgrim Street and in Groat, Cloth and Bigg Markets. The present built fabric of the city incorporates many structural phases. The medieval streets had rows of houses at the heads of the burgage plots, with alleys under and between the houses that gave access to rear gardens or yards and, increasingly with time, outbuildings. That infilling process had begun when the Tudor-period view was drawn (Fig. 4). Thomas Oliver's survey of 1830 shows that by then most of those strips of land were completely built over and the town's buildings had spilled out beyond the town wall. Also outside the town wall was the common pasture, the town moor, much of which is now occupied by the university, Royal Victoria Infirmary, public parks and roads. But great expanses of grass survive, on which Newcastle's freemen still have the right to graze cows.

The present complex of streets and offices and houses, railways and bridges, chares and motorways, rewards the thoughtful visitor with wonderful views in the tight confines of the Tyne Gorge, down the steep hills of 1830s Grey Street and 1780s Dean Street, to the medieval street called the Side, and then across the Tyne to Gateshead. The green hills further south and west form an atmospheric backdrop. Many layers and levels and heights and materials are woven into a rich fabric: but Newcastle's medieval origins can still be found at its heart.

NOTES

1. D. Petts and C. M. Gerrard, *Shared Visions: The North-East Regional Research Framework for the Historic Environment* (Durham 2006); *Frontiers of Knowledge: A Research Framework for Hadrian's Wall*, ed. F. A. Symmonds and D. J. P. Mason (Durham 2009).

2. M. Snape and P. Bidwell et al., 'The Roman Fort at Newcastle upon Tyne', *AA*, 5th ser. 30 (2002) (a special issue of *AA* devoted to various aspects of the excavation of Newcastle's Roman fort); J. Nolan, with B. Harbottle and J. Vaughan, 'The Early Medieval Cemetery at the Castle, Newcastle upon Tyne', *AA*, 5th ser. 39 (2010), 147–288.

3. M. G. Macklin, B. T. Rumsby and M. D. Newson, 'Historical Floods and Vertical Accretion of Fine-Grained Alluvium in the Lower Tyne Valley, North East England', in *Dynamics of Gravel-Bed Rivers*, ed. P. Billi, R. D. Hey, C. R. Thorne and P. Tacconi (Chichester 1992), 573–89; D. G. Passmore and C. Waddington, *Managing Archaeological Landscapes in Northumberland* (Oxford 2010).

4. See, for example, Petts and Gerrard, *Shared Visions* (as n. 1), 197–200.

5. Bede, *EH*, 278–80; J. Nolan and J. Vaughan, 'Excavations at Oakwellgate, Gateshead, 1999', *AA*, 5th ser. 36 (2007), 114.

6. A. Oswald, C. Dyer and M. Barber, *The Creation of Monuments: Neolithic Causewayed Enclosures in the British Isles* (Swindon 2001), 68–69.

7. P. Rush, 'The Roman Pottery', in *Ferrybridge Henge: The Ritual Landscape*, ed. I. Roberts (Leeds 2005), 231.

8. B. Vyner, 'A Great North Route in Neolithic and Bronze Age Yorkshire: The Evidence of Landscape and Monuments', *Landscapes*, 1 (2007), 69–84; D. H. Heslop, 'Newcastle and Gateshead before AD 1080', in *Newcastle and Gateshead before 1700*, ed. D. Newton and A. J. Pollard (Chichester 2009), 1–22.

9. D. N. Hale and D. C. Still, 'Geophysical Survey at Picktree, Chester-le-Street and Humbledon Hill, Sunderland', *Durham Archaeological Journal*, 17 (2003), 1–7; 'An archaeological evaluation at the former Vaux Brewery, St Mary's Way, Sunderland, Tyne & Wear' (unpublished report by Pre-Construct Archaeology Limited 2004), 114.

10. G. Fairclough, 'Tynemouth Priory and Castle: Excavation in the Outer Court', *AA*, 5th ser. 11 (1983), 101–33; R. Bradley, 'Bridging the Two Cultures: Commercial Archaeology and the Study of Prehistoric Britain', *Antiq. J.*, 86 (2006), 1–13. There are enough later defences at Tynemouth to have masked early ditches.

11. I.e. 1499 to 1382 BC–1333 to 1324 BC: see G. Brogan, 'Excavations and Building Recording at 44–48 High Bridge, Newcastle upon Tyne', *AA*, 5th ser. 36 (2010), 333–34, 347, 371.

12. Heslop, 'Newcastle and Gateshead' (as n. 8), passim (religious significance); R. Bradley, 'Bridging' (as n. 10), passim.

13. M. G. Macklin, D. G. Passmore and B. T. Rumsby, 'Climatic and Cultural Signals in Holocene Alluvial Sequences: The Tyne Basin, Northern England', in *Alluvial Archaeology in Britain*, ed. S. Needham and M. G. Macklin (Oxford 1992), 123–40.

14. J. Proctor, *Pegswood Moor, Morpeth: A Later Iron Age and Romano-British Farmstead Settlement*, PCA Monograph 11 (Oxbow Books 2009).

15. *Frontiers of Knowledge* (as n. 1), section 4, 24.

16. S. Willis, 'Sea, Coast, Estuary, Land, and Culture in Iron Age Britain', in *The Later Iron Age in Britain and Beyond*, ed. C. Haselgrove and T. Moore (Oxford 2007), 107–29.

17. J. McKelvey, 'The Excavation of Hadrian's Wall at Nos 24–46, Shields Road, Byker, Newcastle upon Tyne', *Arbeia Journal*, 9 (2010), 151–58.

18. G. R. B. Spain and F. G. Simpson, 'The Roman Wall from Wallsend to Rudchester Burn', in *HN*, XIII, 496–548.

19. C. P. Graves and D. H. Heslop, *The Eye of the North: An Archaeological Assessment of Newcastle upon Tyne* (Oxford forthcoming).

20. J. Quartermaine, 'Excavations at Bottle Bank, Gateshead, Tyne & Wear', *AA* (forthcoming).

21. M. McCarthy, 'The Roman Town of Luguvalium and the Post-Roman Settlement', in *Carlisle and Cumbria*, 2–11.
22. Snape and Bidwell, 'Roman Fort' (as n. 2), passim.
23. Ibid., 275–80.
24. Nolan, Harbottle and Vaughan, 'Early Medieval Cemetery' (as n. 2), passim; Graves and Heslop, *Eye of the North* (as n. 19).
25. Nolan, Harbottle and Vaughan, 'Early Medieval Cemetery' (as n. 2), 254; D. Knowles and R. N. Hadcock, *Medieval Religious Houses in England and Wales* (London 1971), 478 (Monkchester).
26. Bede, *EH*, 294–309.
27. B. Harbottle and P. A. G. Clack, 'Newcastle upon Tyne: Archaeology and Development', in *Archaeology in the North: Report of the Northern Archaeological Survey*, ed. D. W. Harding (Durham 1976), 121; G. McCombie et al., *Newcastle and Gateshead* (New Haven CT and London 2009), 108, 118, 121.
28. McCombie et al., *Newcastle and Gateshead* (as n. 27), 9–10, 108–09.
29. Harbottle and Clack, 'Newcastle upon Tyne' (as n. 27); C. F. O'Brien, L. Bown, S. Dixon and P. Nicholson, *The Origins of the Newcastle Quayside*, Society of Antiquaries of Newcastle upon Tyne, Monograph Series 3 (Newcastle upon Tyne 1988), 156.
30. S. Middlebrook, *Newcastle upon Tyne: Its Growth and Achievement* (Newcastle upon Tyne 1950), 32; Harbottle and Clack, 'Newcastle upon Tyne' (as n. 27), 118.
31. McCombie et al., *Newcastle and Gateshead* (as n. 27), 9.
32. The copy of Buck's engraving consulted for this research is in a volume entitled *Coleraine collection of British topography* in the library of the Society of Antiquaries of London.
33. Today, the surviving towers and much of the western section of the wall are scheduled ancient monuments.
34. McCombie et al., *Newcastle and Gateshead* (as n. 27), 125–27; McCombie, 'The Buildings of Trinity House, Newcastle upon Tyne', *AA*, 5th ser. 13 (1985), 163, 178–84.
35. N. McCord and R. Thompson, *The Northern Counties from AD 1000* (London 1998), 130.
36. Ibid., 132. See also F. W. Dendy, *Three Lectures ... on Old Newcastle, its Suburbs, and Gilds, and an Essay on Northumberland* (Newcastle upon Tyne 1921), *passim.*
37. *North Country Diaries (Second Series)*, ed. J. C. Hodgson, SS 124 (Durham 1915), 15.
38. *The Illustrated Journeys of Celia Fiennes 1685–c.1712*, ed. C. Morris (London 1982), 175–78.
39. D. Heslop, B. Jobling and G. McCombie, *Alderman Fenwick's House: The History of a Seventeenth-Century House in Pilgrim Street, Newcastle upon Tyne, and Its Owners* (Newcastle upon Tyne 2001); McCombie et al., *Newcastle and Gateshead* (as n. 27), 189, 126 (for the early sashes in Trinity House and Plummer Tower respectively), 181 (55–57 Westgate Road).
40. McCombie et al., *Newcastle and Gateshead* (as n. 27), 14–15, 152–66.
41. McCombie, 'The Buildings of Trinity House' (as n. 34), 163–85.
42. R. E. Howard, R. R. Laxton and C. D. Litton, 'Tree-ring analysis of timbers from the rigging loft and chapel undercroft, Trinity House, Broad Chare, Newcastle upon Tyne, Tyne and Wear' (unpublished report by English Heritage 2002).
43. See, briefly, McCombie et al., *Newcastle and Gateshead* (as n. 27), 46.
44. See ibid., particularly Elain Harwood, 'The Byker Estate', 232–36.

By Divine Decree: Roman Sculpture from North-East England

MARTIN HENIG

The sculpture of north-east England, carved in local sandstones, mainly dates from after the construction of Hadrian's Wall and reflects the culture of the frontier zone in the 2nd and 3rd centuries AD. *While most commissions were the work of local sculptors, other traditions from as far away as Syria can be noted. It is important to realize that the quality of the work largely depended on skill and patronage. The best work, mainly embellishing gates and important buildings as well as religious commissions and tombstones, provides impressive testimony to the skill and originality of the artists, working in the forts and garrison-towns of the region. A considerable quantity of Roman sculpture has been salvaged from early churches in the region, especially Jarrow and Hexham (some is still incorporated in the crypt at the latter) and reflects both practical re-use of Roman stone and a possible source of influence on the development of later sculpture.*

UNTIL about fifty years ago the sculpture produced in the Roman Province of Britain was regarded as a rather poor reflection of the sculpture of Metropolitan Rome. Moreover, for the most part, Romano-British art revealed a similar level of competence or rather of incompetence wherever it was encountered. In this respect R. G. Collingwood's diatribe is especially memorable.[1] Excuses might be found, for instance that this was an art 'foreign' to the native genius which lay in 'Celtic', abstract art. Whereas the artistic traditions of the Anglo-Saxons, Vikings and Normans, each of which it could be claimed was equally 'foreign', were admired and regarded as a suitable subject for art-historical study, only the occasional individual, most notably Charles Roach Smith, devoted much attention to Romano-British art, and of course his chief field of interest was south-eastern England.[2]

The north only gained because of its relatively abundant epigraphic record. The inscriptions, so useful for reconstructing some sort of history, were often associated with sculpture, both tombstones and commemorative reliefs, mainly of a military character. John Collinwood Bruce's *Lapidarium Septentrionale* of 1870–75 provides a still valuable corpus of material. Serious analysis of art styles comparable to that expended on later periods of sculpture was a product of the 20th century: here a great deal is owed to the pioneering genius of Professor Jocelyn Toynbee.[3] David Smith isolated two sculptures from South Shields as the work of a Palmyrene (Syrian) sculptor,[4] though the first full-scale study of a sculptural school in Britain was that of John Phillips in a paper which identified a discrete Carlisle school of sculptors, whose work was mainly centred in the region to the west of Hadrian's Wall.[5] Subsequent work on the various fascicules of the British contribution to the *Corpus Signorum Imperii Romani* has made it clear that sculptural workshops in Roman Britain were every bit

BAA Trans., vol. XXXVI (2013), 18–33

as regional as those operating in the Anglo-Saxon and later periods, for the most part dependent on a good nearby source of freestone and artisans trained through long apprenticeship to carve it. In Scotland and the north in general, as well as in the West Midlands, sandstone was invariably employed. In Yorkshire, Lincolnshire and down the Jurassic ridge, limestones were available, softer when quarried and easier to carve. This ready availability of local materials only breaks down in the London region and in parts of the south where stone (mainly limestone) was imported from a distance from the Cotswolds and Northamptonshire as well as from western Gaul.[6]

The British Archaeological Association's Newcastle conference came at an opportune moment in the study of Romano-British sculpture. With the near completion of the 10th fascicule of the *Corpus*, it has become possible to speak and write with some confidence about sculptural traditions throughout the province now that all regions, apart from some of the northern counties south of Hadrian's Wall (work on which is also well in progress) have been surveyed. With regard to the north-east of England, the first region to be covered, the same Edward John Phillips who 'discovered' the Carlisle school produced what still remains as one of the most useful fascicules in the series.[7] Every item is meticulously described and illustrated with half-tones. However, only a dozen lines were accorded to artistic style and nothing was said directly about stone sources, presumably because everything was cut from local sandstones. Moreover, Phillips was sufficiently influenced by older attitudes to see the ill-proportioned bodies of some carved figures as the result of a native aesthetic rather than attributing it to poor or village work found in the sculpture of every period.[8]

SCULPTURE AND THE ROMAN MILITARY COMMUNITY

THE culture-zone of the Roman Wall region was virtually the creation of the Emperor Hadrian. Although there had been a Roman military presence in this region from Flavian times, augmented by the Trajanic frontier with forts along the Stanegate such as Vindolanda, it only really achieved permanence with the construction of the Wall following Hadrian's visit to Britain in AD 122. The wording of the commemorative inscription, perhaps originally at Wallsend, partly preserved in two stones found re-used in St Paul's Church at Jarrow is significant (Fig. 1).[9] It suggests that the necessity (*necessitate*) of keeping the empire within limits had been imposed on the emperor by the will of the gods (*divino praecepto*). The eighty-mile boundary was thus as much a sacred boundary (*limes*) as a political and military one. That considerable numbers of people came to the Wall on pilgrimage or at least to its one generally accessible town, Carlisle, a kilometre to the south, is suggested by a number of enamelled offering vessels inscribed with the names of forts positioned on the western flank of the Wall.[10] But the whole region acted as a close-knit community. Religious monuments as much as the physical presence of soldiers protected the Empire to the south, and the rich iconography of both votive sculpture and personal memorials provides telling testimony to *Romanitas*, despite the complete lack of marble and other exotic freestones of the highest quality. Here, we will concentrate on the eastern side of the Wall, though most of what is written here is true of the western side, too, and was, at least as far as Carlisle was concerned, partly touched on in my contribution to the Association's Carlisle conference to which it is, of necessity, a pendent.[11] With this in mind, the boundaries of the eastern side of the Wall have been drawn somewhat wider to include a few of the well-known forts in the central sector of the Wall, briefly touched on in this earlier paper.

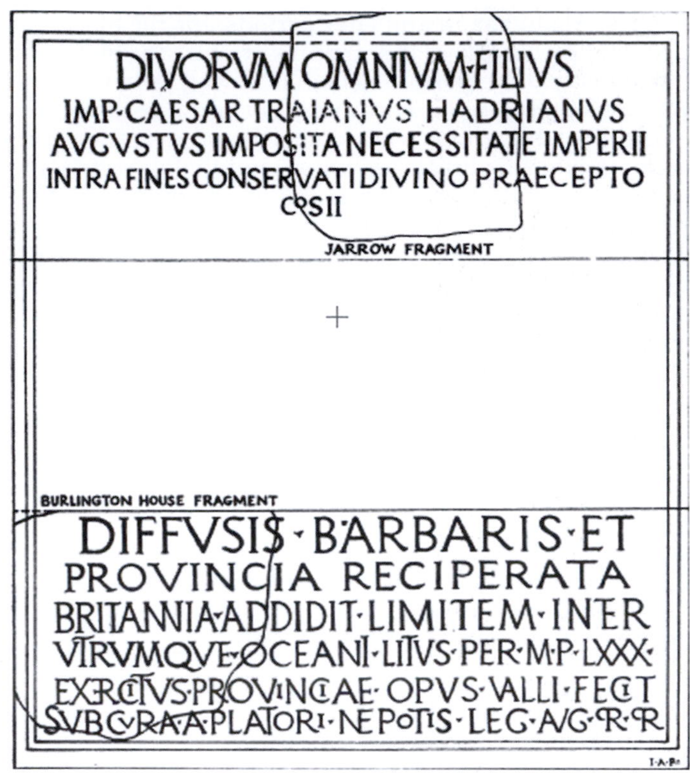

DIVORVM OMNIVM·FILIVS
IMP·CAESAR TRAIANVS HADRIANVS
AVGVSTVS IMPOSITA NECESSITATE IMPERII
INTRA FINES CONSERVATI DIVINO PRAECEPTO
COS II
JARROW FRAGMENT
BURLINGTON HOUSE FRAGMENT
DIFFVSIS·BARBARIS·ET
PROVINCIA RECIPERATA
BRITANNIA·ADDIDIT·LIMITEM·INTER
VTRVMQVE·OCEANI·LITVS·PER·M·P·LXXX·
EXERCITVS·PROVINCIAE·OPVS·VALLI·FECIT
SVB CVRA A·PLATORI·NEPOTIS·LEG·AVG·PR·PR

Fig. 1. Hadrianic dedication commemorating the erection of Hadrian's Wall *Museum of the North*

In terms of quantity, there is less extant Romano-British sculpture even in this region than there is in Anglo-Saxon and later periods where, despite natural losses and deliberate iconoclasm, a great deal survives. We are mainly concerned with carved work from forts and their contiguous *vici* including Housesteads and Vindolanda, or the largely military settlement at Corbridge. Nothing anti-dates the late 1st century (when the Roman army first established settlements), and most must certainly be dated later. To judge from inscriptions, there does not appear to be anything which post-dates the reign of Constantine (306–37), when inscriptions (and sculpture) virtually cease throughout Britain, so virtually all the sculptures can be assigned to a period of two hundred years, mainly within the 2nd or 3rd centuries AD.

The most attractive and successful carvings are those which rely for their effect on texture and line; images in the round or in high relief are inevitably less accomplished in the intractable sandstones of this region, and indeed amongst the best work are those close to (and very probably the products of) the Carlisle school, such as two of the Housesteads memorials depicting men standing and wearing long-sleeved tunics.[12] Something of the same aesthetic can be seen in a relief from Corbridge portraying a female figure, presumably a goddess, stirring a tub.[13] The deity is recognizably the mother goddess associated with Mercury on votive reliefs from Bath and Gloucester, and raises the possibility that the sculptor or more probably his client came from south-western Britain.[14] The head of the god Antenociticus (Fig. 2), part of a sculpture

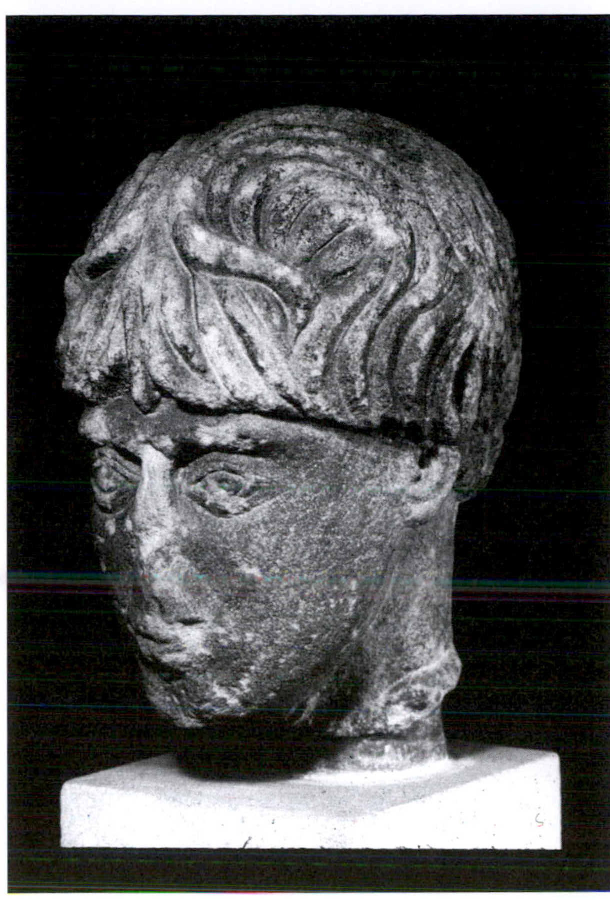

FIG. 2. Head of Antenociticus from Benwell (32 cm high)
Museum of the North

in the round from his temple at Benwell, reveals in its very simplified physiognomy both the limitations of sculptural art in the region and (in the treatment of the hair) an ability to create a lively and imaginative pattern of flowing curves.[15]

Work of high quality is inevitably associated with patronage. The best sculpture in terms of artistry is associated with military units or private commissions by rich army officers or those involved in military supply. One of the most accomplished and almost certainly the earliest relief from the region is the tombstone of a horseman, an *eques*, in the *Ala Petriana*, dated to the Flavian period, a generation before the Wall was built.[16] It shows the deceased wearing a plumed helmet and holding a standard which figures the radiate bust of a divine emperor, perhaps *Divus Augustus*: he is seated astride a richly caparisoned mount which rears over a crouching barbarian. The sculpture is one of a discrete group of cavalry tombstones,[17] and was found in the foundations of the porch to the south transept of Hexham abbey, perhaps taken there from a cemetery outside the early fort at Corbridge.

Such fine sculptures deserve to be taken as the measure of what was possible when high quality and doubtless well-paid craftsmen were available. It is unfair to judge Roman sculpture — as has too often been done — by amateur carvings of deities, for instance in the case of a figure of a Genius from Corbridge,[18] or many of the tombstones, which, although bungling in themselves, demonstrate a desire to ape both in art and literacy the art of the elite.[19] These can be compared with the many crude examples of corbels and other carvings in medieval churches which seem not to receive much attention from architectural historians, who are inevitably attracted to higher quality objects and buildings which are easier to fit into their canons of value.

There are differences in style and competence amongst what must have been significant compositions. One of the best-known and most interesting reliefs is what was probably one of a series of tableaux of the Labours of Hercules which embellished a military headquarters building at Corbridge (Fig. 3). It can be dated to the 3rd century, when Hercules was especially popular as guardian of the Empire.[20] Here it seems that the god or hero (Hercules was envisioned as both) is battling against the Lernian Hydra. He stands frontally, his club raised to dispatch the beast. The vigorous but rough patterning of the club, and indeed of Hercules' hair and beard, reminds me very much of the stylization of cameos depicting Hercules dated to the early 3rd century.[21] The body is rather ill proportioned and perhaps shows rather too much ambition in the sculptor, rather than (as Phillips claimed) a deliberately chosen new aesthetic. He is more successful with the small but by contrast rather dull figure of Minerva who stands beside Hercules to urge him on. The same lumpiness is displayed in a relief of Jupiter, *spolia* from Hexham abbey but probably from Corbridge.[22] The problem lies in a stone which is more difficult to carve smoothly than the softer limestones of, say, the Cotswold region. Perhaps the cragginess and lack of precision mattered less in the case of animals, especially those which nobody had seen. Hence the figure in the round from Corbridge of a lion about to devour a goat, intended for a tombstone but almost immediately re-used for a public fountain, has always been admired.[23] However, other less well-preserved compositions of this type from the same site and from the nearby Shorden Brae tower tomb or mausoleum were probably in the same range of competence.[24]

The most successful and distinctive carving is that which recognizes and works with the limitations of the medium to produce low relief, almost two-dimensional compositions. Pride of place should really go to what can be associated directly with the Legions and official administration, prime examples being a pair of altars dedicated by *Legio VI* which probably stood on the bridge at Newcastle and may very well be Hadrianic, one to Neptune carved with a dolphin and trident and the other to Oceanus displaying an anchor, simple but boldly striking (Fig. 4).[25] The Corbridge eagle standing on a thunderbolt must have been a masterpiece of relief carving, although only the left wing and the flashes on that side of the thunderbolt remain.[26] It clearly embellished a prominent official building. In style it is reminiscent of some of the Dolichene sculpture from the site, and it may date quite late in the 3rd century. Still highly evocative are three pieces of sculpture from a little shrine at Corbridge, evidently dedicated to *Roma Aeterna*. Two panels show respectively a vine growing out of a volute crater and Pan playing double pipes in front of another vine. A pediment portrays the foundation myth of Rome: the *Lupa Romana* with the twins, Romulus and Remus, again amidst vines.[27] These are significant pieces, recalling the pastoral beginnings of Rome as celebrated by the Augustan poets, and the delicate and harmonious carving style must have given the shrine a jewel-like quality. A similar style can be seen in the curly handled vase and linear ornament on an altar from Benwell dedicated by a centurion of *Legio XX* to Antenociticus and the Imperial Numina, although the hand is not the same.[28]

Fig. 3. Relief of Hercules and the Lernean Hydra from Corbridge (89 cm high)
Corbridge Museum

Fig. 4. Altar to Oceanus. Newcastle (120 cm high)
Museum of the North

GODS AND GODDESSES

AS in the case of medieval sculpture, the most iconographically interesting pieces are those sculptures and reliefs which are connected with religious beliefs. These bring us close to the spiritual lives of the people who commissioned and made them. Some are familiar Roman deities, others are native to Britain or north-west Europe, others still are of Oriental origin. Even very simple two-dimensional reliefs can be highly effective and would have been more so when the subjects were picked out in paint. A striking recent find from the Dolichenum at Vindolanda, an altar dedicated by a prefect of *Cohors IV Gallorum* to Jupiter Dolichenus, portrays this originally Eastern deity holding his thunderbolt and standing on a bull, carved in a conservative manner by a sculptor who knew his limitations. The bull can be compared with the animal on an altar to Hercules Invictus from Risingham, dedicated by the tribune of the *Cohors I Vangionum*.[29] The dedicators in each case were important people, Roman citizens, who would not have been satisfied with shoddy work but would have had to limit their ambitions to whatever was available. Also interesting is a relief from High Rochester which portrays Venus in company with two nymphs (Fig. 5).[30] All three

FIG. 5. Venus and the Nymphs from High Rochester (70 cm high)
Museum of the North

figures are depicted frontally, and the half-kneeling Venus is shown somewhat elongated compared to classical models. But the figures are nicely spaced and the restraint of the stone-carver, the low relief of the carving and lack of excessive ornamentation renders this a memorable image. Two seated goddesses on a relief from Housesteads, unfortunately destroyed in a site fire soon after discovery, were realistically portrayed in conversation. They were dressed in highly patterned clothing reminiscent of figures assigned to the Carlisle school, and indeed this relief may be associated with that school.[31] Also from Housesteads are two victories, both carved in high relief within niches, the first fairly static but richly textured, the second a very lively figure standing on a globe with skirts billowing around her ankles.[32] Both must have embellished important buildings in the fort.

More idiosyncratic are the sculptures of native deities. The head of Antenociticus from Benwell (Fig. 2), with mask-like face but hair highly patterned, is a rare surviving example of a cult image in the round, and has already been mentioned. However, most are in relief. A large dedication slab from Risingham is of especial interest for it was collected as early as 1599 by Sir Robert Cotton.[33] It was set up by *Cohors IV Gallorum* and depicted on one side Victory on a globe and on the other Mars, accompanied by his goose.[34] The rich textures of the octagonal border around the central inscription and the artist's desire to fill vacant spaces with apotropaic devices, Hercules knots and tricephales, give a non-Roman quality to an apparently Roman inscription. The goose was especially associated with Celtic and Germanic types of Mars (Mars Lenus, Mars Thincsus). Another example of mixed Roman style and native religion comes from Housesteads, in the form of an arch from the shrine of the German god Mars Thincsus. Here, the god, again with his goose, is figured centrally in the pediment, and two supporters, the *Alaisiagae*, stand on each side.[35] Three nymphs from Coventina's well at Carrawburgh represent the goddess-nymph Coventina in triple form (Fig. 6).[36] Unlike the Risingham relief there is no real attempt here at naturalism, or indeed at differentiating one from the other. The drapery covering the lower parts of their bodies is, however, attractively patterned. Another triad, the *cucullati*, is the subject of another relief, from Housesteads, closely dated to the early

FIG. 6. Three nymphs from Coventina's Well, Carrawburgh (52 cm high)
Chesters Museum

3rd century (Fig. 7).[37] The cloaks of these identically figured *genii* allowed the sculptor to avoid excessive detail and concentrate on their outlines. By contrast, a goddess stirring a tub mentioned above as perhaps a type of deity imported from south-west Britain is richly patterned, as is her background.[38] It is interesting that this deity appears to be one closely associated with the Dobunni in the Cotswold region: it is possible that the patron, if not the sculptor, came from there.

Patterning is employed very effectively for the cloak of the oriental deity Mithras, here equated with the sun god, on an altar set up in the Carrawburgh Mithraeum by a military prefect (Fig. 8).[39] The exceptional image from Housesteads of Mithras Saecularis, born from an egg, is carved almost in the round within a zodiac set in an egg-shaped frame (Fig. 9).[40] The high quality of the carving verges on the metropolitan. Certainly, it does not really belong with the rest of the sculpture considered here, and raises the possibility that other sculptors, possibly from distant parts of the

FIG. 7. Relief of Genii Cucullati from Housesteads (41 cm high)
Housesteads Museum

Fig. 8. Altar to Mithras from Carrawburgh (122 cm high)
Museum of the North

Fig. 9. Mithras born from an egg from Housesteads (112 cm high)
Museum of the North

Empire, were being given employment by rich patrons in the north — the prefects of Auxiliary forts and Legionary officers, for example. It may be noted that some of the sculptures discovered in the London Mithraeum were the work of artists from the Cotswolds, but there were also imported marbles, one of them dedicated by a veteran of *Legio II Augusta*.[41] Housesteads, Carrawburgh and the region in general seem to have been too far away for anyone to have been able to import marble or even more tractable freestones, but certainly the hand of highly skilled foreign sculptors can be distinguished.

SCULPTORS FROM THE EAST

TWO tombstones from South Shields, although employing a confident linearity in design, employ a very different aesthetic that is certainly not British. Rather, it can be matched most easily in Palmyrene art.[42] It is tempting to ascribe the work to a single individual, or at least to his workshop, despite the caution shown by one recent commentator.[43] One of them is a 'banquet' tombstone of Victor the Moor (Fig. 10), a freedman of a soldier in a cavalry regiment.[44] The other is the frontal-facing image of

Regina, freedwoman and wife of a Palmyrene *vexillarius* called Barates; she was a Catuvellaunian from the Verulamium region of south-east Britain (Fig. 11).[45] The type of image is different in that Victor is reclining on a couch, while Regina is seated frontally with a jewel box on one side of her and a basket containing balls of wool on the other. But there are close resemblances between the two reliefs in their architectural settings and the detailed and rich patterning of the draperies of the figures. It is unlikely that there were many *lapidarii* in Britain from so far east, and two unrelated Palmyrene sculptors from the same location would be a real coincidence (though a father-and-son workshop is possible). There are two sculptures, different in kind, but perhaps from the same Syrian group as the South Shields stele. The more impressive is a freestanding image of Juno Regina from the fort at Chesters, much further west (Fig. 12).[46] The goddess is clad in a long patterned tunic with borders of scroll-work somewhat reminiscent of the scrolling tendrils of the plant in the background of the Victor relief, and bearing comparison with the scrolled border of a garment worn by a eunuch on a relief from Palmyra.[47] With it was found a small part of a companion statue of Jupiter Dolichenus.[48] The dating of these sculptures is bound to be circumstantial. It is tempting to ascribe the South Shields stele to the early years of the 3rd century, perhaps during the years when Septimius Severus is thought to have had a base there (209–11); he was accompanied by his sons and his Syrian

FIG. 10. Gravestone of Victor the Moor from South Shields (100 cm high)
South Shields Museum

FIG. 11. Gravestone of Regina from South Shields (125 cm high)
South Shields Museum

FIG. 12. Statue of Juno Regina from Chesters (161 cm high)
Chesters Museum

consort Julia Domna and her entourage, so *Arbeia* is likely to have been especially cosmopolitan at this time.[49] Phillips and Stewart would date the two stele a generation earlier, in the later 2nd century, and this is, of course, possible.[50] On such a small sample it is difficult to decide whether we are dealing with a single artist, a single workshop group or evidence of more than one workshop.

The sculpture associated with the Temple of Jupiter Dolichenus at Corbridge can also be attributed to a sculptor from the East, but in this instance perhaps from Asia Minor. Part of a frieze depicts the sun-god mounted on a winged horse riding towards a building in which one of the Dioscuri stands holding his mount; beyond them Apollo leans against a laurel tree (Fig. 13).[51] The frieze would almost certainly have been completed with further deities, a matching building with the other Dioscurus,

FIG. 13. Frieze from Temple of Jupiter Dolichenus from Corbridge (55 cm high)
Corbridge Museum

and Luna-Diana, the moon-goddess. The crisp, low relief carving is attractive and displays a sound understanding of the medium. The classicizing nature of this fine piece hints at a 2nd-century date. However, other sculptures which have been associated with the Corbridge *Dolichenium* look later. The stylized full-face figure of a Dioscurus wearing a cloak patterned with deeply incised lines, holding the bridle of his mount, and a fragmentary relief depicting the head of a similar horse and its garland, are highly distinctive, as is another section of frieze with a *bucranium*.[52] Both horses have large oval eyes with prominent pupils identical to that of the powerful full-face image of the sun-god, one of the most powerful and vigorous reliefs from the entire Wall region (Fig. 14).[53] All can probably be dated to the end of the 3rd century. Even though the buildings which they ornamented were destroyed in 396, in the aftermath of the overthrow of Allectus, they represent provincial versions of the metropolitan art of the Tetrarchy, and the sun-god relief in particular has been compared with styles of human representation in the age of Constantine.[54]

FINAL CONSIDERATIONS

MOST studies of regional Roman sculpture would simply end at this point. There was a large range of carved stone, of varied competence, but in its better manifestations comparable to the best from workshops elsewhere (bearing in mind limitations of available material). However, that is not all. This paper has been concerned with large-scale sculptures, but carved gems, often of under 2 cm in length, have been found in profusion at Housesteads, Corbridge, South Shields and indeed almost everywhere in the region. They display sophistication in subject matter and in form. From South Shields, we have two cameos and an intaglio which reflect the Severan presence in the early years of the 3rd century. Roman religion and myth are also reflected. Either gems were imported or gem-cutters set up shop with their highly portable stock-in-trade.[55]

Like other archaeological finds from the region, including the writing tablets from Vindolanda, we are seeing in regional art not just the detritus of an unimportant backwater of Empire, but the products of thriving provincial Roman societies expressing themselves in distinctive ways. Indeed, the region is one of the richest in the

FIG. 14. Relief of Sol from Corbridge (52 cm high)
Corbridge Museum

Roman West for uncovering material culture, not just the sculpture which has been the theme of this paper, but metalwork and pottery, too.

I have already hinted in my contribution to the Association's Carlisle transactions that there were continuities between products of the Roman and Christian periods, in the copying of Roman sculptures and the reconditioning of Roman buildings, as well as perhaps employing them as models for the earliest Northumbrian ecclesiastical architecture.[56] This has recently been reiterated by Paul Bidwell's comparison of the vaulting of St Wilfred's crypt at Hexham with that of the Chesters strong-room.[57] We certainly need to ask questions about what the survival of so much of Roman material culture meant in early medieval societies, which valued *Romanitas* highly. As Bidwell rightly remarks, the density of architectural and sculptural remains in the region of the Wall must have been more like the status quo in Italy and parts of Gaul than in many areas further south in Britain.

The use of *spolia* in the surviving crypt at Hexham (and very probably in St Wilfrid's church on the site as well), and also at St Paul's at Jarrow, must in part reflect the very availability of Roman stone including sculptures and inscriptions to serve as building blocks and hardcore.[58] In the case of Hexham, the use of, or rather revival of, *Romanitas*, is manifested by stones taken from nearby *Coria* (Corbridge): the imposing tower tomb (perhaps of a governor) or mausoleum at Shorden Brae, or the bridges over the River Tyne at both Corbridge and Chesters. In the case of Jarrow, it is thought that the *spolia* principally originated in Wallsend. However, it was not always enough simply to use Roman buildings as a quarry. Frieze blocks with vegetal ornament probably taken from the Shorden Brae monument seem to have been deliberately employed for decorative effect in the southern passage and side chamber and the northern passage in the Hexham crypt.[59] Some of the inscriptions at Hexham, for example those in the north passage arch head and the roofing slab in the north side chamber, may have been intended to be visible.[60]

The extant foundation inscription of Jarrow church, originally set in the north wall of the nave, is dated 23 April 685, and may reflect the fact that Roman dedications in Latin were still to be seen adorning the remains of buildings, amongst them, maybe, the two Hadrianic inscribed blocks with which this paper began (Fig. 1). Even as late as the 12th century, William of Malmesbury read, or rather misread, an inscription in a triclinium at Carlisle.[61] Although the Jarrow stones were apparently used simply and unceremoniously as building blocks, like the tooled blocks from the bridges over the river Tyne at Chesters and Corbridge which were employed in the Hexham crypt, it is more than possible that they were first studied by the 7th-century *lapidarii*. Certainly, the style of lettering and spacing in so many extant Romano-British inscriptions bears a marked resemblance to the Jarrow dedication both in the quality of their lettering and lack of word separation; indeed, the upper part of the Hadrianic memorial provides quite a good comparison. Even the chi-rho which begins the Jarrow dedication may have been taken to signify *Romanitas*, for it was the pre-eminent Romano-Christian symbol.[62]

We cannot assume that the Romano-British carvings they saw all around them were without interest to Northumbrian sculptors either. I have suggested as much in the context of the Bewcastle cross.[63] A panel probably from a screen found re-used in the triforium of the south transept of Hexham abbey carved with a rosette could just as easily have been part of a Roman screen from a headquarters building at Corbridge or more probably part of the embellishment of the Shorden Brae mausoleum as a church screen from the 8th century.[64] If the former, it could have influenced later art, and if the latter it may have been influenced by regional Roman sculpture. Although new motifs were undoubtedly imported from the south to influence the Christian art of Northumbria, regional influences which emanated directly or indirectly from the Roman presence in the Wall region deserve to be rigorously examined, and this means a much fuller engagement with the distinctive art of this part of Roman Britain than has previously occurred.

The question of influence, if not continuity, was indeed posed by a small exhibition of Romano-British and Northumbrian work at the Henry Moore Foundation at Leeds, and in its accompanying guide-pamphlet, at the same time as the BAA conference in Newcastle.[65] Among the most intriguing pieces was a fragment of sculpture from Hexham abbey depicting putti amidst vine scrolls, one of them shooting with his bow.[66] While it is hard to find close comparanda amongst Roman sculpture surviving in the region, the trailing vines on the Corbridge shrine of *Roma Aeterna* and a cupid on an altar of Jupiter Dolichenus, also from Corbridge, are significant pointers, as are the rather more elegant cupids which flank an inscription from Housesteads.[67] My feeling is that the Hexham blocks are works of the late 7th century. If so, they certainly raise the question of a lively discourse with the past.

ACKNOWLEDGEMENTS

I am very grateful to all those people who over the years have shown such enthusiasm for my work on Roman sculpture, amongst them current colleagues working for the *Corpus Signorum Imperii Romani*, Penny Coombe, Francis Grew and Kevin Haywood, who have sharpened my perceptions enormously. I am most grateful to those who provided me with photographs for the project: Roger Tomlin, and especially Lindsay Allason-Jones, as well as the present editors, who have greatly smoothed problems of illustrating this contribution.

NOTES

1. See R. G. Collingwood and J. N. L. Myres, *Roman Britain and the English Settlements* (Oxford 1937), 247–50.
2. M. Henig, *The Art of Roman Britain* (London 1995), 9–10, 174–89.
3. J. M. C. Toynbee, *Art in Britain under the Romans* (Oxford 1964): see chapters 3 and 4 on sculpture.
4. D. J. Smith, ' A Palmyrene Sculptor at South Shields?', *AA*, 4th ser. 38 (1959), 203–07.
5. E. J. Phillips, 'A Workshop of Roman Sculptors at Carlisle', *Britannia*, 7 (1976), 101–08.
6. M. Henig, 'Sculptors from the West in Roman London', in *Interpreting Roman London. Papers in Memory of Hugh Chapman*, ed. J. Bird, M. Hassall and H. Sheldon, Oxbow Monograph 58 (Oxford 1996), 97–103. Compare K. Hayward's comments in *CSIR*: *Roman Sculpture from London and South-East England* (vol. 1, fasc. 10), ed. P. Coombe, F. Grew, K. Hayward and M. Henig (Oxford forthcoming).
7. E. J. Phillips, *CSIR: Corbridge. Hadrian's Wall East of the North Tyne* (vol. 1, fasc. 1) (Oxford 1977).
8. A theme he pursued in E. J. Phillips, 'The Classical Tradition in the Popular Sculpture of Roman Britain', in *Roman Life and Art in Britain. A Celebration in Honour of the Eightieth Birthday of Jocelyn Toynbee*, ed. J. Munby and M. Henig, British Archaeological Reports, Brit ser. 41 (Oxford 1977), 35–49.
9. R. G. Collingwood and R. P. Wright, *The Roman Inscriptions of Britain (I): Inscriptions on Stone* (Oxford 1965), 349–51 (no. 1051).
10. M. Henig, 'Souvenir or Votive? The Ilam Pan', *Association for Roman Archaeology Bulletin*, 20 (2010), 11–13.
11. M. Henig, '*Murum civitatis, et fontem in ea a Romanis mire olim constructum*: The Arts of Rome in Carlisle and the Civitas of the Carvetii and Their Influence', in *Carlisle and Cumbria*, 11–28.
12. J. C. Coulston and E. J. Phillips, *CSIR*: *Hadrian's Wall West of the North Tyne* (vol. 1, fasc. 6) (Oxford 1988), 84–85 (nos 202 and 203).
13. Phillips, *CSIR: Corbridge* (as n. 7), 42–43 (no.115).
14. B. W. Cunliffe and M. G. Fulford, *CSIR: Bath and the Rest of Wessex* (vol. 1, fasc. 2) (Oxford 1982), 11 (no. 39); M. Henig, *CSIR*: *Roman Sculpture from the Cotswold Region* (vol. 1, fasc. 7) (Oxford 1993), 26–27 (no. 78).
15. Phillips, *CSIR: Corbridge* (as n. 7), 82–83 (no. 232).
16. Ibid., 26–27 (no. 68).
17. M. Mackintosh, 'The Sources of the Horseman and Fallen Enemy Motif on the Tombstones of the Western Roman Empire', *JBAA*, 139 (1986), 1–21. The Hexham tombstone is listed at 15–16 (no. 8).
18. Phillips, *CSIR: Corbridge* (as n. 7), 3 (no. 5).
19. Ibid. , 98–99 (no. 267, from Risingham), 100–01 (no. 273, from High Rochester).
20. Ibid., 3 (no. 6).
21. Compare M. Henig, 'Caracalla as Hercules? A New Cameo from South Shields', *Antiq. J.*, 66 (1986), 378–80. pl. lxiva.
22. Phillips, *CSIR: Corbridge* (as n. 7), 6 (no. 12).
23. Ibid., 31–32 (no. 82).
24. Ibid., 30–31 (nos 79–81).
25. Ibid., 71–72 (no. 213), 74 (no. 216).
26. Ibid., 53 (no. 170).
27. Ibid., 12–13 (nos 38 and 37 respectively).
28. Ibid., 81 (no. 230).
29. A. Birley and A. Birley, 'A Dolichenum at Vindolanda', *AA*, 5th ser. 39 (2010), 35–36 (see no. 1, fig. 1); Phillips, *CSIR: Corbridge* (as n. 7), 63 (no. 190).
30. Ibid., 74–76 (no. 218).
31. Coulston and Phillips, *CSIR: Hadrian's Wall West* (as n. 12), 128 (no. 349).
32. Ibid., 36–38 (nos 99, 100).
33. G. Davies, 'Sir Robert Cotton's Collection of Roman Stones: A Catalogue with Commentary', in *Sir Robert Cotton as Collector*, ed. C. J. Wright (London 1997), 132–36 (no. 1).
34. Phillips, *CSIR: Corbridge* (as n. 7), 72–74 (no. 215).
35. Coulston and Phillips, *CSIR: Hadrian's Wall West* (as n. 12), 65 (no. 161).
36. Ibid., 34–35 (no. 93).
37. Ibid., 61–62 (no. 152).
38. Phillips, *CSIR: Corbridge* (as n. 7), 42–43 (no. 115).
39. Coulston and Phillips, *CSIR: Hadrian's Wall West* (as n. 12), 47–48 (no. 122).
40. Ibid., 49–50 (no. 126).
41. Collingwood and Wright, *Roman Inscriptions* (as n. 9), 1–2 (no. 3).

42. Smith , 'A Palmyrene Sculptor' (as n. 4); M. A. R. Colledge, *The Art of Palmyra* (London 1976), especially 231–33.

43. P. Stewart, '*Totenmahl* Reliefs in the Northern Provinces: A Case-Study in Imperial Sculpture', *Journal of Roman Archaeology*, 22 (2009), 267, 268–69.

44. Compare Victor the Moor with banquet reliefs from Palmyra itself (Colledge, *Art of Palmyra* (as n. 42), pls 150 and 61, 62, 102).

45. Compare the stele of Regina with that of Ra'ateh from Palmyra (Colledge, *Art of Palmyra* (as n. 42), pls 149, 74). However, Malku's wife portrayed on a funerary plaque from Palmyra (Colledge, *Art of Palmyra* (as n. 42), pl. 98) sits in a basket chair like Regina.

46. Coulston and Phillips, *CSIR: Hadrian's Wall West* (as n. 12), 44–45 (no. 117).

47. Colledge, *Art of Palmyra* (as n. 42), pl. 91.

48. Coulston and Phillips, *CSIR: Hadrian's Wall West* (as n. 12), 45 (no. 118).

49. M. 'Mattern, 'Die Reliefverzierten römischen Grabstelen der Provinz Britannia: Themen und Typen', *Kölner Jahrbuch für Vor- und Frühgeschichte*, 22 (1989), 789–91 (nos 116, 117).

50. Phillips, *CSIR: Corbridge* (as n. 7), 29–30 (no. 75); Stewart , '*Totenmahl* Reliefs' (as n. 43), 266–69.

51. Phillips, *CSIR: Corbridge* (as n. 7), 18–19 (no. 52).

52. Ibid., 19–20 (nos 53–55).

53. Ibid., 20–21 (no. 56).

54. M. Henig, 'Relief Carving of Sol', in *Constantine the Great. York's Roman Emperor*, ed. E. Hartley, J. Hawkes, M. Henig and F. Mee (York 2006), 196, 198 (no. 179). Compare the image of Christ in the Hinton St Mary mosaic: M. Henig, 'Central Roundel of Floor Mosaic', in ibid., 204–06 (no. 190).

55. M. Henig, 'Gem Workshops in the Provinces: Roman Britain', in *Aquileia e la glittica di età ellenistica e romana*, ed. G. Sena Chiesa and E. Gagetti (Trieste 2009), 142 (fig. 2), 145–46.

56. Henig, '*Murum civitatis*' (as n. 11), 18–28.

57. P. Bidwell, 'A Survey of the Anglo-Saxon Crypt at Hexham and its Reused Roman Stonework', *AA*, 5th ser. 39 (2010), 53–145, especially figs 34–36.

58. T. Eaton, *Plundering the Past. Roman Stonework in Medieval Britain* (Stroud 2000), 104–05, 128.

59. Ibid., 117, fig. 62; Bidwell, 'Anglo-Saxon Crypt' (as n. 57), 118–20, figs 38, 39.

60. Bidwell, 'Anglo-Saxon Crypt' (as n. 57), 119; Collingwood and Wright, *Roman Inscriptions* (as n. 9), nos 1122, 1151.

61. Compare Henig, '*Murum civitatis*' (as n. 11), 13.

62. R. Cramp, *County Durham and Northumberland*, Corpus of Anglo-Saxon Stone Sculpture in England 1 (Oxford 1984), 113–14 (no. 17), 524 (pl. 98); E. Okasha, 'Spaces between Words: Word Separation in Anglo-Saxon Inscriptions', in *The Cross Goes North. Processes of Conversion in Northern Europe, AD 300–1300*, ed. M. Carver (York 2003), 341, pl. 21.1.

63. Henig, '*Murum civitatis*' (as n. 11), 20–23.

64. Phillips, *CSIR: Corbridge* (as n. 7), 55–56 (no. 180); compare Bidwell, 'Anglo-Saxon Crypt' (as n. 57), 72, and Cramp, *County Durham* (as n. 62), 186 (no. 22).

65. C. Karkov and E. Tait, *Roman to English. The Migration of Forms in Early Northumberland* (10 July–10 October 2010).

66. Ibid., no. 2. See also Cramp, *County Durham* (as n. 62), 185 (no. 21a–c).

67. Phillips, *CSIR: Corbridge* (as n. 7), 12–13 (no. 38), 17–18 (no. 51); Coulston and Phillips, *CSIR: Hadrian's Wall West* (as n. 12), 98 (no. 241).

Stones of the North: Sculpture in Northumbria in the 'Age of Bede'

JANE HAWKES

The stone sculpture surviving in Bernicia from the 'Age of Bede' makes it clear that the Church in north Northumbria adopted rich and varied means in its initial displays of public art in sculptural form during the later 7th and 8th centuries. The ways in which the medium represented, at the time, a new and innovative art has allowed insight into the potential significances of its materiality as a result of its means of transmission, as have the motives informing the selection of the various monument forms, and the motifs and images used to decorate them. It is argued here that the results of such experimentation may well have included the deliberate manipulation of the art of carved relief and the presentation of the human form, which was originally highly coloured and inset with other materials, and it is suggested that this phenomenon should be understood to represent conscious attempts to recreate the painted icon: panels familiar in ecclesiastical contexts that played a specific role in sacred settings as the image made 'material'.

INTRODUCTION

WHEN Bede died in 739, the carved stone monuments of Anglo-Saxon Northumbria, which have come to be identified as definitive of the material culture of the region, were perhaps not as numerous or significant a part of the landscape as they were to be by the end of the 8th century. Yet, the means by which the ecclesiastical culture of Northumbria, or more specifically Bernicia, would come to be cast in stone had been established: churches, with their architectural and liturgical furnishings, had been constructed in stone, as had funerary monuments and the freestanding monumental high crosses now associated most intimately with the public arts of Anglo-Saxon England.

Bede's own centre of Jarrow-Wearmouth, with its stone churches and associated chapels, had been standing for over fifty years (Wearmouth being founded, *c.* 674, and Jarrow, *c.* 682),[1] as had the slightly older church of St Andrew's at Hexham (founded *c.* 672), with its crypt, carved architectural decoration, and frith stool.[2] At St Peter's (Wearmouth) there was the monumental figure in the gable of the entrance porch, itself decorated with interlaced zoomorphs whose tails form Tau crosses flanking the threshold;[3] and, among the carved fragments from the site, which include the remains of an elaborate stone bench-throne,[4] is the funerary marker commemorating the priest Herebercht, its central cross enclosed by two zoomorphs with serpentine bodies and the heads of birds of prey.[5] At St Paul's (Jarrow), the church was recorded, in stone, as having been dedicated during the time of the ecclesiastical prelate (Ceolfrith) and the secular ruler (Ecgfrith);[6] and it too was adorned with carved sculptures, as well as

BAA Trans., vol. XXXVI (2013), 34–53

liturgical furnishings such as the *schola sanctorum*,[7] and a stone reredos (Fig. 1).[8] The central cross of this latter piece is flanked by an inscription recalling the words reputedly heard by Constantine prior to his victory at the Milvian Bridge in 306: IN HOC SINGULARI SIGNO VITA REDDITUR MUNDO (In this unique sign life is returned to the world). By the early decades of the 8th century this would have had particular resonance against the backdrop of the Good Friday liturgy of the Lateran which saw the Lateran relic of the True Cross process from the Church of Christ Saviour to Sta Croce in Hierusaleme (known simply as 'Jerusalem' at this time), where it was placed on the altar alongside the relic thought to have been brought to Rome by Constantine's mother, Helena, and venerated by the Pope. As Ó Carragáin has shown, this was a ritual that would have been observed in Rome by Wilfrid and Benedict,[9] and knowledge of it was here being commemorated and invoked in stone in the sacred space of St Paul's.

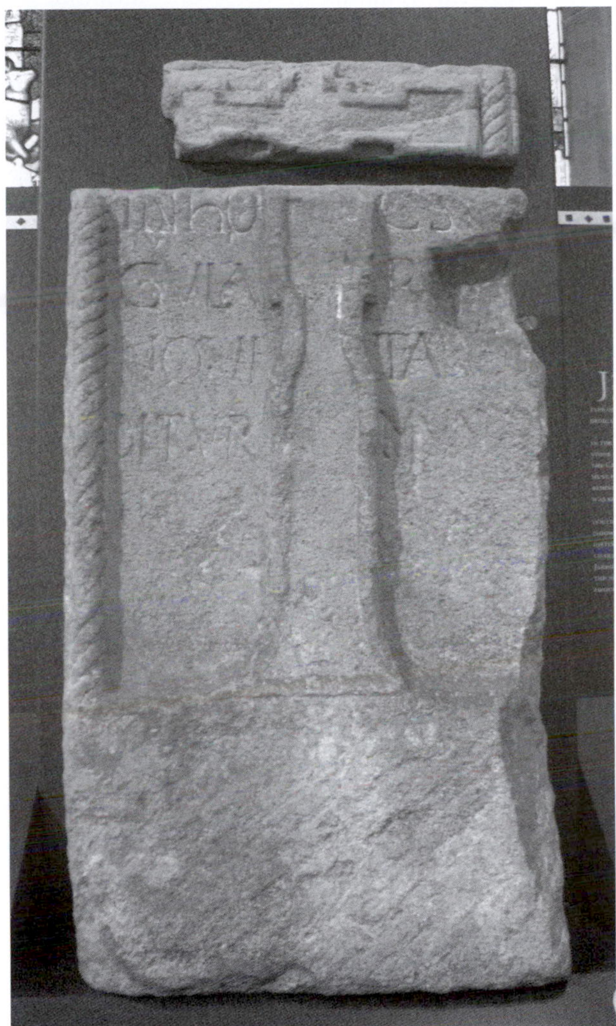

FIG. 1. Reredos, Jarrow, St Pauls, late 7th century
Photo: author

There were, of course, other centres marked by stone buildings and public stone monuments: the late 7th- or early 8th-century church at Escomb (County Durham), for instance, often associated with the Jarrow-Wearmouth centre, survives in its entirety in stone, and includes material from the Roman fort of *Vinovium* (Binchester),[10] some of which was reconstructed as the chancel arch. The remains of various sculptural monuments (all dated to the 8th century)[11] also preserved there include parts of a liturgical screen (one of the upright pilasters and the remains of a light socket),[12] and a funerary monument.[13] Now set as a reredos to the high altar, this presents a stepped-base cross flanked by symbols of the sun and moon, and thus references the general resurrection at the end of time.[14] And there is the 8th-century stone church at Corbridge (Northumberland), which stands in the *vicus* area of the Stanegate fort of *Corstopitum*, and preserves Roman material in the form of the extremely large and imposing arch at the west end of the nave.[15]

At a number of these sites there are also the remains of the stone monuments erected during the course of the 8th century that have come, in the scholarship, to define the sculptural arts of the period: namely, the freestanding monumental high stone crosses. Thus, the remains of carved monumental cross-shafts have survived at Escomb,[16] some of which have been related stylistically to the contemporary cross standing in the nearby church at Auckland St Andrew;[17] and, although no stone crosses seem to have survived at Jarrow-Wearmouth, the carved remains there link the centre with the production of the well-known 8th-century monuments that have survived elsewhere: at Ruthwell (Dumfriesshire), Bewcastle (Cumberland), and Rothbury (Northumberland).[18]

Thus, although at the time of Bede's death, the stone buildings and monuments which have come to be identified as definitive of the material culture of Anglo-Saxon Northumbria were perhaps not as familiar as they were to be a century later, the earliest articulations of these public art forms were clearly present, and were, moreover, manifesting some of the extraordinary inventiveness that characterizes the early Christian art of the region.

THE NEW ART OF STONE IN EARLY CHRISTIAN ANGLO-SAXON ENGLAND

IT is perhaps worth noting here that, when these stone monuments and buildings first began to appear over the course of the 7th century, they represented an entirely new and innovative art form. The art of working in stone is generally understood to have been one *not* practised by the early Germanic settlers in the region in the immediate post-Roman period. But, as a result of contacts with peoples in the west and north-west, the establishment of the papal mission in the south at the turn of the 7th century, and other encounters with the sub-Roman world, stone came to be a medium embraced by the Anglo-Saxons for public art.[19]

Those living in the west and north-west, for instance, had continued to use stone as a medium for erecting churches and funerary monuments. At Whithorn (Galloway), as even Bede was forced to admit, the 'Southern Picts':

> had embraced the truth, by the preaching of Ninias, a most reverend bishop and holy man of the British nation, who had been regularly instructed at Rome, in the faith and mysteries of the truth; whose episcopal see, named after St Martin the bishop, and famous for a stately church (wherein he and many other saints rest in the body), is still in existence among the English nation. The place belongs to the province of the Bernicians, and is generally called the White House (*candida casa*), because he there built a church of stone.[20]

Putting to one side the rhetorical contortions by which Bede identifies Ninian with Christianity, the Roman Church, Britons and Northumbria, it is clear that in the north-west stone was used to construct buildings. Furthermore, at this site, and elsewhere in the region, funerary monuments still survive that also demonstrate a continuum of working in stone for commemorative purpose.[21]

Nevertheless, it was with the arrival and establishment of the papal mission that stone as a medium for art and architecture was re-introduced into the Anglo-Saxon territories on a large scale: the churches of the monastery at Canterbury were erected with re-used Roman material, as was the Church of Christ Saviour, set up within the walls of the old Roman cantonal capital, to serve as the headquarters of the mission.[22] Most significantly, there was the church — built of stone from the foundations — which was dedicated to the Four Crowned Martyrs.[23] This is an unusual dedication which existed only in Pannonia, where the saints in question were martyred under Diocletian in 305, and Rome. Here, a 4th-century *titulus* on the Coelian Hill was rededicated to *Coronati Quattuor* in the early decades of the 7th century to mark the translation there of the martyrs' relics. While it has been suggested that the Canterbury dedication may mark the further translation of some of these relics in 601, what is important is that the martyrs in question were understood to be stonemasons.[24] A new stone church dedicated to these specific saints, set up *within* the confines of the Romano-British cantonal capital of Canterbury, whose landscape had been systematically redefined by its new stone churches, clearly reflects the importance that was being placed on that medium in the first papal ecclesiastical centre in Anglo-Saxon England.

PRECEPTS AND PERCEPTIONS OF THE NEW ART OF STONE

THE construction of this stone church also reflects, as has been argued elsewhere, the importance invested in the medium of stone by early Anglo-Saxon churchmen due to its perceived potential to express things Roman.[25] Bede makes this clear in his explicit association of stone with Rome in his account of the stone churches set up under Benedict and Ceolfrith at Jarrow and Wearmouth.[26] Here the Roman associations were further expressed through the use of *opus signinum*,[27] not only encountered in Rome, but also still visible in the flooring of the Roman remains in the landscape of the north-east: at *Vinovium*, for instance, from where stones were taken for display in the fabric of the church at Escomb.[28] There was also the covered walkway linking St Peter's with the monastic settlement to the south of the church at Wearmouth,[29] echoing those that linked the Roman funerary churches of San Lorenzo and Old St Peter's with the city of Rome;[30] and there was the use of the western *porticus* as a burial place for eminent churchmen.[31] As Ó Carragáin has demonstrated, this was a practice which, found elsewhere in early Christian contexts in Anglo-Saxon England at Canterbury,[32] can be traced back to the use of the eastern *porticus* of St Peter's in Rome as the place of burial of popes, from the time of Leo I onwards.[33]

Association with imperial and papal Christian Rome is also reflected in the design of the stone monuments that began to be erected in Northumbria at this time. Apart from the clear Constantinian references incorporating contemporary papal liturgical ritual in the Jarrow reredos, analogous associations may also lie in the form and decoration of the stone high crosses that were unique to the insular world until the 11th or 12th century. For among the monument forms that would have been encountered by those visiting Rome were the obelisks; with their squared, tapering monolithic form they had become ubiquitous signifiers of imperial victory. And they included in their number the obelisk that stood to the south-west of St Peter's until the 16th century (Fig. 2), being associated with the martyrdom of Peter who, it was recorded, was crucified '*inter duas metas*' (between the two metae), that is, in the spina of Nero's circus, at an equal distance from the two end goals; in other words, he was executed at the foot of the obelisk which now stands before the church — originally raised by Constantine over the necropolis on the slopes of the Vatican hill, to the north of the circus, leaving only the obelisk in its original setting as part of the commemorative and triumphal Christian appropriation and dedication of the overall site.[34] With these associations, and that of Constantine with the 'victory sign' of the cross in Anglo-Saxon England, it is not inconceivable that the form of the obelisk may have played a part in the development of the squared and slightly tapered monumental stone crosses that were set up in Northumbria during the course of the 8th century. Indeed, such connections may well have influenced the contemporary references to, and perceptions of, these crosses. The runic inscription at Bewcastle (Fig. 3), for instance, refers to the cross unequivocally as *þis sigbecn* (victory sign).[35]

Certainly, the decorative motifs and iconographic schemes carved on the crosses reveal the strong influence of the Roman world — imperial and Christian. As

FIG. 2. Obelisk, St Peter's, Rome
Photo: author

FIG. 3. Cross-shaft, Bewcastle, Cumbria, west face, early 8th century
Photo: author

Nordhagen noted in 1969, any consideration of the inhabited plant-scrolls (Fig. 4), which are so ubiquitous to the cross-shafts, and serve to transform them at one level into the Tree of Life, should include the pilasters arranged in the Oratory of John VII in St Peter's between 705–07 (Fig. 5).[36] These comprised five 1st-century spoliated pilasters, and a sixth, commissioned by John, to complete the set. Square in section and standing upright along the wall, these made prominent the motif of a plant-scroll growing from the ground-level upwards, filled with all variety of animals, birds and even human figures. While the inspiration for the individual designs presented on the Northumbrian sculptures may lie in a complex genealogy of sources,[37] it is not

FIG. 4. Cross-shaft, Bewcastle, Cumbria, east face, early 8th century
Photo: author

FIG. 5. Pillaster from Oratory of John VII, Old St Peters, Vatican, Rome, 705–07
Photo: author

unlikely that the association of the motif with one of the most important spaces in St Peter's will have played a part in decisions to adopt and display the plant-scroll in the Anglo-Saxon north. And, as far as the figural images are concerned, the influence of the Roman world can be seen in the production of individual images as well as iconographic schemes — as at Rothbury, where the iconography of imperial rule, from an object such as an imperial diptych, was adapted to present the divine rule of Christ (Fig. 6).[38]

THE NEW ART OF THE STONE ICON

AGAINST this background, of potential inspiration, appropriation, adaptation and innovation in the material, form and decoration of the art of stone sculpture in the 7th and 8th centuries in Anglo-Saxon Northumbria, the art of relief carving itself perhaps deserves further consideration. For not only was it an innovative art form in its early stages, it was also highly polychromed and incorporated multiple media in its presentation. In their original state the stone monuments would have stood, brightly coloured and inset with paste glass and/or pieces of metal.

FIG. 6. Adoration of Christ, Rothbury, Northumberland, late 8th century
Photo: author

Numerous pieces of sculpture attest to its coloured appearance: as Bailey has noted, the shaft of the cross from Ruthwell, which was preserved in the church after its demolition in the 17th century, is recorded in the 18th century as still retaining green paint on its surface;[39] while the base of the slightly later 8th-century cross-shaft at Rothbury still retains traces of red paint.[40] Later sculptures, such as the early 9th-century fragments from Reculver (Kent)[41] and the 10th-century pieces from Burnsall (West Yorkshire) also preserve traces of gesso and polychromy.[42] And, of course, the early 9th-century shrine fragment preserving a carving of the angel of the Annunciation from Lichfield[43] provides perhaps the best-known instance of the phenomenon, as well as giving clear insight into the quality of painterly techniques — subtle shading, gradations of colour, and fine-line highlighting — that could be brought to bear in this medium.

Furthermore, the deeply drilled eyes of many of the figures, such as the Lichfield Angel and all the figures preserved on the Rothbury fragments (Figs 6, 8, 9, 12, 13), attest to the use of insets, likely in the form of paste glass, rendering them analogous to the studded eyes of contemporary ivories, such as the 8th-century Northumbrian Genoels Elderen diptych now in Brussels, in which the eyes of Christ Triumphant, the angel of the Annunciation, the Virgin, Elizabeth and the handmaiden (of the Visitation) are all inset with bright blue glass.[44] Most remarkably, recent conservation of the fragment from Aberlady, East Lothian, at the National Museum of Scotland has revealed the presence of a tin casing within the drilled pupil of one of the birds decorating the stone; this has been identified as having held just such an inset.[45] Moreover, the presence of additional recesses and drilled holes (on the Reculver fragments, or the 8th-century cross-head from Lastingham in North Yorkshire), bear witness to the appliqués that were attached to the stone carvings — a metal cross held by Christ on one of the Reculver pieces;[46] and a metalwork boss set at the centre of the Northumbrian cross-head (Fig. 7).[47] The fragmentary and monochrome remains that today provide evidence of the existence of Anglo-Saxon stone sculpture are clearly far removed in appearance from what was once set up in the churches and across the landscape.

The bright colours and (occasionally) glittering nature of the freestanding crosses would have made them instantly visible to those encountering them, whether this occurred within ecclesiastical enclosures, as suggested by the situation of the Ruthwell

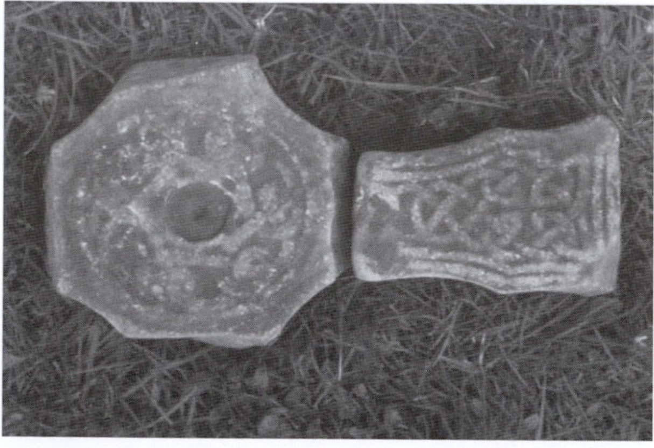

FIG. 7. Cross-head, Lastingham, Yorkshire, 8th century
Photo: author

and Bewcastle monuments,[48] or on landed estates, as suggested in the Life of Willibald, which recounts how, as an infant, Willibald was set at the foot of just such a cross (albeit not identified as stone) in the early 8th century (i.e. *c.* 703) and miraculously healed of a life-threatening illness:

> When his parents in great anxiety of mind, were still uncertain about the fate of their son, they took him and offered him up before the holy cross of our Lord and Saviour. And this they did, not in the church but at the foot of the cross, for on the estates of the nobles and good men of the Saxon race it is a custom to have a cross, which is dedicated to our Lord and held in great reverence, erected on some prominent spot for the convenience of those who wish to pray daily before it.[49]

Alternatively, the monuments could have been encountered within the churches themselves, as indicated by the cross from Rothbury which preserves in the arms of its cross-head holes for candles or floating wicks (Fig. 8).[50] Here, the effect of glittering candlelight would certainly have lent considerable power to the carvings on the monument, not least of which is the visceral representation of the Damned in Hell (Fig. 9), their paste-glass eyes reflecting light from the cross-head above, and their naked genitalia threatened by the jaws of the serpentine creatures whose coils entrap the Damned, and whose eyes would also have glittered in the (candle)light.[51]

With this in mind, it is possible to turn to consider the figural carvings themselves, although here the preconceptions that underpin understanding of much of this sculpture need first to be addressed. For the way in which the carvings have been deemed

FIG. 8. Top of cross-head, Rothbury, Northumberland, late 8th century
Photo: author

FIG. 9. Damned in Hell, Rothbury, Northumberland, late 8th century
Photo: author

to conform, or not, to certain classical norms has considerable bearing on the present discussion of their presentation and effects. In the early scholarship the 'barbarity' of the carved figures was, at best, noted, but was more often castigated for its inability (or, more accurately, the inability of the carvers) to produce figures carved in relief that replicated the perceived, although resolutely undefined, refinement of classical carving.[52] These deficiencies — lack of proportion, stylization and flattening — were cited as proof of the influence of the barbaric arts of the Germanic peoples who were incapable of achieving the heights of civilized cultures as expressed in the public arts. Now, while it might be recognized that these attitudes are perhaps best considered as the products of the time in which they were published (in the years leading up to, during, and in the immediate aftermath of the Second World War), and the rhetoric used to frame the premise dismissed, it remains the case that much discussion of Anglo-Saxon art generally has regarded the tendency to render figures and animals as less than realistic or naturalistic entities, as a result of the Germanic Anglo-Saxon tendency to abstraction and stylization evident in the traditional arts of the metalworker.[53]

While this may indeed be the case, it was certainly not a characteristic unique to the arts of the Anglo-Saxons. For a brief consideration of the carvings circulating in the late Roman, early Christian world of the 5th and 6th centuries demonstrates many features analogous to those identified in the Northumbrian carvings. The consular diptychs for instance (Fig. 10), which were re-used on the altars of Anglo-Saxon churches in the 7th and 8th centuries,[54] are characterized by considerable stylization, abstract flattening, and odd proportions. In the context of representing the apparently 'real' event of the inaugural games organized and officiated by the consul, the diptychs, like that of Areobindus (506),[55] present man and games 'non-realistically' by elevating and enlarging the consul with the symbols of his office and magisterial authority, and isolating him from the inaugural circus depicted below. In turn, the circus is reduced to a series of diminutive figures placed as a semicircular frame demarcating the arena, itself filled with further diminutive figures and animals presented in awkward and 'un-naturalistic' poses. The lion, for instance, is presented much like the creatures on the Rothbury cross (e.g. Fig. 9):[56] its body stands in profile, but its head, set between its forelegs, is turned to face the viewer and so is seen full-on from above.

The overall organization of the scene negates any notion of perspective, of the games taking place within the arena before the consul enthroned in his box. Events taking place in three-dimensional space have been effectively reduced to a two-dimensional planar surface. The result is the articulation of the visual rhetoric of *aulic* art that distorts representations of space and form to emphasize, in this case, the consul's majesty and authority within the imperial hierarchy. In this act of visual relocation, of removing the subject from the visual illusion of 'real' time and space, the figure has been rendered all important, and the authority inherent in his office has been foregrounded — situated in the space between the viewer and the two-dimensional plane of the ivory. At the same time, however, by retaining reference to the space of the arena by means of the figures placed in a semicircle, the viewer is able to intuit that particular space, and with that awareness the representation of the arena is transformed in the mind of the viewer into a circular structure that obtrudes horizontally from the vertical plane of the ivory diptych.[57] Thus, without the use of linear perspective an understanding of perspectival space is achieved, while at the same time social and cultural hierarchies are also being expressed by means of the manipulation of scale.

With this in mind, it is worth reconsidering the 'style' of the Northumbrian carved figures, for if they can be removed from the scholarly categories of 'inadequate' classicism, or cultural hybridity, it is possible that they, too, may be usefully regarded as reflecting quite deliberate visual manipulation. In the panel containing the *Majestas* standing over the beasts at Ruthwell (Fig. 11), for instance, the figure, enlarged within the frame, his arms held tightly at his side, has been reduced to the absolute essence of majesty and authority, in a manner analogous to, but perhaps articulated with even more emphasis than that expressed on the diptych. Yet at Ruthwell the deeply dished halo stands distinctively forward of the frame, thus dissolving it and allowing the figure to move from one plane into another; in effect, situating the Divine within the space that lies between sculptural surface and viewer.

Elsewhere, the crucifixion in the arms of the cross-head from Rothbury employs a similar strategy, albeit articulated more emphatically (Fig. 12). For here an angel enclosed in the inner moulding framing the upper cross-arm grasps the upper rim of the deeply dished cruciform halo of Christ that extrudes over the upper intersection of the frames at the centre of the cross-head, extending almost to the outer edge of the stone. As at Ruthwell, the result is such that the frame, here the cross of the crucifixion itself, recedes and the figure of the Crucified crowned by the triple cruciform halo of divine majesty[58] is physically thrust forward to stand as Christ resurrected, and so demonstrates the theological paradox that the death on the cross was understood to be the means to everlasting life. In effect, cross and crucifixion recede into the past, while Christ is resurrected in Majesty in the future.

Below, at the top of the shaft, the unusual half-length figure of the *Majestas* continues the presentation of shifting planes of existence (Fig. 13).[59] In this panel, instead of raising his right hand in blessing, Christ holds it across his body with his index finger extended and laid (uniquely in the iconography of the *Majestas*), on the book held over his chest in his left hand; literally pointing to the Word of the gospels. This arrangement makes for a unique set of iconographic references, but it also ensures that the body of Christ is enclosed firmly within the arched frame that surrounds him; and unlike the standing figure at Ruthwell the halo does not obtrude over that frame. In fact, the body is further contained by the presence of two buds on long stems that extend between the figure and the frame, with the buds lying on either side of the halo under the arch. While these appear, however, to emphasize the confinement of Christ, the fact that the stems are carved as if emerging from behind his body also makes it seem that his body is thrust forward to emerge from the frame and stand in front of it. In effect, although adopting different strategies from those employed in the cross-head above and at Ruthwell, the relief carving of the *Majestas* at Rothbury has also been manipulated to present the body of Christ as if it inhabits a plane of existence between the carved surface of the cross-shaft and the viewer. The result in all cases is a three-dimensional icon, which achieves a complex re-presentation of the Divine.

And here the term 'icon' perhaps needs to be explored further. For, in considering the manner in which the art of relief carving on these Northumbrian sculptures has been exploited to present the figure in three-dimensional space against a two-dimensional background surface, together with the fact that the carvings were likely originally highly coloured, which would have articulated the figures as clearly contained by, or emerging from, the frames delineating the panels, we perhaps have an insight into the reasons lying behind this quite specific method of presentation.

Fig. 10. Diptych of Consul Areobindus, 506 (Constantinople)
Musée national du Moyen Âge – Thermes et Hôtel Cluny, Paris, France

Fig. 11. *Majestas Christi* (Christ over the Beasts), Ruthwell, Dumfries., early/mid-8th century
Photo: author

FIG. 12. Crucifixion, Rothbury, Northumberland, late 8th century
Photo: author

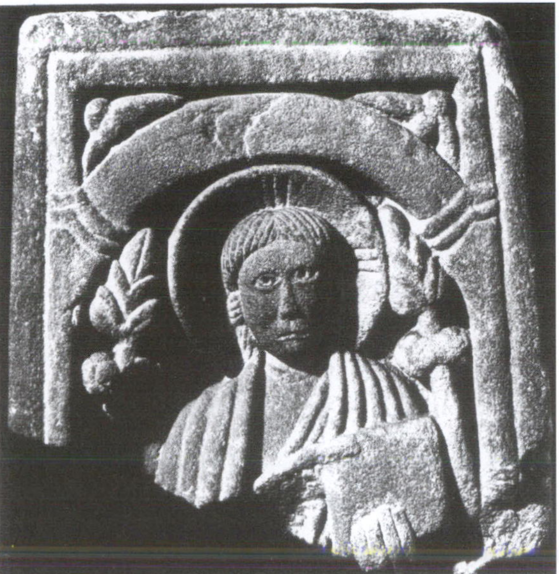

FIG. 13. *Majestas Christi*, Rothbury, Northumberland, late 8th century
Photo: author

Evidence from the 6th century onwards provides many examples of the painted panels which are understood to be 'icons': wooden boards painted with depictions of a holy being or object. The most common subjects were Christ, the Virgin, Saints, Angels and the cross; but events such as the crucifixion were also included.[60] Yet, while it is the painted wooden board that is commonly considered to constitute the material icon, it is clear that they could be constructed in other media, and still serve the same function: as the means by which the viewer could contemplate, and so come to understand the nature of the Divine.

The paintings (whether on wooden boards or some other medium; whether depicting a figure or an event) were considered to be like writing in that they induce remembrance and so elicit understanding.[61] Like text, the picture was deemed to recall what has happened in the story of salvation, which, as Belting put it, 'is more than a historical fact'; the act of viewing the image/icon allows the observer to recall to memory the person or event depicted, and so to recall the Divine in his heavenly glory.[62] In effect, the icon could refer to both the past and future presences of the Divine in the life of humanity, something that could be experienced only indirectly in the present.[63] As the image was viewed, a person (such as Christ) or event (such as the crucifixion) from the past was called to mind by the observer in the present, enabling the future significance of that event or person in the history of salvation to be recalled. Put another way, the icon functioned as a portal through which the human viewer could gain proper understanding of the Divine through contemplation and remembrance, processes that made present the past and future. The act of viewing the image thus enabled imagined movement through time and planes of existence:

between past, present and future; the human (and the material) and the Divine (and immaterial).

Thus, in Rome during the 7th and 8th centuries, painted panel icons, generally of the Virgin and Child but also of Christ,[64] became prominent features in sacred spaces, their confines delineated by the edges of the wooden board, or — as is the case with the 7th-century life-size icon of the Virgin and Child in Sta Maria in Trastevere — by elaborate frames. This particular icon, however, was not merely a painted wooden panel with a gold-painted frame; the cross originally held by the Virgin formed a metalwork appliqué, which was only subsequently replaced by the painted version. At the same time, icons in other media were also venerated: one example can be seen in the almost life-size 8th-century panel in the Catacomb of Comodilla (Rome), which depicts the widow Turtura standing before the Virgin and Child, flanked by saints Felix and Adautto; contained within its painted frame, this image is set on the wall of the chamber at human height and eye level. Graffiti nearby testifies to the presence of Anglo-Saxon visitors to and viewers of the image.[65] Elsewhere, at Sta Maria Antiqua, the church serving a papal *diaconium* and so frequented by early pilgrims to Rome,[66] are a number of icons of 7th-century date all of which are enclosed within painted frames: the Annunciation, set at floor level on the south pier to the left of the Sanctuary area; the Virgin *Eleousa*, painted at eye level on the circular surface of the south-west column of the right aisle (the space for the female congregation); the Three Holy Mothers (set low down in the north-west wall of the right aisle); and the Virgin and Child (Fig. 14). This latter has been painted, in a frame, on the back wall of a small niche, low down on the south face of the north-west pier, demarcating the narthex from the main body of the nave and the aisle on the right, and preserves the remains of a fixture holding a hanging that would have covered the icon, and a small indentation before it, on the ledge below.[67]

FIG. 14. Virgin and Child Niche Icon, Sta Maria Antiqua, Rome, 705–07
Photo: author

In each case there is a strong sense of frontality, with the gaze of the painted figures engaging with that of the viewer, while the figures themselves fill but are contained firmly within the space of the painted panel, be that on wood, stone or brick. All serve the purpose of facilitating access by the viewer to the Divine; to understanding the idea that, in the incarnation of Christ, the Second Person of the Trinity was united to human nature, thus making salvation possible by breaking down the wall separating God and man, and the past and future from the present.

Thus, images defined by multimedia, polychromy, and the clearly defined limits of a framed space, are all aspects of the icons familiar in the context of Christian spaces in the 7th and 8th centuries. These are also the self-same features that define the figural carvings of Northumbrian sculpture. But here the art of relief carving has in some cases been exploited to enable the figures to break through the frames confining them, so that they appear to physically inhabit the space between the Divine and the human — something that can only be intimated in the two-dimensional medium of the flat painted surface. In manuscript contexts, for instance, it is suggested in portrait pages, such as that of the Evangelist, Mark, in the 8th-century Lichfield gospels where the left foot of the evangelist is painted so as to obtrude over the frame containing him.[68]

Furthermore, we know that panel paintings of divine figures and salvationary episodes were known in Anglo-Saxon England; the earliest account of Christian art in the region is, after all, Bede's description of the Augustine mission's progress to their headquarters within Canterbury bearing a panel painting of Christ;[69] the most famous such painting, was of course, the 6th- or 7th-century icon now displayed in the Lateran Sancta Sanctorum.[70] There is also the often-cited account of painted boards publicly displayed in the chapel of St Mary at Wearmouth and the church of St Paul at Jarrow, which included not just figures of Christ, the Virgin and Saints, but events such as the crucifixion.[71] Furthermore, in one of his more extensive defences of the role of figural art in sacred spaces, as part of the contemporary debate concerning icons within the Church, Bede invoked these self-same images in a manner that is not irrelevant to consideration of the figural sculptures:

> If it was permissible [he says] to lift up a brazen serpent on a piece of wood [. . .] why should it not be allowable to recall to the memory of the faithful, by a painting, that exaltation of our Lord Saviour on the cross through which he conquered death, and also his other miracles and healings through which he wonderfully triumphed over the same author of death, and especially since their sight is wont also to produce a feeling of great compunction in the beholder [. . .] And again, if it was not contrary to that same law to make historiated sculptures [. . .] why should it be considered contrary to the law to sculpture or to paint as panels the stories of the saints and martyrs of Christ, who by their observance of the divine law, have earned the glory of an eternal reward?[72]

On the one hand this passage makes clear that in early 8th-century Northumbria, for Bede at least, images could be justified because they allow, by engaging the memory, the production of 'a feeling of great compunction' — that specific feeling which was inspired by the act of contemplation, and which, as Gregory the Great put it, was the means by which 'we rise to the love of God'.[73] In other words, contemplating images was, for Bede, the very process by which icons, through engaging the memory and enabling the mind to transcend human time, were deemed to facilitate access to and understanding of the Divine.

On the other hand, and perhaps more remarkable, is the fact that — in the only surviving reference we have to carved sculpture *per se* in the pre-Viking world — we find it being invoked as painted panels, as synonymous with the painted wooden panels more generally understood to be icons. This strongly implies that the sculptured (historiated) reliefs were, in some cases, understood to function as icons, and this may well explain the distinctive manner in which they have been carved. It is, after all, the distinctive manner in which the figural relief carvings have been manipulated that enables them to allude, visually and physically, to the processes understood to be involved in viewing an icon.

SUMMARY

IT is certainly clear from this review of the Anglo-Saxon sculpture of Bernicia in the 'Age of Bede' that the Church in north Northumbria adopted rich and varied means in its initial displays of public art in sculptural form during the later 7th and 8th centuries. The ways in which the medium represented, at the time, a new and innovative art form has allowed some insight into what its materiality might have signified, as a result of its means of transmission, to both those responsible for its production, and those who might have been expected to view it. Insight is also gained from an exploration of the motives informing the selection of the various monument forms, and the motifs and images used to decorate them. In the light of these observations, it is also clear that the results of such experimentation may well have included the deliberate manipulation of the art of carved relief and the presentation of the human form, which was originally highly coloured and inset with other materials. It may be that this phenomenon should be understood to represent conscious attempts to recreate the painted icon: panels familiar in ecclesiastical contexts that played a specific role in sacred settings as the image made 'material'. Here, in the medium of carved relief these images were presented as performative; as mimicking, in the way they are carved to appear as if they inhabit more than one plane of existence, the process by which the viewer, engaging in the (theologically crucial) act of contemplation, was expected to move beyond the material surface and the human present, through towards an understanding of the immortal and immaterial that existed in the past and will be made manifest again in the future.

NOTES

1. R. Cramp, *County Durham and Northumberland*, Corpus of Anglo-Saxon Stone Sculpture in England 1 (Oxford 1984), 106–34, pls 90–107, 110–25; eadem, *Wearmouth and Jarrow Monastic Sites*, 2 vols (Swindon 2005–06).
2. R. N. Bailey and D. O'Sullivan, 'Excavations over St Wilfrid's Crypt at Hexham, 1978', *AA*, 5th ser. 7 (1979), 145–57; Cramp, *County Durham* (as n. 1), 174–93, pls 167–88; R. N. Bailey, *Saint Wilfrid's Crypts at Ripon and Hexham* (Newcastle upon Tyne 1993); P. Barnwell, 'A Survey of the Anglo-Saxon Crypt at Hexham and its Reused Roman Stonework', *AA*, 5th ser. 39 (2010), 53–145.
3. R. N. Bailey, 'Sutton Hoo and the Seventh Century', in *Sutton Hoo: Fifty Years After*, ed. R. Farrell and C. Neuman de Vegvar, American Early Medieval Studies 2 (Oxford, OH 1992), 33, fig. 2a; J. Hawkes, 'Symbolic Lives: The Visual Evidence', in *The Anglo-Saxons from the Migration Period to the Eighth Century: An Ethnographic Perspective*, ed. J. Hines (Woodbridge 1997), 325, figs 10–16.
4. Monkwearmouth 15: Cramp, *County Durham* (as n. 1), 129–30, pls 122–23.
5. Monkwearmouth 5: Cramp, *County Durham* (as n. 1), 124, pl. 110; Bailey, 'Sutton Hoo' (as n. 3), 35, fig. 3; Hawkes, 'Symbolic Lives' (as n. 3), 322, figs 10–13.

6. Jarrow 17: Cramp, *County Durham* (as n. 1), 113–14, pl. 524; I. Wood, *The Most Holy Abbot Ceolfrid* (Jarrow 1995), 1–2.

7. Jarrow 30a–y: Cramp, *County Durham* (as n. 1), 120–21, pls 103–06; eadem, *Wearmouth and Jarrow* (as n. 1), II, 184–91.

8. Jarrow 16: Cramp, *County Durham* (as n. 1), 112–14, pl. 96; eadem, *Wearmouth and Jarrow* (as n. 1), II, 199; J. Hawkes, 'The Anglo-Saxon Legacy', in *Constantine the Great: York's Roman Emperor*, ed. E. Hartley, J. Hawkes and M. Henig (London 2006), 108–09, fig. 45.

9. É. Ó Carragáin, *The City of Rome and the Age of Bede* (Jarrow 1994), 10–11; idem, *Ritual and the Rood: Liturgical Images and the Old English Poems of the 'Dream of the Rood' Tradition* (London 2005), 189–201.

10. H. M. Taylor and J. Taylor, *Anglo-Saxon Architecture*, 2 vols (Cambridge 1965), I, 234–38.

11. Cramp, *County Durham* (as n. 1), 77–79.

12. Escomb 3–4: Cramp, *County Durham* (as n. 1), 78, pls 54–55.

13. Escomb 7: Cramp, *County Durham* (as n. 1), 79, pl. 270.

14. R. N. Bailey, 'St Cuthbert's Relics: Some Neglected Evidence', in *St Cuthbert, His Cult and His Community to AD 1200*, ed. G. Bonner, D. Rollason and C. Stancliffe (Woodbridge 1989), 238–43, fig. 14.

15. Taylor and Taylor, *Architecture* (as n. 11), I, 172–76.

16. Escomb 1–2, 5–6: Cramp, *County Durham* (as n. 1), 77–79, pls 53–54, 56.

17. Auckland St Andrews 1: Cramp, *County Durham* (as n. 1), 37–40, pls 1–5.

18. R. Cramp, *Early Northumbrian Sculpture* (Jarrow 1965), 5–12; eadem, *County Durham* (as n. 1), 220–21; R. N. Bailey and R. Cramp, *Cumberland, Westmorland and Lancashire North-of-the-Sands*, Corpus of Anglo-Saxon Stone Sculpture in England 2 (Oxford 1988), 65–71; J. Hawkes, 'Viewed Through a Glass Darkly: The Questionable Movements of Art in Anglo-Saxon England', in *Freedom of Movement in the Middle Ages*, ed. P. Horden, Harlaxton Medieval Studies 25 (Donnington 2007), 27–31.

19. Cramp, *Northumbrian Sculpture* (as n. 18), 5; R. N. Bailey, *England's Earliest Sculptors* (Toronto 1996), 22–41; J. Hawkes, '*Iuxta Morem Romanorum*: Stone and Sculpture in the Style of Rome', in *Anglo-Saxon Styles*, ed. G. H. Brown and C. Karkov (Albany, NY 2003), 76–78.

20. 'Namque ipsi australes Picti, qui intra eosdem montes habent sedes, multo ante tempore, ut perhibent, relicto errore idolatriae fidem ueritatis acceperant, praedicante eis Verbum Nynia episcope reuerentissimo et sanctissimo uiro de natione Brettonum, qui erat Romae regulariter fidem et mysteria ueritatis edoctus; cuis sedem episcopates, sancti Martini episcope nomine et ecclesia insignem, ubi ipse etiam corpora una cum pluribus sanctis requiescit, iam nunc Anglorum gens obtinet. Qui locus, ad prouinciam Berniciorum pertinens, uulgo uocatur Ad Candidam Casam, eo quod ibi ecclesiam de lapide [. . .] fecerit.' Bede, *EH*, 222–23; see also P. Hill, *Whithorn and St Ninian: The Excavation of a Monastic Town, 1984–91* (Stroud 1997), 143.

21. C. Thomas, *Whithorn's Christian Beginnings*, Whithorn Lecture 1 (Whithorn 1992), 3–10; D. Craig, 'The Provenance of the Early Christian Inscriptions of Galloway', in Hill, *Whithorn* (as n. 20), 614–20; G. Henderson and I. Henderson, *Art of the Picts: Sculpture and Metalwork in Early Medieval Scotland* (London 2004), 159–96.

22. Bede, *EH*, 114–15; Hawkes, '*Iuxta Morem Romanorum*' (as n. 19), 72.

23. Bede, *EH*, 158–59.

24. E. Cambridge, 'The Architecture of the Augustine Mission', in *St Augustine and the Conversion of England*, ed. R. Gameson (Stroud 1999), 231; Hawkes, '*Iuxta Morem Romanorum*' (as n. 19), 72–73.

25. Hawkes, '*Iuxta Morem Romanorum*' (as n. 19).

26. Bede, *Historia Abbatum*, in *Venerabilis Baedae Opera Historica*, 2 vols, ed. C. Plummer (Oxford 1896), I, 368.

27. Cramp, *Wearmouth and Jarrow* (as n. 1), II, 54.

28. I. Ferris and R. Jones, 'Transforming an Elite: Reinterpreting Late Roman Binchester', in *The Late Roman Transition in the North: Papers from the Roman Archaeology Conference, Durham 1999*, ed. T. Wilmott and P. Wilson, BAR Brit. ser. 299 (Oxford 2000), 1–11. For Anglo-Saxon ecclesiastical visitors to Roman ruins, see *Two Lives of Saint Cuthbert*, ed. B. Colgrave (Cambridge 1940), 122–23, 242–45; and Bede, *EH*, 440–41.

29. Cramp, *Wearmouth and Jarrow* (as n. 1), 53–54.

30. R. Krautheimer, *Rome, Profile of a City, 312–1308* (Princeton, NJ 1980), 24–26; Hawkes, '*Iuxta Morem Romanorum*' (as n. 19), 75.

31. Taylor and Taylor, *Architecture* (as n. 11), I, 432–46; Cramp, *Wearmouth and Jarrow* (as n. 1), I, 69–70.

32. Taylor and Taylor, *Architecture* (as n. 11), I, 134–39.

33. É. Ó Carragáin, 'The Term *Porticus* and *Imitatio Romae* in Early Anglo-Saxon England', in *Text and Gloss: Studies in Insular Learning and Literature Presented to Joseph Donovan Pheifer*, ed. H. Conrad O'Briain, A. M. D'Arcy and J. Scattergood (Dublin 1999), 13–34.

34. R. Lanciani, *Pagan and Christian Rome* (Boston and New York 1892), 127; J. Mitchell, 'The High Cross and Monastic Strategies in Eighth-Century Northumbria', in *New Offerings, Ancient Treasures. Studies in Medieval Art for George Henderson*, ed. P. Binski and W. Noel (Stroud 2001), 88–114.

35. Bailey and Cramp, *Cumberland* (as n. 18), 61, 65.

36. P. J. Nordhagen, 'A Carved Marble Pilaster in the Vatican Grottoes: Some Remarks on the Sculptural Techniques of the Early Middle Ages', *Acta ad Archaeologiam et Artium Historia Pertinentia*, 4 (1969), 113–20.

37. E. Kitzinger, 'Anglo-Saxon Vine-scroll Ornament', *Antiquity*, 10 (1936), 61–71; this will be the subject of a future study by John Mitchell in *The Staffordshire Hoard and Anglo-Saxon Art: Material, Contexts and Interpretations*, ed. L. Cleaver (Turnhout forthcoming).

38. Rothbury 1: Cramp, *County Durham* (as n. 1), 217–21, fig. 20, pls 211–15; J. Hawkes, 'The Rothbury Cross: An Iconographic Bricolage', *Gesta*, 35 (1996), 84–85; eadem, 'The Iconography of Passion or Power?', in *The Insular Tradition*, ed. C. Karkov, R. T. Farrell and M. Ryan (New York 1997), 27–44.

39. R. N. Bailey, 'Anglo-Saxon Art; Some Forms, Orderings and Meanings', in *Form and Order in the Anglo-Saxon World, AD 600–1100*, ed. S. Crawford, H. Hamerow and L. Webster, Anglo-Saxon Studies in Archaeology and History 16 (Oxford 2009), 26 n. 48.

40. Although not recorded by Cramp, *County Durham* (as n. 1), 219, the gesso and red paint are still visible on the base of the shaft standing as the pedestal of the font within the church.

41. J. Hawkes, 'Reculver Column, in six pieces', in *Constantine the Great* (as n. 8), 247–50, cat. 267–72.

42. Burnsall 2, 5: E. Coatsworth, *Western Yorkshire*, Corpus of Anglo-Saxon Stone Sculpture 8 (Oxford 2008), 108–10; E. Coatsworth, R. Wood and L. Butler, *Early Sculptures in Burnsall Church* (Skipton 2005), 10–11.

43. W. Rodwell, J. Hawkes, R. Cramp and E. Howe, 'The Lichfield Angel: A Spectacular Anglo-Saxon Painted Sculpture', *Antiq. J.*, 88 (2008), 14–19.

44. *The Making of England: Anglo-Saxon Art and Culture, AD 600–900*, ed. L. Webster and J. Backhouse (London 1991), 180–83, cat. 141.

45. This will form the subject of a forthcoming paper by Alice Blackwell of the National Museum of Scotland, Edinburgh; I am grateful to her for the chance to view her work prior to publication.

46. Reculver 1b: D. Tweddle, M. Biddle and B. Kjølbye-Biddle, *South-East England*, Corpus of Anglo-Saxon Stone Sculpture 4 (Oxford 1995), pl. 116; Hawkes, 'Reculver Column' (as n. 41), 249–50, cat. no. 270.

47. Lastingham 4: J. Lang, *York and Eastern Yorkshire*, Corpus of Anglo-Saxon Stone Sculpture 3 (Oxford 1991), 169, pls 582–83; Bailey, *Earliest Sculptors* (as n. 19), 7–9, fig. 3; J. Hawkes, 'Statements in Stone: Anglo-Saxon Sculpture, Whitby and the Christianisation of the North', in *Anglo-Saxon Archaeology: Basic Readings*, ed. C. Karkov (New York 1999), 413–14, pl. 15.8.

48. Ó Carragáin, *Ritual and the Rood* (as n. 9), 54–78; although see also F. Orton and I. Wood with C. Leeds, *Fragments of History: Rethinking the Ruthwell and Bewcastle Monuments* (Manchester 2007), 13–31.

49. 'Cumque parentes eius magna mentis excess suspense et de incerta filii sui evasion ambiguous, summentes filium suum, obtulerunt illum coram illam dominicam sanctamque crucem Salvatoris. Qui, sicut mos est Saxanice gentis, quod in nonnullis nobelium bonorumque hominum predibus non aecclesia, sed dancte crucis signum Deo dicatum cum magno honore almum in alto erectum ad commode diurni orationis sedulitate habere solent.' 'Vita Willibaldi episcope Eichstetensis', *Monumenta Germaniae Historica Scriptores*, 15 (Hanover 1887), 88; trans. C. H. Talbot, ed., *The Anglo-Saxon Missionaries in Germany* (New York 1954), 154–55.

50. Cramp, *County Durham* (as n. 1), 221, pl. 212.

51. Hawkes, 'Rothbury Cross' (as n. 38), 88–90; eadem, 'The Road to Hell: The Art of Damnation in Anglo-Saxon Sculpture', in *Listen, O Isles, Unto Me: Studies in Medieval Word and Image in Honour of Jennifer O'Reilly*, ed. E. Mullins and D. Scully (Cork 2011), 236–42.

52. See, for example, A. W. Clapham, *English Romanesque Architecture Before the Conquest* (Oxford 1930); T. D. Kendrick, *Anglo-Saxon Art* (London 1939); F. Saxl, 'The Ruthwell Cross', *Journal of the Warburg and Courtauld Institutes*, 6 (1943), 1–19; F. Saxl and R. Wittkower, *British Art and the Mediterranean* (Oxford 1948); see also M. Schapiro, 'The Religious Meaning of the Ruthwell Cross', *Art Bulletin*, 26 (1944), 232–45.

53. L. Webster, 'Encrypted Visions: Style and Sense in the Anglo-Saxon Minor Arts, A.D. 400–900', in *Anglo-Saxon Styles* (as n. 19), 11–30; Hawkes, 'Symbolic Lives' (as n. 3); eadem, 'Design and Decoration:

Revisualising Rome in Anglo-Saxon Sculpture', in *Rome Across Time and Space. Cultural Transmission and the Exchange of Ideas, c 500–1400*, ed. C. Bolgia, R. McKitterick and J. Osborne (Cambridge 2011), 201–12.

54. A. Maskell, *Ivories* (London 1905), 47–81; W. Levison, *England and the Continent in the Eighth Century* (London 1946), 101; D. Gaborit-Chopin, *Ivoires du Moyen Âge* (Fribourg 1978), 22–24; T. Klauser, *A Short History of the Western Liturgy*, trans. J. Halliburton (London and New York 1979), 61; Hawkes, 'Rothbury Cross' (as n. 38), 85; eadem, 'Iconography' (as n. 38), 37–39; see also P. Williamson, *Medieval Ivory Carvings. Early Christian to Romanesque* (London 2010), 43–45.

55. *Rome and the Barbarians*, ed. J. Aillagon (Milan 2008), 210, cat. II.16.

56. Cramp, *County Durham* (as n. 1), pls 213–15.

57. I am grateful to Meg Boulton for discussion of this subject.

58. Hawkes, 'Rothbury Cross' (as n. 38), 77–80, fig. 1.

59. Cramp, *County Durham* (as n. 1), 217–19, pl. 214; Hawkes, 'Rothbury Cross' (as n. 38), 80–81, fig. 3.

60. E.g. 8th-century icon of the crucifixion, Sinai (*Sinai. Treasures of the Monastery of Saint Catherine*, ed. K. A. Manafis (Athens 1990), pl. 9).

61. See further below, n. 73.

62. H. Belting, *Likeness and Presence: A History of the Image Before the Era of Art* (Chicago 1994), 10.

63. Belting, *Likeness and Presence* (as n. 62), 11.

64. For icons of Virgin and Child, see those at the Patheon, Sta Maria Nuovo, and Sta Maria in Trastevere (ibid., pls I and II, facing 264); for that of Christ, see the Lateran Sancta Sanctorum icon (L. Nees, *Early Medieval Art* (Oxford 2002), pl. facing 137).

65. G. Matthiae and M. Andaloro, *Pittura Romana del Medioevo, vol. 1: Secoli IV–X* (Rome 1987), 120–21, tav. 8.

66. Krautheimer, *Profile of a City* (as n. 30), 81; B. Brenk, 'Papal Patronage in a Greek Church in Rome', in *Santa Maria Antiqua al Foro Romano, cento anni doppo*, ed. J. Osborne, J. Rasmus Brandt and G. Morganti (Rome 2004), 113–27.

67. Overall, see P. J. Nordhagen, *The Frescoes of John VII,* A.D. *705–707, in S. Maria Antiqua in Rome*, Acta ad Archaeologiam et Artium Historia 3 (Rome 1968); Belting, *Likeness and Presence* (as n. 62), 115–21; and Ann Van Dijk, 'Type and Antitype in Santa Maria Antiqua: The Old Testament Scenes on the Transcenae', in *Santa Maria Antiqua* (as n. 66), 113–27, pl. on 112, fig. 1 (on Annunciation panel); P. J. Nordhagen, 'Is Empiricism Really Worth the Trouble? On the Documentation Techniques Employed in the Study of Santa Maria Antiqua', in *Santa Maria Antiqua* (as n. 66), 215–16, fig. 2a–b.

68. Lichfield, Cathedral Library (Book of St Chad), p. 182; J. J. G. Alexander, *Insular Manuscripts, 6th to the 9th Century* (London 1978), pl. 80, cat. 2. See further current work by Nick Baker on the evangelists in Anglo-Saxon art; I am grateful to him for the opportunity to discuss this issue.

69. Bede, *EH*, 74–75.

70. Nees, *Early Medieval* (as n. 64), 138–39.

71. Bede, *Historia Abbatum*, in *Venerabilis Baedae* (as n. 26), 373.

72. 'Si enim licebat serpentem exaltari aeneum in ligno quem aspicientes filii Israhel viverent, cur non licet exaltationem domini saluatoris in cruce qua mortem uicit ad memoriam fidelibus depingendo reduci vel etiam alia eius miracula et sanationes quibus de eodem mortis auctore mirabiliter triumphauit cum horum aspectus multum saepe compunctionis soleat praestare contuentibus et eis quoque qui litteras ignorant quasi uiuam dominicae historiae pandere lectionem? [. . .] Si licuit duodecim boves aeneos facere qui mare superpositum ferentes quattuor mundi plagas terni respicerent, quid prohibet duodecim apostolos pingere quomodo euntes docerent omnes gentes baptizantes eos in nomine patris et filii et spiritus sancti uiua ut ita dixerim prae oculis omnium designare scriptura? Si eidem legi contrarium non fuit in eodem mari scalpturas histriatas [. . .] quomodo legi contrarium putabatur si historias sanctorum ac martyrum Christi sculpamus siue pingamus in tabulis qui per custodiam diuinae legis ad gloriam meruerunt aeternae retributionis attingere.' *Bedae Venerabilis Opera. Pars II. Opera Exegetica 2A*, ed. D. Hurst, Corpus Christianorum Series Latina 119A (Turnhout 1969), 212–13; translation in *Bede: On the Temple*, ed. and trans. S. Connolly (Liverpool 1995), 91–92.

73. *Moralia in Job*, ed. M. Adriaen, Corpus Christianorum Series Latina 143 (Turnhout 1979), 326; see also *Gregorius Magnus Homiliae in Hezechihelem Prophetam*, ed. M. Adriaen, Corpus Christianorum Series Latina 142 (Turnhout 1971), 37–38; J. Hawkes, 'Gregory the Great and Angelic Mediation: The Anglo-Saxon Crosses of the Derbyshire Peaks', in *Text, Image and Interpretation: Studies in Anglo-Saxon Literature in Honour of Éamonn Ó Carragáin*, ed. A. Minnis and J. Roberts (Turnhout 2007), 438–42.

Eyes of Light: Colour in the Lindisfarne Gospels

HEATHER PULLIAM

The brilliant and varied colours of the Lindisfarne Gospels are one of the manuscript's most celebrated features, and yet the question of their meaning and role within the iconographic programme has been largely neglected in existing scholarship. In part this is due to the fact that colour studies are an intensely problematic field of inquiry, necessitating an interdisciplinary approach that is also inherently dependent upon scientific analysis. Advances in Raman microscopy have enabled non-invasive testing for the first time, and in the past ten years the Lindisfarne Gospels and a number of other Insular manuscripts have undergone testing at the British Library and Trinity College Dublin. This essay offers a preliminary examination of the relationship between colour, iconography and meaning within the Lindisfarne Gospels, before proceeding to an in-depth analysis of the portrayal of eye colour within the manuscript. This analysis explores the connections between colour, material, early medieval epistemology, optics and exegesis.

DESPITE the many publications that discuss the Lindisfarne Gospels, relatively little consideration has been given to the relationship between colour and meaning within the manuscript. This lacuna in the literature is particularly notable given that its colour is one of the manuscript's most frequently lauded features. Typical of facsimile commentary volumes, both the 1956 and 2003 commentaries discuss colour within the context of pigment analysis, stylistic comparisons and verbal descriptions of the images.[1] Investigations into the iconographic meaning of its images, however, largely treat the pages as if they were without colour.[2] This omission is relatively common within the field of early medieval art history due to a host of issues that are too numerous to list here in their entirety.[3] Colours transform over time; perceptions of colour vary depending on the viewer and lighting conditions; conservation issues frequently prevent access to the original; colour reproductions are unreliable and frequently unavailable — the list is a long one. Moreover, linguistic studies of colour vocabulary and literature provide an additional layer of uncertainty.[4]

It seems unlikely, however, that the colour of the Lindisfarne Gospels was applied casually or without thought. Recent colour reports suggest that the remarkable range of colours present within the manuscript was created via the sophisticated and careful application of very few original pigments.[5] Unlike the later middle ages, when the roles of colourist, draughtsman and designer were usually distinct, it has frequently been argued that a single individual, the bishop Eadfrith, was responsible for all aspects of the Lindisfarne illuminations. In other words, the well-educated, literate artist who designed and executed the manuscript's complex iconography with its multivalent meaning also selected and applied its remarkable range of colours.

BAA Trans., vol. XXXVI (2013), 54–72

Modern audiences should be reminded that technologies have struggled to replicate the subtle and sophisticated colour range found in the Lindisfarne Gospels. The tunic worn by the evangelist Matthew on fol. 25v, for example, is a purple-plum colour in facsimile images, but appears red in the British Library 'Turning the Pages' online exhibition and a number of other publications (Fig. 1 and Col. Pl. IV in print edn).[6] Equally, the outer garment worn by John on fol. 209v is a blue-violet colour in both facsimiles, but red on the British Library website and most other publications (Fig. 4 and Col. Pl. VII in print edn). This garment seems particularly difficult to reproduce, and even the new high-resolution images that were placed online during the course of writing this article fail in this respect. Additionally, while colour studies have repeatedly demonstrated that medieval descriptions and use of colour indicate that brightness, saturation and texture were often prioritized over hue, modern reproductions have not managed to capture the striking variations in intensity and texture present within the manuscript. Of the various reproductions available, the 2003 facsimile most closely matches the original.[7]

Refinements to Raman microscope technology in the 1990s have made it possible to identify a range of pigments with relative accuracy for the first time. Previously, analyses had depended almost exclusively upon visual identification and an understanding of chemistry and medieval recipes. As a number of recent publications have noted, observations based on this method have been insufficiently questioned.[8] As Cheryl Porter has pointed out, the appearance of mineral pigments may change significantly due to oxidization, while organic pigments tend to fade over time; a single pigment can create a wide range of colour and even hue, depending on the binder, medium and amount of grinding; and medieval recipes are frequently vague, often mistranslated (or untranslatable) and at times even misleading. Fortunately, a few years ago, the pigments of the Lindisfarne Gospels were analysed using Raman microscopy. The 2004 report confirmed the need to question long-held assumptions based on visual inspections, reversing at least two popular assumptions about the manuscript's pigments.[9]

Much of this paper will focus upon the use of blue and green within the evangelist portraits. The published Raman microscopy analysis reports two types of green present within the manuscript. The bright leek-green colour of the outer rim of Mark's halo on fol. 93v and of the book held by Luke's evangelist symbol on fol. 137v both registered as verdigris, a copper-based pigment (Figs 2, 3 and Col. Pls V, VI in print edn). The muddier, darker green of the bench frames in the Mark and Luke portraits registered as vergaut, a mixture of yellow orpiment and a woad-based pigment.[10] The leek-green colour of the verdigris in the Lindisfarne Gospels is quite striking and its brightness relatively unusual. Surviving forms of green from the Insular period typically have a deeper, darker colour. One of the most surprising and important findings of the 2004 microscopy report was the absence of lazurite. The brilliant range of blues that are present within the manuscript had long been believed to have been composed of lapis lazuli, suggesting an extensive trade route, but the report discovered that they were organic rather than mineral. They have the chemical compound $C_{16}H_{10}N_2O_2$, and are most likely derived from the rather less exotic woad plant.[11]

While analyses using Raman microscopy technologies are far more accurate than those based upon visual inspection, the results are not absolute. A number of pigments, especially organic plant-based ones, produce visible colour in concentrations that are too low for detection via this technology.[12] Of the mineral pigments, verdigris is particularly difficult to identify. Raman microscopy proved inconclusive, for example, in a recent investigation of the use of green within the Book of Durrow, although the subsequent X-ray fluorescence analysis did detect copper.[13] The identification of verdigris within the Lindisfarne Gospels, however, was further confirmed when green sweepings from the gutter on fol. 93v were analysed and identified as verdigris ($Cu_2(O_2CCH_3)_4{*}Cu(OH)_2$).[14] The bright leek-green found in the Lindisfarne Gospels also appears in a number of places within the manuscript, but only a few of these instances were tested. Prominent examples from the portrait pages include Matthew's pallium, the majority of books held by the various figures, the corners of the frames for Matthew and John's portraits, the rim of Mark's halo and, possibly, the eyes of the four evangelists (Figs 1–4 and Col. Pls IV–VII in print edn).[15] While acknowledging the hazards of visual identification that are outlined above, it seems relatively safe to assume that these areas of leek-green are also verdigris or some similar copper-based pigment, especially when we consider that the artist who created the Gospels was working with a limited range of pigments. Additionally, this leek-green colour, most likely because of its copper content, tends to show through on the reverse side of the vellum in quite a distinct and recognizable fashion.

One of the most striking features of the Lindisfarne evangelist portraits is the brightly and varicoloured robes of the evangelists (Figs 1–4 and Col. Pls IV–VII in print edn). Scholars have frequently dissected, classified and analysed the theological meanings conveyed in the poses, attributes and even hairstyles of evangelists represented in Insular, Carolingian and late Anglo-Saxon manuscripts; however, as suggested above, the insightful discussions of the complex theological meaning inherent within these images never focus on and rarely even discuss the brilliant colours used in these portraits.[16] Within the Lindisfarne Gospels, each portrait is surrounded by a relatively simple frame that surrounds a plain, pale pink background. With the exception of the Matthew portrait, the imagery is limited to the figure of the evangelist, a simple stool and footrest, writing materials and evangelist symbol. Against this stark regularity, individual differences of poses are marked and meaningful.[17] Equally noticeable against the plain backgrounds of each portrait are both the vibrancy and distinct colour combinations that change from evangelist to evangelist.

At the most basic level, the manuscript's array of colour conveys variety and opulence; however, it might also be understood as a reference to the concord of the gospels, which was the subject of a number of patristic works, most notably Augustine's *Harmony of the Gospels*. As a number of scholars have demonstrated, this theme played a central role in Insular art, liturgy and literature, emphasizing that, while each gospel has a distinct voice, together they create a harmonious testimony to the life of Christ.[18] Similarly, in the Lindisfarne Gospels, each of the evangelists has his own unique colour 'palette', but certain rhythms and patterns weave the four portraits together into a harmonious whole. John's clothing is the inverse of Matthew's but with some minor variations: his purple robe appears slightly bluer and the folds of his clothing are indicated via blue and white highlights, whereas Matthew's are delineated by black. Their haloes are similarly aligned. Matthew's nimbus is coloured with yellow but has a red rim; John's is red with a yellow rim. Mark and John sit on blue cushions; Matthew and Luke on red ones.

Significantly, one of the most influential early medieval discussions of colour symbolism, Bede's *Explanation of the Apocalypse*, emerged from the same cultural milieu as the Lindisfarne Gospels. In it, Bede explores at length the symbolism of the twelve stones of the walls of the Holy City (Revelation 21:19). The tunic colours of each of the four evangelists roughly parallel the colours of the first four stones: the first stone, jasper for Matthew; the second stone, sapphire for Mark; the third stone, chalcedony

Fig. 1. Lindisfarne Gospels, British Library Cotton MS Nero D.IV, Matthew Portrait page, fol. 25v

Fig. 2. Lindisfarne Gospels British Library Cotton MS Nero D.IV, Mark Portrait page, fol. 93v

Fig. 3. Lindisfarne Gospels, British Library Cotton MS Nero D.IV, Luke Portrait page, fol. 137v

Fig. 4. Lindisfarne Gospels, British Library Cotton MS Nero D.IV, John Portrait page, fol. 209v

for Luke; and the fourth stone, emerald for John. While there is some question as to what colour jasper and chalcedony were thought to be, Bede and others undoubtedly perceived sapphires as blue and emeralds as green. Bede describes the former as the colour of sky on a clear day, and the latter as greener than the greenest foliage.[19] His descriptions could easily be applied to the bright blue of Mark's tunic and intense green of John's garment. It is perhaps worth noting that chalcedony was frequently noted for its paleness, which is a distinctive feature of Luke's tunic.[20]

John's association with the emerald is explicitly referenced in both the Lindisfarne Gospels and Bede's commentary on the Apocalypse. Within the manuscript, each of the gospels is demarcated by a carpet page surrounded by a rectangular frame with ornament at its four corners and at the four cardinal points (Fig. 5 and Col. Pl. VIII in print edn). As has frequently been noted, the decoration at the four cardinal points closely resembles examples of Anglo-Saxon metalwork. In the John carpet page, on fol. 210v, at the top and bottom of the frame, are two beast-heads. Unique to John's gospel, the interlace forms a faux metalwork socket that contains a single green stone (Figs 5–6 and Col. Pls VIII, IX in print edn). Again, it seems likely that these stones, along with the green in the four squares that compose the majority of the carpet page, are coloured with a copper-based pigment, as their colour closely matches the areas identified as verdigris and is clearly visible on the reverse of the page.

In his commentary on the stones of the Apocalypse, Bede notes, 'since such exalted faith is made known throughout the whole world through the gospel, and that there are four books of the gospel, the emerald is placed in fourth place'.[21] A Greek source associates the emerald specifically with John, stating that the stone 'is green in colour and when rubbed with oil it receives a brilliant shine and beauty. We believe that this stone indicates the proclamation of the Evangelist John'.[22] A number of Latin texts, including Bede's, associate the emerald with oil, and Irish commentaries similarly connected the evangelist John to oil.[23] In the later middle ages green robes become a fixed part of John's iconography, and the colour is typically interpreted as a sign of faith in this context.[24]

The association between John and the colour green can be seen elsewhere in Insular and late Anglo-Saxon art. In the Cambridge-London Gospels, a green frame and four green crosses surround John's eagle.[25] Unfortunately, John's is the only extant symbol, and so it is not possible to compare it with the other evangelist symbols originally contained in this manuscript. Having said this, what survives of the Mark symbol appears to be executed in red and yellow, although the page was badly damaged by fire. The Echternach Gospels, which are so frequently compared to the Cambridge-London Gospels, offer little help in ascertaining the Cambridge-London colour scheme as they are executed entirely in yellow, red and purple.[26] The association between John and the colour green is more evident in manuscripts from the later Anglo-Saxon period. In New York, Pierpont Morgan Library, MS 709, for example, John appears on fols 1v and 77v, wearing a green robe. In a related manuscript also held at the Morgan Library, MS 708, John's portrait is framed in green and gold.[27]

While John's eyes provide the most intense green stare, the other evangelists' eyes appear to be a pale bluish-green, as do those of the figure peering from behind the curtain in the Matthew portrait (Figs 7–10 and Col. Pls X–XIII in print edn).[28] One simple, pragmatic explanation might be that the artist had a personal preference for light eyes. While less common than brown eyes, conceivably there would have been quite a few blue- and even green-eyed people in Northumbria! More surprising,

Fig. 5. Lindisfarne Gospels, British Library Cotton MS Nero D.IV, John carpet page, fol. 210v

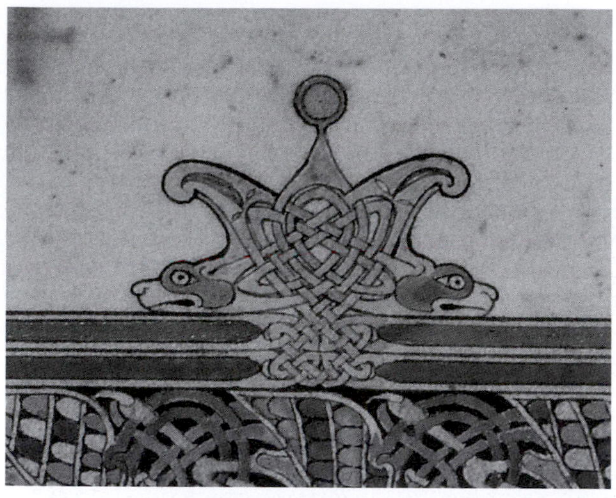

FIG. 6. Lindisfarne Gospels, British Library Cotton MS Nero D. IV, John carpet page, fol. 210v, detail

however, is the fact that the eyes of Matthew's angel and Luke's ox are similarly coloured (Figs 8, 10 and Col. Pls XI, XIII in print edn). While the linguistic evidence shows an awareness of pale-eyed (glass-eyed) horses, it seems likely that as is the case today, this permutation would be fairly exceptional.[29] Perhaps even more odd is the fact that, although the lion symbol has black eyes, it appears to have blue-green 'shadows' around its eyes (Fig. 9 and Col. Pl. XII in print edn), a trait it shares with all four evangelists.

While much of Insular art is characterized by an abstract use of colour, the naturalistic colour found within the Lindisfarne Gospels' evangelist portraits is one of the manuscript's most distinctive features. Flesh-tones are carefully applied. The hair of both Mark and Luke is a subtle shade of dark ash-blond, while John's is a slightly richer chestnut brown. Matthew's hair is not simply grey, but 'salt-and-pepper' grey. The realism of the Lindisfarne portraits is most evident in the colouring of the evangelist symbols. The lion's pelt is not rendered in the usual bright yellow orpiment found in other Insular manuscripts, but rather a surprisingly subtle dun colour. This is the only instance of this colour within the manuscript,[30] suggesting the lengths to which the artist went in order to create suitable colour. Equally, the careful and intricate gradations of colour within the wings, fur, hooves and talons of the calf and eagle symbols are incredibly life-like. This realism is most readily apparent when contrasted to the bright reds, yellows and blues of the birds and beasts in other Insular gospel-books, and even within the carpet pages of the Lindisfarne Gospels. Clearly, great pains have been taken to achieve this remarkably naturalistic colour. In such a context, the depiction of a green-eyed ox and a lion wearing bright blue-green 'eye-shadow' is a significant deviation that merits consideration.

The unusual emphasis given to the eyes of the evangelists and their symbols, especially the unusual bluish-green 'shadow', is best understood through early medieval and patristic discussions of the eye, where it is repeatedly associated with light and the state of the soul. In Matthew 6:22 and Luke 11:33, Christ states that the 'eye is the light of the body'. In his oft-consulted *Etymologies*, Isidore of Seville writes:

Eyes are called *oculi* [...] because they have a hidden, *occultus*, light, that is one placed secretly, or within. These, among all the senses, are very close to the soul [*animae*]. In the eyes is every

FIG. 7. Lindisfarne Gospels, British Library Cotton MS Nero D.IV, John Portrait page, fol. 209v, detail

FIG. 8. Lindisfarne Gospels, British Library Cotton MS Nero D.IV, Matthew Portrait page, fol. 25v, detail

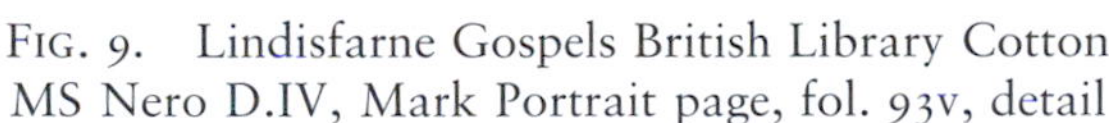

FIG. 9. Lindisfarne Gospels British Library Cotton MS Nero D.IV, Mark Portrait page, fol. 93v, detail

Fig. 10. Lindisfarne Gospels, British Library Cotton MS Nero D.IV, Luke Portrait page, fol. 137v, detail

disclosure of the mind [*mentis*], whence the disturbance or joy of the animus appears in the eyes. The eyes are also *lumina*. They are called this because light, *lumen*, emanates from them; or because in the beginning, they hold light closed within them; or having received it from outside, they pour it back, exposing it to sight.[31]

Isidore's description of the eye hints at several key features of vision as it was understood in the early medieval period.[32] The mind focuses and wills rays of light from the eyes to the object, touching the object and bringing some aspect of it — its form or image — back into the viewer's body. In so doing, the viewer takes on some characteristics of what s/he has seen, and the object is imprinted — medieval writers frequently use the metaphor of a wax and seal — onto the viewer. Augustine, and a number of other medieval writers, cite the example of the chameleon that looks at a certain hue and then transforms into that hue as well as to the mistaken belief that the visual 'caprices' of a pregnant mother alter the appearance and form of her unborn child.[33]

In a similar vein, biblical passages repeatedly connect the eye with light, purity and God's teachings. In the gospel passages mentioned above, Christ states, 'If your eye is wholesome, your entire body will be filled with light. But if it is wicked, then even your body will be darkened' (Matt. 6:22). In the psalms, which were such an integral part of monastic life, the narrator repeatedly calls for God to 'enlighten my eyes'.[34] Elsewhere he asks God to 'light my lamp' and praises God for enlightening the blind.[35] When the faithful turn towards Christ and his teachings, they look upon the truth and the light and thus their eyes are filled with light. Most relevant to the evangelist portraits, Psalm 18 states that 'the precepts of the Lord are brilliant, enlightening the eyes [*illuminans oculos*]' while the popular Psalm 118 adds 'your word is a lamp [*lucerne*] to my feet and a light [*lumen*] to my paths'. This theme is expanded by St Paul, who describes the wicked as the blind in whom 'the light of the Gospel of the glory of Christ [*illuminatio Evangelii gloriæ Christi*], who is the image of God' does not shine. Conversely, the good carry in 'earthen vessels, this treasure', that is, the light that God 'has shined [. . .] into our hearts, to illuminate the knowledge of the splendor of God, in the person of Christ Jesus' (II Cor. 4:4, 6–7).

This theme is most explicitly set out in Augustine's commentary on the opening of John. In his second treatise, commenting on John 1:8 ('He was not the Light, but he was to offer testimony about the Light'), Augustine writes: 'An enlightened man is as called a light; but the true light is that which enlightens'.[36] He goes on to note that eyes are called lights, but that they are open in vain unless they have some other source of illumination such as a lamp or the sun. In his first treatise, he explains at great length that the teachings of scriptures and men such as John the Baptist and John the Evangelist are like mountains that are illuminated by and thus reflect the light of God to smaller men.[37] He goes on to caution that, although shining, they are not the source of the light, citing John 1:9: 'The true Light, which illuminates every man, was coming into this world'. He urges his audience to lift their eyes and bodily senses to the light of the evangelist and his gospel while raising their hearts to its source, the Lord.

As John Gage has noted, gospel books were associated with light, and their gold covers symbolically conveyed Christ's claim, 'I am the light of the world'.[38] In a number of early medieval images, gospel books are shown studded with emeralds, which are often four in number or arranged in clusters of four.[39] It seems likely that this custom similarly indicates that the gospels shine with the light of God, drawing upon the belief that the emerald was the brightest gemstone. This may explain the unusual choice of green for the covers of the majority of books that are portrayed within the Lindisfarne Gospels. Moreover, according to both Bede and Isidore, the emerald 'imbues the reflected air around it with greenness'.[40] Similarly, the evangelists and their gospels enlighten those who heed their teachings. While not specifically referring to the evangelists, Bede writes that the emerald represents those who 'strive the more to conceive in their mind by hope "the unfading and eternal inheritance which is reserved in heaven," and extend it to their neighbours by preaching'.[41]

In the Lindisfarne Gospels, the artist's use of the colour articulates the union between the evangelist and the light of Christ to which the gospels give witness. Three of the four evangelists stare directly at their holy texts, absorbing the light of the word (Figs 1–4 and Col. Pls IV–VII in print edn). The lion with the blue-green 'eye-shadow' and green-eyed ox stare out towards the viewer, prominently holding their green books between their paws and hooves (Figs 9, 10 and Col. Pls XII, XIII in print edn). In Matthew's portrait page, his angel and the mysterious figure peering from behind the curtain also hold onto green books, the former staring outwards and the latter gazing intently at Matthew's gospel (Fig. 1 and Col. Pl. IV in print edn). In both cases, the figures' eye colour seems to reflect that of the green books which they carry. The evangelists and their symbols bear witness to the truth and light that is Christ, and some aspect of his glory is imprinted upon them. It is perhaps worth noting at this point that the only use of gold writing in the manuscript is on the incipit pages where the evangelists' names are written in gold so that they literally reflect light.[42] As we have seen, according to late antique and early medieval theories of vision, the object is not only touched by the eye's rays but its form is 'absorbed into' the body. Although with significant differences, spiritual sight similarly allows the light of Christ to enter into the soul of the 'viewer' and facilitates a union between object and audience.[43]

The specific use of blue and/or green to convey God's light is unsurprising. In Exodus 24:10 and Ezekiel 10:1–4, the glory of God is described as having the likeness of a sapphire. In his discussion of sapphires, Bede cites both passages, saying that 'the glory of the Lord consists of this colour, which bears the image of the super-celestial'.[44] Similarly, the emerald was associated with the radiance of the enthroned Christ due to the description in Revelation 4:3, 'And there was an rainbow [*iris*] surrounding the throne, in aspect similar to an emerald'. In mosaics, the triumphal *crux gemmata* is frequently studded exclusively with emeralds, sapphires and pearls.[45] In a number of Byzantine, Anglo-Saxon and Carolingian artworks, Christ is shown surrounded by a green mandorla or aura, and the haloes of both him and his saints are usually gold or green.[46] Similarly, Christ's halo was often shown studded with green emeralds.[47] Within the Lindisfarne Gospels, Mark and John, the two evangelists who were associated with the resurrected and glorified Christ, sit on blue cushions and wear blue and green tunics (Figs 2, 4 and Col. Pls V, VII in print edn).[48] As I have noted elsewhere, the Grandval Bible similarly distinguishes the two 'divine' evangelists from the two 'mortal' evangelists through material and colour, where the former have gold haloes and the latter have silver ones.[49]

Moreover, the Lindisfarne Gospels are not unique in portraying Christ and his saints as having light-filled, or light-emitting, eyes. It has frequently been suggested that Insular figurative sculpture with drilled eyes would have had insets of some kind, presumably glass, as is the case elsewhere, and the National Museum of Scotland's recent discovery of a complete tin sleeve in the drilled socket that forms the eye of the Aberlady angel would seem to confirm this.[50] In the Durham Crucifixion page, despite its badly deteriorated colour, Christ's eyes — or specifically the disproportionately large irises of his eyes — are a notable green colour, as are those of the evangelist symbols in the Book of Durrow (Figs 11, 12 and Col. Pls XIV, XV in print edn).[51] The latter should perhaps be discounted as the options for eye colour are somewhat restricted due to the manuscript's limited colour range. The Durham Crucifixion page, however, makes use of a number of colours including green, black, orange, yellow,

FIG. 11. Book of Durrow, Dublin, Trinity College Library, MS A. 4. 5. (57), fol. 21v

and brown, and the practice of leaving the eye without colour and simply delineating the pupil in black or brown was certainly an option as it was a relatively common convention in this period. In another example from Rome, the four evangelist symbols in the 7th-century Oratory of San Venanzio in the Lateran, rather disconcertingly, have bright red eyes.[52] In metalwork, on the lower cover of the Lindau Gospels, four champlevé busts emerge from the central square of the boss.[53] Although all four of the figures are identified by the Morgan Library as representing Christ, it seems more

Fig. 12. Book of Durrow, Dublin, Trinity College Library, MS A. 4. 5. (57), fol. 84v

Fig. 13. Durham Cathedral Library A. II.17, Crucifixion page, fol. 38v

likely, given Insular practice, that these busts are multivalent, portraying the four evangelists as embodying the various aspects of Christ. The eyes of the figures are outlined in blue while the irises, not unlike the Lateran mosaic, are an iridescent orange colour. In these latter two examples, what is remarkable is not the presence of colour within the eye, but its otherworldly and unnatural hue.

While acknowledging the limited colour range of the Book of Durrow, the representation of Matthew's symbol suggests that the green eyes of the evangelist symbols might not be mere coincidence (Fig. 11 and Col. Pl. XIV in print edn). Wearing a brilliant cloak, the figure stares directly out at the spectator with bright green eyes and wears a matching green 'X' or 'Chi' over his chest. In Psalm 4:7, the narrator asserts that 'the light of your countenance, Lord, has been sealed upon us'. Both Augustine and Cassiodorus in their commentaries on this verse make the analogy to a coin that is stamped with the emperor's image. Cassiodorus writes that the 'cross leaves its mark, the light is of God's countenance' shining within the good Christian. Augustine notes that, when the Christian soul carries the light of God's countenance, it is stamped within, in 'his very heart, that is, in that chamber where we are to pray'.[54] The evangelist symbol of Matthew literally bears the imprint of Christ's cross of light in his heart.[55]

While it has been suggested that the areas of green and/or blue-green that surround the eyes of the human figures should be explained as a rather singular reflection of Byzantine modelling,[56] it is better understood as a reference to the light of the church and her teachings shining out from the eyes of the evangelists, which — like the emerald — imbues the air reflected around it with light and colour. In the Crucifixion page of the Durham Gospels, Christ's bright green eyes are given similar emphasis (Fig. 13 and Col. Pl. XVI in print edn). Almost invisible in reproductions of this badly damaged page, Christ's eyes are surrounded by minute, dense, parallel, vertical striations. The manner in which the lines are arranged at the sides of the eyes clearly indicates that they are not intended to represent eyelashes and so may similarly reflect the radiance of Christ's eyes. Even in its current condition, with the majority of its colour stripped from it, the page with its undulating aura surrounding the head and shoulders of Christ and his rippling garment suggest brilliant light emitting from him.

The Lindisfarne Gospels' selection of blue and/or green for the iris and surrounding eye area of the evangelists and their symbols makes a great deal of sense. Gregory the Great writes, 'He strengthens the minds of His preachers in the love of internal greenness, so that they despise all transitory things [. . .] Hence the shepherd of the Church himself, calling his hearers to pastures of eternal greenness'.[57] Similarly, in his commentary on the Apocalypse, after Bede compares the sapphire to the light of the skies on a clear day, he goes on to say that the holy man, 'When struck by the rays of the sun, emits a radiant brightness from himself; because the mind [*animus*] of the saints, which is always intent on heavenly things, in that it is daily renewed by the rays of divine light [. . .] diligently seeks for the things eternal, and commends them to others for their seeking'.[58] Earlier in the commentary, when discussing the emerald rainbow, Bede writes that it represents the saints whom God has enlightened, noting that it is therefore appropriate that they are compared with 'an emerald, a stone of a deep green'.[59]

Most relevant to the faux emeralds that appear in the John carpet page, both emeralds and the colour green were celebrated for their ability to heal and refresh strained eyes. Pliny, in a work that may well have been known by Bede, writes that the emerald is of such a beautiful green that strained eyes can be restored by merely gazing upon it.[60] Isidore similarly praises the emerald's ability to soothe eyestrain.[61] In this context, it is unsurprising that John, the evangelist associated with clear vision and whose gospel was thought to heal the sick, wears a bright green tunic, while the John carpet page is studded with faux emeralds. Perhaps coincidentally, Augustine's commentary on John repeatedly describes Christ's incarnation as an eye-salve (*collyrium*).[62]

In terms of pose, as Michelle Brown has pointed out, the most notable distinction occurs in the John portrait where the Evangelist's singular frontal pose and direct gaze demarcate him as the beloved apostle who wrote the Book of Revelation.[63] As such, John was seen as one gifted with special vision. This conceit is a standard motif in Insular and early medieval exegetical literature and art, where John's symbol, the eagle, is described in terms of the creature's ability to see long distances and its habit of staring directly at the sun.[64] Augustine's homily on John 1:1, which is clearly referenced in the John Portrait within the Book of Kells, famously expounded at length upon John's sight and the nature of 'inner' or 'spiritual' vision.[65] In the Lindisfarne Gospels, John's frontal gaze is rendered in a fully saturated, clear green that matches his tunic and the book held by his symbol. Only this green colour and the bright red of John's halo are clearly perceptible on the reverse of the page. While it is impossible to know whether this effect was immediate, the resulting ghostly image with its large green eyes that seem to burn through the page is quite disconcerting.

Unlike the other three evangelists in the Lindisfarne Gospels, John does not look down at his text but instead seems to stare directly out at the viewer, which Brown interprets as John inviting 'the onlooker to partake in the inspiration of the gospel' (Figs 4, 7 and Col. Pls VII, X in print edn).[66] As I have discussed elsewhere, Insular art often depicts saints, scribes and evangelists with a lowered gaze, looking at some intermediary object that affords them an indirect, inner vision or glimpse of the Godhead.[67] In the two surviving evangelist portraits from the Book of Kells, Matthew and John stare directly out at the manuscript's audience. In both cases, the complex iconography makes clear that what the viewer sees in the image is only a glimpse of the inner vision beheld by the evangelist. The iconography of the John portrait and its incipit on the opposite verso do this through extremely complex visual exegesis that draws directly from Augustine's commentary on John 1:1.[68] More simply, and similar to John's gesture in the Lindisfarne Gospels, Matthew obscures his right hand under his outer garment to touch his breast, a gesture that George Henderson has interpreted as possibly indicating 'the hidden counsels of God, not yet revealed'.[69] While the hand of John in the Lindisfarne Gospels emerges from under his outer garment, it also rests on his chest. Both gestures surely denote that true understanding and vision of the scriptures are housed within the chest, which in the medieval period was seen as the 'secret', 'inner chamber', a treasure house in which true wisdom was kept.[70] John's bright green under-tunic, matching his eyes, suggests an inner light that burns brightly.

While John's gaze conveys an inner vision, it equally suggests a looking outwards. Unlike the other evangelists who regard their work, we cannot see the object of John's gaze. In part, this indicates John's longing and unfulfilled desire, characteristics that were thought to be essential aspects of spiritual vision. John's eyes reach out like an unanswered question, and we empathically follow his gaze in its search for an object. Again, parallels can be found in Augustine's commentary on the beginning of John's gospel, where the patristic writer explains to his audience that, while they should look to the evangelist and his gospel with their bodily sight, their inner eye should follow John's gaze, seeking the source of his illumination.[71] In another sense, however, John's eyes do find and engage with an object, and that object is us. Augustine, in his many analyses of spiritual vision, suggests that, while Christians cannot 'presently' look fully upon God, they can glimpse God in each other. Love is the key component of spiritual sight, and in loving a neighbour, according to Augustine, one is able to glimpse God.[72] It seems unsurprising, then, that John, the evangelist who was so commonly associated with love,[73] stares directly at the manuscript's audience while reflecting the glory of God.

By way of conclusion, it is helpful to return to the distinctive varicoloured robes discussed at the beginning of this paper. Although described as 'illogical' and 'indiscriminate' shadows, it seems more likely that the bright red folds of John's tunic represent light.[74] Similar lines of red, green, white and blue appear on the robes of all four evangelists, and it has even been suggested that they may represent shot silk (Figs 1–4 and Col. Pls IV–VII in print edn).[75] Whether or not this is the case, surely the striations of bright green, blue and red indicate heavenly light and radiance rather than dark shadow. With the exception of blue, these are the colours used in the manuscript to portray the heavenly auras that surround the evangelists and their symbols. As we have seen, green and blue were colours associated with the brilliance of the heavens and divine light. Artists commonly used red to convey firelight, sunlight and the brilliance of gold.[76] Additionally, with the notable exception of Matthew's deep plum-coloured robe and its black striations,[77] the colours of the folds and the garments that they appear on come from opposite sides of the colour-wheel — red and blue; green and red — creating the optical effect of simultaneous contrast whereby colours intensify one another, giving the illusion of flux.[78] As a result, the four men appear to wear living robes of light, fulfilling the instructions that Christ gave during his Sermon on the Mount: 'You are the light of the world [...] Let your light stand before the eyes of men so they may see [...] and praise your father in heaven'.

ACKNOWLEDGEMENTS

I would like to thank Catherine Turner and Gabriel Sewell at Durham Cathedral Library and the Special Collections staff at the University of Edinburgh for all of their help and patience. A number of people were extremely generous in answering my many queries. They include Alice Blackwell, Susie Bioletti, Susanna Kirk, Bernard Meehan, George Henderson, Kathleen Doyle, Robin Clark, and Michelle Brown. While writing this article, I was fortunate to attend Cheryl Porter's 'Medieval Palette' course run in conjunction with the Montefiascone conservation project. Versions of this paper were given at the University of Glasgow 'Colour Studies Group', the University of Edinburgh Medieval Art Seminar and the British Archaeological Association Conference. I am most grateful for the comments from participants of all three groups as well as those from the anonymous reviewer of this article.

NOTES

1. *Evangeliorum Quattuor Codex Lindisfarnensis*, ed. T. D Kendrick, 2 vols (Olten and Lausanne 1956–60); Michelle Brown, *The Lindisfarne Gospels: Society, Spirituality and the Scribe* (London 2003). The scientific analyses published in the 2003 monograph have proved revolutionary to our understanding of colour.

Equally valuable, however, is Bruce-Mitford's 'Decoration and Miniatures', published in the 1956 commentary volume to *Evangeliorum Quattuor* (see above), in which he offers careful observations and detailed description of colour, even observing the lighting conditions under which he viewed the manuscript.

2. There are notable exceptions to this in Brown's work: see, for example, her discussion of purple (Brown, *Lindisfarne* (as n. 1), 335, 369).

3. For a more in-depth discussion of these issues and overview of published scholarship on medieval colour, see H. Pulliam, 'Color', *Medieval Art History Today — Critical Terms* (a special issue of) *Studies in Iconography*, 33 (2012), 3–14.

4. See, for example, N. Barley, 'Old English Colour Classification: Where Do Matters Stand?', *Anglo-Saxon England*, 3 (1974), 16; C. Biggam, *Blue in Old English: An Interdisciplinary Semantic Study*, Costerus 110 (Amsterdam 1997); *The Realms of Colour*, ed. A. Portmann and R. Ritsema (Leiden 1974), especially P. Dronke, 'Tradition and Innovation in Medieval Western Colour-Imagery', 51–107; J. André, *Étude sur les termes de couleur dans la langue Latine*, Études et commentaires 7 (Paris 1949); A. George, 'Calligraphy, Colour and Light in the Blue Qur'an', *Journal of Qur'anic Studies* 11 (2009), 75–125; H. A. Lazar-Meyen, 'Colour Terms in Táin Bó Cúailnge', in *Ulidia: Proceedings of the First International Conference on the Ulster Cycle of Tales, Belfast and Emain Macha, 8–12 April 1994*, ed. J. Mallory and G. Stockman (Belfast 1994), 201–05; L. James, *Light and Colour in Byzantine Art* (Oxford 1996). There has been some debate as to how applicable paradigms found in language are to visual images as well as to what extent language reveals a culture's conceptualization of colour.

5. Brown, *Lindisfarne* (as n. 1), 281.

6. For the BL online images, three websites are now available (the first requires a plug-in that can be downloaded from the webpage): <http://www.bl.uk/onlinegallery/ttp/ttpbooks.html>, <http://www.bl.uk/onlinegallery/ttp/accessiblettp.html> and <http://www.bl.uk/manuscripts/Viewer.aspx?ref=cotton_ms_nero_d_iv_fs001r>. For an example of the type of colour distortion common in most print reproductions of the manuscript's pages, see C. Nordenfalk, *Celtic and Anglo-Saxon Painting: Book Illumination in the British Isles, 600–800* (London 1977).

7. This conclusion is based upon my own comparison between the original manuscript and the facsimile.

8. K. L. Brown and R. J. H. Clark, 'The Lindisfarne Gospels and Two Other 8th Century Anglo-Saxon/Insular Manuscripts: Pigment Identification by Raman Microscopy', *Journal of Raman Spectroscopy*, 35 (2004), 4–12; C. Porter, 'You Can't Tell a Pigment by its Color', in *Making the Medieval Book: Techniques of Production: Proceedings of the Fourth Conference of the Seminar in the History of the Book to 1500, Oxford, July 1992*, ed. L. Brownrigg (Los Altos Hills, CA 1995), 111–16.

9. Brown and Clark, 'The Lindisfarne Gospels' (as n. 8).

10. The published colour reports use the term 'indigo' as a blanket term for the pigment produced from both indigo and woad plants, but woad is used here to distinguish between the two plants.

11. Brown and Clark, 'Lindisfarne Gospels' (as n. 8), 7.

12. Ibid., 9.

13. Personal communication with Susie Bioletti, Trinity College Dublin. See also L. Burgio, S. Bioletti and B. Meehan, 'Non-destructive, In Situ Analysis of Three Early Medieval Manuscripts from Trinity College Library Dublin (Codex Usserianus Primus, Book of Durrow, Book of Armagh)', in *Making Histories: Proceedings of the Sixth Insular Art Conference*, ed. J. Hawkes (York forthcoming).

14. Brown and Clark, 'Lindisfarne Gospels' (as n. 8), 9.

15. Of these instances, the eyes are the most difficult to classify (see discussion below).

16. See, for example, J. J. G. Alexander, 'The Illumination of the Gospels', *The York Gospels: A Facsimile With Introductory Essays By Jonathan Alexander, Patrick McGurk, Simon Keynes & Bernard Barr*, ed. N. Barker, J. Alexander, P. McGurk, and C. Barker (London 1986), 65–74; J. O'Reilly, 'St John as a Figure of the Contemplative Life: Text and Image in the Art of the Anglo-Saxon Benedictine Reform', in *St Dunstan: His Life, Times and Cult*, ed. N. Ramsay and T. Tatton-Brown (Woodbridge 1992), 165–85; Michelle P. Brown, *The Book of Cerne: Prayer, Patronage, and Power in Ninth-Century England* (London 1996); J. Rosenthal and P. McGurk, 'Author, Symbol and Word: The Inspired Evangelists in Judith of Flanders's Anglo-Saxon Gospelbooks', in *Tributes to Jonathan J. G. Alexander: The Making and Meaning of Illuminated Medieval & Renaissance Manuscripts, Art & Architecture*, ed. S. L'Engle and G. B. Guest (London 2007), 185–202.

17. Brown, *Lindisfarne* (as n. 1), 346–70. Laura Kendrick's discussion of these four evangelist pages is also extremely enlightening but often overlooked: L. Kendrick, *Animating the Letter: The Figurative Embodiment of Writing from Late Antiquity to the Renaissance* (Columbus, OH 1999), 161–64.

18. R. McNally, 'The Evangelists in the Hiberno-Latin Tradition', in *Festschrift Bernhard Bischoff zu seinem 65. Geburtstag*, ed. J. Autenrieth und F. Brunhölzl (Stuttgart 1971), 111–22; J. O'Reilly, 'Patristic and Insular Traditions of the Evangelists: Exegesis and Iconography', in *Le Isole britanniche e Roma in etá Romanobarbarica*, ed. A. Fadda and É. Ó Carragáin (Rome 1998), 49–94; '"*Traditio evangeliorum*" and

"*Sustentatio*": The Relevance of Liturgical Ceremonies to the Book of Kells', in *The Book of Kells: Proceedings of a Conference at Trinity College Dublin, 6–9 September 1992*, ed. F. O'Mahony (Aldershot 1994), 398–436; J. Cronin, 'The Evangelist Symbols as Pictorial Exegesis', in *From the Isles of the North: Early Medieval Art in Ireland and Britain: Proceedings of the Third International Conference on Insular Art, Held in the Ulster Museum, Belfast, 7–11 April, 1994*, ed. C. Bourke (Belfast 1995), 111–17.

19. On sapphires, he cites Exodus 24:10, 'Under his feet was a paved work of sapphire stone, or like the sky, when it is serene', and on emeralds, he writes, 'Smaragdus nimiae viriditatis est, adeo ut herbas virentes, frondesque et gemmas superet omnes, inficiens circa se viriditate repercussum aerem, qui merito et viridi proficit oleo, quamvis natura imbuatur': *PL*, XCIII, cols 198b, d. For English translations of Bede's text, see <http://www.apocalyptic-theories.com/theories/bede/bede.html> (accessed 1 November 2012).

20. See for example *PL*, XCIII, col. 197d.

21. '[T]anta fidei sublimitas per Evangelium mundo innotuit, apte, propter quatuor Evangelii libros, quarto loco smaragdus ponitur': *PL*, XCIII, col. 199b.

22. W. Weinrich, *Revelation*, Ancient Christian Commentary on Scripture 12 (Drovers Grove, IL 2005), 375.

23. See McNally, 'The Evangelists' (as n. 18) and *PL*, XCIII, col. 198c. I am grateful to George Henderson for pointing out that oil was associated both with the evangelist John and the emerald.

24. A. Petzold, '"Of the Significance of Colours": The Iconography of Colour in Romanesque and Early Gothic Book Illumination', in *Image and Belief: Studies in Celebration of the Eightieth Anniversary of the Index of Christian Art*, ed. Colum Hourihane (Princeton 1999), 130–31.

25. Cambridge, Corpus Christi College MS 197b, fol. 1r, and BL, MS Cotton Otho C V: see M. Brown, *Manuscripts from the Anglo-Saxon Age* (London 2007), pl. 31.

26. Paris, Bibliothèque nationale, MS Latin 9389 (images of this and the other Bibliothèque nationale manuscripts cited in this paper are available at: <http://mandragore.bnf.fr/jsp/rechercheExperte.jsp> (accessed 1 November 2012)).

27. Images of these pages are available via the Pierpont Morgan's online resource, CORSAIR, at <http://corsair.morganlibrary.org/> (accessed 1 November 2012).

28. Because the eye area is quite small and less intensely coloured in these other examples, it is not possible to state with certainty whether the eyes are blue, green or a shade of blue-green. The 2004 colour report describes the eye area of Mark as 'possibly verdigris' and that of Luke as 'indigo'. It is not clear, however, whether the tested area was the 'shadowed' skin between the eye and the eyebrow or the iris itself. The version as published in Michelle Brown's monograph does not include the Luke test site but does indicate the test areas more specifically, making it clear that it is the skin surrounding Mark's eye that is coloured indigo (woad). Brown and Clark, 'The Lindisfarne Gospels' (as n. 8), 6–7, and Brown, *Lindisfarne* (as n. 1), 437–51. Additionally, the colour terms in both Old Irish and Anglo-Saxon show considerable slippage between these two hues, see Biggam, *Blue in Old English* (as n. 4) and A. K. Siewers, 'The Bluest-Greyest-Greenest Eye: Colours of Martyrdom and Colours of the Winds as Iconographic Landscape', *Cambrian Medieval Celtic Studies*, 50 (2005), 31–66.

29. C. P. Biggam, 'Ualdenegi and the Concept of Strange Eyes', in *Lexis and Texts in Early English: Studies Presented to Jane Roberts*, ed. J. Roberts, C. Kay and L. Sylvester (Amsterdam 2001), 34–35.

30. Bruce-Mitford, 'Decoration', in *Evangeliorum Quattuor* (as n. 1), I, 134.

31. *Isidore of Seville's* Etymologies*: The Complete English Translation of* Isidori Hispalensis Episcopi Etymologiarum sive Originum Libri XX, trans. P. Throop, 2 vols (Charlotte, VT 2005), II, XI.1.31: 'Oculi vocati [...] quia occultum lumen habent, id est, secretum, vel intus positum. Hi inter omnes sensus viciniores animae existunt; in oculis enim omne mentis indicium est, unde et animi perturbatio vel hilaritas in oculis apparet. Oculi autem iidem et lumina. Et dicta lumina quod ex eis lumen manat, vel quod initio sui clausam teneant lucem, aut extrinsecus acceptam visui proponendam refundant'. *PL*, LXXXII, cols 401c–402a.

32. The following summary draws heavily upon M. Miles, 'Vision: The Eye of the Body and the Eye of the Mind in Saint Augustine's "De Trinitate" and "Confessions"', *The Journal of Religion*, 63 (1983), 125–42.

33. Ibid., 130.

34. See, for example, Psalm 12:4: 'Enlighten my eyes [*illumina oculos meos*]' and Psalm 18:9, 'The precepts of the Lord are brilliant [*lucidem*], enlightening the eyes [*illuminans oculos*]'.

35. Psalm 17:29: 'For you illuminate my lamp [*illuminas lucernam*]'; Psalm 145:8: 'The Lord enlightens (*illuminat*) the blind'.

36. *St. Augustin. Homilies on the Gospel of John; Homilies on the First Epistle of John, Soliloquies*, ed. Philip Schaff, A Select Library of the Nicene and Post-Nicene Fathers of the Christian Church 7 (Whitefish, MO 2010), 15. 'Quia et homo illuminatus dicitur lux; sed vera lux illa est quae illuminat.' *PL*, XXXV, col. 1391.

37. *PL*, XXXV, cols 1379–88.

38. John Gage, *Colour and Culture: Practice and Meaning from Antiquity to Abstraction* (London 1993), 45.

39. See, for example, the famous mosaics at Ravenna (the book held by the figure to the right of Maximian in San Vitale; each of the gospels held by the four evangelist symbols in the mosaics from the archiepiscopal chapel), and also the book held by Christ in the clypeus above the apse at San Apollinare in Classe. In a more tangible manifestation, the gold cover of the Codex Aureus of St Emmeram depicts Christ in Majesty surrounded by four large green gemstones.

40. *Isidore of Seville's* Etymologies (as n. 31), II.XVI.7.1. '[I]nficiens circa se viriditate repercussum aerem': *PL*, LXXXII, col. 517a. Bede text, cited in n. 19.

41. See the online translation (as n. 19). '[T]entantur, eo amplius haereditatem immarcescibilem et aeternam conservatam in coelis et mente concipere sperando, et in proximos satagunt spargere praedicando': *PL*, XCIII, cols 198c–d.

42. Brown, *Lindisfarne* (as n. 1), 278, 332.

43. For an explanation as to the relationship between spiritual and physical vision as discussed by Augustine, see Miles, 'Vision' (as n. 32).

44. See the online translation (as n. 19). 'Et gloria Domini in hoc colore consistat, qui portat imaginem supercoelestis': *PL*, XCIII, col. 198a. Cf. Exodus 24:10: 'And they saw the God of Israel. And under his feet was something like a work of sapphire stone, or like the sky, when it is serene'; Ezekiel 10:1: 'And I saw, and behold, in the firmament that was over the heads of the cherubim, there appeared above them something like the sapphire stone, with the sight of the likeness of a throne'.

45. Well-known examples of the *crux gemmata* include the cross under the arch of the apse of S. Vitale in Ravenna and the great jewelled cross that dominates the apse of S. Apollinare in Classe.

46. See, for example, the mandorla of Christ in Majesty in the Sacramentary of Charles the Bald (Paris, Bibliothèque nationale, MS Latin 1141, fol. 6r); Paris, Bibliothèque nationale, MS Latin 9385, fol. 197v; the New Minster *Liber Vitae* (BL, MS Stowe 944, fol. 6r); the halo of the crucified Christ and those of the four evangelists in the so-called Gospels of François II (Paris, Bibliothèque nationale, MS Latin 257, fol. 12v); and the haloes of the four evangelists in an 11th-century enamel pectoral cross from the State Pushkin Museum.

47. See, for example, Christ's halo in the presbytery and apse mosaics of San Vitale, Ravenna.

48. Gregory the Great, for example, in his commentaries on Ezekiel, explained that Mark as the lion represents Christ waking at his resurrection while John as the eagle symbolizes Christ's ascension into the heavens: *PL*, LXXVI, cols 815a–d. Brown has argued that Mark and John lack facial hair because they represent the 'youthful, immortal types of the resurrected Christ': Brown, *Lindisfarne* (as n. 1), 350.

49. H. Pulliam, 'Looking to Byzantium: Light, Color, and Cloth in the Book of Kells' Virgin and Child Page', in *Insular and Anglo-Saxon Art and Thought in the Early Medieval Period*, ed. C. Hourihane (University Park, PA 2011), 59–78.

50. For a discussion of possible paste additions to Insular sculpture, see R. N. Bailey, *England's Earliest Sculptors* (Toronto 1996), 5–11. Analyses of the Aberlady fragment were undertaken as a part of the National Museums of Scotland-Glenmorangie Research project: see A. Blackwell, 'Individuals', in A. Blackwell, D. Clarke and M. Goldberg, *Early Medieval Scotland: Individuals, Communities and Ideas* (Edinburgh 2012).

51. Durham, Cathedral Library, MS A. II. 17, fol. 38v, and Dublin, Trinity College, MS A. 4. 5. (57), fols 21v, 84v. Due to the deteriorated state of the Durham crucifixion page, reproductions frequently alter its colour so as to increase the legibility of both the image and the text that surrounds it. As a result the colour is exaggerated in most publications, while in others it severely diminished. My observations are based on a close inspection of the manuscript.

52. See C. Pietrangeli, *San Giovanni in Laterano* (Firenze 1990), 58. I am grateful to my colleague Claudia Bolgia for directing me to this mosaic.

53. Image online at the Pierpont Morgan Library website, <http://www.themorgan.org/collections/collections.asp?id=67> (accessed 1 November 2012). See also *The Making of England: Anglo-Saxon Art and Culture* AD *600–900*, ed. L. Webster and J. Backhouse (Toronto 1991), 170. Because of the even distribution of orange, it appears that this was the original colour of the enamel, although some red enamels do corrode to yellow and conceivably orange (personal communication with Dr Susanna Kirk, National Museums of Scotland).

54. *Saint Augustin: Expositions on the Book of Psalms*, trans. A. C. Coxe, A Select Library of the Nicene and Post-Nicene Fathers of the Christian Church 8 (Edinburgh 1996), 10. '[I]n ipso corde, id est, in illo cubili ubi orandum est loquebatur': *PL*, XXXVI, col. 82.

55. Nordenfalk, *Celtic* (as n. 6), pl. 4.

56. Brown, *Lindisfarne* (as n. 1), 286.

57. *Homilies on the Book of the Prophet Ezekiel: Saint Gregory the Great*, trans. T. Tomkinson (Etna, CA 2008), 355. 'Quia praedicatorum illius mentes internae viriditatis amore solidavit, ut transitoria cuncta despiciant [...] Unde et ipse pastor Ecclesiae, auditores suos ad pascua aeternae viriditatis vocans': *PL*, LXXVI, cols 999b–c.

58. 'Qui radiis percussus solis, ardentem ex se emittit fulgorem. Quia coelestibus semper intentus sanctorum animus, divini luminis quotidie radiis innovatus [...] ardentior aeterna perquirit, aliisque inquirenda suadet': *PL*, XCIII, col. 198a.

59. '[S]maragdo lapidi nimiae viriditatis': *PL*, XCIII, col. 143b.

60. Pliny the Elder, *Natural History: A Selection*, trans. J. F. Healy (London 2004), 372 (from chapter 16 of book 33). Although it has been suggested that Bede was only familiar with the earlier books of Pliny's *Natural History*, his commentary on the Apocalypse draws heavily upon the later books: see P. Kitson, 'Lapidary Traditions in Anglo-Saxon England: Part II, Bede's *Explanatio Apocalypsis* and Related Works', *Anglo-Saxon England*, 12 (1983), 73–123.

61. *PL*, LXXXII, col. 517a.

62. Specifically, treatises 2.16, 34.9, and 35: *PL*, XXXV, cols 1395, 1655 and 1660.

63. Brown, *Lindisfarne* (as n. 1), 369.

64. Ibid., loc. cit.; O'Reilly, 'St John' (as n. 16); J. Hamburger, *St. John the Divine: The Deified Evangelist in Medieval Art and Theology* (Berkeley, CA 2002). See also n. 48 above.

65. H. Pulliam, *Word and Image in the Book of Kells* (Dublin 2006), 180–85.

66. Brown, *Lindisfarne* (as n. 1), 369; Kendrick, *Animating the Letter* (as n. 17), 161–64.

67. H. Pulliam, '"The Eyes of the Handmaid": The Corbie Psalter and the Ruthwell Cross', in *Listen O Isles Unto Me: Studies in Medieval Word and Image in Honour of Jennifer O'Reilly*, ed. E. Mullins and D. Scully (Cork, 2011), 253–62.

68. Pulliam, *Word and Image* (as n. 65), 180–85.

69. Henderson's explanation is complex, drawing upon Psalm 73:11 ('why do you not withdraw your right hand from your bosom'), and the so-called Christ in Majesty page on fol. 32v, suggesting: 'if the first figure on 28v [the Matthew Portrait] and the second on f. 32v are indeed seen in the same setting — one enthroned, surrounded by beasts, the other, certainly Christ, acclaimed by angels — and form a sequence, the almighty enthroned of Chapter 4, and the Lamb, as it had been slain, of Chapter 5, then the gesture of the concealed hand could represent the hidden counsels of God, not yet revealed'. G. Henderson, *From Durrow to Kells: The Insular Gospel-Books, 650–800* (London 1987), 157.

70. M. Carruthers, *The Book of Memory: A Study of Memory in Medieval Culture*, Cambridge Studies in Medieval Literature 10 (Cambridge 1990), 53–57.

71. *PL*, XXXV, cols 1379–88.

72. Miles, *Vision* (as n. 32), 135.

73. For an overview of this association between John and love, see Brown, *Lindisfarne* (as n. 1), 369.

74. See, for example, Bruce Mitford's description in *Evangeliorum Quattuor* (as n. 1), I, 128.

75. G. R. Owen-Crocker, *Dress in Anglo-Saxon England* (Manchester 1986), 302.

76. Gage, *Colour* (as n. 38), 26.

77. For an explanation as to this deviation, see Pulliam, 'Color' (as n. 3), 7–10.

78. This may simply be a case of simultaneous contrast, or equally it could be an example of chromostereopsis.

Apostolically Inscribed: St Cuthbert's Coffin as Sacred Vessel

JENIFER NÍ GHRÁDAIGH and JULIET MULLINS

Although its iconography is widely discussed, St Cuthbert's reliquary coffin has never been acknowledged for what it really is: the vessel for a miraculously incorrupt body. Its 'humble' graffito technique has also been misread as lacking in artistic ambition, rather than as an opportunity to place the epigraphy and the representational art on an equal basis and, moreover, to mirror some of the most striking visual experiences of the early medieval pilgrim to the Roman catacombs. By comparing the coffin with a liturgical vessel, the Ardagh Chalice, which likewise bears a litany of apostles, the purpose of such litanies' depiction as communion rather than simply invocation is explored. The importance of the viewer's own gaze upon the coffin and the witnessing power of the angels and apostles are also considered in the light of hagiographic and apocryphal sources.

THE reliquary coffin of St Cuthbert, reliably datable to 698 and provenanced to Lindisfarne, should be considered as one of the most telling witnesses to the 7th-century Anglo-Saxon cult of the saints, as well as being a unique testament to skilled monumental wood carving of the period (Fig. 1 and Col. Pl. XVII in print edn). However, although it has excited interest within the narrower context of St Cuthbert's cult, the coffin has failed to attract as wide an audience as the embroidered textiles found within it, or to arouse such intense levels of scholarly interest as have the impressive stone crosses of Ruthwell and Bewcastle.[1] This must be due in part to the inadequacy of the published photographs of the coffin, which do it little justice as an artwork; and in part to its fragmentary state, recomposed from some of the 6,000 pieces of oak which were recovered after the excavations of St Cuthbert's burial in 1827 and 1899.[2] A general art-historical tendency to value the plasticity of relief sculpture over the linearity of incised works has also contributed to its relative neglect, and is apparent in C. R. Dodwell's negative assessment of its 'unsophisticated style'.[3]

A brief description of the coffin and its iconography will help to illustrate the argument of this paper. The coffin is a tapered or trapezoidal chest, with a maximum length of 1.69 m, a maximum height of 0.46 m, and a width of 0.41 m at the 'angel' end, tapering to 0.38 m at the 'Virgin' end.[4] It was constructed originally of six oak planks, of which five have been certainly identified: the long sides, ends and lid. The base has been provisionally identified with a cross-inscribed board, separately assembled in the 1930s. Ernst Kitzinger felt this board could not have belonged to the original coffin for iconographic reasons, a point since disproved.[5] It will here be assumed, following Richard Bailey, J. M. Cronyn and C. V. Horie, that this was indeed the original coffin base. The lid shows a standing figure of Christ with the symbols of the evangelists about him, accompanied by inscriptions in a mixture of

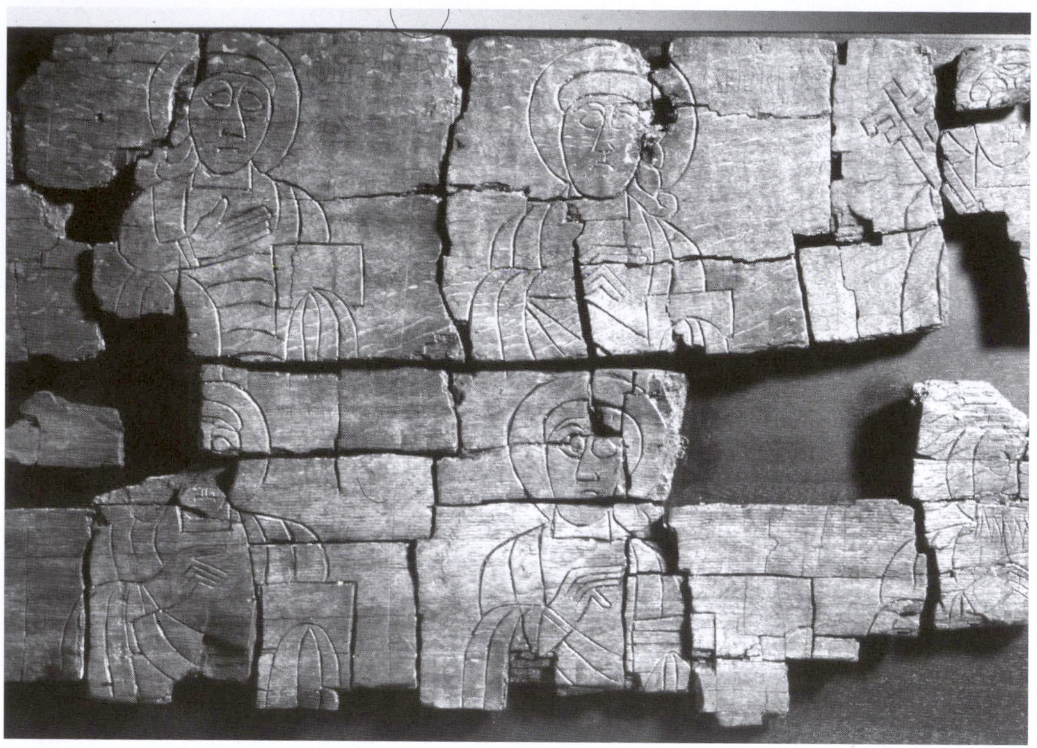

FIG. 1. Detail of the apostles, John and Andrew. St Cuthbert's Coffin
By kind permission of the Dean and Chapter, Durham

Roman and runic script: Matheus and Marcus above his head, Lucas and Iohannis beneath his feet.[6] The narrower end of the coffin shows the Virgin and Child (Fig. 2); the Virgin is seated in profile but her shoulders and head are turned to face the viewer fully.[7] The Apostles panel, probably originally on the right side of the coffin, shows two rows of six half-length figures, of which Peter and Paul are distinguished from the others, Peter by his keys and hairstyle, Paul by his hairstyle alone.[8] As with the other images, these are accompanied by their names.[9] The wider end panel shows two angels, identified by inscription as Michael and Gabriel. The long panel opposite the apostles continues the sequence with another five angels, Raphael and Uriael identified by inscriptions, the other three unfortunately lacking identifiers, apart from an ambiguous UMIA (which Kitzinger suggested could have come from the name Rumiel), and the letters A[.]VRI[.]IA, whose meaning is not known.[10] It would seem likely that the seven archangels represent the seven angels of the apocalypse described but unnamed in Revelation 8:2 and 15:1 and given various names in a broad tradition of apocryphal texts.

BODILY PARTS: THE COFFIN AND ITS DECORATION

CUTHBERT'S coffin has a longer historiography than any other extant medieval Insular artwork. Initially described by Bede in the 8th century, it was also mentioned

Fig. 2. The Virgin and Child, St Cuthbert's Coffin
By permission of Durham University

in the anonymous account of the 1104 translation and commented upon in greater detail by Reginald of Durham in his account of the same event (composed between 1165 and 1172), in a chapter dedicated to 'his coffin and how it was constructed and carved in a marvellously diverse way'. Because a tendency to exaggeration is often found in hagiography, Dodwell counselled caution in our interpretation of Reginald's description of the coffin. Nevertheless, as a significant medieval example of an aesthetic reaction to an extant work, it ought to be considered on its own merits. Reginald stated that 'The whole [coffin] is engraved on the outside with the most marvellous carving, which is of such fine and subtle craftsmanship that it may be considered more consistent with a state of ecstasy than the knowledge or resources of a sculptor'.[11]

Meyer Schapiro noted that it was the style of the carvings and not their meaning which enthused Reginald, whose other comments on the fabrics and comb preserved within the coffin show him capable of discerning and sensitive judgement.[12] Indeed, bearing in mind differences of medium and scale, it may be observed that there is little to distinguish the figural style of the Lindisfarne Gospels, which is clearly sophisticated and of high quality, from that of the coffin.[13] The arguments presented below should show that, in terms of both style and meaning, the coffin is one of the most original and ambitious artworks of the 7th century.[14]

The importance of the iconography of Cuthbert's coffin has been most fully explored by Ernst Kitzinger, who was surely right in stressing that analogues for the archangels and the apostles in the form of prayers and litanies are key to our understanding of the iconography of the whole.[15] Kitzinger's interpretation of the coffin ascribes an apotropaic function to it. The apostles and archangels provide a sort of visual litany which the figures on the lid — Christ, the Evangelists, the Virgin and Child — complement. The litany of the saints had no fixed form at this early stage, and was subject to local and regional variation, but it seems to have held a special place in Insular devotion, and influenced works of art in various media.[16] In the case of the coffin, as Kitzinger suggests, the visualization of the litany not only encourages the viewer to appeal to the figures depicted for mercy and protection, but also suggests the fulfilment of these prayers through the figures' very presence. The cross-inscribed base complements this scheme by infusing it with the idea of God's triumph and protective power.[17]

While we may concur with Kitzinger in his analysis both of the source of the figural scheme and its ultimate function of manifesting divine presence, the purpose of that presence as purely protective is problematic. For, despite the exhaustiveness of his commentary on the coffin, Kitzinger did not acknowledge that the relics of Cuthbert were themselves a source of miraculous power and the saint himself was considered to be an influential intercessor. The need of protective images is thus placed in doubt. Furthermore, the coffin is first and foremost a site of burial, and this must not merely influence our reading of it, but suggests that other funerary works and sepulchral sites should be compared with it.[18] The iconography of the coffin can only be understood properly if we bear in mind its function as a container for a sacred body. As such, the imagery cannot be immediately compared (as some have done) to that of apsidal mosaics or frescoes, chancel screens or gospel books, each of which has a very different purpose.[19] Moreover, the physical presence of the body within the casket and the strong tradition of its incorrupt state — witnessed at the saint's translation in the 7th century and again in the 11th and 12th — have important implications for our understanding of the coffin's iconographic scheme and its relationship to the relics within.[20] Before turning to the question of interpretation, however, the decision to incise rather than sculpt the coffin must be accounted for.

THE QUESTION OF INCISION

AT the beginning of this article, it was suggested that St Cuthbert's coffin is comparatively little known because it is sculpted in a linear, two-dimensional idiom. The plasticity of the carving on the Ruthwell and Bewcastle crosses, which may be as early as the coffin (although likely dating to *c.* 730–60), reveals sculptors with great facility for deep relief carving.[21] This raises a simple question: why incise, when carving was possible? Given the proficiency of both the Anglo-Saxons and the Irish with wood, it seems unlikely that a lack of available skilled craftsmen was the issue. It is difficult to agree with Kitzinger's judgement on the matter. According to him, '[i]t is the use of the graffito technique, often employed in Early Christian art for the most stenographic kind of sign language, which stamps our figures as works of humble standing, with no pretension except that of giving visible form to prayer'.[22] Kitzinger compared the style of the coffin to the graffiti on the grave slabs of the Roman catacombs, and this suggestion is one to which we shall return. Regarding his other claims, however, there is sufficient evidence that this was not considered a humble work, and that, at least in the 12th century, it was not perceived as such. Therefore, we must look for a more convincing reason for the technique of its decoration.

Because of the unique way in which it is carved, Cuthbert's coffin has not been given its due as a work of art by scholars used to dealing with Insular stone sculpture. However, there is one context in which incision is the norm and not the exception, and this is epigraphic inscriptions. It may be no coincidence that the earliest datable Anglo-Latin inscription extant is that from the dedication stone of St Paul's church at Jarrow, which bears the date of 23 April 685. This names not simply the dedicatee, St Paul, but also King Ecgfrith and Abbot Ceolfrith as joint founders, 'with God as authorizer'. Its triple form of dating, mentioning the reigns of king and abbot and the date (the ninth day of the kalends of May), suggests a deliberate emulation of Luke's gospel, where such triple dating is also used.[23] Whether or not the numerology of the inscription is as complex as has been argued, the care taken over the composition of this dedication stone demonstrates the importance given to monumental inscriptions in Northumbria at the precise time of the coffin's manufacture. Such value is further suggested by Bede's transmission (*sub anno* 688) of the epitaph of King Ceadwalla from St Peter's, Rome, in its entirety in his *Historia ecclesiastica*.[24] This is especially striking as Bede's transcription was not a direct one, but derived from a *silloge*, a manuscript collection of such epitaphs, which must have been present in Northumbria shortly after Ceadwalla's death.[25] Such *sillogae* testify to a continuing interest in epigraphy, and particularly in Roman epigraphy, initially sparked in the 4th century by Pope Damasus's composition of inscriptions celebrating the tombs of the martyrs, but evidently still eagerly pursued by the Anglo-Saxons in the 7th century.[26] This strong interest in epigraphy leads to consideration of the possible importance of the inscribed names on the coffin, their implications, and also whether a wish to foreground the inscriptions may have been amongst the reasons for the decision that the whole coffin should be an incised work and not a sculpted one. The combination of three-dimensional carving contrasted with incised lettering is not unknown in Northumbria at this period, as shown, for example, by the inscribed Jarrow cross slab. At Jarrow, however, the dominance of the cross, emphasized by its relief, is the very aspect which the inscription celebrates.[27]

If a desire to emphasize the inscriptions was the primary catalyst for the incised form of the overall decoration, then two of their aspects strike one as puzzling. First, the inscriptions are much more lightly cut than the drawings, which makes them difficult to read; and second, in the case of the archangel Raphael, the division of the inscription around the angel's body shows that it was certainly made after the carving.[28] One phenomenon that may have a bearing on the matter is the collection of graffiti inscriptions carved by Anglo-Saxon pilgrims onto the walls of the catacombs of Rome, to which Kitzinger drew attention.[29] Much art-historical emphasis has been placed on the influence of Roman sarcophagi on visiting pilgrims from Ireland and England.[30] With the exception of Wilfrid's crypt at Hexham, less attention has been paid to the influence of the Roman catacombs within an Anglo-Saxon context. In the catacombs, the majority of Early Christian sepulchral monuments are not elaborately carved sarcophagi, but simple incised slabs, while paintings attracted the most attention from pilgrims intent on inscribing their names. The incised technique of Cuthbert's coffin may thus reflect both experience of monuments in the catacombs and the appearance of graffiti. Reference to the monuments and quasi-sacred inscriptions of the Roman catacombs would have been both appropriate and edifying in the context of this major sepulchral object; and the names of the apostles, faintly inscribed in the manner of pilgrim-graffiti, must have powerfully evoked the presence and authority of the apostles at Cuthbert's side.

In general, names might be inscribed upon objects so as to indicate ownership, name the craftsman and, occasionally, identify the subject. As evidenced by the Jarrow inscription cited above, they might also be added so as to ascribe patronage and authorization to an object.[31] From one perspective, inclusion of names on the coffin was surely not required: any literate viewer ought to have been able to identify these figures as the apostles by their number, St Peter's oversized keys, and St Paul's dramatic beard.[32] Given the other and more common circumstances of inscribing names, here at some level the names of the apostles, archangels and Christ may imply ownership, patronage and authorization, not simply of the coffin, but of its contents.[33] Such an interpretation must be considered in the light of the iconography of the coffin discussed below, as well as the claims presented by Cuthbert's incorrupt body within.

EXPLORING THE ICONOGRAPHY

The lid of the coffin

THAT the relationship between Cuthbert's body (no mere fragment, but whole and incorrupt) and the iconographical scheme of the coffin is key to our understanding of both is suggested by the emphatically corporeal manner of the coffin's iconography. Here are shown not merely the names of the angels and apostles but their physical appearance, and that with some attention to specifics of physiognomy and hairstyle. This suggestion is further supported by the two scenes chosen for depiction upon the coffin's lid and end: Christ with the evangelists and the Virgin and Child. Only Christ is depicted twice, and this double depiction has sometimes been glossed over as an unfortunate iconographic 'error' due, perhaps, to problems with the lack of appropriate models.[34] Yet, it will be argued here that these two images are central to our understanding of the coffin's iconography and the Christological message carried therein, which in turn frames (in every sense of the word) the body of Cuthbert and the saint's emerging cult.

In the upper image, Christ stands between the four symbols of the evangelists in a scene that appears to depict him in glory at the Second Coming. All elements of the imagery combine to reinforce this reading. The tetramorphs derive from the apocalyptic beasts of Revelation 4:6–8; the standing figure of Christ is paralleled on the doors of Santa Sabina in Rome in a scene which has been interpreted as the Second Coming; and the whole appears to derive from an earlier 'majestas' composition.[35] In the lower image, the Virgin and Child are depicted in a scene that emphasizes the importance of the incarnation and the humanity of Christ. The effect of the two combined is not dissimilar to that of the paired images of Christ crucified and enthroned in glory in the 8th-century Irish St Gall gospels, where through the use of two distinct images the complex duality of Christ's humanity and divinity is conveyed.[36] On the coffin, the two images and the two facets of Christ's persona are linked by the position of his hands (the right hand raised in blessing, the left bearing a scroll) and the cross-inscribed halo that circles his head in both. The unusual inclusion of the cross on this halo recalls the moment when the humanity and divinity of the Son are most potently displayed, in the defining moment in Christian salvation that underpins all else: the crucifixion of Christ. It is thus a resonant feature of this work that uniting the Christological images on the coffin is the cross depicted on the coffin's base, a symbol and sign which despite its structural simplicity combines the theological complexity of the Christological message conveyed above it.

That 8th-century Northumbria was fully attuned to this message is suggested by the iconography of monuments such as the Ruthwell Cross and the poem to which it is related, *The Dream of the Rood*, in which the glory and humanity of Christ are evocatively combined in the heroic mode. The importance of the incarnation and judgement in contemporary Northumbrian art is also alluded to by Bede, who in his *Lives of the Abbots of Wearmouth and Jarrow* records that the paintings which Benedict Biscop brought from Rome to adorn St Peter's Church at Wearmouth allowed all who saw them:

> to contemplate the dear face of Christ and His saints, even if only in a picture, *to put themselves more firmly in mind of the Lord's incarnation* and, as they saw the decisive moment of the Last Judgement before their very eyes be brought to examine their conscience with all due severity.[37]

The pictorial representation of Christ and the saints evokes the dual ideas of Christ's corporeality through his incarnation and his divinity, which will only be fully revealed to mankind at the Second Coming, which in turn causes the believer to consider the bodily resurrection of the individual at the end of time, and under the threat of judgement.

The apostles and the archangels

THE themes of incarnation and judgement, humanity and divinity, that are depicted on the coffin's lid, end and base are picked up in the depiction of the seven archangels and twelve apostles that gaze out from the sides as they do in numerous other continental and Insular depictions of the *parousia*. As Kitzinger noted, the list of apostles derives from the litany of the canon of the Roman Mass, which dates back at least to the time of Gregory the Great. Many of the earliest examples of this litany (which differs from the list of apostles found in Matthew 10, for example, by excluding Judas the traitor and replacing him with Paul the apostle who, together with Peter, heads the saints) have Insular connections. One example is found in the Bobbio Missal, compiled at the monastery of Echternach, founded by the Northumbrian missionary Willibrord *c.* 700. Another is found in the preface to the Hieronymian Martyrology, which is known to have reached Northumbria by the 7th century where the text acquired a number of accretions, including the addition of local Northumbrian saints.[38] The litany of the saints can therefore be shown to derive from a very specific liturgical context, and one which we might assume was familiar to a Northumbrian audience. The same is not, alas, true of the archangels, who aside from Michael are not commemorated in any of the martyrologies or calendars associated with early Northumbria. The angels are named in a number of Irish sources, but only Michael is commemorated in the 8th-century *Martyrology of Tallaght* (based upon an exemplar derived from Lindisfarne that passed through Bangor and Iona), Bede's *Martyrology*, or any of the later Anglo-Saxon litanies for that matter.[39] Nevertheless, it is clear that the seven archangels have particularly strong apocalyptic associations, for they appear as heralds to the end of time in the apocryphal 1 Enoch, a book well known to the Anglo-Saxons, the influence of which has been charted in *Beowulf*, the works of Bede and the 9th-century Book of Cerne.[40] The apocalyptic associations of these particular angels is neatly underscored by a verse in the 9th-century Irish lorica known as 'Patrick's Breastplate' or *Faíd Fiada* ('The Deer's Cry'), in which the supplicant claims: 'Today I gird myself / With the power of the order of the cherubim, / With the obedience of angels, / With the ministry of the archangels, / With the expectation of resurrection, / For the sake of a reward'.[41]

The believer's expectation of resurrection is central to the iconography of this coffin and to the body within. The belief that the shrine of a saint represented his *locus resurrectionis* is well attested in early medieval Ireland and derives, ultimately, from accounts of the tomb of Christ found in Adomnán's *De Locis Sanctis*. A copy of this text was presented to King Aldfrith of Northumbria in 698 and used by Bede for his own account of the holy places. The *locus resurrectionis* was foreordained by God, and the saint was usually guided to it by an angel. In the case of the *Life of Senán*, the angel is explicitly named as Raphael the archangel.[42] If we understand the coffin of Cuthbert as an expression of his *locus resurrectionis*, then the resonance of the incarnation and judgement, with the apocryphal archangels and apostles looking on, is all the more striking.

As was noted above, the image of Christ with his mother is linked to the image of him between the evangelists by the position of his hands and the cross-inscribed halo common to both. The archangels and apostles are linked in a similar manner: the same model is used for all of them, with only Peter and Paul differentiated by their hair. One striking difference between the archangels, as against the apostles, lies in their eyes: five of the angels have drilled pupils, but none of the apostles do (Fig. 3).[43] The effect of this is not simply to increase the life-like qualities of the angels, but also to impute greater powers of vision to them; that is, to emphasize their significance as witnesses. The quotation from Bede's *Lives* cited above highlights the importance of sight and the gaze to early Northumbrian spirituality. As Bede makes clear, Christ's bodily suffering and the viewer's possible own are implicitly juxtaposed: sight leads to somatic response. In the mid-7th century, the primacy of sight was similarly accepted by the Irish monk Cummian in his letter on the Easter controversy; those who go to Rome are capable, because of what they have seen, of testifying to the truth.[44] It is, of course, most boldly expressed in John 20:8, where Christ's *absent* body

Fig. 3. The archangels, St Cuthbert's Coffin
By permission of Durham University

is the source of conviction to two of the disciples. It is also possible to link sight explicitly with Cuthbert's body and cult: Bede records that Cuthbert's hair was the source of a miraculous cure for a young monk in Dacre suffering from a tumour on his eye. Thus, in 8th-century Northumbria, believing and seeing are causally linked, just as seeing and believing are.[45] Further, the linking of sight and witness with artistic production is revealed in the Old English poem *Andreas*, in which carved angels that adorn the walls of the temple are miraculously brought to life to testify to Christ's own divinity.[46] Dodwell has suggested that this description of sculpted Cherubim and Seraphim, who replace sphinxes in the original apocryphal source, may be an interpolation influenced by the striking qualities of contemporary sculpture.[47] Whether or not this is the case, it certainly suggests that, to the Anglo-Saxons, angelic witnesses were particularly highly regarded, while also demonstrating a belief in the agency of the image, here miraculously revealed, but always implicit. In this context, the decision to drill the pupils of the angels on Cuthbert's coffin may have real significance: it is an attempt to represent the angels' penetrating vision. They stand as witnesses both to Christ's divinity and Cuthbert's sanctity.

INVOCATION OR COMMUNION?

ONCE we accept that the coffin is a vessel for a sacred body, we can start to place the litanies, particularly the litany of the apostles, within a more meaningful context.

As Kitzinger noted, the inclusion of Paul in place of Judas and the likely order of the apostles derives from the *Communicantes* hymn from the canon of the Mass; the list of angels also probably derives from a prayer, but one which must have non-Roman, possibly Irish, origins.[48] The order of the apostles is taken by reading from right to left, with the apostles in pairs, one above the other (see Appendix below). Plotted thus, the list begins with Peter and Paul, and can be seen to correspond exactly to the order in the canon of the Mass, of the eucharistic prayer of the Roman rite: the *Communicantes* hymn. It should be noted, however, that the coffin does not maintain the genitive endings of the list of names in the hymn, but corrects these to the nominative, although whether this shows a consultation of the list of apostles in Matthew 10:2–4, or simply the ironing out of what could be considered a grammatical anomaly, or indeed an intention not to imply that the coffin was 'of' the saints so named, is difficult to ascertain.[49] Contemporary graveslabs in Latin and Old English do not routinely inscribe the names of those buried beneath them in the genitive, as the names are usually given within a longer formula; however, on ogham stones the names are always in the genitive, and such a form does, comparisons aside, imply ownership.[50] By listing the names of the saints in the genitive, it might have been open to a mistaken reading: that this coffin was not Cuthbert's, but a reliquary of all the apostles. Such an implication was avoided by the correction to the nominative.

The notation of the names in the nominative as opposed to the genitive may seem a minor matter, but it is worth emphasizing because it provides a point of contrast with the closest comparable list found on another artefact: the list of names inscribed beneath the decorative interlace girdle of the bowl of the 8th-century Ardagh Chalice (Figs 4, 5), now in the National Museum of Ireland, Dublin.[51] This ministerial chalice is one of the finest to survive from the early medieval West, and may have been indicative of an Insular tradition of ministerial chalices now lost. Only eight Insular chalices now survive, of which the silver Ardagh Chalice discussed here, the 8th-century Tassilo Chalice (Kremsmünster abbey, Austria) and 9th-century Derrynaflan Chalice (also National Museum of Ireland) are by far the most elaborate.[52] The chalice which was buried with St Cuthbert does not, however, appear to have been of a similar form.[53]

Although the list of names on the Ardagh Chalice is the same as on the coffin, on the chalice the order is amended from the *Communicantes* to correspond (excepting Paul's inclusion) with the list as given in Matthew 10:2-4. However, its origin in the *Communicantes* hymn is preserved for us by the use of genitive endings in all but the two final names. Thomas O'Loughlin has suggested that the degree of concern thus displayed in the choice of the list of names (despite the final carelessness of inconsistency) — which shows both consultation of the liturgy and a comparison of this against the canonical scriptural list — allows us to infer that the list itself was carefully chosen and imbued with significance.[54] It was no mere decoration but instead was a direct invocation of the prayer, a logical ornament considering the use of the chalice in the eucharistic rite.[55] It is also important to state that while the Ardagh Chalice is now unique in bearing an inscribed list of the apostles' names, it may not always have been so; few elaborate chalices survive. Hints suggesting that other chalices could have borne similar inscriptions include the various letters used to aid the assembly of the parts of the elaborate 8th-century Derrynaflan Paten, which presupposes literate craftsmen, as does also its microscopic inscribed invocation.[56] Inscriptions are indeed commonplace on reliquaries across the Insular world, although

FIG. 4. The Ardagh Chalice
© *National Museum of Ireland*

FIG. 5. Detail of the inscription on the Ardagh Chalice
© *National Museum of Ireland*

they are usually of a commemorative nature.[57] In the case of the Ardagh Chalice, the inscription of the litany from the *Communicantes* was clearly related to function, but we can be more precise. Thomas O'Loughlin has elucidated the evidence of the specific understanding of this prayer in an 8th-century Insular context by reference to the Stowe Missal. It should be understood first to stress comradeship between those conducting the liturgical action in the present and the saints named, and secondly to connect that liturgical action with the original events being recalled, of the Last Supper itself.[58]

While the coffin is, and likely always was, unique, the chalice very possibly follows an established tradition. Even if this is not the case, the inscription is more easily explicable in the context of a chalice, where it makes unproblematic liturgical sense. Such a citation on the coffin makes larger claims, invoking the presence of the apostles around Cuthbert's body as around Christ's.

In drawing a comparison between the chalice and the coffin, it is imperative to note that both of these items come from a joint Insular context: in Northumbria the strands of Anglo-Saxon and Irish culture were irrevocably intertwined. The question now arises as to whether the coffin was intended to evoke ideas of a chalice, as both were vessels for sacred bodies, or whether the correspondences are less precise. It is tempting to see the coffin specifically *as* a chalice, given the symbolism which Catherine Karkov has traced from chalices depicted on sarcophagi in the early Christian world to the chalice-like terminals of the crosses of sepulchral slabs, including Northumbrian name-stones. Three from Lindisfarne itself are of this form and, she has argued, relate to the use of the chalice in a funerary context, and to its uniting of the death of the individual with the crucifixion of Christ.[59] Whether or not the litany of the apostles was sufficient to create the coffin as chalice for the monastic viewer must depend on the frequency of such iconography on chalices, and this is unprovable.

It is perhaps more useful to note that both chalice and coffin operate within a funerary context and convey similar ideas of the body of Christ tied to embodied believers, whose own ultimate fate will depend on the judgement and resurrection following Christ's Second Coming. It has recently been argued that a similar logic lies behind the representation of the saints as Christ-like figures (bare-chested and clad in loincloths) on the tent-shaped, 12th-century Lemanaghan Shrine (Fig. 6). Positioned about the cross, these figures await their resurrection at the Second Coming, and thus imply that St Manchán too will arise with them, Christ-like, at this time.[60] Although the Lemanaghan Shrine post-dates the coffin by some five centuries, its form is deliberately antiquated, and based on now-lost earlier models. Indeed, the shrine of Adomnán from Iona (of *c.* 704–27) may have been broadly similar in shape, if the finials from St-Germain-en-Laye are indeed fragments of it.[61] Although utilizing an entirely different visual language, the snake motif from this shrine fragment similarly promises resurrection through allusion to Christ on the Cross as Moses' brazen serpent. This exegetical reading of Numbers 9 was first suggested by Christ himself and is discussed by Bede in his commentary on Genesis. Further afield, this equation of snakes with Christ's Passion and our redemption has been proven in the Columban sphere by the use of the motif in the Passion texts from the Book of Kells.[62] Thus Cuthbert's coffin may be placed within a wider tradition of grandiose saintly claims being staked at this time in Northumbria and the northern Insular world.

CONCLUSION

CUTHBERT'S reliquary coffin is an object lesson in every sense: it is an indictment of the fragmentation of academic disciplines which has divided its epigraphy from its representational art, and has treated its oaken planks as artistic support alone. As has

Fig. 6. Detail of saints on the Lemanaghan Shrine
Photo: Griffin Murray. Reproduced by kind permission of the Bishop of Ardagh and Clonmacnoise

been shown above, its iconography can only be fully apprehended by acknowledging both the hidden body within, and the embodied viewer without. The bodily emphasis of the coffin's decoration should not, therefore, be taken as indicative simply of a preference for mediterranean or classical models; to read it as a partisan artistic statement of Irish or Roman allegiance is not only anachronistic, but underestimates the sophistication of the artistic milieu in which the coffin was composed. As noted above, unlike gospel books, particularly the Lindisfarne Gospels, with which it can be compared, and with which it does indeed have very close stylistic parallels, here there is no decorative ornament: neither interlace nor spirals nor triskeles detract or distract from the bodies which surround those of Cuthbert himself. This is surely no coincidence.

The dialogue generated between body and coffin is not unique to Cuthbert's reliquary coffin. A correlation between the incorrupt body and the vessel intended for it is also evident in Bede's description of Æthelthryth's elevation sixteen years after her death, once her body was found incorrupt.[63] Here the vessel prepared for her was a re-used Roman marble sarcophagus from the ruins of Grantchester: 'a coffin beautifully made of white marble with a close-fitting lid of the same stone'.[64] The intact sarcophagus mirrors Æthelthryth's miraculously intact body, which is chaste, incorrupt and even cured of the neck wound which had marred her corpse originally.[65] The intended metaphorical reading of Æthelthryth's sarcophagus is clear; that of Cuthbert's less so. However, the parallelism so evident in Bede's description of the two events enforces the view that the correct reading of Cuthbert's coffin is one which is firmly cognizant of the coffin's precious bodily cargo.

The correspondence between the Ardagh Chalice and its litany, and those on the coffin has been shown not merely to relate to a common interest in the apotropaic power of litanies of the saints, but also as bringing Cuthbert into communion with the heavenly court. The engraved style of the coffin is moreover a choice which emphasizes Cuthbert's continuity with the earlier martyrs of the Roman catacombs, while the light graffiti of the saints' and angels' names suggests to the viewer that they have physically inscribed their presence on the coffin, as pilgrims were wont to make their mark in sacred places.

APPENDIX

INSCRIPTIONS ON THE COFFIN COMPARED WITH THE APOSTOLIC NAMES IN THE *COMMUNICANTES* HYMN FROM THE CANON OF THE MASS IN THE ROMAN RITE

COFFIN

PETRUS PAulus ANDREAS [?] IOHANNIS THOMAS IAcoBUS philipPUS BARtholomaeus MATHEAE [....]NUS [?]

COMMUNICANTES HYMN

Petri Pauli Andreae Jacobi Johannis Thomae Jacobi Philippi Bartholomaei Matthaei Simonis Thaddaei

NOTES

1. The most detailed treatment of the coffin remains that of Ernst Kitzinger, 'The Coffin-Reliquary', in *The Relics of Saint Cuthbert*, ed. C. F. Battiscombe (Oxford 1956), 202–307. See also M. Werner, 'The *Madonna and Child* Miniature in the Book of Kells Part I', *The Art Bulletin*, 54 (1972), 14–19; R. N. Bailey, 'St Cuthbert's Relics: Some Neglected Evidence', in *St Cuthbert, His Cult and His Community to AD 1200*, ed. G. Bonner, D. Rollason and C. Stancliffe (Woodbridge 1989), 231–46; J. M Cronyn and C. V. Horie, 'The Anglo-Saxon Coffin: Further Investigations', in ibid., 247–56; R. I. Page, 'Roman and Runic on St Cuthbert's Coffin', in ibid., 257–65; J. Higgitt, 'The Iconography of St Peter in Anglo-Saxon England, and St Cuthbert's Coffin', in ibid., 267–85.

2. The poor quality of the published photographs, which make difficult any analysis, was noted by D. H. Wright, '[Review of] The Relics of Saint Cuthbert by C. F. Battiscombe', *Art Bulletin*, 43 (1961), 147. For the reconstruction, see Cronyn and Horie, 'Anglo-Saxon Coffin' (as n. 1), 247, 249; not all of the fragments belonged to the reliquary coffin.

3. C. R. Dodwell, *Anglo-Saxon Art: A New Perspective* (Manchester 1982), 20.

4. Dimensions are taken from Kitzinger, 'Coffin-Reliquary' (as n. 1), 212–16. As Kitzinger notes, however, the lid does not appear to taper and is of slightly broader dimensions at the Virgin end than the chest itself.

5. Kitzinger, 'Coffin-Reliquary' (as n. 1), 218; Cronyn and Horie, 'The Anglo-Saxon Coffin' (as n. 1), 249, 253, 256; Bailey, 'St Cuthbert's Relics' (as n. 1), 238–43.

6. Kitzinger, 'Coffin-Reliquary' (as n. 1), 228–48.

7. Ibid., 248–64.

8. Ibid., 265–73; Higgitt, 'The Iconography of St Peter' (as n. 1), 270.

9. E. Okasha, *Hand-List of Anglo-Saxon Non-Runic Inscriptions* (Cambridge 1971), 67–69; Page, 'Roman and Runic' (as n. 1), 257–65.

10. Kitzinger, 'Coffin-Reliquary' (as n. 1), 273–77; Cronyn and Horie, 'The Anglo-Saxon Coffin' (as n. 1), 253.

11. 'De illius theca intima, quam mirandi generis diversitate sit composite ac celata'; 'Haec tota [theca] exterius premirabili celatura desculpitur, quae adeo est minuti ac subtilissimi operis, ut plus stupori quam scientiae aut possibilitati sculptoris convenire credatur.' *Reginaldi monachi Dunelmensis libellus de admirandis b. Cuthberti virtutibus*, ed. J. Raine, SS 1 (London 1835), ch. 43. (We are grateful to Dr David Woods for his advice on the translation of the Latin.)

12. M. Schapiro, 'On the Aesthetic Attitude in Romanesque Art', in idem, *Romanesque Art: Selected Papers* (London 1993), 11–12, 17–18.

13. See most comprehensively M. P. Brown, *The Lindisfarne Gospels: Society, Spirituality and the Scribe* (London 2003).

14. The physical reconstruction of Cuthbert's coffin in 1938 was carried out by a Mr Padgham of the British Museum, in conjunction with Ernst Kitzinger's scholarly reconstruction. C. F. Battiscombe wrote to Audrey Baker, in a letter dated 12 September 1938: 'At the end of this month or the beginning of next we are starting here in Durham to reconstruct the coffin and are employing a Mr. Padgham, one of Dr Plenderleith's staff, to do this work'. Durham Cathedral Library MS LIB 4/6B. This was slightly but not substantially amended in 1978.

15. Kitzinger, 'Coffin-Reliquary' (as n. 1), 279, 280. The choir of saints often performs an intercessory role in early medieval religion: see J. Hennig, 'Studies in Early Western Devotion to the Choirs of Saints', *Studia Patristica*, 8 (1963), 239–47.

16. See *Anglo-Saxon Litanies*, ed. M. Lapidge, Henry Bradshaw Society 106 (Woodbridge 1991). Litanies are invoked in Aldhelm's 7th-century prose and verse *De Virginitate*, and in the 12th-century epilogue to the Irish *Martyrology of Óengus*. Deshman has argued that the 10th-century litany illuminations added to the Athelstan Psalter (BL, MS Cotton Galba A. XVIII), are modelled after lost earlier Insular models, in the context of deliberate artistic revivalism of the time: R. Deshman, 'Anglo-Saxon Art after Alfred', *Art Bulletin*, 56 (1974), 179–83.

17. See R. M. Liuzza, 'Prayers and/or Charms to the Cross', *Cross and Culture in Anglo-Saxon England: Studies in Honor of George Hardin Brown*, ed. K. L. Jolly, C. E. Karkov, and S. Larratt Keefer (Morgantown, WV 2007), 279–323, and the other essays in this volume.

18. Kitzinger notes on several occasions that parts of the iconographic scheme employ models found in early Roman cemeteries and catacombs, but makes no comment as to how the coffin itself functions within a funerary context. See, for instance, his discussion of the Virgin and Child in 'Coffin-Reliquary' (as n. 1), 251.

19. See L. Nees, 'The Iconographic Program of Decorated Chancel Barriers in the Pre-Iconoclastic Period', *Zeitschrift für Kunstgeschichte*, 46 (1983), 20–23; Werner, 'The *Madonna and Child* Miniature' (as n. 1), 14–19. This is not to detract from the usefulness of Nees's or Werner's contributions to our understanding of the coffin.

20. According to William of Malmesbury (12th century), the holiness of five English saints was marked by the preservation of their bodies incorrupt after death: the virgins Æthelthryth and Werburg, Edmund the Martyr, Archbishop Elphage and Cuthbert. William of Malmesbury, *Gesta Regum Anglorum: The History of the English Kings*, ed. and trans. R. A. B. Mynors, R. M. Thomson and M. Winterbottom, 2 vols (Oxford 1998), I, 386–87.

21. For Ruthwell's date, see most recently and with references *Theorizing Anglo-Saxon Stone Sculpture*, ed. C. E. Karkov and F. Orton (Morganstown, WV 2003).

22. Kitzinger, 'Coffin-Reliquary' (as n. 1), 298.

23. Luke 3:1–2. D. Howlett, *Insular Inscriptions* (Dublin 2005), 83–84. Howlett proposes a complex numerology of this inscription, based on letter numbers, spaces and biblical parallels.

24. R. Sharpe, 'King Ceadwalla's Roman Epitaph', in *Latin Learning and English Lore: Studies in Anglo-Saxon Literature for Michael Lapidge*, ed. K. O'Brien O'Keeffe and A. Orchard, 2 vols (Toronto 2005), I, 171–93. We are most grateful to Dr Mark Faulkner for drawing this article to our attention.

25. Sharpe posits that such a *silloge* may have been brought to Northumbria by Bishop Wilfrid after his final visit to Rome in 703; 'Ceadwalla's Epitaph' (as n. 24), 185.

26. Ibid., 172.

27. IN HOC SINGVLARI SIGNO VITA REDDITVR MVNDO, 'In this singular sign life is given back to the world'. Transcription from Howlett, *Insular Inscriptions* (as n. 23), 92. The cross is described in detail in Rosemary Cramp, *County Durham and Northumberland*, Corpus of Anglo-Saxon Stone Sculpture 1 (Oxford 1977), 112–13, nos 16a and 16b.

28. Page, 'Roman and Runic' (as n. 1), 264.

29. J. Osborne, 'The Roman Catacombs in the Middle Ages', *Papers of the British School at Rome*, 53 (1985), 278–328; R. Derolez, 'Anglo-Saxon Runes in Rome', *Old English Newsletter*, 21 (1987), 36–37; C. Carletti, 'Viatores ad martyres: testimonianze scritte altomedievali nelle catacombe romane', in *Epigrafia medievale greca e latina. Ideologia e funzione, Atti del seminario di Erice (12–18 settembre 1991)*, ed. G. Cavallo and C. Mango (Spoleto 1995), 197–225. See now L. Izzi, 'Anglo-Saxons Underground: Early Medieval Graffiti in the Catacombs of Rome', in *England and Rome in the Early Middle Ages: Piety, Politics and Culture*, ed. F. Tinti (Turnhout forthcoming). We are most grateful to Dr Izzi for access to this, and discussion of the implications of her research, prior to publication.

30. For instance, D. H. Verkerk, 'Pilgrimage *ad Limina Apostolorum* in Rome: Irish Crosses and Early Christian Sarcophagi', in *From Ireland Coming*, ed. C. Hourihane (Princeton 2001), 8–26.

31. Okasha, *Hand-List* (as n. 9), 7–9.

32. D. Ó Cróinín, 'Cummianus Longus and the Iconography of Christ and the Apostles in Early Irish Literature,' in *Sages, Saints and Storytellers: Celtic Studies in Honour of Professor James Carney*, ed. D. Ó Corráin, L. Breatnach and K. McKone (Maynooth 1989), 268–79.

33. On a cautionary note, it should be added that all surviving inscriptions referring to makers and owners are 9th-century and later.

34. For a reading of the entire iconography of the coffin as relating to Incarnation and Judgement, but oblivious to the corporeal context suggested here, see Werner, 'The *Madonna and Child*' (as n. 1), 14–18.

35. See Kitzinger, 'Coffin-Reliquary' (as n. 1), pp. 229, 245, 246.

36. A similar effect is achieved in the crucifixion scene in the Durham Gospels: see J. O'Reilly, 'Early Medieval Text and Image: The Wounded and Exalted Christ', *Peritia*, 6–7 (1987–88), 72–118.

37. Our emphasis: 'uel semper amabilem Christi sanctorumque eius, quamuis in imagine, contemplarentur aspectum; uel dominicae incarnationis gratiam uigilantiore mente recolerent; uel extremi discrimen examinis quasi coram oculis habentes, districtius se ipsi examinare meminissent'. *Historia Abbatum auctore Baeda*, in *Venerabilis Baedae Opera Historica*, ed. C. Plummer (Oxford 1896), ch. 6; translation from *Lives of the Abbots of Wearmouth and Jarrow*, trans. D. H. Farmer in *The Age of Bede* (London 1988), 193.

38. One of the earliest manuscripts of the *Hieronymian Martyrology*, Paris, Bibliothèque nationale de France, MS lat. 10837, was written at Willibrord's monastery in Echternach in the early 8th century. See P. Ó Riain, 'A Northumbrian Phase in the Formation of the Hieronymian Martyrology: The Evidence of the Martyrology of Tallaght', *Analecta Bollandiana*, 120 (2002), 311–63; M. Lapidge, 'Acca of Hexham and the Origin of *The Old English Martyrology*', *Analecta Bollandiana*, 123 (2005), 45–52.

39. For an early discussion of the names of the angels, see M. R. James, 'Names of Angels in Anglo-Saxon and Other Documents', *Journal of Theological Studies*, 11 (1910), 569–71.

40. A twenty-five-line fragment of the Book of Enoch survives in an 8th-century English manuscript, BL, MS Royal 5 E XIII): see *Apocrypha Anecdota: A Collection of Thirteen Apocryphal Books and Fragments*, ed. M. R. James (Cambridge 1893), 146–50; D. Dumville, 'Biblical Apocrypha and the Early Irish: A Preliminary Investigation', *Proceedings of the Royal Irish Academy*, 73 (1973), 299–338. For the influence of the text more widely, see F. Biggs, '1 Enoch', in *Sources of Anglo-Saxon Literary Culture: A Trial Version*, ed. F. Biggs, T. Hill and P. E. Szarmach (Binghamton, NY 1990), 25–27; R. E. Kaske, '*Beowulf* and the Book of Enoch', *Speculum*, 46 (1971), 421–23; B. Bischoff, 'Turning-Points in the History of Latin Exegesis in the Early Middle Ages', in *Biblical Studies: The Medieval Irish Contribution*, ed. M. McNamara (Dublin 1976), 159 n. 126.

41. Atomriug indiu / Niurt gráid hiruphin, / I n-aurlataid aingel, / I frestul inna n-airchaingel, / I freiscisin esséirgi / Ar chiunn fochraicce. 'Faeth Fiada: Patrick's Breastplate', in J. Carey, *King of Mysteries: Early Irish Religious Writings* (Dublin 2000), 131.

42. 'Life of Senán, son of Gerrcenn' / 'Betha Shenain meic Geirrginn', in *Lives of Saints from the Book of Lismore*, ed. W. Stokes (Oxford 1890), 66, 213 (lines 2194–96).

43. Kitzinger, 'Coffin-Reliquary' (as n. 1), 282–84 noted this but considered it simply a stylistic preference of one of the two artists who he proposed had jointly worked on the coffin.

44. *Cummian's Letter 'De Controversia Paschali' Together with a Related Irish Computistical Tract, 'De Ratione Computandi'*, ed. M. Walsh and D. Ó Cróinín (Toronto 1988), 93–95; this passage is discussed by

Verkerk, 'Pilgrimage *ad Limina Apostolorum*' (as n. 30), 11. See also C. Hahn, 'Seeing and Believing: The Construction of Sanctity in Early-Medieval Saints' Shrines', *Speculum*, 72 (1997), 1079–1106.

45. Bede, *EH*, book IV, ch. 32.

46. 'Andreas', in *Andreas and the Fates of the Apostles*, ed. K. R. Brooks (Oxford 1961), 1–55 (23–26) (lines 706–810). Translated in *Anglo-Saxon Poetry*, trans. and ed. S. A. J. Bradley (London 1982), 110–53 (129–31).

47. Dodwell, *Anglo-Saxon Art* (as n. 3), 121.

48. Kitzinger, 'Coffin-Reliquary' (as n. 1), 269, 274.

49. Excepting Math[e]ae.

50. Okasha, *Hand-List* (as n. 9), 8–9; A. Harvey, 'Problems in Dating the Origin of Ogham Script', in J. Higgitt, K. Forsyth and D. N. Parsons, eds, *Roman, Runic and Ogham: Medieval Inscriptions in the Insular World in Context* (Donington 2001), 37–50 (40).

51. M. Ryan, *Early Irish Communion Vessels* (Dublin 2000), 12–16, 34–38; idem, 'The Formal Relationships of Insular Early Medieval Eucharistic Chalices', *Proceedings of the Royal Irish Academy*, 90C (1990), 281–356.

52. Ryan, 'The Formal Relationships' (as n. 51), 282.

53. Dodwell, *Anglo-Saxon Art* (as n. 3), 208.

54. T. O'Loughlin, 'The List of Saints on the Bowl of the "Ardagh Chalice"', *The Journal of Celtic Studies*, 5 (2005), 107–13 (112). See also the Earl of Dunraven, 'On an Ancient Chalice and Brooches Lately Found at Ardagh, in the County of Limerick', *Transactions of the Royal Irish Academy*, 24 (1873), 433–55.

55. T. O'Loughlin, 'The Praxis and Explanations of Eucharistic Fraction in the Ninth Century: The Insular Evidence', *Archiv Für Liturgie-Wissenschaft*, 45 (2003), 1–20; P. Ní Chatháin, 'The Liturgical Background of the Derrynavlan Altar Service', *Journal of the Royal Society of Antiquaries of Ireland*, 110 (1980), 127–48 (138–39).

56. M. Brown, '"Paten and Purpose": The Derrynaflan Paten Inscriptions', in R. M. Spearman and J. Higgitt, eds, *The Age of Migrating Ideas* (Edinburgh 1993), 162–67.

57. Okasha, *Hand-List* (as n. 9); R. Ó Floinn, *Irish Shrines and Reliquaries of the Middle Ages* (Dublin 1994), 38–41; P. E. Michelli, 'The Inscriptions on Pre-Norman Irish Reliquaries', *Proceedings of the Royal Irish Academy*, 96C (1996), 1–48.

58. O'Loughlin, 'The List of Saints' (as n. 54), 113.

59. C. Karkov, 'The Chalice and Cross in Insular Art', in Spearman and Higgitt, *Age of Migrating Ideas* (as n. 56), 237–44 (237, 241–42).

60. T. Ó Carragáin, *Churches in Early Medieval Ireland* (London 2010), 76.

61. D. MacLean, 'Snake-Bosses and Redemption at Iona and in Pictland', in Spearman and Higgitt, *Age of Migrating Ideas* (as n. 56), 245–53 (251).

62. MacLean, 'Snake-Bosses and Redemption' (as n. 61), 251.

63. Bede, *EH*, book IV, ch. 19.

64. 'locellum de marmore albo pulcherrime factum, operculo quoque similis lapidis aptissime tectum'.

65. C. E. Karkov, 'Exiles from the Kingdom: The Naked and the Damned in Anglo-Saxon Art', in *Naked Before God: Uncovering the Body in Anglo-Saxon England*, ed. B. C. Withers and J. Wilcox (Morgantown, WV 2003), 182.

Henry II, Anglo-Scots Relations, and the Building of the Castle Keep, Newcastle upon Tyne

STEVEN BRINDLE

The castle keep at Newcastle upon Tyne is one of the finest and best-preserved Anglo-Norman keeps in existence. Clearly dated from the Pipe Rolls to 1172–79, it was added by Henry II to the castle established by Robert Curthose in 1095. This paper considers the complex background to its construction in the disputes between the kings of England and Scotland over possession of the earldom of Northumbria, the evidence for its construction, and Henry's possible motives in building it. The building's remarkable design is considered in relation to its apparently intended use as a palatial residence, setting for ceremony and prison. Aspects of its original design are also discussed.

INTRODUCTION

THE castle keep at Newcastle upon Tyne almost perfectly fulfils our image of what an Anglo-Norman donjon should be, its height, regular square plan, turrets, steep entrance steps and self-contained air all suggesting the harsh realities of 12th-century power politics. The 19th-century restorations, whatever one may think of their more speculative elements, create an illusion of completeness and help the keep stand up to its surroundings: even the brutal proximity of the 19th-century railway viaducts does not dilute its air of power. This is no sad, overshadowed ruin (Fig. 1 and Col. Pl. XVIII in print edn).

When Henry II built the keep *c.* 1172–79 the *nova castella supra Tinam* was no longer new, having been there for almost a century: it was already one of the principal centres of royal authority in the north of England. Why did Henry add this remarkable building to it? The background lies in the initial difficulties that the Anglo-Norman state had experienced in establishing its authority north of the Tyne and in the threat, which remained live until 1174, that the Scots kings would retake Newcastle together with the earldom of Northumbria, both of which they had recently held.

THE POLITICAL BACKGROUND

THE earldom of Northumbria had been the most independent satrapy of the old English kingdom, up to the death of Earl Tostig fighting for the Norwegian king Harald Hardrada at Stamford Bridge in 1066. After the Norman Conquest, William I was too preoccupied with matters further south to come north in person: he appointed

BAA Trans., vol. XXXVI (2013), 90–114

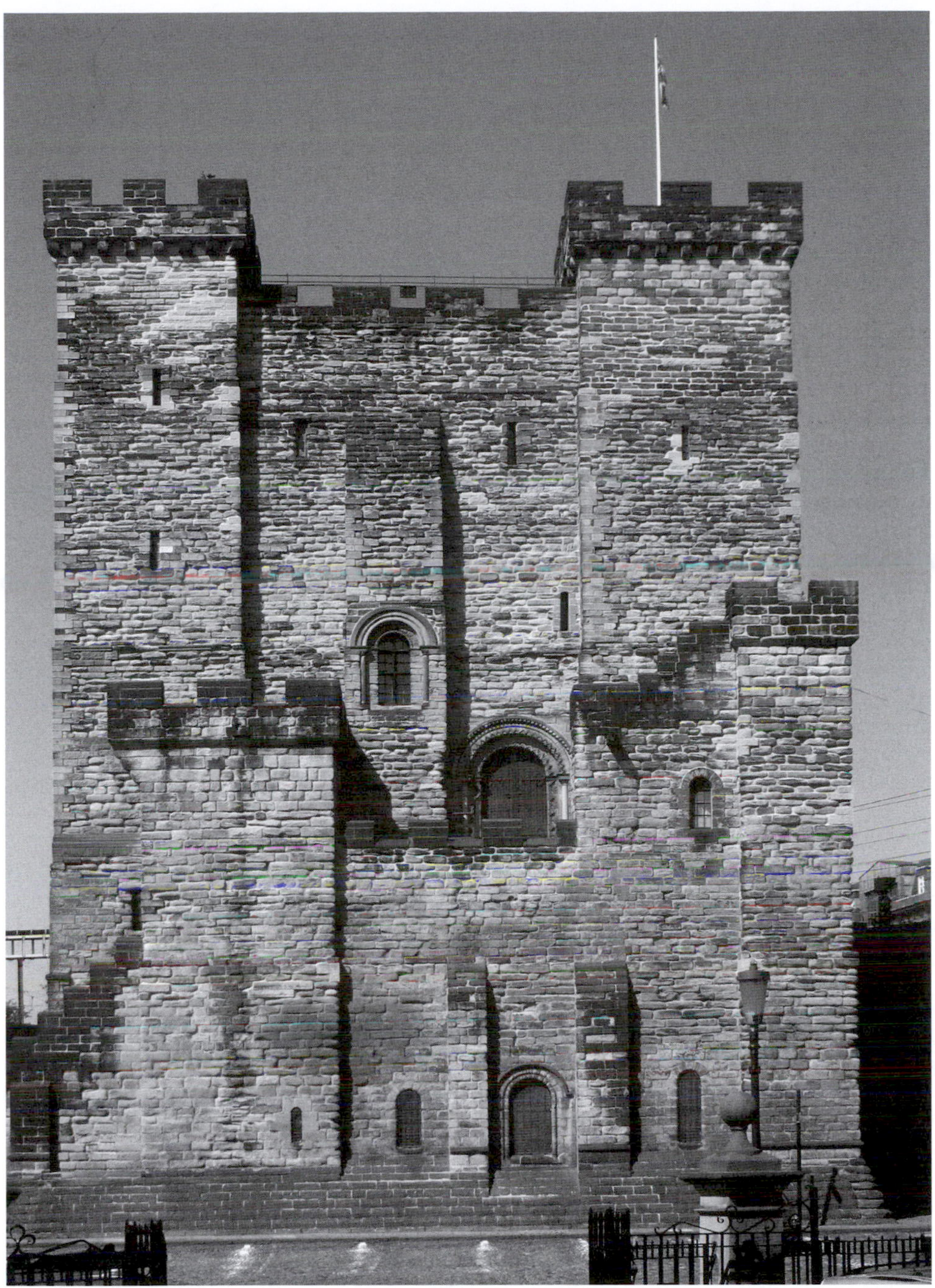

FIG. 1. The castle keep, Newcastle upon Tyne, from the south-east

two native earls in succession, Oswulf and Gospatrick, and then a Norman earl, Robert de Comines. Robert was ejected in the great uprising of 1069–70. After suppressing it, the Conqueror appointed another English earl, Waltheof, son of a previous earl, Siward. The Conqueror marched into Scotland, intimidating Malcolm III Canmore into doing homage to him at Abernethy in 1072.[1] However, Waltheof joined Robert FitzOsbern's rebellion in 1075, and was captured and executed in 1076.[2] The Conqueror tried yet another tack, vesting the military and civil powers of the earldom in Walcher, bishop of Durham. This experiment, which may be seen as the origin of the palatine status of the bishops of Durham, lasted four years, until Walcher was murdered attempting to escape from a burning church in Gateshead, in 1080.[3]

William I was recently reconciled with his eldest son, Robert Curthose, and the latter led another expedition to restore royal authority in the north, marching as far as Edinburgh in 1080. On his way south, Curthose founded the 'New Castle upon the Tyne'.[4] Around the same time, the Conqueror made a second attempt to appoint a Norman baron to the earldom in the person of Aubrey de Coucy. Aubrey despaired of the attempt, resigning the earldom the same year and forfeiting the rest of his estates as a result. He was replaced with a third Norman candidate, Robert Mowbray. The revolving-door succession of earls of Northumbria from Tostig to Robert Mowbray hints at the difficulty the Conqueror experienced in projecting his authority this far north. As David Douglas has observed, Curthose's placing of the castle on the Tyne rather than anywhere further north suggests that the area northwards was still a debatable land.[5]

When Malcolm III Canmore of Scotland raided England for a fifth time in 1093, he was trapped and killed at Alnwick with his eldest son Edward, by Earl Robert. At last the king seemed to have an earl who was capable of doing his job, but it did not last. Robert Mowbray rebelled in 1095, attempting to garrison the castles of Newcastle, Tynemouth and Bamburgh in the process. On his defeat and capture in 1095, the earldom was left vacant.[6]

William II had founded the first baronies north of the Tyne.[7] Henry I built on his achievements by building keeps and creating further baronies. He travelled north to Carlisle in 1122, and probably began the keep there.[8] It is likely that he was responsible for building the great keep at Bamburgh: the ancient seat of the Northumbrian kings was the principal royal castle in the north-east, and the seat of the sheriffs of Northumberland.[9] In 1121 he authorized (and may have ordered) Bishop Ranulf Flambard to build Norham castle, the first attempt by an Anglo-Norman to build a fixed defence on the Tweed.[10] He established two more baronies in the far north for trusted 'new men', Walter Espec at Wark on Tweed, just south of Coldstream, and Eustace de Vesci at Alnwick. English sovereignty in the far north was hardening.

The Norman kings clearly had no more use for earls of Northumbria. However, David I, who succeeded to the throne of Scotland in 1124, had provided himself with a claim to the earldom by marrying Matilda, daughter of Waltheof, last native earl of Northumbria and also earl of Huntingdon.[11] On 1 January 1127, the Melrose chronicle tells us, David, together with the elite of England, swore fealty to the Empress Matilda, daughter of Henry I, as heiress to the English throne.[12] However, on Henry I's death in 1135 and the succession of King Stephen instead of the empress, David was able to resume his father's aggressive policies. He invaded early in 1136; Stephen marched north; there was a conference at Durham. David's heir Henry did homage to Stephen at York, and was invested with the earldom of Huntingdon.[13] David was evidently dissatisfied or sensed further opportunities, for in 1138 he invaded again: a terrible devastation of Northumberland ensued. Stephen was beset by other enemies in the south, and it was left to Archbishop Thurstan of York to lead the northern barons and defeat David in the Battle of the Standard at Northallerton on 22 August.[14] The victory did not drive David from the north, though; Walter Espec's castle at Wark fell, and Eustace Fitz John at Alnwick went over to his side. In April 1139 a new settlement was negotiated by Stephen's queen Matilda, who was David's niece. David's son Henry was recognized as earl of Northumbria, saving the crown's rights, the loyalties of the Norman barons and the castles of Bamburgh and Newcastle. It was not long, however, before both castles were in Scots hands. Only the bishops of Durham stood between the Scots king and complete control of the north.[15]

As David Crouch has pointed out, in legal fact Henry held Northumbria, like the county of Huntingdon, as an English earl.[16] In practice, it is hard to avoid thinking that Stephen's authority in the north was severely compromised: not a single castle remained in royal hands north of the Tees. David I could hardly have achieved the successes he did without the disastrous circumstances (for England) of Stephen's reign. Yet there were other factors which made him such a formidable opponent. Educated by his English mother and brought up partly at the Anglo-Norman court, he was the first Scots king to live and rule like a European monarch. He invited Norman families to settle in Scotland, and from their ranks he drew his household knights and household officers. Against this background the prospect of Northumbria and Cumbria (which King David probably regarded as part of the earldom) reverting to the royal house of Scotland for good may not have seemed that outrageous to the Anglo-Norman baronage in the north.[17]

For the young Henry of Anjou, this civilized-looking king was a crucial ally. In 1149 he travelled to Carlisle. The Hexham and Melrose chronicles tell us that David 'entertained him with great respect and sumptuous provision of costly munificence'.[18] These chroniclers and Robert of Torigny simply tell us that David knighted the sixteen-year-old Henry.[19] William of Newburgh and Roger of Howden add that at the same time David extracted an oath from him that, if he became king of England, he would cede Newcastle and all Northumbria, and 'allow him and his heirs to possess all the land between the Tyne and the Tweed in peace without calumny [*sine calumnia*] in perpetuity'.[20] This formula would in principle be compatible with continued English sovereignty over the region, in the same way that the duchy of Normandy or the county of Anjou were legally part of the French crown, allowing David's heirs a like degree of independence.

When his son and heir Henry, earl of Huntingdon died in 1152, David I invested his younger grandson William with the earldom of Northumbria at Newcastle. He subsequently took his elder grandson, Malcolm, on a tour of Scotland as heir to the kingdom. The compliance of the Anglo-Norman barons on the former occasion seems like the surest proof of David's success.[21] When David died at Carlisle castle in 1153, it must have seemed like a secure possession, and his heirs' border might well have remained on the Ribble and the Tees. However, his heir Malcolm IV was only twelve years old, and, from 1154, facing him was Henry of Anjou, who swiftly established his credentials as the most formidable ruler of the age.

The first years of Henry II's reign were marked by his determined efforts to restore the authority that the crown had lost during the previous reign, a policy which paid little heed to previous promises or commitments: the years 1154–57 witnessed him make short work of potential opponents such as William of Aumale, Henry of Blois, his own brother Geoffrey, and Stephen's younger son William of Blois.[22]

In 1157 Henry demanded that Malcolm restore Cumbria and Northumbria to him, a flagrant breach of his promise made to David I at Carlisle in 1149. Malcolm IV was then sixteen years old. That summer he surrendered Newcastle, Bamburgh and Carlisle, and travelled south. He awaited Henry at Peak in Derbyshire and accompanied him to Chester, where he did homage. The Melrose chronicle says that he 'became his vassal upon the same terms as his grandfather had been the vassal of the old King Henry, preserving in every respect his dignities'.[23] Henry returned the earldom of Huntingdon to him, and Malcolm presumably did homage for this. Meanwhile his brother William, the actual earl of Northumbria, received the lordship of Tynedale in compensation for its loss. Archibald Duncan has pointed out that Henry's resumption of Northumbria, while returning Huntingdon to Malcolm, can be seen as in line with his established policy of returning the situation in feudal tenure to the status quo in the time of his grandfather, Henry I.[24] It remains unclear whether Malcolm was here performing any further homage, in the way that Malcolm III Canmore had to William I at Abernethy in 1072: however, only one chronicler claimed that Malcolm was performing homage for Scotland, and Duncan has argued persuasively that the homage was purely for Huntingdon, his 'dignities' being his rights as king of Scotland to dignified reception in England.[25]

Malcolm seems to have accompanied Henry on his campaign in North Wales, and was still travelling with him when the king reached Carlisle, in January 1158. However, relations seem to have become strained. Henry II knighted William, earl de Warenne at Carlisle, but he and Malcolm 'were not friends, and so the king of Scots was not yet made a knight'.[26] It does look rather pointed: Henry had refused to knight Malcolm in the same place (probably in the same building) that he had himself been knighted by Malcolm's grandfather David nine years previously, on which occasion he had promised to leave David's descendants in peaceful possession of Northumbria, a promise which he had just flagrantly broken. Everyone present would have been aware of all this. Had Malcolm protested about the oath-breaking, and was this the cause of the row?

From Carlisle, Henry probably travelled eastward. He travelled via Wark on Tweed, taking Walter Espec's old castle (destroyed by the Scots in 1138) back into crown hands and ordering a keep to be built.[27] He may have ordered Hugh le Puiset to refortify Norham castle around this time. The king turned south to Newcastle: the charter evidence shows that he was accompanied by a formidable group of earls and bishops.[28] Henry is not known to have visited Newcastle again, and the likelihood seems to be that he did not. The only subsequent occasion on which he is known to have travelled to the north of England was in the summer of 1175, when he was in York in August.

Despite Henry II's apparent snub in refusing him knight in 1157, Malcolm IV followed his feudal lord's summons, and followed Henry on his ill-fated Toulouse campaign in 1159. At last Henry knighted him, at Périgueux in south-western France. The Melrose chronicle says that on his return to Scotland several Scots lords were angry at him, for his submission to the Angevin king.[29] Despite this, Malcolm had substantial successes in Galloway and Argyll in the last years of his reign. He did homage to Henry on at least one more occasion, at Woodstock on 1 July 1163, when he gave his younger brother and some young nobles as hostages.[30] Malcolm died in 1165, leaving a stable inheritance to his more dynamic brother, William 'the Lion'.

It was William who had actually been deprived of the earldom of Northumbria in 1157, and, as Archibald Duncan has pointed out, his desire to regain it dominated the politics of his reign.[31] Nevertheless, he seems initially to have followed his brother's policy of cooperation with the Angevins. In 1166 he crossed the sea to France with Henry, possibly in support of the latter's Breton campaign. Relations were evidently not smooth, to judge from Henry's outburst of temper against Richard du Hommet at Caen for speaking out in support of the Scots king (this was the famous 'chewing the straw of his couch' incident).[32] There cannot have been an open breach, though, for William came south again early in 1170: his brother David was knighted by Henry at Windsor on 31 May.[33] On 15 June, William and David both did homage to Henry the Young King, this being the day after his controversial coronation at Westminster Abbey by the archbishop of York in Becket's absence. Together with the earls and barons of England, they 'became the new king's men', but again, we cannot be entirely sure what they were doing homage for.[34]

It was probably sometime in 1171 that Henry took the decision to build the keep at Newcastle. He had spent the first half of his reign restoring the authority of the English crown, and extended its reach in new and undreamed of directions; in the process he racked up an impressive list of enemies. William II of Scotland, as it turned out, was one of them. When the 'Young King' Henry and Louis VII launched the uprising of 1173, he was swift to join them, invading the north and threatening Newcastle and Carlisle, but failing to take either of them. In the summer of 1174 he invaded again, was taken by surprise at Alnwick on 13 July and taken prisoner. On 26 July he was delivered, bound, to Henry II at Northampton.[35]

In this great crisis, the northern barons had generally stayed loyal to Henry II, hence William's disaster. Bishop Hugh le Puiset of Durham had played the most discreditable role, sitting on the fence with his castles garrisoned in 1173 to see how far William would get, not lifting a finger to resist him, and arranging to have his nephew Hugh, count of Bar, bring a force of forty knights and five hundred Flemish foot-soldiers or mercenaries to England in the spring of 1174 for certain unspecified purposes. By quite spectacular bad luck, they landed in England on the same day that William II was taken prisoner.[36]

Henry's triumph was complete. He met Hugh le Puiset and William the Lion at Northampton in July 1174. Bishop Hugh surrendered his castles of Durham, Norham and Northallerton and sent his nephew home.[37] William was taken to Normandy in Henry's train as his prisoner, and forced to agree to the Convention of Falaise. Any doubt about his status and that of his realm was removed: he was to be Henry's liege man, owing him homage for Scotland and all his other territories. The churchmen of Scotland were obliged to do homage, too: the Church in Scotland was declared to be subject to the Church in England. All the earls and barons of Scotland were to do homage to the king of England, too. No fugitives from English justice might be harboured in Scotland. Hostages, including William's brother David and four Scots earls, were to be given. William had to cede the castles of Roxburgh, Berwick, Jedburgh, Edinburgh and Stirling, only being released on their cession. And so on. The earldom of Huntingdon was taken from William and given to Simon de Senlis; William remained in possession of Tynedale. Of the earldom of Northumbria, there was no mention: in all probability, Henry had never acknowledged William's possession of it. The Convention was ratified in York Minster in August 1175, and at last William was free to go home.[38] No more complete assertion of overlordship could have been devised, short of Henry attempting to replace the Scots king altogether. So by the time the great tower of Newcastle was finished in 1178, the threats to Angevin rule in the north had been effectively neutralized. Henry's dominion over the king of Scots and his realm was a legally established fact.

THE BUILDING OF THE CASTLE

SOON after the 'New Castle' was established by Robert Curthose, elaborate arrangements were made to provide castle-guard for it: twelve baronies were set up, covering much of the southern part of the present county of Northumberland, somewhat like the baronies established to owe castle-guard to Dover. So the 'new castle' seems to have been permanently warded from the outset. What was around it as its immediate setting is a matter of some doubt. Certainly, Robert Curthose established the castle there as it overlooked an existing bridge, the lowest crossing on the Tyne, occupying the site of the original 2nd-century *Pons Aelius*. A little way to the north of the castle site the Roman wall ran east–west, probably standing and visible. There had been some kind of settlement here: the chronicler Simeon of Durham calls it Monkchester.[39]

The site that Curthose chose had some natural strength, and land falling away southwards towards the Tyne and eastwards into a narrow valley. To the north and west it lacked natural defences, so deep ditches were dug. An Anglian cemetery covered part of the site: some of it was disturbed by the works, and some of it was buried more deeply. A small church on the site was left standing, enclosed by the new defences. In the 18th century there were remains of a mound in the south-west portion of the site, but modern scholars have doubted whether this was an 11th-century motte: the castle may have been a ring-work. The original entrance was probably on the west side, the site of the later Bailey Gate.[40]

The castle occupies a triangular site, with its base at its south end about 104 m wide at the top of the steep slope down to the Tyne, and measuring about 128 m to its apex at the north, where the Black Gate now stands. At some point, it was enclosed with stone walls, substantial sections of which remain today. There is no clear evidence of their date, but their massive chamfered plinths and square enclosed mural towers suggest that they, too, could date from the reign of Henry II. As W. H. Knowles noted, the references in the Pipe Roll of 1167–68 to considerable sums spent on 'the work of the castle' at Bamburgh and Newcastle could refer to its walls, as this predates the clear references to 'the tower of the New Castle' (see below). It is possible, stylistically, that these defences were begun in the reign of Henry I, but there is no proof of this (Fig. 2).[41]

Most of the south curtain wall survives, with an impressive 12th-century postern gate towards its eastern end. At the south-east corner there was a massive circular bastion, the Half-Moon battery, which was removed in 1810 to make room for the city's moot hall. Much of the northern part of the east curtain wall remains, including a section beneath the railway arches with a massive plinth with nine chamfered offsets. At the northern apex of the site was a subsidiary gateway, also of 12th-century date, to which the Black Gate was added in the 1240s. Only traces of the west curtain have been found, but enough of it was recorded by 19th-century antiquaries for its line to be known with some certainty. About half-way down on the west side was Bailey Gate, the principal entrance prior to the addition of the Black Gate. Its appearance is known from a drawing made *c.* 1810, just before the demolition of this whole stretch of wall, and it, too, was of the 12th century, with a semicircular arch framed by two plain orders.[42] During the construction of the railway viaduct, the footings of a detached square stone tower were found, immediately to the north of the keep, an apparently early structure whose relationship to the walls is unclear (Fig. 3).

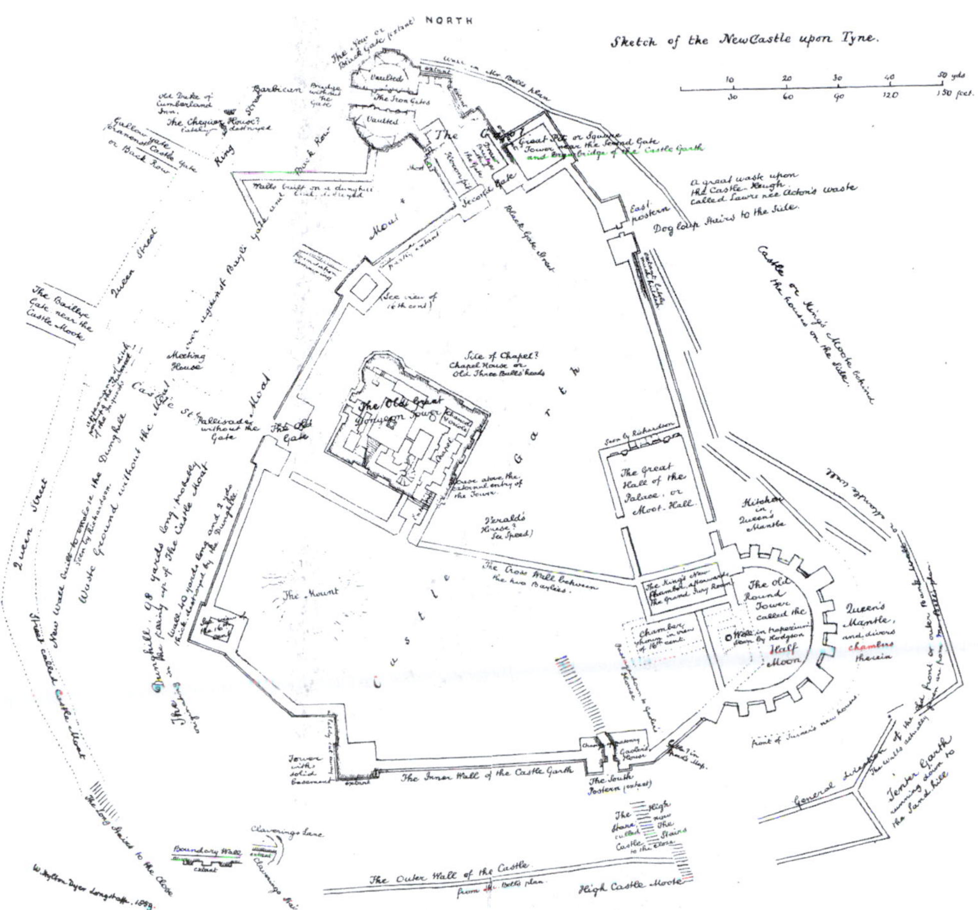

FIG. 2. A plan reconstructing the medieval layout of the castle at Newcastle upon Tyne, compiled by the Newcastle antiquary W. H. D. Longstaffe, *c.* 1860, on the basis of antiquarian observations made over a long period. In Longstaffe's day only the keep, the Black Gate at the northern end of the bailey and parts of the south and east curtain walls remained standing and visible

Henry II's great keep was set down within this triangular enclosure. At some point, whether before the building of the keep or around the same time, the enclosure was divided by a further wall into an 'Inner Bailey' to the north and an 'Outer Bailey' to the south.[43] The 'Bailey Gate' led straight into the Inner Bailey, right next to the eventual site of the keep. Furthermore, it seems to have been on the side away from the town; in other words, the castle was entered from outside the town. In both these respects, Newcastle's planning echoed that of Carlisle castle.[44]

The keep stood about 6 m to the north of this dividing wall: its fore-building seems to have had an outer section linked to it. By the 18th century, the keep had become surrounded by houses, butting up to it on all sides, which evidently incorporated

BAILEY GATE OF THE NEW-CASTLE.

on Stone by John Storey from a drawing by Mr. Jefferson, in the possession of Thomas Bell Esqre.

FIG. 3. The Bailey Gate and castle keep, Newcastle upon Tyne, drawn *c.* 1810, shortly before the demolition of the Bailey Gate and the attached section of curtain wall, which had then recently been exposed by the demolition of various adjacent houses. The demolitions left the keep standing in isolation for the first time in its history

sections of the outer curtain and dividing wall, and perhaps other medieval structures. All of this was cleared away without record *c.* 1810. Two 18th-century Newcastle historians make tantalizing references to an inner line of defence around the keep, Bourne saying that 'there were two great strong walls which surrounded the Castle. The interior wall was of no great distance from the Castle itself, as may still be seen in several places'.[45] Brewer referred to the keep being approached by two portals, the first set in a great wall 'which, at a few yards distance, has inclosed [*sic*] the whole keep'.[46]

On the basis of these cryptic references, a Mr J. Ventress made a model of the castle in the 1850s, which is preserved in the keep today. This shows the keep surrounded by a square inner enclosure or chemise, and reconstructs the west curtain wall on the wrong alignment. However, there seems to be no archaeological evidence for an inner wall completely enclosing the keep. Not long after this, W. H. D. Longstaffe published his magisterial article, which remains probably the fullest published statement of historical evidence for the castle, and included a careful review of the archaeological evidence then available. He concluded that the keep had only been flanked by the west curtain wall, with the dividing wall to the south, and all scholars since have followed his basic plan (Fig. 2).[47]

The great keep at Newcastle is one of Henry II's finest surviving buildings, but, as noted above, the king is only known to have visited the place once, well before it was built, in the spring of 1158 (thirteen years before work commenced on it). This remarkable building was an exercise in patronage by remote control. The key figures in its construction were the justiciar, Richard de Lucy, and the sheriffs: William de Vesci, from around Michaelmas 1157 to Easter 1170, Roger de Stutevill from Easter 1170 to Easter 1185, and Roger de Glanvill, from Easter 1185 to Michaelmas 1189. The Pipe Roll for 1167–68 has William accounting for £30 of works at Bamburgh and £23 7s. 4d. at Newcastle, while the sheriffs of Lancashire accounted for a further £151 for works at Bamburgh and Newcastle: all this was done at Richard de Lucy's order, not the king's.[48] The next two years have no references to work at Newcastle, and only minor works at Bamburgh.

The Pipe Roll for 1171–72 then has the first reference to 'the work of the tower of the New Castle above the Tyne': £58 14s. 0d. spent by the king's brief.[49] From then on, there are explicit references to 'the tower of Newcastle upon Tyne' in each year until 1177–78.[50] These total £903 4s. 7d., somewhat less than other computations of its cost, presumably because these included sums which were not expressly stated as for the tower.[51] It seems significant that all the references to spending on the tower without exception were made 'by the king's brief', while the earlier references, and a reference to a payment of £20 for keeping soldiers there in 1172–73, were made at Richard de Lucy's brief. From 1175–76, the sheriff Roger de Glanville was paid £30 a year for keeping the castle, and this became a regular annual charge. The sum of £903 does not seem particularly large, given that the great tower at Dover, evidently modelled on that of Newcastle, cost four times at much. However, as Nicholas Vincent has pointed out, there are dangers in over-reliance on the Pipe Roll evidence, as we do not have the accounts of spending from the king's chamber, which could have added a great deal more.[52]

We do not know if Henry II ever saw the completed building: there are no documented references to his visiting Newcastle after the initial visit in 1158.[53] There are no major payments for work at Newcastle in the later years of Henry II's reign, and

Northumberland is missing from the Pipe Rolls for 1191–95, but thereafter regular payments of £30 a year for the custody of the New Castle on the Tyne are resumed. There are only relatively minor payments for repairs to the castle in the reigns of Richard and John, which suggest that the curtain walls probably can be dated to the reign of Henry II, as well as the keep. There are, however, a number of references to repairs to the 'King's houses' and to the gaol, suggesting that these were separate buildings within the castle.[54] One other reference in the Pipe Roll for 1202–03 makes very interesting reading: 56s. by King John's brief, for the expenses of six soldiers for taking prisoners from 'Mirebel' to Newcastle and Lancaster.[55] This can only refer to John's surprise attack on the rebel forces led by Geoffrey de Lusignan, which were besieging the dowager queen Eleanor in the castle of Mirebeau in Anjou, on 31 July 1202. John captured his ill-fated nephew Arthur, duke of Brittany together with Geoffrey and the whole of their force.[56] The 'prison', and probably the well-appointed cells in the keep at Newcastle, were to be put to good use.

There is no space or scope here to discuss the keep and the rest of the castle's very complex and interesting later history, except in so far as it affected the present appearance of the building. The key dates are 1810–11, when the buildings abutting the keep were demolished (with grievous losses to archaeology) and the building was re-roofed by an anonymous surveyor working for the City corporation, and 1846, when the Newcastle architect John Dobson carried out further restoration for the Society of Antiquaries of Newcastle, which had taken a lease of the building.[57]

THE ARCHITECTURE OF THE KEEP

THE keep was sited on the highest part of the castle site close to the western curtain wall. It loomed above the Bailey Gate, which was probably the main entrance. It is oblong in plan, 17.84 m from north to south and about 25 m from east to west for the main tower, with the fore-building filling the whole of its eastern face and adding another 4.57 m to the width. From the basement floor to the 19th-century roof platform it is 26 m high. The building has a single main compartment to each floor, but the immensely thick walls, up to 5.5 m thick at ground-floor level, have numerous mural chambers and passages.

Exterior

THE building presents a formidable and regular appearance. The yellow-brown sandstone laid in regular courses has been much eroded, and there are large areas of 19th- and 20th-century refacing. It rises from an impressive battered plinth, 1.7 m high and projecting by 0.75 m.[58] The building is four storeys high, with openings at all four levels: those at the ground floor were originally narrow slits, now mostly widened. At the south-west, south-east and north-east corners there are square turrets, projecting very slightly from the main body. The north-west turret, for no obvious reason, has a hexagonal, faceted shape. The hall at second-floor level was given impressive two-light windows beneath semicircular relieving arches on its north, east and south sides (Fig. 1 and Col. Pl. XVIII in print edn).

Newcastle's keep followed those of Bamburgh and Carlisle: it is argued here that they were both probably the work of Henry I. Bamburgh's keep is a good deal larger, with a complex three-compartment plan, although its dramatically stepped plinth has some similarity to that of Newcastle.[59] Newcastle departed from these models in its elaborate entrance arrangements: neither Carlisle nor Bamburgh originally had a fore-building, being entered by simple doorways at ground level. At Carlisle, however, there is clear evidence of a fore-building being planted against the east face of the building, probably at a fairly early stage: it seems likely that this was done to provide a more impressive entrance, and this could reasonably be attributed to Henry II, although there is no documentary evidence for this.[60] Newcastle's most direct architectural antecedent was Henry II's keep at Scarborough, dated to 1157–69.[61] Scarborough, with its regular appearance, finely finished masonry and architectural ornament, may be seen as prefiguring Newcastle, although it had a relatively conventional first floor entrance through a fore-building. Given Scarborough's completion date of *c.* 1169, it is possible that this was Master Maurice's previous major project.

Chapel

ONE of the building's many singular features is the splendid chapel at ground-floor level beneath the fore-building steps. This had its own entrance, fitted in rather uncomfortably to the left of the entrance steps. Originally, this would have been further enclosed by the lost outer part of the fore-building. The chapel may have been separate from the rest of the ground floor: the door which now links it to the adjacent mural chamber is said by some authorities to be secondary, but the evidence for this seems unclear.[62]

The chapel's entrance door has a drawbar slot: it could be securely barred from inside, although one wonders in what circumstances anyone would ever have needed to bar themselves inside. Its two-bay nave measures approximately 4.9 m by 4.1 m. There is a square chancel, about 3.6 m square, of one principal bay with a half-bay off to one side. The blind arcading and the chancel arch have vigorous chevron ornament, and the thick vaulting-ribs have ball-ornament: much of this is original, although it was fairly sensitively restored *c.* 1846–47 by John Dobson as part of his restoration of the building for the town's Corporation and the Society of Antiquaries of Newcastle.[63]

Ground floor

THE ground floor has a main chamber measuring about 8.2 m by 6.25 m. Traditionally known as the Garrison Room, it has a central cylindrical column 762 mm in diameter, with a finely carved base with torus and scotia mouldings and a shallow, scalloped capital. Eight thick vaulting ribs radiate from this springing from corbels at varying heights, although the crowns of their arches are at a common level. Light is provided by two loops high in the east and south walls with deep, splayed and stepped openings. The column was made hollow, so as to accept a water-pipe conducted from the well-chamber on the second floor, which simply emerges through a hole low down on the west side of the column: if there was a basin to catch the water, there is now no sign of it.

The mural chamber to the east, which today communicates with the chapel, opens off the foot of the spiral stair. A blocked opening next to its door may have been a half-height internal window: its appearance suggests a 'buttery bar', so this may have been a pantry or buttery space. As discussed above, it is not clear whether the door linking it to the chapel is primary, although the lack of a door rebate would certainly seem odd if it were. The mural chamber in the north wall was evidently built as part of the first-floor suite, approached by a staircase from above. Finally, the mural chamber in the west wall had a draw-bar slot outside its door: it was a cell, albeit a well-appointed one with an en-suite garderobe. The external door which opens off this garderobe is clearly a much later feature, probably cut through in the 17th or 18th century to link these spaces with one of the houses which then abutted the keep on all sides.

First floor

THE main room on the first floor is oblong, measuring 8.8 m by 6.85 m: its larger dimensions relating to the main walls being about 0.6 m thinner here. The cylindrical column and arches which run north–south, dividing it into equal halves, look fairly convincingly medieval, but were actually added in the early 19th century when the building was renovated by the town's Corporation: at different stages the room has housed the town's female debtors, a charity school, and the library of the Society of Antiquaries of Newcastle. The fireplace in its east wall is also of the 19th century.[64]

The room is approached by a short passage from the south-east spiral stair. There is a large window embrasure here, which seems to present a doorway rather than a window to the outside. W. H. Knowles thought that this was indeed originally a doorway which linked the keep at first-floor level to the curtain wall dividing the two baileys outside.[65] The short passage would have been the only access to the room, whose appearance has been much altered by the breaking-through of two gaps in its east and west walls. In the east wall there is another mural chamber, directly above the one at ground-floor level and of similar dimensions. Doorways have been cut through from the fore-building steps to this room, and from this room to the main first-floor chamber, and this now forms the visitor entrance. Originally, the mural chamber was approached from the spiral stairs, and before the gap was cut in its west wall there was a row of small wall-cupboards there. Some storage function seems likely.

A second mural chamber in the north wall, 9.15 m long and just 2.13 m wide, has three north-facing windows and a fine, original fireplace. It was served by a garderobe within the west wall, and had a subsidiary chamber beneath it (the north mural chamber at ground-floor level), approached by a dedicated stair. The first-floor rooms seem to have been designed as a self-contained suite for a person of high rank, although the accommodation here is slightly inferior to that on the second floor, an impression reinforced by its position on this floor, hence presumably the idea that this was the 'Queen's Chamber' (so-called). Curiously, the water supply arrangements do not seem to have served this floor.

Second floor

THE greatest peculiarity of the keep's planning is the way that the entrance stairs go all the way up to the second floor. The entrance door there was evidently the main, and quite possibly the only entrance to it, if the chapel with its separate entrance door really was isolated from the rest of the building (Figs 4, 5 and Col. Pls XIX, XX in print edn).

The second floor is signalled as the grandest in status by the great height of its main chamber, which measures 9.15 m from north to south, 7.24 m from east to west, and 9.15 m to the springing of the 19th-century vault: it would have risen about 12.19 m high to the apex of the original roof. A barrel-vaulted passage, 1.83 m wide, leads

FIG. 4. A conjectural reconstruction of the south-east side of the castle keep as it was first built, showing it with higher battlements and turrets. The lost outer part of the fore-building, connecting it to the dividing wall between the two baileys, is also shown

FIG. 5. A conjectural reconstruction of the south-east side of the castle keep, taking a section through the fore-building steps and showing the chapel beneath the steps, the putative upper chapel opening off the landing, and reconstructing the lost entrance to the doorway over the fore-building

from the richly moulded entrance door. The entrance door has no evidence of a draw-bar slot: it would have been protected by the outer doorways, but this nevertheless seems odd.

In the south-west corner of the hall, there is a door to a long mural chamber in the thickness of the south wall. It is known as the King's Chamber, and corresponds in many respects to the first-floor Queen's Chamber (although it is in the south wall, where the Queen's Chamber is in the north wall). It is 9.45 m long and just 2.13 m wide, with four windows: even before they were widened, it would have been light by Norman standards, with views to the south over the river. It is equipped with a fireplace (somewhat smaller than that in the first-floor chamber, but similar in its mouldings) in the window wall, and a garderobe, separated from the main room by a lobby, and by at least one door.

A garderobe opens off the west side of the hall: this seems to represent the only common provision for the keep, as all the other garderobes open off mural chambers. At the opposite (north-east) corner of the hall is the door to the well chamber, occupying the north-east corner of the building. Steps lead up to a platform before the well-head: the well is 762 mm in diameter, lined with beautifully finished ashlar and 30.18 m deep, with about 15.24 m depth of water in it. The masonry to either side has evidence of some kind of windlass. There are two niches in the chamber walls, each with a stone basin. A drain leads from each basin via lead pipes set in the thickness of the walls, which thus formed part of the original construction. The pipe from the basin on the right leads down through the hollow column in the ground floor 'Garrison Room', to the spout in its south face (see above). The basin on the left leads to a basin in a doorway over the fore-building (see below). Master Maurice carefully contrived this system to provide water to these two particular places, but did not provide a supply to the King's Chamber, Queen's Chamber, or the main first-floor room.

The main hall has a remarkable and elaborate design. It was remarkable for its height: although there are beam-slots part-way up the wall, these relate to the insertion of a floor in the 17th century. Despite the provision of fireplaces in the two most important mural chambers, the hall did not originally have a fireplace: the chimney-breast in the west wall is of the 19th century and the present fire-surround is of the 20th century. So the room presumably had a central hearth with a louver high above. What makes the room more remarkable is the dramatic treatment of the window embrasures, which are splayed and given deeply stepped sills, and merge with wall-passages and flights of steps to provide a range of spatial experiences in a manner reminiscent of Baroque architecture. It also makes for dramatic lighting of the room, which would have been controllable when the windows had shutters. In the south wall there are two deep window embrasures, originally with two-light windows: a mural passage runs through the wall, spanning the embrasures, forming a gallery which overlooks the hall from high up. This gallery was evidently intended to lead on up to third-floor level via stairs in the west wall, but the idea was abandoned during construction, and the stairs left incomplete.

Steps lead up into a further deep window embrasure in the wall, and give access to a mural chamber at a mezzanine level in the west wall. This, too, had a door which could be barred from the outside, and was thus designed as a cell, and like the one at ground-floor level, it had its own garderobe. The east wall has a large, arched window embrasure, its sill well above the floor. The embrasure is crossed by a mural staircase which leads upwards, from the south-east spiral stair to the third-floor mural gallery.

So as one ascends the stairs there is another dramatic spatial effect: one looks down into the hall to one's left, or up to a window on one's right.

The third floor, roof level and turrets

AT third-floor level, a mural gallery runs around the building, with loopholes in the outer walls and larger openings looking into the interior space, which today look down into the main hall beneath the present brick vault dating from 1811. Originally there was a steeply pitched counter-sunk roof at this level: the openings in the end (north and south) walls would indeed have looked down into the hall, but the openings in the longer, east and west walls, would have looked onto the outer faces of this roof, and provided access to its gutters (Fig. 6 and Col. Pl. XXI in print edn).

Despite the insertion of the vault, the evidence for the original roof is fairly clear. First, there are wall-scars showing the line of a roof at about a 53° pitch on both end walls. Secondly, the original drainage channels to drain the gutters have both been found, just beneath the floor of the mural gallery: the east gutter was drained northwards, and the west gutter was drained westwards. Thirdly, the sockets for the principal rafters are all visible, apart from those for the middle five on the west wall which were blocked by the 19th-century chimney-breast.

FIG. 6. A conjectural reconstruction of the original 12th-century roof over the keep, based on contemporary examples in Normandy and the evidence of the beam sockets

There are two tiers of sockets on each side relating to fifteen trusses or rafter-pairs, closely spaced at approximately two-foot centres. The lower sockets are relatively deep, the upper ones are smaller and approximately square, but both seem to be shaped for timbers which rake upwards. Although several of Newcastle's antiquaries have made beautiful survey drawings of the keep, none of them seems to have attempted a reconstruction of the roof-structure: a reconstruction is presented here, based on the surviving 12th-century roofs at Kempley church, Gloucestershire, and Lisieux cathedral, Normandy.[66]

The south-east spiral stair, 4 m in diameter, rises all the way from the ground floor to the roof (Fig. 4 and Col. Pl. XIX in print edn). At second-floor level a mural stair rises through the east wall (spanning the window-embrasure as described), and leads to a further spiral stair in the north-east turret. This is a curious elaboration, for all it does is provide a secondary route from the third-floor gallery to the parapet-level: it could not be extended downwards, for the well chamber is immediately below it. The ground floor and first floor, representing much of the space within the building, were only reached by a single flight of stairs. Getting from the mural gallery to the parapets, for whatever reason, required two!

Today, the keep has a level roof platform over the 1811 brick vault. Originally, the roof would have been counter-sunk within the third storey, surrounded by mural galleries and with parapet-walks overlooking it from all four sides. Parapets and low turrets were also reinstated in 1811. These make a major contribution to the keep's impressively regular and complete appearance, but they are probably incorrect in almost every detail, and, unfortunately, the work was apparently not accompanied by any record of its previous state.[67] The battlemented parapets are much too low; in modern times they have had to be supplemented with railings. The corbelling-out of the parapets is anachronistic: the original parapets probably rose in the same plane as the wall below, and may indeed have had a slight inwards offset. Finally, the turrets are diminutive, only rising slightly above the main level of the roof. The surviving corner turrets at Rochester, the White Tower, Hedingham and Dover are proportionally much higher (Fig. 4). Given the Newcastle keep's carefully considered design, it seems likely that its original turrets did, indeed, rise substantially higher.

Finally, the north-west turret, for no apparent reason, was built with a different, faceted shape. The 1813 restorers used this as a cue to provide it with an upper stage rising higher than the other turrets, a visual effect one associates more with later-medieval architecture (compare the gatehouses at Dunstanburgh or Lancaster) than with the 12th century.

The fore-building and entrance steps

THE strangeness of the entrance arrangements at Newcastle has already been referred to. In order to get the entrance steps all the way to second-floor level within the depth of the building, Master Maurice was forced to make them very steep, and to have steps rising through the fore-building arch with only the narrowest possible landing-space to allow for the opening arc of the doors. Even so, he could not quite do it, and the last few risers are actually within the main second-floor doorway (Fig. 5 and Col. Pl. XX in print edn).

The fore-building arch, just referred to, is too narrow to have a full chamber over the arch. It does, however, house a tiny lobby with a doorway, which now looks out into thin air, just above and to the left of the actual archway. Two corbels, below the doorsill, confirm that the doorway must have led onto a narrow timber gallery (Fig. 7). There is some rather vague pictorial evidence that spur walls projected to either side of the fore-building steps, forming an outer part of the fore-building and linking it to the curtain wall between the baileys (Fig. 3). So, this door and gallery led to the wall-walk on this curtain, and perhaps also to some kind of platform, over this outer part of the fore-building (Figs 4, 5 and Col. Pls XIX, XX in print edn).

The strangest point of all is that just within this tiny lobby there is a stone basin set into the wall, with a lead pipe bringing water from the second-floor well chamber. All of this is evidently original fabric. Why on earth did Henry II or his representatives want a water supply here, in a tiny lobby immediately above the main entrance? Some thoughts in relation to this question are offered below, but ultimately the matter remains obscure.

Near the top of the fore-building steps, a plain and narrow doorway leads into an oblong room directly above the chapel sanctuary. This is decorated with mural arches with zigzag ornament: the whole of this is replacement 19th-century masonry from John Dobson's restoration, but is said to be a fairly faithful restoration of what he found there. The mural decoration has led to suggestions that this was a further chapel or oratory, although its narrow doorway seems to sit a little oddly with this identification.[68] This brings us to the entrance door itself, its elaborate Romanesque ornament also restored by Dobson: Lewis Vulliamy's engraving suggests that here, too, Dobson copied the historic forms fairly faithfully.

AN INTERPRETATION

THE keep at Newcastle was planted by Henry II at great cost within a fortress that was had been founded a century previously and was well established, with Bamburgh, as one of the crown's two main fortresses north of the Tees. Henry himself had probably not seen Newcastle since 1158, shortly after he intimidated Malcolm IV into returning the northern counties, including Newcastle, and doing homage to him.

The castle's curtain walls are undated, but their form and the lack of evidence for them in the Pipe Rolls for the reigns of Richard I and John suggests that they probably predated the keep. They may, perhaps, be attributed to the earlier part of Henry's reign. So the keep may have represented the last element in a general rebuilding of the castle in stone. On the other hand, it may not have been initially intended, and have been added as an afterthought. However, unlike the previous works at the castle, the payments for it in the Pipe Rolls were all made 'by the king's brief'. The keep was built under the direction of a French mason, Maurice, who was presumably Henry's choice. The keep contains several highly idiosyncratic features: it seems unlikely that these could have been made without the king's knowledge and permission, even given that, so far as we know, all this was done without a single royal visit.

The keep at Carlisle seems to have had a first-floor hall and a second-floor chamber. Newcastle's planning is closer to the keep at Bamburgh, which seems to have had suites of two or three rooms at both first- and second-floor levels. However, Newcastle has major differences: despite the parity of accommodation between the two floors, the second-floor entrance imposes a clear hierarchy on them. They might be interpreted as for the king and the sheriff, or the king and an eminent guest. The second-floor entrance is without apparent precedent, and evidently created problems. The steepness of the entrance was evidently not seen as a drawback: possibly the

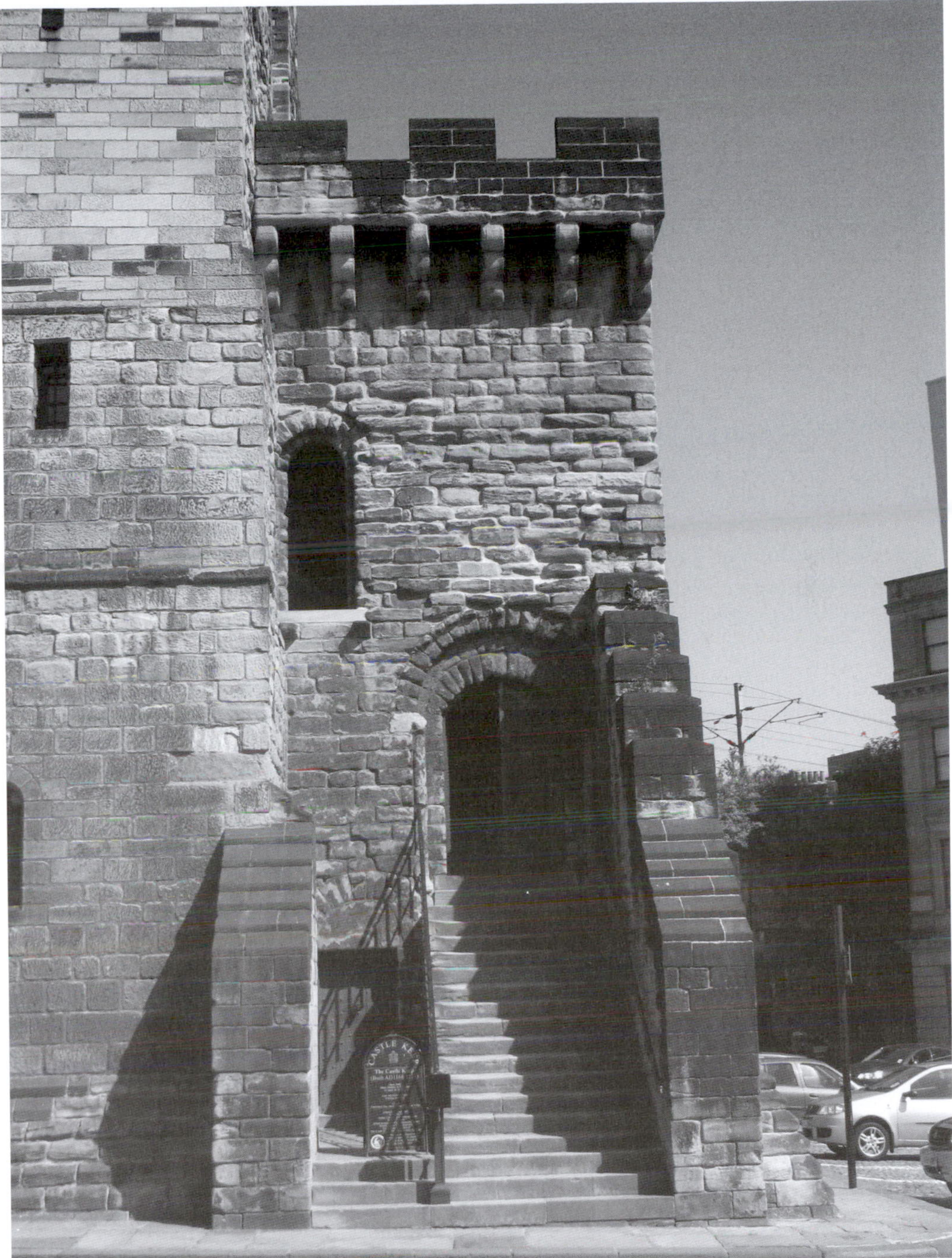

FIG. 7. The entrance to the keep fore-building, showing the small doorway above the entrance with corbels to support a lost balcony or walkway

reverse, if the intention was to make those approaching feel impressed, even dwarfed, as they struggled up the precipitous steps. Indeed, the fact that Newcastle's 'second-floor entrance' planning was followed at Dover suggests that it was considered to be successful.

If the keep was intended as a setting for ceremonial, one might think that the victory of 1174 and the Convention of Falaise of 1175 would have made a difference, as they markedly shifted the power-relationships in question. However, there is no evidence that the keep's design was materially changed during construction: on the contrary, the chapel interior all seems to be primary and intended from the outset. This in turn suggests that the steps above it, and thus the whole remarkable second-floor entrance, were part of the original design. It is possible that the design was 'tweaked' after 1174–75, but we have no way of knowing this.

The keep overlooks the bridge and the road south to Durham. In 1171, Hugh le Puiset was the greatest potentate in the north of England after the king, and a figure with close links to the rival house of Blois whose uncertain allegiance was demonstrated in 1173–74. If the keep was a statement of Henry's determination to control the north, Bishop Hugh was probably one of the main intended recipients of the message. However, any such statement would surely have been aimed primarily at the king of Scots. As outlined above, the deep background to its construction lies in Anglo-Scots relations, and the turbulent history of Northumbria. The earldom had proved beyond even William the Conqueror's ability to control effectively, and after Robert Mowbray's disgrace in 1095, William II and Henry I let it go into abeyance. However, David I equipped himself with a genealogical claim to the earldom which he then made good, to the point of investing his son and grandson with this honour in Newcastle itself.

In this story Newcastle and Carlisle play parallel roles, it being at Carlisle that Henry was obliged to promise to leave David's heirs in quiet possession of the earldom while receiving knighthood from King David. Carlisle already had a grand keep, where David I himself died in 1153. It was also at Carlisle that Henry refused knighthood to Malcolm IV in 1157, shortly after breaking this promise and wresting back Northumbria. Carlisle keep was originally approached by a simple doorway: at some early stage a fore-building was added to make a grander entrance. It is tempting, in considering Newcastle's keep and the emphasis placed on its entrance, to attribute this to Henry II, too.

From 1139 until 1157 the heir to the Scots throne held Northumbria of the English crown, effectively extending Scots power to the banks of the Tyne. Henry would have had a keen awareness of how undesirable this situation was, for it was from a similar position, as holder of multiple fiefdoms in France, that he tormented and undermined his own overlord, Louis VII. By the time the Newcastle keep was finished, Henry had completely turned the tables: Northumbria was back in his own hands, the Convention of Falaise had been ratified, and the King of Scots' personal homage to Henry and his ancestors, however this might have been interpreted, had been converted into the subordination of the Scots crown to the English crown. At one level, the context for the building of Newcastle may have been a wish to defy and efface the memory of David I's triumph, of his son's and grandson's tenure of the earldom, of Henry's obligations to him, and of Henry's breach of the oath which had apparently accompanied his own knighthood in 1149. The resumption of Northumbria was also a reassertion of the situation when Henry's grandfather, Henry I, was king, the standard or litmus test so often referred to or appealed to by Henry II.

A number of questions remain open. Why did the magnificent keep at Bamburgh not suffice for this purpose? It was the ancient capital of Northumbria, and was probably built by Henry's grandfather, Henry I, whom he revered. Bamburgh keep is visible for miles, and flanked the road south from Edinburgh. Yet under Henry II, Newcastle supplanted Bamburgh as seat of the sheriff, perhaps because it was more directly on the road south to Durham and York. But another explanation could be that it was because the principal scenes of David I's triumphs had been Carlisle and Newcastle, not Bamburgh: so that was where Henry had to plant his standard, architecturally speaking.

Finally, what can be said about that basin in the lobby over the fore-building? The lobby would have communicated with a balcony-like space over the lost, outer part of the fore-building, potentially a suitable place for formal public appearances. It seems impossible, given the basin's small size and location, that it was for an everyday practical purpose. One is put in mind of the ceremonies of hand-washing which formed such an important part of 12th-century court life: the problem with this idea is that the washing of the royal hands at the Angevin court, so far as we know, was the jealously guarded preserve of certain household officers, notably the Lord Butler and the Lord Steward and their proxies who actually served at court on a day-to-day basis. We do not know of any specific ceremonial context which would explain this feature. Nevertheless, ritual and ceremony, in particular the ceremonies of homage and hospitality, were the outward expressions of power-relationships in the 12th century, and each major ceremony was carefully planned and eagerly watched. Faced with a feature as strange as this one, it seems natural to look in this direction for a solution.

For the present, we may conclude that the keep at Newcastle was designed to serve as a setting for ceremonial, with a likely emphasis on ceremonies of fealty and homage, though there is little or no evidence of it actually being used in this way. The steep entrance route and deliberately dramatic lighting of the main interior seem intended to enhance this ceremonial purpose. It was evidently intended as an occasional royal residence with primary and secondary suites of accommodation, a pattern later repeated at Dover. It was also intended to receive some eminent but rather more reluctant guests, to judge by the two well-appointed cells. On a day-to-day basis, it was designed as the place from which the sheriffs of Northumberland would exercise the crown's authority, in the pointed absence of an earl of Northumbria: it was a monumental expression of Henry II's determination to control the North directly. This remarkable building, it may be suggested, was the expression in stone of Henry's view of the proper relationship between England, Northumbria and Scotland.

ACKNOWLEDGEMENTS

I am very grateful to Dr Jeremy Ashbee for his advice and encouragement, and to Dr Nat Alcock, Dr Chris Currie and Dr John Gillingham for their help and advice in the preparation of this article.

NOTES

1. *The Ecclesiastical History of Orderic Vitalis*, ed. M. Chibnall, 6 vols (Oxford 1969–80), II, 263; D. C. Douglas, *William the Conqueror* (London 2004), 211–13; A. A. M. Duncan, *The Kingship of the Scots 842–1272: Succession and Independence* (Edinburgh 2002), 45; F. M. Stenton, *Anglo-Saxon England* (Oxford 1971), 601–05.

2. *Orderic Vitalis* (as n. 1), II, 321–23; Douglas, *Conqueror* (as n. 1), 225–26; Stenton, *Anglo-Saxon* (as n. 1), 610–12.

3. Douglas, *Conqueror* (as n. 1), 232–23; Stenton, op. cit., 613–15.

4. Douglas, *Conqueror* (as n. 1), 233.

5. Ibid., loc. cit.

6. D. Carpenter, *The Struggle for Mastery: The Penguin History of Britain 1066–1284* (London 2003), 121, 131.

7. William II created a series of baronies in northern England in the wake of his successful expedition to Carlisle in 1092, settling the Balliols at Bywell and Mitford, and Robert de Umfraville in Redesdale, further north. The twelve baronies in the south of Northumberland owing castle-guard service to Newcastle do not seem to be securely dated, but may in part date from his reign: F. Barlow, *William Rufus* (New Haven, CT, and London 2000), 297–98.

8. M. McCarthy, H. R. T. Summerson and R. G. Annis, *Carlisle Castle: A Survey and Documentary History* (London 1990), 119; J. A. A. Goodall, 'The Great Tower of Carlisle Castle', in *Carlisle and Cumbria*, 39–62.

9. R. A. Brown, H. M. Colvin and A. J. Taylor, *The History of the King's Works: The Middle Ages*, 2 vols + plans (London 1963), II, 554–55; Goodall, 'Great Tower' (as n. 8). The dating of the keep at Bamburgh is a well-known problem. Early scholars including G. T. Clark believed it to be by Henry II, but Brown, Colvin and Taylor, citing evidence from Pipe Rolls of the 1160s which clearly documents repairs to an already-existing building, argue it was possibly built by Henry, earl of Northumbria and heir to the Scots throne, during his occupation in the 1140s. The present author is more inclined to agree with Dr Goodall, 'Great Tower' (as n. 8), 51–52, in attributing it to Henry I. Its lower, broader proportions (that is, lower and broader than those of Newcastle), evident architectural debt to the White Tower, the simplicity of its window mouldings, and the apparent evidence for Henry I having ordered the keep at Carlisle to be built, all appear to support this conclusion. Furthermore, there is no evidence that either David I of Scotland or his son Henry built donjons anywhere else, other than a single chronicle reference to David building the keep at Carlisle (which may refer to works to complete it): McCarthy, Summerson and Annis, *Carlisle Castle* (as n. 8), 119. In any case, it seems reasonable to doubt whether Henry, earl of Huntingdon, would have had the resources to build this behemoth.

10. A. Saunders, *Norham Castle* (London 1998).

11. Carpenter, *Struggle for Mastery* (as n. 6), 130–32.

12. *The Church Historians of England*, ed. and trans. J. Stevenson, 5 vols in 8 (London 1853–58), IV.1, 122 (this volume includes the chronicles of John and Richard of Hexham, and Melrose). Duncan, *Kingship* (as n. 1), points out that this was for the earldom of Huntingdon, and not necessarily for Scotland. I am not aware of any evidence as to whether Henry I accepted David I's claim through marriage to the earldom of Northumbria.

13. D. Crouch, *The Reign of King Stephen 1135–1154* (London 2000), 39–41.

14. Carpenter, *Struggle for Mastery* (as n. 6), 166–68; A. L. Poole, *Domesday Book to Magna Carta, 1087–1216*, 2nd edn (Oxford 1955), 270–72.

15. G. W. S. Barrow, 'The Kings of Scotland and Durham', in *Anglo-Norman Durham 1093–1193*, ed. D. Rollason, M. Harvey and M. Prestwich (Woodbridge 1994), especially 318–20. David I's unsuccessful attempt to get his nominee, William Cumin, elected to the see in 1141, and the election of Hugh le Puiset, cadet of the house of Blois and natural ally of King Stephen, in 1152, were both blows to Scots influence in the north.

16. Crouch, *King Stephen* (as n. 13), 73–83, 323.

17. Carpenter, *Struggle for Mastery* (as n. 6), 178–86; Poole, *Domesday* (as n. 14), 273–75; Barrow, 'Kings of Scotland' (as n. 15), 321.

18. *Church Historians* (as n. 12), IV.1, 27 (Hexham chronicle, *sub anno* 1150: quotation), 127 (Melrose chronicle, *sub anno* 1149).

19. *Chronicles of the Reigns of Stephen, Henry II and Richard I*, ed. R. Howlett, 4 vols, Rolls series 82 (London 1884–90), IV, 159 (chronicle of Robert of Torigni).

20. *Chronica Magistri Rogeri de Hovedene*, ed. W. Stubbs, 4 vols, Rolls series 51 (London 1868–71), I, 211. William of Newburgh repeats the story.

21. *Church Historians* (as n. 12), IV.1, 29–30.

22. E. Amt, *The Accession of Henry II in England: Royal Government Restored, 1149–1159* (Woodbridge 1993), 27.

23. *Church Historians* (as n. 12), IV.1, 130. The story is repeated in *Rogeri de Hovedene* (as n. 20), I, 216, but it seems clear that he was simply repeating the Melrose chronicle. I am grateful to Dr John Gillingham for pointing this out to me, as for much else.

24. Duncan, *Kingship* (as n. 1), 72.

25. Poole, *Domesday* (as n. 14), 275. Poole notes the ambiguity as to what Malcolm had done homage for, noting that Hugh the Chanter, alone of the chroniclers, claimed that he had done homage for Scotland:

Historians of the Church of York, ed. J. Raine, 3 vols, Rolls series 71 (London 1879–94), II, 215; Duncan, *Kingship* (as n. 1), 72.

26. *Rogeri de Hovedene* (as n. 20), I, 216. The Melrose chronicle says substantially the same thing: 'they parted from each other not upon the best of terms, and therefore the King of Sots was not made a knight at this time.' (*Church Historians* (as n. 12), IV.1, 130.)

27. *Church Historians* (as n. 12), IV.1, 130; Brown et al., *King's Works* (as n. 9), II, 852–53.

28. R. W. Eyton, *Court, Household and Itinerary of King Henry II* (London 1878), 33. Henry issued a charter to Hubert de Vallibus at Newcastle on Tyne, attributed by Eyton to the summer of 1158: it was witnessed by the archbishop of York, the bishops of Durham and Lincoln, Hugh, earl of Norfolk, Aubrey de Vere, earl of Oxford, Geoffrey de Mandeville, earl of Essex, Richard de Lacy, Manasser Biset, Henry de Essex and others.

29. *Chronicles of the Reigns* (as n. 19), II, 47; IV, 202–03; *Rogeri de Hovedene* (as n. 20), I, 217.

30. *Chronicles of the Reigns* (as n. 19), II, 58–59.

31. Duncan, *Kingship* (as n. 1), 99.

32. *Chronicles of the Reigns* (as n. 19), II, 73. The Melrose chronicler was somewhat vague about the episode: Henry crossed the sea and was followed by William, king of Scots, 'the business of his lord so requiring it, but he returned ere long, after some military exploit had been attempted'. *Church Historians* (as n. 12), IV.1, 131.

33. *Church Historians* (as n. 12), IV.1, 132.

34. *Rogeri de Hovedene* (as n. 20), II, 4–5.

35. *Chronicle of the War between the English and the Scots in 1173 by Jordan Fantosme*, ed. F. Michel (London and Edinburgh 1840), 81–3; *Rogeri de Hovedene* (as n. 20), II, 63–64.

36. G. V. Scammell, *Hugh de Puiset, Bishop of Durham* (Cambridge 1956), 38–39; *Rogeri de Hovedene* (as n. 20), II, 63.

37. *Rogeri de Hovedene* (as n. 20), II, 64; Scammell, *Hugh de Puiset* (as n. 36), 41–43.

38. *Rogeri de Hovedene* (as n. 20), II, 80–82, gives the complete text of the convention as ratified at York. Duncan, *Kingship* (as n. 1), 99–100, points out that the provisions concerning the church were not carried out, and indeed that the pope forbade the archbishop of York to attempt to exercise authority in Scotland.

39. *Symeon of Durham: Historia Regum*, ed. T. Arnold, 2 vols, Rolls series 75 (London 1882–85), II, 211; H. Bourne, *History of Newcastle upon Tyne* (Newcastle 1736), 5–9; B. Harbottle, 'The Medieval Archaeology of Newcastle', in *Newcastle and Gateshead before 1700*, ed. D. Newton and A. J. Pollard (Chichester 2009).

40. Harbottle, 'Medieval Archaeology' (as n. 39), 23; eadem, and M. Ellison, 'An Excavation in the Castle Ditch, Newcastle upon Tyne, 1974–6', *AA*, 5th ser. 9 (1981), 75–250.

41. W. H. Knowles, 'The Castle, Newcastle upon Tyne', *AA*, 4th ser. 2 (1926), 1–51 (esp. 4–8).

42. Ibid., 4–8; W. H. D. Longstaffe, 'The New Castle upon Tyne', *AA*, 2nd ser. 4 (1860), 45–139.

43. The Newcastle antiquary William Hylton Dyer Longstaffe made the first full compilation of evidence for the castle's layout and published the first accurate plan in 1860 ('New Castle', as n. 42). His plan has only been slightly altered by more recent investigations.

44. Carlisle castle also occupies a triangular site at one end of the city. The castle was divided, apparently from a very early stage, into an inner and outer bailey, and the principal entrance was originally into the east end of the inner bailey. This early gatehouse was blocked by or in the early 14th century, and converted into the 'Queen of Scots Tower': McCarthy et al., *Carlisle Castle* (as n. 8), 98, 121.

45. Bourne, *History of Newcastle* (as n. 39), 118.

46. J. Brewer, *History of Newcastle* [vol. I] (Newcastle upon Tyne s.d.), 143 (I found a copy of this work in the Society of Antiquaries of Newcastle upon Tyne's library at the Hancock Museum of the North, Newcastle, but am unable to find it in the catalogue on their website, or in the BL main catalogue).

47. Longstaffe, 'New Castle' (as n. 42).

48. *The Great Roll of the Pipe for the Fourteenth Year of the Reign of King Henry the Second:* A.D. *1167–1168*, s.e., Pipe Roll Society 12 (London 1890), 169. (Hereafter, references to the Pipe Rolls will be given in the form '*Pipe Roll 14 Henry II: 1167–68*'.)

49. *Pipe Roll 18 Henry II: 1171–72*, Pipe Roll Society 18 (London 1894), 66.

50. *Pipe Roll 19 Henry II: 1172–73*, Pipe Roll Society 19 (London 1895): work of the tower, £167 14s. 5d.; purprestures, work of the tower, £54 10s. 11d.; *Pipe Roll 20 Henry II: 1173–74*, Pipe Roll Society 21 (London 1896): work of the tower, £7 15s. and 100s. 10d.; *Pipe Roll 21 Henry II: 1174–75*, Pipe Roll Society 22 (London 1897): work of the castle, £50; work of the tower, £25 13s. 6d., 'and to Maurice the Mason for the same tower, 20s. by the king's gift by the king's brief'; purprestures, work of the tower, £11 22d.; *Pipe Roll 22 Henry II: 1175–76*, Pipe Roll Society 25 (London 1904), 37–38: work of the tower, £133 7s. 6d.; £80 and 23s. 6d.; purprestures, £17 22d.; £144 15s 4d; *Pipe Roll 23 Henry II: 1176–77*, Pipe Roll Society 26 (London, 1905), 82: works of the tower, £141 12s. 11d.; *Pipe Roll 24 Henry II: 1177–78*, Pipe Roll Society 27 (London 1906), 59: work of the New Castle, £97 0s. 1d.

51. Brown et al., *King's Works* (as n, 9), II, 746, calculate the cost at £1144.

52. N. Vincent, 'In the Shadow of the Castle Wall: King Henry II and Dover, 1154–1179', in *Henry II and the Great Tower of Dover Castle*, ed. S. Brindle and P. Pattison (London forthcoming).

53. R. W. Eyton, *Court, Household and Itinerary of King Henry II* (London 1878), used as a standard source by several generations of scholars, has no further references to visits to Newcastle. However, this is now generally regarded as unreliable, given the extensive assumptions made by attempting to relate the evidence of charters (which give locations but are mostly undated) to that of chronicles. There are long periods for which we actually have very little idea where Henry II was.

54. *Pipe Roll 6 Richard I: 1194–95*, Pipe Roll Society 43 (London 1928), 132–33: £15 for custody of the castle for half a year, and 18s. 2d. for repair of the king's houses; *Pipe Roll 7 Richard I: 1195–96*, Pipe Roll Society 44 (London 1929), 24–25: £30 for custody, 40s. for repairs of the king's houses at Newcastle, 4s. 5d. for repair of the gaol at Newcastle; *Pipe Roll 8 Richard I: 1196–97*, Pipe Roll Society 45 (London 1930), 9, 11: £30 for custody; 37s. for repair of the tower.

55. *Pipe Roll 4 John: 1202–03*, Pipe Roll Society 53 (London 1937), 48.

56. W. L. Warren, *King John* (Harmondsworth 1966), 92–95.

57. Newcastle upon Tyne and its castle have been extremely well served by generations of excellent local historians, centred on its Society of Antiquaries. On the later history of the castle: Bourne, *History of Newcastle* (as n. 39); Brewer, *History of Newcastle* (as n. 46); Longstaffe, 'New Castle' (as n. 42); Knowles, 'The Castle' (as n. 41); J. C. Bruce, *Guide to the Castle of Newcastle upon Tyne* (London, 1847).

58. These figures, here rendered in metric, are taken from one of the outstandingly good early 20th-century survey drawings by W. H. Knowles in the Society of Antiquaries of Newcastle's collections: Woodhorn Colliery, Northumberland County Records, 21/4/2/2/4.

59. Goodall, 'Great Tower' (as n. 8), 46 and n. 29.

60. McCarthy, Summerson and Annis, *Carlisle Castle* (as n. 8), 69, 91–92.

61. Brown et al., *King's Works* (as n, 9), II, 830–31.

62. The doorway in question has what looks like primary masonry in both jambs. In the room on the other side, the cornice is interrupted by the doorway, which is given an arch rising from the cornice: all of this looks reasonably convincing as a primary feature. Against this is the curious fact that the doorway has absolutely straight sides with no rebate for a door. One would have thought that a chapel would require a door, to protect its status and prevent interruptions to services. Knowles, in his careful and thorough description of the keep (see 'The Castle' (as n. 41)), marks the doorway in his plan as a later feature, but does not refer to it in his text. Of course, the original lack of a door (for whatever reason) would provide a full explanation for the chapel needing a draw-bar on its outer doorway.

63. *Memorial of the Society of Antiquaries of Newcastle upon Tyne to the Town Council relative to the restoration of the Norman Keep of the Castle of that Town, and Report of the Sub-Committee of the Society upon the Same*, s. a. (Newcastle upon Tyne 1847); T. Faulkner and A. Grey, *John Dobson, Architect of the North-East* (Newcastle upon Tyne 2001), 76, 81, 106. Dobson had made drawings of the keep when young (*c.* 1811), 'when it was more perfect'. In 1846 he restored a number of features, including the chapel, the 'upper chapel' and the main entrance door, for the Society of Antiquaries on the basis of these drawings. Unfortunately, his drawings do not seem to survive in the society's collections, now in Northumberland County Records at Woodhorn Colliery.

64. Longstaffe, 'New Castle' (as n. 42), 84–85.

65. Knowles, 'The Castle' (as n. 41), 23.

66. I am very grateful to Dr Nat Alcock and Dr Chris Currie for their advice in relation to this: any errors in the reconstruction, which is very tentative, are the author's responsibility.

67. For Dobson's (lost) juvenescent drawings of the keep, see above, n. 59. In 1817 Lewis Vulliamy made a beautiful series of survey drawings of the keep for the Society of Antiquaries of London, which remain in its library. Vulliamy carefully distinguished between original masonry and the new work at high level, suggesting that he may have had access to some kind of record of the keep's previous state, but there is no indication what this might have been: perhaps he was simply estimating the level of survival of historic masonry from the outer surfaces.

68. The author of the *Memorial of the Society* (as n. 63) calls this room the oratory, while doubting that it was one and suggesting that it was a guard chamber. He includes it on his list of things to be restored. An indistinct illustration by Dobson in E. Mackenzie, *A Description and Historical Account of the Town and County of Newcastle upon Tyne*, 2 vols (Newcastle upon Tyne 1827), I, 102, suggests that it did have wall-arcading with chevron ornament. Knowles, 'The Castle' (as n. 41), 13–15, identifies the room as a guard chamber. It is not clear, however, why a guard chamber should have been given blind arcading.

The Construction of the Gothic Priory Church of Hexham

JENNIFER S. ALEXANDER

The priory church of Hexham which survives from the late 12th to early 13th century is an ambitious building of some size that derives its architectural design from buildings in the north of England and Scotland. The choir and transepts were planned together but there is evidence in the fabric that a change was introduced during the building of the north transept, and it is suggested that this was due to the replacement of the master mason. The construction sequence can be understood from a detailed examination of the fabric, and from a survey of its masons' marks.

INTRODUCTION AND HISTORY

HEXHAM priory was an early foundation, and the first records of building work relate to the period of St Wilfrid in the 7th century, from which the crypt survives.[1] Its position close to the Scottish border has meant that it suffered raids both to its outlying properties and to its urban site, with consequent periods of financial hardship and of repair, or reconstruction, of its church and claustral buildings. The documentary history was transcribed by James Raine in the 1860s and needs only brief mention here.[2] The most significant event in its early history was its refoundation *c.* 1113 as an Augustinian house, by which time Hexham had been removed from Durham and placed in the see of York. This does not seem to have been the stimulus for an immediate reconstruction of the church and we hear only that the claustral buildings were rebuilt in stone by Asketill, the first prior, who died in 1130. Instead, surviving Anglo-Saxon work, of unspecified date, seems to have been refurbished in the late 11th century.[3] There may have been a partial rebuilding of the choir in connection with the translation of the relics of Hexham's saints to a site close to the high altar in 1155, from which the apse has been found, but it was swept away in a complete reconstruction of the choir and transepts in the late 12th and early 13th century (Fig. 1).[4]

No documentation exists for the building work of the current church, but the evidence for the raid in 1296 when the Scots attacked the region, and the priory church was burned, can be seen in the area around the crossing.[5] There is fire damage to the rear of the triforium arcade in the south-west choir bay and on the east triforia of both transepts, probably caused by burning roof timbers. The north side was the most affected and all the sub-arches of its triforium arcade are 14th-century replacements, apart from one group of shafts in the north bay. Repairs had been set in hand promptly and new altars consecrated in 1310, but the priory and its lands were subjected to further attacks until the middle of the 14th century.[6] The erection of a series of eastern chapels under a pitched roof against the east wall of the choir, together with a small sacristy on the outside of the choir south wall in *c.* 1350, presumably marked a

BAA Trans., vol. XXXVI (2013), 115–140

Fig. 1. Hexham priory church exterior from the north

return to more peaceful times.[7] The late 13th-century west cloister was also remodelled around the middle of the 14th century, dated by the capitals which have bubbly, seaweed foliage. The nave had certainly been started in the early 13th century, and has fabric from the late 14th to early 15th century, which suggests that some rebuilding had taken place, but it was ruined by the 18th century and the current version is that erected by Temple Moore in 1907–09.[8] Two new windows were installed in the choir during the Perpendicular period, one in the south-east end of the aisle and the other in the main east wall and both have since been replaced.[9]

CHOIR

THE decision to rebuild the Romanesque church at Hexham was made in a period of calm, and it is clear that the canons were embarking on a large and costly enterprise in which new ideas might be expected to appear. The choir is an ambitious building, six bays in length and aisled, and is considerably longer than its Romanesque predecessor (Fig. 1). The initial layout and first building campaign show signs of uninterrupted work with a consistency of design and construction evident on the exterior walls, but there are anomalies in the interior which suggest that subsequent work was more protracted. The aisle walls with flat pilaster buttresses and lancet windows finished with moulded arches on chalice or waterleaf capitals and monolithic shafts, place the start of work in the last two decades of the 12th century (Figs 2, 3).

Hexham's stylistic affinities are with buildings in the north of England and Scotland, as will be discussed below, but it departs from these prototypes in the plan of its east end, as it had neither a projecting unaisled presbytery, nor an eastern aisle. Hexham's flat east wall with its two levels of tall lancet windows is the result of an 1860 remodelling by the Newcastle architect, John Dobson, as the replacement for a high gable and the late medieval row of chapels aligned across the east end of the building, which had become derelict (Figs 4, 6).[10]

Evidence for the earlier appearance of the east end is in the antiquarian record. Daniel King's 17th-century view shows a broad five-light Perpendicular window above the row of chapels, and this in turn had been partly filled in and replaced before 1809 as early engravings show the cusping from its outer edge surviving on either side of a strange four-light window (Fig. 5). The narrower window had been built during a major refurbishment of the 1720s and was perhaps derived from Kirkwall's east window.[11] A version of it remained until Dobson removed the chapels and remodelled the east wall, as can be seen in a photo from *c.* 1858 (Fig. 6). Also visible in the pre-restoration photo are the two buttresses of the centre section of the choir wall and these are clearly flat pilasters with angle shafts, compatible with a late 12th-century date and probably from the original east wall. The damaged lower parts of the buttresses are shown in Hodges's drawing of 1888.[12]

FIG. 2. Choir exterior from north-east

FIG. 3. Capital from the interior of a choir south aisle window

Fig. 4. Choir exterior east wall

Fig. 5. Detail of a drawing by W. Brown, published in 1809, showing the east window flanked by tracery from an earlier east window

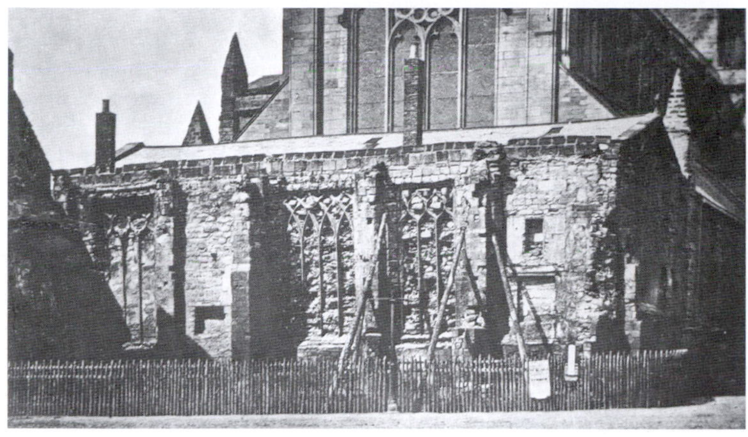

FIG. 6. Photograph taken in *c.* 1858 before the removal of the 14th-century chapels built against the east end of Hexham

Although the masonry of the exterior has been replaced, the inner faces of the walls of the choir triforia are medieval and the east walls are in bond with the ends of the triforia arcades, demonstrating that the original east wall must also have been of full height. Hexham is an early example of a building with this feature, and its context needs to be established. The more usual design of east end for early Gothic Augustinian churches is one where the presbytery projects beyond the end of the choir aisles, seen, for example, at Lanercost.[13] In departing from this model Hexham sacrificed the banks of windows around the sanctuary for the more diffused light entering through aisle windows, but gained circulation space in the east bays where the relics would have been housed.

One source cited for Hexham's plan is Ripon, which also has a six-bay choir with side aisles, but it has been shown to have had a rectangular ambulatory in the last bay and not a flat east end.[14] Alternatively, Hexham's origin may have been in late-12th-century unaisled choirs like Brinkburn's (probably in building after 1188),[15] but the structural, and visual, differences between east walls without aisles which are usually no more than about 10–14 m in width and Hexham's wall which cannot have been less than about 23 m wide, make a direct connection seem unlikely.

Full height east walls including aisles are more common in the 13th than in the late 12th century, although Romanesque builders did sometimes use the design, for example at St Cross, Winchester. The building that established the concept in the north, and provides the immediate context for Hexham, is Jervaulx's four-bay choir, dated to *c.* 1190–1200, although little is still standing.[16] Coming out of a late 12th-century period of ambitious Cistercian building, Jervaulx should be seen as part of, or perhaps the stimulus for, a group of buildings in the north of England with imposing choirs which end in high east walls in the early Gothic period, not all of which are Cistercian. One such is Kirkham where the plan changed from an eastern ambulatory to a full-height wall during the construction of its eight-bay choir in the first quarter of the 13th century, or Whitby and Rievaulx which have long aisled choirs (both of seven bays) ending in cliff walls from *c.* 1220 and *c.* 1220–30 respectively.[17] Since there is no firm date for Hexham, it is not possible to determine its precise place within the development of northern flat-ended choirs, but the architectural detailing of its lateral walls would suggest that it belongs to the end of the 12th century, and this would place it at an early stage.

CONSTRUCTION SEQUENCE

THE interior of the choir has a three-storeyed elevation, with side aisles under stone rib vaults, but the main space covered by a wood roof with the principal trusses supported on wall shafts (Fig. 7). The spacing of the clerestory bays and the design of its arches might suggest that a stone vault had been considered at some point, but the piers behind the triforia arcades show no traces of the necessary abutment and the exterior buttresses are insufficient for its support. As Peter Draper has noted, the absence of a stone high vault is not of itself evidence for a lack of ambition or of a shortage of funds, and is a feature commonly found in the northern abbey churches.[18] Its three-storeyed elevation, of an arcade supported on clustered piers, with round arched triforium openings and a clerestory wall passage, is that found widely in northern England in the early 13th century, for example at Whitby, Jedburgh, and Lanercost choir.

The choir piers consist of coursed keeled shafts in two sizes and resemble those of St Andrews from *c.* 1170, Jedburgh's nave from the 1180s, and Arbroath, although the capitals at Hexham are of a later form.[19] The north arcade capitals are more varied than those on the south, and include some stiff-leaf foliage (albeit heavily restored), and both combine square and keel-shaped abaci, while the arch mouldings

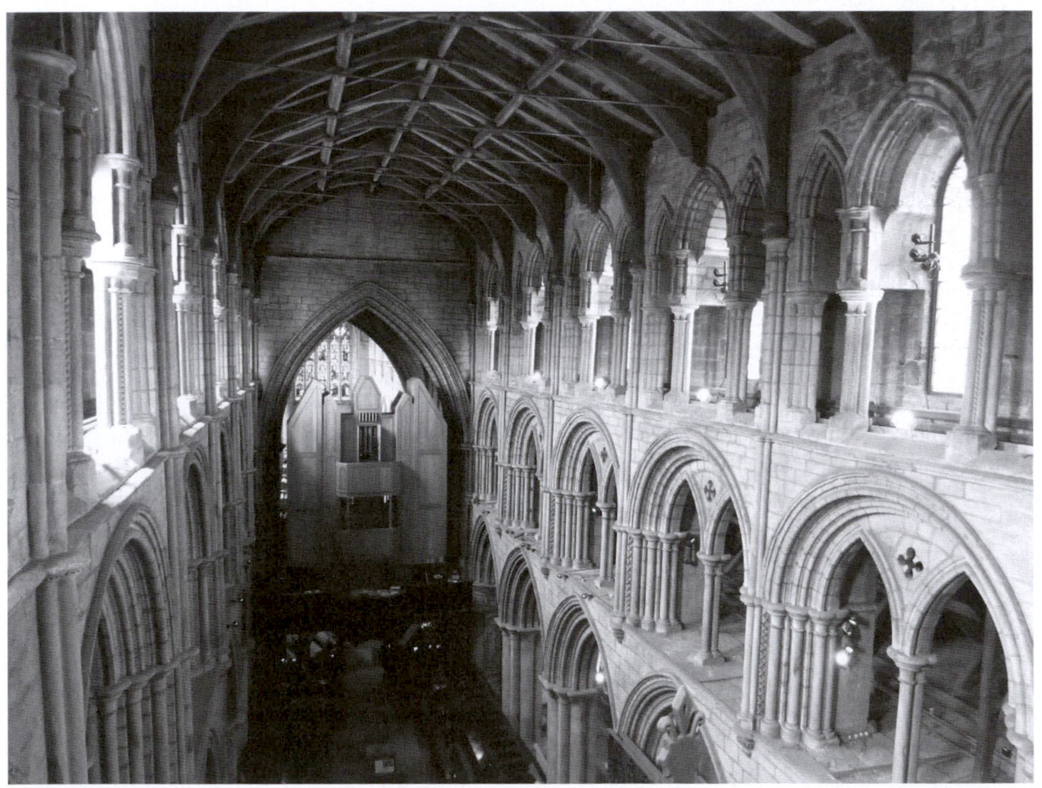

FIG. 7. Choir interior from the south-east

differ between the two sides (Fig. 8). Stepped bases above square plinths are described as unique to Hexham, but only one pair of pier bases has this design and the rest are square.[20] Construction of the arcade was from east to west, with a pause while the Romanesque east end was removed and the last two bays were then built.[21] The coursing in the spandrels between the arcade arches on the south is mostly regular until the fourth bay from the east where it changes, and the last two bays have been built from west to east (Fig. 9).[22] Masons' marks suggest that all the piers belong to the same phase, with the marks repeated along, and across, the arcades, but in no particular pattern. There are no marks on the western responds.[23]

The triforium followed with masons from the piers joined by others for its construction. A building break evident in bay four on the south, in line with that of the arcade beneath, has the same masons' marks on either side of the break suggesting that it was not of long duration. There is no corresponding break on the north. The west bay on the south and all the north bays have an order of dogtooth flanking slender shafts between the bays and both sides have narrow bands of nailhead in each arcade arch. Dogtooth is used in a similar way in a number of other northern abbeys,

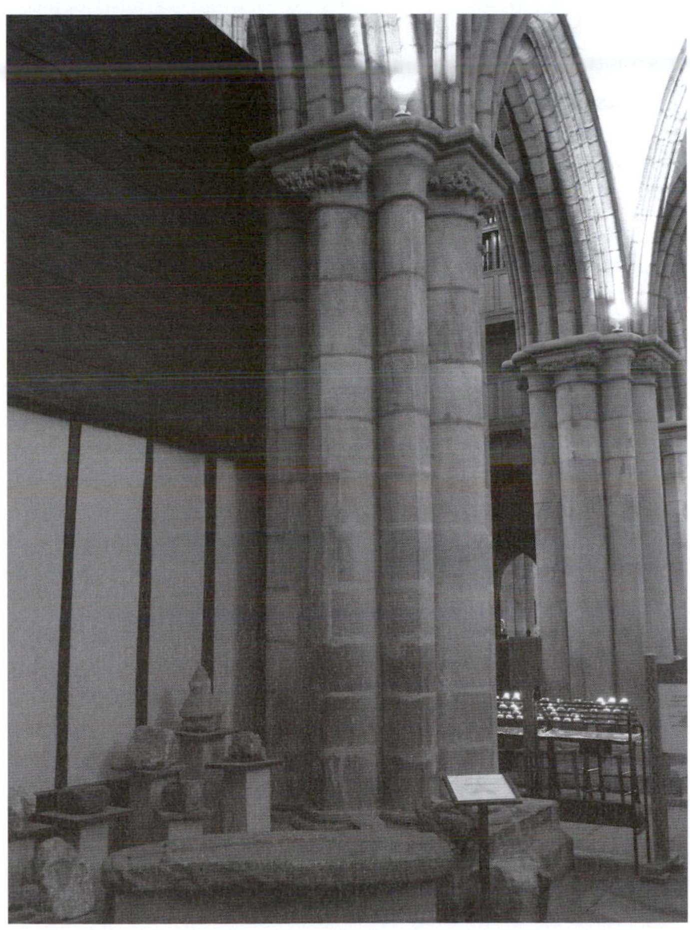

FIG. 8. Choir north arcade piers from the aisle

FIG. 9. Choir south arcade from the north-west, with the building break above the fourth arch from the left

between the shafts of the lay-brothers' door at Jervaulx, on the processional cloister door at Whitby, and in the clerestory at Tynemouth. The roof shafts are grouped monoliths at triforium level but change to coursed ones in the clerestory where they separate the bays of a tall two-storeyed triple arcade of two blind arches flanking a window, with a wall passage (Fig. 7).

The clerestory shows signs of hasty construction, with a rough finish to the inner wall surfaces and no masons' marks. The clerestory arcade design can be seen as a development of the wall arcade at Coldingham Priory, where a two-storeyed arrangement is used for the larger arches of the windows in the unaisled choir (Fig. 10). Coldingham was a daughter house of Durham, founded after 1098, and the two surviving walls of the choir are probably from the decade around 1200.[24] Hexham's arrangement uses lobed rather than square abaci, but it retains the sense of visual continuity effected by the use of grouped single-sized shafts at wall-passage height.

Overall, Hexham's closest stylistic links are with Arbroath, a royal foundation of 1178 of magnificent size with which it shared a patron, and which reflected the influence of St Andrews and Jedburgh.[25] As Richard Fawcett has established, Arbroath's piers are of the same form as Hexham's (but use octagonal bases), and the triforium of the nave is similar in both design and proportion to Hexham's choir, although more heavily built (Fig. 11). Arbroath's clerestory does not survive well enough to establish whether the two were similar. The completion date of Arbroath is not recorded: the east end was in a sufficient state to receive the burial of its founder in 1214 and it was consecrated in 1233, by which time the building was probably

Fig. 10. Drawing of Coldingham priory church from the west, by W. K. Hunter, published in 1858

complete. The interior of Hexham's choir is stylistically later than its aisle walls and belongs to a second campaign that was probably begun in the first or second decade of the 13th century.

One feature clearly adopted by Hexham from Arbroath (and St Andrews) is the type of respond used at the crossing.[26] At both Scottish sites a type of pier based on half an octagon with slender coursed shafts sunk, rather than inset, into the angles is used as a transept respond (Fig. 12). Hexham takes the idea further to create a new version in which the bases and separate capitals are removed, leaving the shafts to rise directly out of the pier base and to be subsumed into the pier core below the level of the single, large, moulded capital (Fig. 13). It is used opposite two different designs of arcade pier, in choir and transept, and makes no visual connection with either, or with the shafts of the eastern crossing pier to which it is attached, or with any of the four different arch mouldings which it supports.

CROSSING

THE crossing area is not fully consistent and bears evidence of changes of plan during its construction. The unusual crossing piers, made up of a square core to which are attached separate clusters of five round shafts towards the nave and transepts under

FIG. 11. Arbroath abbey church, nave, north-west bay
Photo by Richard Fawcett

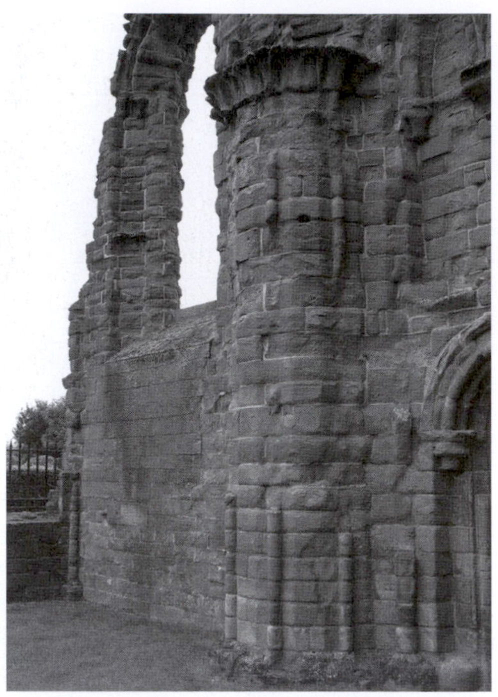

FIG. 12. Arbroath, south transept respond
Photo by Richard Fawcett

round abaci to the east and lobed ones to the west, were not all built at the same time (Fig. 14). Neither of the eastern piers is coursed in with the masonry of the adjacent transept walls, the north-west pier is only in bond until a few courses above the arch into the nave aisle, whereas the south-west pier is fully coursed into the corner of the nave and south transept for its entire height. Masons' marks are shared between the two eastern piers and the east arch, but only one of these marks appears on the lower courses of the north-west pier and the south-west pier has no marks. The sequence of construction is that the eastern crossing arch and its piers were built with the end of the choir, including the western faces of the piers and the transept responds, plus the first few courses of the mouldings of the main north and south arches and the toothings of the corner above. The transept east walls were built up against the standing piers, with the result that there are butt-joints between the arcade spandrels and the piers and disturbed areas of masonry in the upper levels (Fig. 15).[27] The western piers were then raised, with the corner of the south transept, and the crossing arches completed to a simpler design that replaced the roll mouldings of the outer orders with chamfers.

TRANSEPTS

THE plan of the transepts is as ambitious as that of the choir, with a four-bay arcade leading into an eastern aisle on each transept, a type that is only found otherwise on

FIG. 13. Hexham south choir aisle respond

FIG. 14. Hexham crossing piers from the south

major buildings in the region, such as St Andrews, Durham, and York. Work on the early stages of the south transept seems to have preceded that of the north since the design of the choir aisle exterior wall continues with only minor changes on to its east wall, whereas the north transept's aisle is very different to that of the choir and work was clearly halted at the end of the north choir aisle.[28] The slype was brought inside the building and occupies the end bay of the south transept.

On the interior the choir elevation is retained for the transept arcades with slight variations; new designs are used for the piers and the arcade arches have three orders of chamfer for the south and a complex series of narrow roll-mouldings for the north (Fig. 16 and Col. Pl. XXII in print edn). There is visual continuity in the triforium through the use of paired arches with a pierced spandrel under a round enclosing arch, with minor differences between the two sides, for example, the south side adopts the sunken shaft feature from the crossing responds, whereas the north does not.[29] The choir clerestory design is simplified for the transepts while retaining the basic concept of three tall openings in front of a central window. The roof supports repeat the form of the choir ones and change from detached to coursed shafts at the base of the clerestory in the south transept, but not in the north where they are detached for their entire length.

SOUTH TRANSEPT

THE south wall demonstrates a sophisticated and perfectly aligned relationship between the two upper storeys in which the inner side of the arch jambs on one level

FIG. 15. North transept, east wall, bay next to the crossing

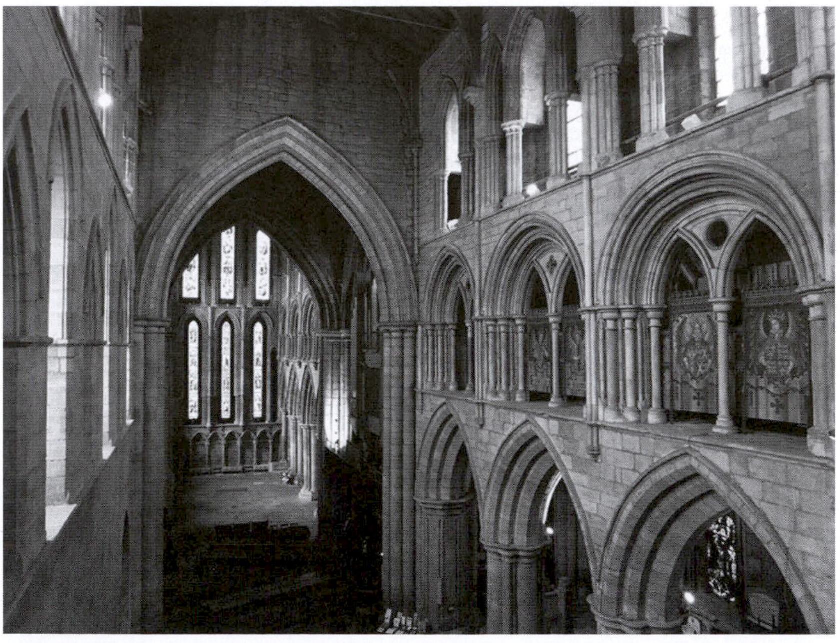

FIG. 16. View across the eastern side of the transepts from the south-west

FIG. 17. South transept from the north

line up with centres of the arches on the other (Fig. 17). Its debt to Coldingham's east wall is evident in the relationship between the arches framing the passage and those set at a higher level that frame the windows of the clerestory (compare Fig. 10). The two upper storeys derive their levels from the east wall, and a subtle adjustment was made to the length of the corner shafts in the clerestory to effect the transition to a different proportion scheme on the south wall (Fig. 18). It was repeated in reverse for the west clerestory.

The west wall presents a marked contrast with a conspicuous lack of alignment between the two upper levels (Fig. 19). The triforium string-course drops down in the corner to allow the west windows to be longer, and the arcade design of the south wall continues for part of the first bay, but then changes to a plainer form without shafts, deep mouldings, or vertical divisions into bays. At no point are the clerestory windows in line with any of the triforium openings, as is apparent on the exterior where the two levels of windows are clearly out of alignment (Fig. 20).

FIG. 18. South transept east and south clerestories, with the stepping up of the capital height in the south-east corner

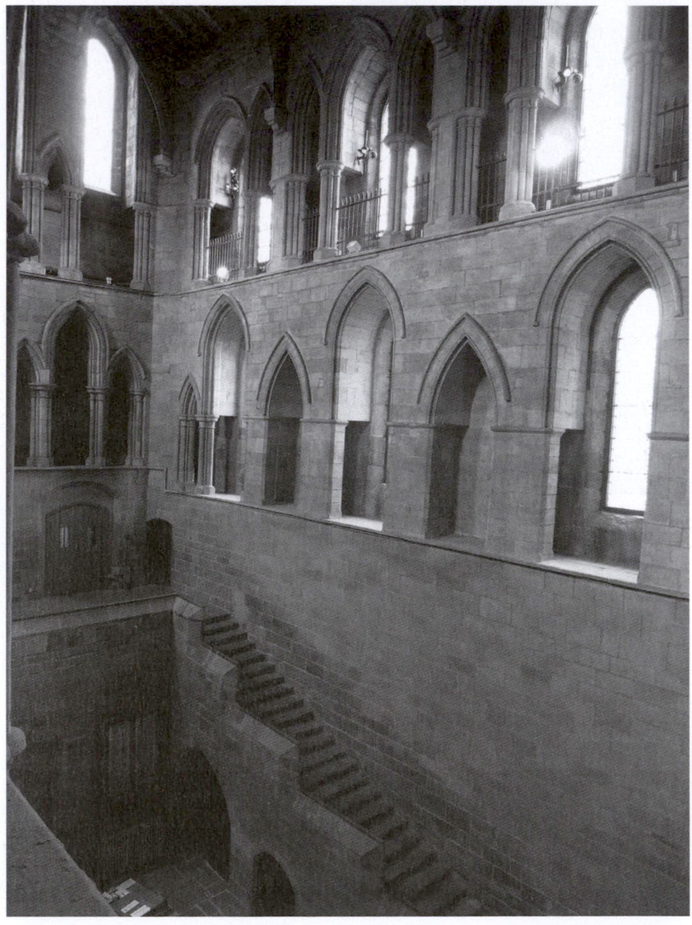

FIG. 19. South transept west wall from the north-east

FIG. 20. Exterior west wall of the south transept from the cloister site

It seems to have been the siting of the most northerly window very close to the end of the triforium, to provide light for the crossing area, that has resulted in the misalignment. The clerestory window could not be sited above it since the tower stair, that rises from the clerestory passage, is positioned in the corner and the security of the tower would have been compromised by having another void there.[30]

The cloister wall arcade is also irregular and its groups of arches reflect the different functions of the transept, slype and east range rather than form a regular row. The left six arches include a processional door from the cloister (as at a number of other Augustinian sites with a single aisle to the nave, such as Brinkburn, Lanercost, Newstead and Bolton), and starts with an additional half-bay, due partly to the increased width of the arch over the door, but also to a failure to account for the thickness of the nave wall at the planning stage. To the right the slype wall arcade is steeper and surrounds its doorway. The last of its arches on the right is smaller and originally formed part of an alternating sequence with the larger openings that flanked the chapter-house vestibule door, which have not been restored.[31]

The masons' marks on the south transept reveal a consistency in its construction with the same marks occurring on all the elevations and at each level. Connections between the three walls are strong, and virtually all the clerestory marks are also present in the triforium and on the ground level. There is no evidence for the upper levels, or the whole elevations, being built at different times. In particular, the marks on the west wall demonstrate that there is a marked consistency between its three levels, and that there was no interruption during their construction.

SOUTH SIDE OF THE NAVE

THERE is some evidence for the elevation of the south wall of the early 13th-century nave preserved at the crossing. The end of the west triforium passage passes behind the crossing pier from the south transept and continues for about 1.5 m (5 ft), before being blocked. The coursing is continuous and the passage runs at the same horizontal level as that of the west side of the transept. There is a second passage at clerestory level and the unaisled side of the nave must therefore have had an elevation with two articulated upper storeys above the blank wall covered by the cloister alley on the exterior. Traces of the string-courses for each level can still be seen on the exterior wall, together with the jamb of one clerestory window.

NORTH TRANSEPT

THE north transept was intended to be the more important liturgical space, with discrete chapels in the aisle that were separated by low walls, as at Lincoln cathedral, and a greater elaboration of its surfaces at ground level through the addition of wall arcades. Both transept aisles have rib vaults but the north has carved bosses, and ribs that spring from sculpted corbels, whereas the south is plainer. The construction of the north transept seems to have been more protracted than that of the south with much less consistency in the masons' marks.

It is probable that the spacing of the south transept arcade piers, which made all the bays the same width, was an error, since it compromised the end bay of the choir aisle vault and required the addition of an extra rib to support it. This is not repeated on the north, and the treatment of its elevations reveals a different approach to alignment. The most marked contrast is between the western exteriors of the two transepts, with the irregular spacing of the south not repeated on the north and instead, tall buttresses rising up to create bays with two tiers of perfectly aligned lancets.

The north facade uses the classic early Gothic design of two levels of tall lancets seen, for example, at York, Whitby, or Lichfield in the first half of the 13th century (Fig. 1). Whitby's north transept (Fig. 21), with its eastern aisle and similar design of wall arcade, bears some resemblance to Hexham's, but the tall vertical shafts that link the two levels at Whitby end abruptly at the string-course when used at Hexham because the upper windows are not aligned with the lower ones there (Fig. 22).[32] Hexham's south transept scheme of continuing the triforium and clerestory at about the same level across all three walls, which Whitby shares, is not followed for the north transept, and only the north and west walls maintain the same levels for the upper storeys. The east elevation has little in common with them. In part this is due to a change in design for the north wall, but it is clear that the original design only included a continuation of the level of the clerestory, and not the triforium.

Building work began with the aisle outside wall, which included the return wall on the north, and the two large buttresses there, together with the arcade respond, the toothings for the three levels of the east elevation, and part of the north wall, and the sites of the arcade piers.[33] The east arcade and the triforium were then built from the crossing at the same height as those of the south transept and choir and problems were encountered when the north bay was reached. The arch supported by the north respond was taller than the other arches, and had already been partly raised on its centring to await the arrival of the voussoirs supported on the pier, and the end of

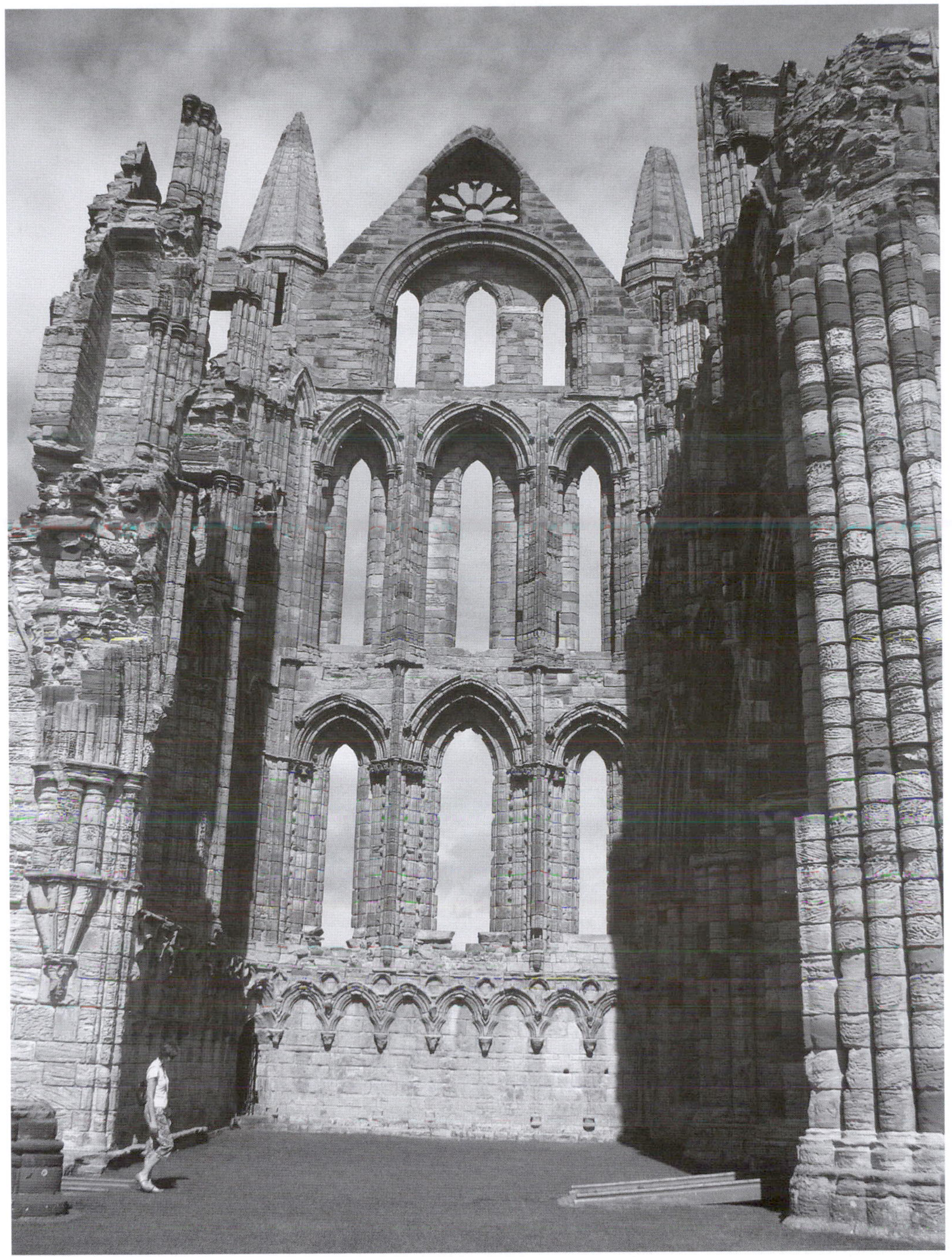

FIG. 21. Whitby abbey, north transept

FIG. 22. Hexham, north transept north and east walls

the triforium had been set at the higher level.[34] Once the arch was built the string-course at the base of the triforium had to rise to clear it and the detached shafts of one side of the triforium arch were shortened (Fig. 23). The clerestory, to the same design as those of the south transept, was then built between the two fixed points of the crossing pier and corner of the north elevation (Fig. 15).

The design of the north wall was changed at that stage, and the low blind arch on the extreme end of the lower lancets modified (Fig. 22). The arch is of a simpler design than those of the second scheme and consisted of a group of slender shafts rising from an octagonal base above the dado with capitals supporting the arch head, of which one remains. The new design took the stilted arches on shafts of the east clerestory windows and elongated the mouldings further to frame the lancet windows. On the exterior there are the remains of the framing for the first scheme, which would have

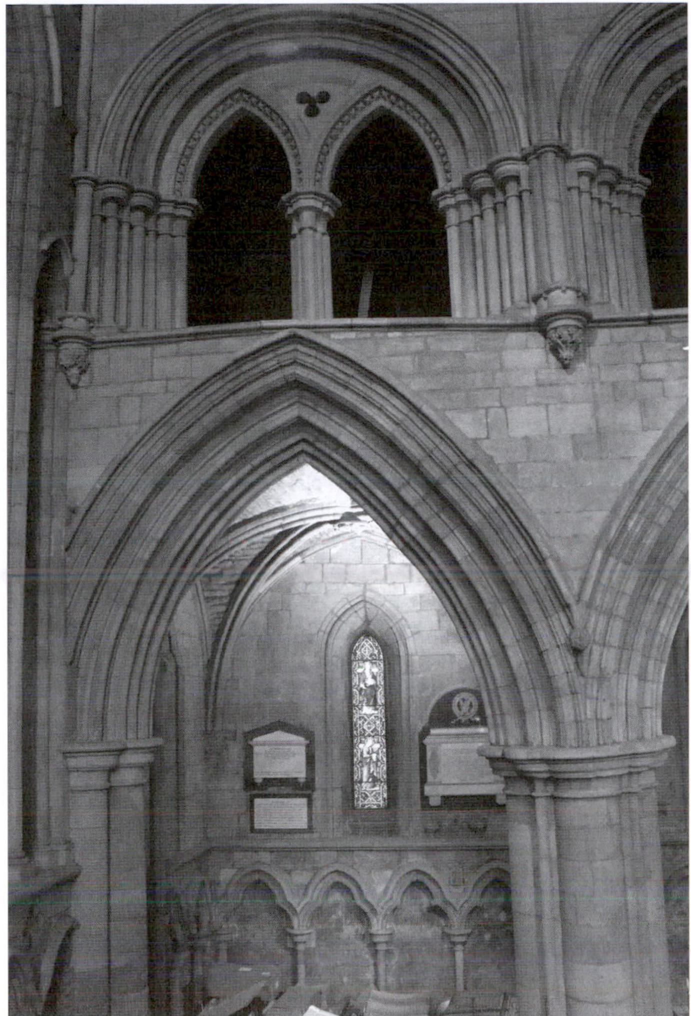

FIG. 23. Hexham north transept north-east bay with distortion to the right side of the arch and raised string-course

resembled that of Brinkburn's west facade, and consist of the annulets for the detached shafts of the arch, their bases, and one capital with a second one moved up to support a blind arch at the new level, with its original site still visible as a disturbance in the masonry (Fig. 1). Since the first scheme would have accommodated a row of windows with flanking blind arches of similar width but lower height to those built, it is possible that the arched heads are those designed for the original windows.[35]

The north clerestory was intended to be at the same height as the eastern one, but the new design required slightly longer windows and so an extra sub-base was installed in the north-east corner, the string-course was stepped down and all the arches of the second phase were sprung from a lower point.[36] It seems likely that the stones for all the northern shafts had already been cut since their length and design remain the same as those of the east clerestory and the bases are the same octagonal shape (Fig. 22).

The most profound change, however, was to the number of storeys. The original design was meant to include a narrow fourth storey to the north wall, sited between the two levels of lancets and would, most probably, have consisted of a row of arches fronting a wall passage, or perhaps a row of windows as at Salisbury cathedral. The height of the storey would have been less than that of the triforium of the east wall (Fig. 24), so it is unlikely to have continued its design across on to the north wall, but a row of narrow lancets, as used for the north wall of Lincoln's west transept, is possible (Fig. 25). The blocked entry to the wall passage running westwards above the original low arch survives in the north-east corner, and the masons' marks on it demonstrate that the change of design happened at the same time as the north bay of the east triforium was built. The same masons went on to cut the stone for the second phase of the north wall. The west wall continues the second design of the north wall, with its triforium based on the new north clerestory design in which tall, narrow arches that are open to the rear wall flank the windows (Fig. 26).

It seems probable that the design is the work of a second master mason, who was recruited after the east side of the north transept had been constructed, since the second phase brings in a new sense of lightness and a much greater voiding of the wall made possible by abandoning the fourth storey. The increase in the height of the triforium, so that it starts above the wall arcade, results in it having a remois passage rather than a triforium one, and, while Lincoln's west transept has a passage at a similar height, it is at the base of a lower arcade since its elevation has three levels of windows above the dado (Fig. 25). The contrast between the triforium designs for the west walls of the two arms of the transept, the mass and solidity of the south side and the transparency of the north, and the alignments of their relative levels, strongly suggest that they are the work of two different master masons (compare Figs 19 and 26).

THE SEQUENCE OF CONSTRUCTION OF THE EAST END

THE phasing of the building programme can now be summarized, drawing together the archaeological and stylistic analysis combined with the evidence of the masons' marks mentioned briefly above. The distribution of the marks shows that, although work on the building was not continuous, it was undertaken within the working lives of a group of masons whose marks can be found across the Gothic building. A total of sixty-two different marks was found in the building, of which sixteen were only on one stone and thus excluded from the analysis, although it is probable that other examples of their work may exist in inaccessible places.

Building work began at the east end with the choir aisles and east wall, including the south transept aisle wall. No masons' marks were found there, but the wall surfaces are very abraded and marks may have been lost. After an interval a second campaign was started in which the choir piers of the first three bays from the east were raised, to be followed by the last two pairs, after the Romanesque choir had been removed, and then the eastern crossing piers and arch. The west crossing piers and the remaining arches had to wait until the west sides of the transepts were under construction. The north transept aisle and its north-east corner were then built, ahead of the arcade. It is evident that the transepts were started before the choir was finished, since some of the choir pier masons moved directly on to the transept arcades, which followed on from the north transept aisle wall, while others started work on the triforium of the choir, and then joined the transept team.[37]

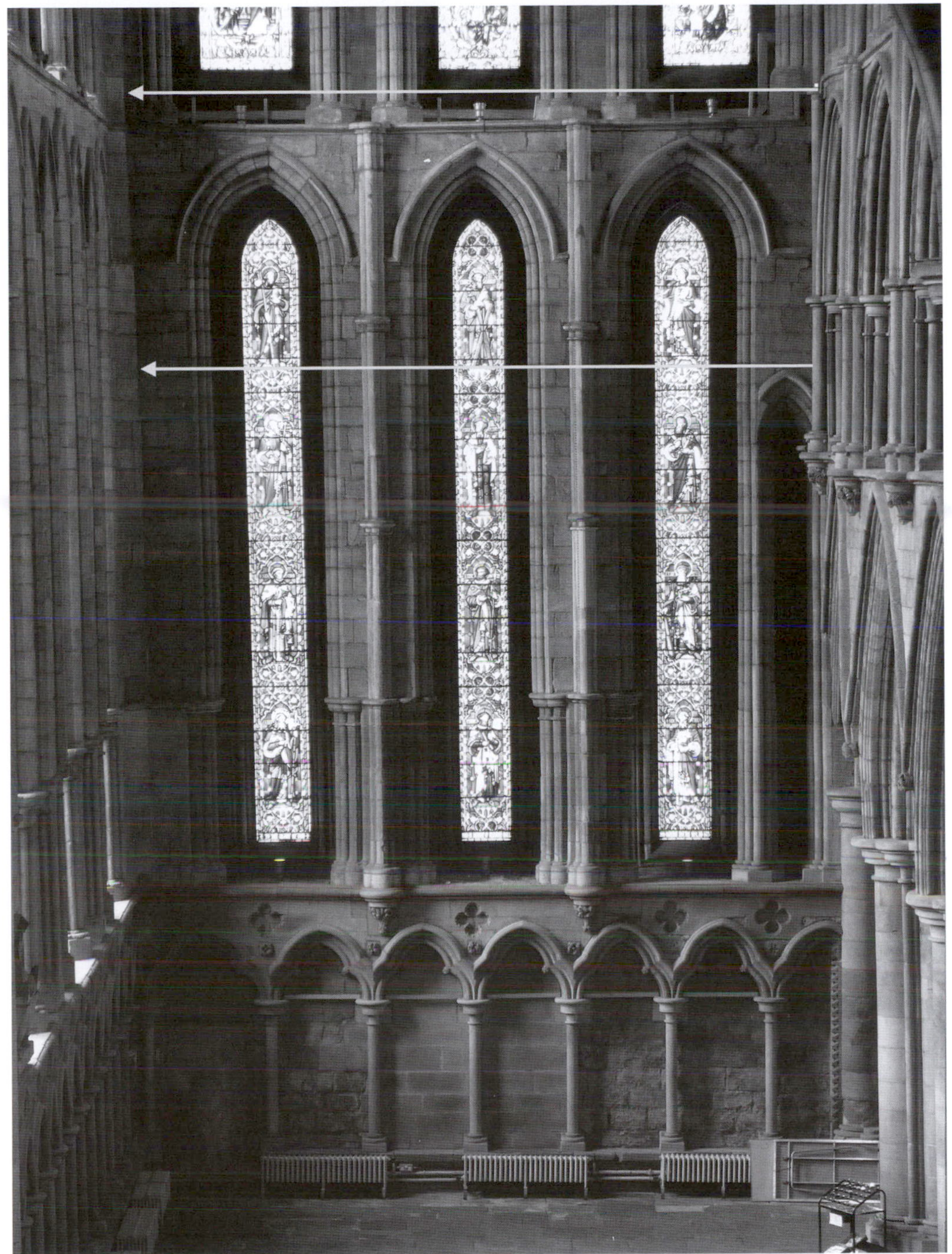

Fig. 24. Site of the intended fourth storey of the north transept north wall

FIG. 25. Lincoln west transept from the south

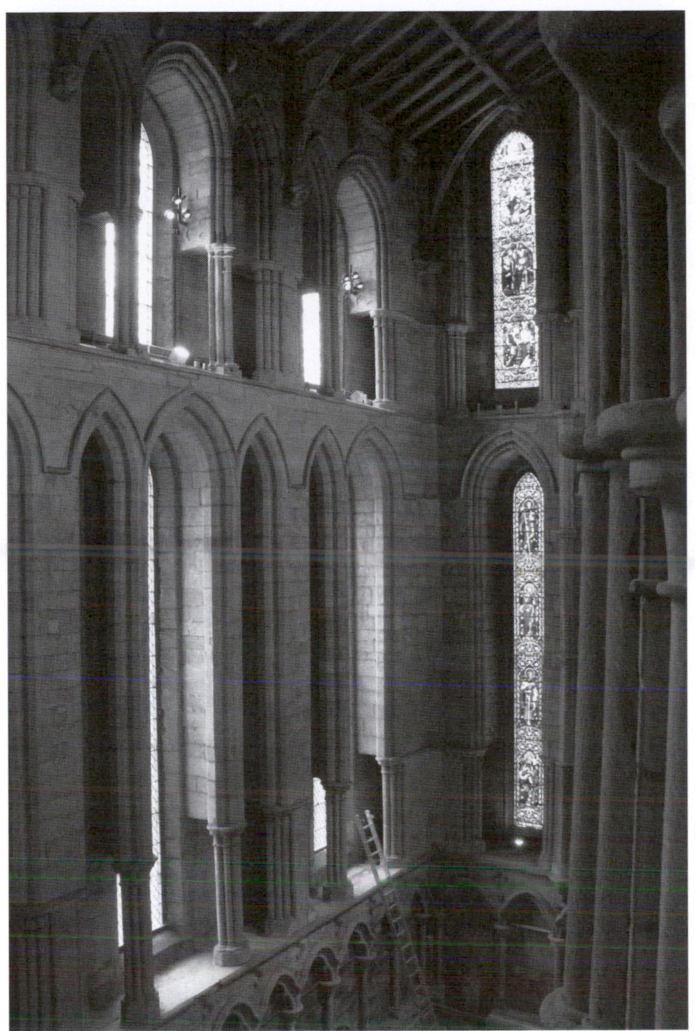

Fig. 26. Hexham north transept west wall from the south east

The choir workforce increased to work on the transepts and only two choir masons did no further work on the building, with a core team of masons providing continuity between the projects by working on the choir and both transepts. The choir triforium continues without a break into the south transept with the same masons working on stone for both, but this is not the case on the north where the marks change after the bay next to the crossing to marks from the lower levels of the south transept.

The south transept was built rapidly by a large team of masons who moved between work on the three elevations, whereas the north transept is much less consistent. Some masons worked on both transepts, but since most of their work was concentrated on one side, usually on the south, it is more probable that two teams were at work.[38] Far fewer marks can be found on the north transept, with whole areas, such as the west clerestory, not marked, which suggests that the change in design, here attributed to a replacement of the master mason, was also accompanied by a different scheme for paying the masons.

CONCLUSION

HEXHAM'S building programme was an ambitious project that was started in the late 12th century and continued into the early 13th. The work progressed as far as the nave, which seems to have been a more modest undertaking than the east end. It is uncertain how far this had progressed before the start of a period of bloodshed and unrest which must have had a catastrophic effect on the canons and their tenants. Repairs were made, and some new projects started, but the opportunities for building work on the scale of that undertaken in the early Gothic period were never to be available again.

ACKNOWLEDGEMENTS

I am grateful to the staff of Hexham priory in allowing me complete access to all parts of the building and to Professor Richard Fawcett and Stuart Harrison for sharing their knowledge of northern buildings with me.

NOTES

1. A description of the church built by Wilfrid in 674–78 is in *The Life of Bishop Wilfrid by Eddius Stephanus*, trans. B. Colgrave, (Cambridge 1927), 44–46.

2. *The Priory of Hexham: Its Chroniclers, Endowments, and Annals*, ed. J. Raine, 2 vols, SS 44, 46 (Durham 1864–65). The relevant documents are in the Appendix to vol. I.

3. Ibid., II, xxvii–xxviii, from the annals of the priory, written by Prior Richard (1141–*c.* 1160). Two doorways with round heads in the west cloister range may have been part of Asketill's work: E. Cambridge and A. Williams et al., 'Hexham Abbey: A Review of Recent Work and its Implications', *AA*, 23 (1995), 83.

4. *Priory of Hexham* (as n. 2), I, lxxiii, 194. The translation was described by Aelred of Rievaulx and by Prior Richard, but neither makes any reference to a new building in which the events took place. Fabric evidence is slight. The robbed-out remains of the apse were rediscovered in 1908 under the west bays of the current choir, immediately to the east of an earlier apse, and assumed therefore to have come from a Romanesque building. Eric Cambridge's 1984 excavation of the chapter-house vestibule area found slight traces of fabric identified as 12th-century, and he interpreted these as the east wall of a cloister, part of a building previously excavated by C. Hodges and associated with the church which ended in the apse, Cambridge and Williams, 'Hexham' (as n. 3), 83–86. A western respond base surviving from the medieval nave is illustrated in E. S. Savage and C. C. Hodges, *A Record of All Works Connected with Hexham Abbey since January 1899 and Now in Progress* (Hexham 1907), pl. xx. It has a square core to which are attached bases for three half-shafts of similar size, all having a double-hollow moulding, regarded by Rigold as having a late 11th-century date, S. E. Rigold, 'Romanesque Bases in and South-east of the Limestone Belt', in *Ancient Monuments and their Interpretation: Essays presented to A. J. Taylor*, ed. M. R. Apted, R. Gilyard-Beer and A. D. Saunders (Chichester 1977), 110.

5. '[. . .] barbara feritate flammis aedificia sacrata destruentes', *Priory of Hexham* (as n. 2), I, xxiv–vi, and 'Prioratum cum tota villa incendio destruxerunt', ibid., I, lxxxi, quoting the chronicle of Thomas of Walsingham.

6. The canons were dispersed to other Augustinian houses in early 1298 since, as well as their house, their lands had been plundered and crops destroyed (*Priory of Hexham* (as n. 2), I, xxvi–xxvii). In 1301 a canon who had retained some of his patrimony was required to donate five marks to the works on the cloister roof and to the church fabric fund (ibid., xl–xli). In 1310 Archbishop Greenfield ordered the consecration of altars

within the priory at Hexham 'de novo constructa seu noviter reparata' (ibid., xlv–xlvi, lxxx–lxxxiii). In 1314 the area was under Scottish occupation and the canons of Hexham were unable to collect rents or produce from their lands, requiring Archbishop Greenfield to lend them £40 in February 1315 to tide them over (ibid., lx). The canons were unable to support themselves despite this and Greenfield again made provision for Augustinian houses in Yorkshire to provide temporary shelter for them (ibid., lx–lxi). The Scots withdrew later in 1315 and the archbishop wrote to the prior in September encouraging him to return to Hexham (ibid., lx, note). The peace was short-lived. In 1317 Archbishop Melton recorded the destruction at Hexham in a letter, in which he described their houses and manors reduced to cinders ('redactic in cineres') and the canons dispersed again (ibid., lxi–lxii). Further problems were encountered around 1320 with more raids, and the priory lands were affected by a cattle murrain which devastated their herds, leading to another dispersal of the canons (ibid., lxiii–lxv). In 1335 and 1336 canons visited Yorkshire and the provinces to raise funds for restoration (ibid., xcv); a further raid in 1346 left the church despoiled (ibid., xcvii).

7. For the sacristy, see P. Ryder, 'The Sacristy/Chapel', in Cambridge and Williams, 'Hexham Abbey' (as n. 3), 99–100; for the east chapels, see below and n. 10.

8. The donation of 400 marks towards the building works in 1429 almost certainly refers to work on the nave: E. Cambridge, 'C. C. Hodges and the Nave of Hexham Abbey', *AA*, 5th ser. 7 (1979), pp. 158–68. As Raine pointed out, the destruction of the nave in 1296 can only be ascribed to tradition (*Priory of Hexham* (as n. 2), lxxxii, note *h*). For the 13th-century period, see further below.

9. See further below, and n. 10. The most important antiquarian texts are: A. B. Wright, *An Essay Towards a History of Hexham in Three Parts* (Alnwick 1823); C. C. Hodges, *The Abbey of St Andrew Hexham* (London 1888); idem, *Guide to the Priory Church of St Andrew, Hexham* (Hexham 1913); idem, and J. Gibson, *Hexham and its Abbey* (Hexham 1919); idem, *Guide to the Priory Church of St Andrew, Hexham*, 2nd edn, rev. J. Gibson (Hexham 1921); idem, 'The Conventual Buildings of the Priory of Hexham, with a Description of a Recently Discovered Twin Capital from the Cloisters', *AA*, 3rd ser. 21 (1924), 214–23.

10. N. Coldstream, 'The Eastern Chapels', in Cambridge and Williams, 'Hexham Abbey' (as n. 3), 95–99. By 1823 the chapels had passed out of use for services and were not included in the 18th-century restoration of the choir; Wright, *Hexham* (as n. 9), 63–64. The restoration also increased the height of the gable, which necessitated the raising of the roof of the east bay; the east aisle bay was rebuilt on both sides; the Perpendicular window in the south-east bay was replaced by a lancet; the east bay of the clerestory was refaced.

11. Masons, carpenters, plumbers and smiths were at work on a substantial restoration campaign that continued under the patronage of a local magnate from the 1720s to 1740 when the choir was given galleries, and by the end of the 18th century the east wall had been panelled and a triple pulpit and the reredos installed: Northumberland Record Office, QSB, Northumberland Quarter Sessions, 'Midsummer at Hexham 1720' (includes a report of Hexham priory church being much out of repair, followed by accounts for building work totalling over £4,000, 2–3); Wright, *Hexham* (as n. 9), 82.

12. Hodges, *Abbey of St Andrew* (as n. 9), pl. 37, fig. 1. It is possible to read the groups of shafts shown in Hodges' reconstruction drawing of the interior wall, as part of a lower row of blocked lancets, but there is no other evidence for this feature.

13. Described as being 'almost uniformly adopted' by the English Augustinians, M. F. Hearn, 'The Rectangular Ambulatory in English Mediaeval Architecture', *Journal of the Society of Architectural Historians*, 30 (1971), 201. Its use is not confined to the order, however, it can also be found for example at Benedictine Tynemouth at a similar date, *c.* 1190–1220, and it was used in Scotland at St Andrews, *inter alia*. For Lanercost, see H. Summerson and S. Harrison, *Lanercost Priory, Cumbria, a Survey and Documentary History*, Cumberland and Westmorland Antiquarian and Archaeological Society Research Series 10 (Kendal 2000).

14. Hearn's reconstruction of Ripon with a full-height east wall has been challenged by S. Harrison and P. Barker, who argue for an eastern aisle instead. M. F. Hearn, 'Ripon Minster: The Beginning of the Gothic Style in Northern England', *Transactions of the American Philosophical Society*, 73/6 (1983), 1–140; S. Harrison and P. Barker, 'Ripon Minster: An Archaeological Analysis and Reconstruction of the 12th-Century Church', *JBAA*, 152 (1999), 49–78.

15. See A. B. E. Clark, *Brinkburn Priory, Northumberland*, 2nd edn (London 1992).

16. P. Fergusson, *Architecture of Solitude, Cistercian Abbeys in 12th-Century England* (Princeton 1984), 84.

17. G. Coppack, S. Harrison and C. Hayfield, 'Kirkham Priory: The Architecture and Archaeology of an Augustinian House', *JBAA*, 148 (1995), 55–136; A. Clapham, *Whitby Abbey, Yorkshire* (London 1952); P. Fergusson and S. Harrison, *Rievaulx Abbey, Community, Architecture, Memory* (New Haven 1999). Carlisle's seven-bay choir, as originally built in the middle of the 13th century, had a short projecting eastern bay.

18. P. Draper, *The Formation of English Gothic: Architecture and Identity* (London 2007).

19. L. Hoey, 'Pier Design in Early Gothic Architecture in East-Central Scotland, *c.* 1170–1250', in *Medieval Art and Architecture in the Diocese of St Andrews*, ed. J. Higgitt, *BAA Trans.*, XIV (Leeds 1994), 85.

20. Hoey, 'Pier Design (as n. 19), 95 n. 14.

21. The apse was in the fourth bay from the east, Hodges, *Guide* (1913) (as n. 9), 32–34. The lack of alignment between the piers and responds at the west end of the aisles, most noticeable on the north, can be attributed to the construction of the aisle walls before the apse had been removed.

22. Construction of the north side seems to have been more piecemeal, with little consistency between the masonry of the spandrels.

23. Masons' marks are usually associated with piecework, since masons on regular wages had less need to record their output for a pay-master. See J. S. Alexander, 'Masons' Marks and the Working Practices of Medieval Stonemasons', in *Who Built Beverley Minster?*, ed. P. Barnwell and A. Pacey (Reading 2008), 21–40. Of the eleven masons who worked on the piers, only two are not found elsewhere in the building. Repairs to the piers may have distorted the evidence, but it is clear that one was on site for some time as his work can be seen on seven piers, whereas the other only worked on one and may therefore have only worked for one season.

24. R. Fawcett, *Scottish Medieval Churches* (Stroud 2002), 330. Fawcett has reconstructed the unaisled presbytery at Jedburgh with a similar elevation to Coldingham, although without the upper shafts: R. Fawcett, *Scottish Abbeys and Priories* (London 1994), 50.

25. R. Fawcett, 'Arbroath Abbey: A Note on its Architecture and Early Conservation History', in *The Declaration of Arbroath: History, Significance, Setting*, ed. G. Barrow (Edinburgh 2003), 50–85. William the Lion, founder of Arbroath, was also a patron of Hexham: *Priory of Hexham* (as n. 2), xv.

26. Fawcett, *Abbeys and Priories* (as n. 24), 44.

27. It is most obvious above the north-east crossing pier, the equivalent area above the south-east pier has been disturbed by the later cutting in of a corner shaft.

28. The interior is less consistent on the south and the string-courses beneath the windows are at different heights in the choir and transept aisles.

29. The spandrel piercings have been reproduced in the replaced sub-arches on the north.

30. Lanercost's south transept also has a triforium window in the same position and the clerestory window is similarly offset to avoid structural problems.

31. Visible in Grimm's drawing from his Northumberland Sketchbook: see London, British Library, MS Additional 15543, fol. 39 (reproduced as pl. 13 of Hodges, 'Conventual Buildings' (as n. 9)).

32. In most facades with two levels of lancets, the windows do not line up since the upper windows are often of a different width than the lower ones, and Whitby's use of the shafts on the inner wall accentuates the fact that the lancets there are aligned.

33. The respond has a simpler design than the arcade piers, although its base was intended for one that matched. It is possible that it may be a later replacement since it is not coursed in to the masonry around it, but the south aisle also has a different respond to its arcade piers. The arch into the nave aisle has the same design as the transept arcade piers for the north jamb and a different one to the south.

34. A lack of suitable foundations caused the pier to sink towards the north and twist its side of the arch, presumably as the weight of the arch settled on it, and some voussoirs slipped. The arch did not fail, however, and the coursing of the spandrel blocks reveals little distortion, although problems are visible in the aisle vault, and the stair behind the respond has been filled in. The arch is asymmetric, as is the arch at the other end of the arcade which was built with the crossing pier to which it is attached, although that one is lower, which suggests that their geometry had been calculated before that of the main arcade arches.

35. These arches are replacements, but earlier ones are shown in 18th-century drawings, for example, Grimm's Northumberland Sketchbook, BL, MS Additional 15543, fol. 18. A second set of bases, with an annulet on a narrow course has partly been modified to support the taller arch on the right hand side of the arcade. The original design continues that of the transept aisle exterior where there is an arcade of arches on detached shafts surrounding the windows.

36. It is distinctly different to the treatment of the clerestory in the south transept where the string-course remains at the same height and the transition to a taller proportion for the terminal wall is effected by lengthening the shafts in the adjacent bays.

37. The choir clerestory has no marks and must have been built under a different payment scheme that did not require the masons to mark their stone.

38. One mason, who marked seventy-two stones, only has one sited in the north, with sixty-seven in the south and four in the crossing; another has twenty-six blocks in the south transept and only two in the north; a third mason's work consists of twelve marks in the south and a single one in the north.

Medieval Saints' Cults at Hexham

JOHN CROOK

This is a study of the physical setting of the saints' cults of Hexham priory. The veneration of relics appears to have been an important factor in the design of the well-known late 7th-century crypt, perhaps designed to house relics of saints that St Wilfrid had brought back from Rome. Hexham is also significant for its local cults: at least seven of its twelve Anglo-Saxon bishops were later regarded as saints, and the cults of Acca, Eata and Ealhmund were promoted by translations and enshrinements in the 11th century and again in the 12th century when new reliquaries were prepared. Very little physical evidence survives for these cults, and the movement of the relics and the way the saints were venerated must be worked out from documentary sources alone.

ON the north side of the choir of St Andrew's priory church at Hexham,[1] above the late medieval 'Great Pulpit', are seven 15th-century painted panels which, unusually given their subject matter, survived the Reformation. Their original location within the church is unknown; in the late 18th century they were at the east end of the choir aisles, and between 1870 and *c.* 1910 they served to screen off the vestry.[2] The panels portray, from west to east, full-length portraits of 'S. Alcmundus, S. Eata, S. Wilfridus, S. Johannes, S. Acca, S. Tondbertus, S. Cuthbertus'. Such is the last physical manifestation of what in the high middle ages was arguably the most impressive collection of saints' relics in the north of England. Hexham is unusual amongst English churches in that at least seven of the twelve bishops who had their seat there between 681 and around 820 were regarded as saints and were the subject of a local cult.[3]

In this paper I examine the documentary evidence for the saints' cults of Hexham and attempt to characterize the physical setting of those cults and the nature of the shrines where the saints' remains, their 'relics', were located. I look in particular at three periods in Hexham's history: the construction of the church under St Wilfrid and especially his crypt, the elevation of the relics of saints Acca, Ealhmund, and Eata in the 11th century, and two further translations of the relics in the 12th century. The task is not an easy one because so much of the great church has been rebuilt since the 11th century. The interpretation has to be teased out from the limited documentary record and such archaeological observations as have from time to time been made, mostly during construction projects. Where possible I have tried to place the Hexham cults in the wider context by comparing them with contemporary cults in other locations.

That the cult of saints was central to Hexham's life and activities from the outset is evident from the construction of its early crypt, the only part of the Anglo-Saxon church to have survived, apart from a few wall footings (Fig. 1). The crypt has aroused much scholarly interest since it was rediscovered in 1725,[4] and it has recently been the

BAA Trans., vol. XXXVI (2013), 141–151

FIG. 1. St Wilfrid's crypt: the north passage looking east

subject of a major study by Paul Bidwell for Tyne and Wear Archaeology, who has examined in detail the source of the recycled Roman masonry of which it was built.[5] The attribution of the crypt to St Wilfrid, founder of the church, relies mainly on the posthumous biography by his friend Stephen, the deacon of Ripon (known to earlier scholars as 'Eddius Stephanus').[6] Stephen professed himself overwhelmed by the quality of the stonework, the subterranean crypts, and the complexity of the church above ground. Any doubts that Wilfrid commissioned Hexham's crypt are dispelled by the fact that it shares several constructional idiosyncrasies with the crypt of his other church at Ripon, notably the use of an unusual ribbed technique for the vaulting, a feature which Bidwell suggests is of Mediterranean origin. Both crypts appear therefore to have been under construction in the 670s. The Hexham crypt must comprise the earliest phase of the church built on a site given to Wilfrid by Queen Æthelthryth, the future saint of Ely (where she is better known by her Latin name, St Etheldreda).

It is, indeed, the *Romanitas* of the two crypts that is their most obvious characteristic. They are the expression of a personality. Wilfrid must be regarded in the same light as those great church builders, such as Gregory the Great or Charlemagne, who imposed their own will on architecture, shaping buildings in a manner hitherto unknown. Stephen of Ripon emphasizes the point. No professional designer was involved: Wilfrid himself, instructed by the Holy Spirit, had considered how to carry out the works, and the result was unique. Stephen had not heard of any other building on this side of the Alps built in such a way. He was probably right in this perception, for in terms of architectural development the two crypts were indeed without issue.

It is in Rome that the sources of the crypt at Hexham are to be found. The point that emerges again and again in Stephen's biography is the way Wilfrid was influenced by Rome. In particular, his visit to that city as a twenty-year-old in 654–55 marked him indelibly: it had a direct effect on ecclesiastical policy in Northumberland, with Wilfrid's success at the Synod of Whitby, and it ensured that on two subsequent occasions, when insoluble conflicts occurred, Wilfrid returned to Rome to seek papal support. There Wilfrid's devotion to the cult of saints developed: Stephen tells us that for many months he went each day to pray at the 'places of the saints' (*loca sanctorum*), and he brought back to England a carefully catalogued collection of relics of Roman saints. He had a special devotion to St Andrew, and it was in that saint's oratory, a great rotunda on the south side of St Peter's basilica, that Wilfrid vowed to spread the Gospel — it is highly significant that the two major churches that he later founded in England, Ripon and Hexham, were dedicated to Saints Peter and Andrew respectively.

The 'places of the saints' would have included the pilgrimage churches that had been constructed over the extramural burial places of saints, frequently over former Roman catacombs. By the time of Wilfrid's visit most had become centres of pilgrimage cults, with churches erected directly above the tombs of the Roman martyrs. These pilgrimage sites included the churches of San Lorenzo, San Sebastiano, SS. Marcellino e Pietro, and, especially, San Pancrazio and Sant'Agnese, which had been reconstructed by Pope Honorius I only twenty to thirty years before Wilfrid's first trip to Rome. In all these churches, the guiding principle was that the graves of the titular martyrs should not be disturbed: the position of the high altar was therefore determined by the grave, which required careful architectural planning.

What Wilfrid achieved at Hexham was a Roman catacomb in miniature. The asymmetry of the access passages probably reveals a deliberate intention to disorient the visitor and to produce the kind of sensations Wilfrid would personally have experienced in the Roman churches. One is reminded of the way visitors to Old Minster, Winchester, at the end of the 10th century were similarly disoriented, requiring the help of a kindly guide to get them out.[7] The culmination of a visit to Hexham was when the pilgrim entered the main chamber, which in its design may have been inspired by the Merovingian shrine-crypts Wilfrid almost certainly saw on his way to and from Rome.

The crypt must therefore be regarded as the expression of Wilfrid's devotion to saints, in particular those of Rome. However, Hexham was not a church established on the site of a pre-existing local cult; the dedication was to an apostle whose supposed remains reposed in Constantinople, though a relic had presumably been brought to Rome to consecrate the oratory next to St Peter's. Thus, at Hexham we have a reversal of the situation in Rome. There, the churches were built over saintly relics which remained undisturbed; at Hexham, the church determined the position of the relic chamber, placed (we may reasonably assume) directly beneath the high altar.

Wilfrid ended his days as fifth bishop of Hexham (from 706), but he died at Ripon, so no major relic cult could develop in the Northumbrian church. That honour would be reserved to the succession of bishops of Hexham between 682 and *c.* 821. Some of those sainted bishops, whose portraits appear in the 15th-century panels in the chancel, also had cults elsewhere, such as St Cuthbert (later of Durham) and John of Beverley. Five of them were, however, buried at Hexham and three (Acca, Ealhmund and Eata) became the subject of major local cults in the mid-11th century.

These cults were largely due to the efforts of the sacrist of Durham cathedral, Alfred son of Westou (fl. *c.* 1025–60). His principal responsibility at Durham was the shrine of St Cuthbert, and to enhance that cult he travelled throughout Northumbria, hunting down relics that would be placed near to the main shrine as a supporting cast. Several of them feature in a relic list appended to one of the manuscripts of Symeon's *Libellus* in the late 12th century.[8] These secondary relics remained close to St Cuthbert's tomb-shrine throughout the middle ages, preserved in reliquary cupboards (*armoires*) on the feretory platform in Durham cathedral.

As well as being the Durham sacrist, with responsibility for Cuthbert's shrine, Alfred was also one of the hereditary priests of Hexham, and there were several potential saints in that church. Symeon of Durham tells us that amongst the many saints of Northumberland that Alfred 'raised from the earth' were the bishops of Hexham, Acca and Ealhmund.[9] Symeon's rather brief account was greatly amplified by two passages of uncertain date that were subsequently inserted into the *Historia Regum* that he had written *c.* 1129. The earliest manuscript in which the interpolations appear is late 12th century, but they were probably written at Hexham somewhat earlier. One of them describes the elevation of Bishop Acca (709–31), who had been buried outside the church in around 740, after nine years in retirement. His grave was marked with two marvellously carved Anglo-Saxon stone crosses, one of which was inscribed with his name (Fig. 2).[10] A cross-shaft fragment embellished with double vine-scroll that survives in Hexham church is traditionally identified as one of these crosses, though the identification must be regarded as an act of faith at best (Fig. 3).[11] Acca's sanctification followed the usual medieval formula of miraculous revelation ('invention'), exhumation ('elevation'), transfer into the church (*adventus*), and enshrinement: such was the way a local saint was created before canonization was reserved to the papacy in the mid-13th century. Given that the grave was marked, its discovery can scarcely be regarded as miraculous, nevertheless the interpolator stresses that the place where the future saint lay was revealed to 'a certain priest' (Alfred) by heavenly intervention. When the tomb was opened, Acca's chasuble, dalmatic and maniple (*sudarium*) were discovered, still intact, and his winding-sheet was also undamaged. Such survival was also a hagiographical commonplace. These items were still displayed in the church in the mid-12th century, when they were said to be as good as new.[12] Parts of them found their way to Durham, where they were mentioned in a late 14th-century relic list: 'an ivory casket with relics of St Acca the Bishop, with portions of his face-cloth and chasuble, which were in the ground for 300 years'.[13] Also within the tomb was a portable altar formed of two hinged wooden panels, bearing the legend 'Almæ Trinitati, agiæ Sophiæ, sanctæ Mariæ'.[14] Perhaps Acca had acquired it during one of his travels abroad with St Wilfrid, whom he accompanied to Rome.

The account of the elevation of Bishop Ealhmund (767–80/81) is very similar: originality was not regarded as a virtue in hagiographical writing; rather, conformity was an indication that the individual really was a saint.[15] The bishop had been buried next to Bishop Acca. In perhaps the 1040s he appeared to a local resident in a dream, instructing him to ask Alfred Westou to translate his remains into a worthier place within St Wilfrid's church. Such supernatural instructions, passed on to the main

FIG. 2. Acca cross shafts

FIG. 3. Detail of the larger Acca cross

protagonist at second hand, are another *topos* of hagiography and derive ultimately from an account of the elevation of St Stephen's relics in 415, as recorded later in the century by Gennadius of Marseilles.[16] A large crowd witnessed the proceedings at Hexham: the bones were exhumed, wrapped in a cloth, and placed in a casket (*scrinium*) supported on a bier (*feretrum*) which was carried into the *porticus* of St Peter, on the south side of the church, pending the ceremonial entry into the body of the building. During the vigil, whilst other watchers were asleep, Alfred removed a finger bone from the relics, intending to take it back to Durham. The saint was evidently displeased, and next morning the bier proved to be immovable — only when Alfred returned the relic was it possible to carry the relics into the church. The anecdote is another hagiographical commonplace; numerous examples could be given of saintly coffins which miraculously increased in weight because their occupants did not wish to be moved or had some concern that needed to be resolved.

The interpolator does not state where the shrines were placed within the church, but practice elsewhere suggests that they were placed at the high altar. Prior Richard, writing in the twelfth century, affirmed that Alfred had translated the remains into 'the more remote parts within the church' ('intra ecclesiam in remotioribus partibus'), but added that that they had subsequently been placed in the sanctuary: Acca to the right (south side) of the high altar, and Ealhmund to the left.[17] He may simply have been mistaken about this, for, as we shall see, by the early 12th century both sets of bones had been enshrined in a single reliquary behind the high altar.

Another Hexham saint was, however, enshrined not at the high altar but in a completely different part of the church. This was Bishop Eata. He was arguably Hexham's most prestigious saint, given that he had been a pupil of St Aidan at the abbey of Lindisfarne. He rose to the position of abbot of Melrose, where his pupils included two future saints: his prior, Boisil, and the young Cuthbert. Subsequently, Eata was appointed bishop of Lindisfarne then — for little more than a year — of Hexham, where he died in 686.

Eata's cult appears to have followed a somewhat different course from Acca and Ealhmund. According to his Life, probably a 12th-century compilation, he was originally buried 'next to the sanctuary of the aforesaid church of Hexham, on the south side, and a small stone chapel was built over his tomb';[18] later his remains were placed together with due honour within the church (*intra ecclesiam*). The author of the Life thought it likely that Alfred Westou was also responsible for this translation,[19] though had this been the case, one might have expected his grandson, Ailred of Rievaulx, or that great historian Symeon of Durham to have mentioned it. Prior Richard makes it clear, however, that the shrine was in a *porticus* on the south side of the presbytery: it was perhaps the *porticus* of St Peter where Ealhmund's body temporarily rested on the eve of his translation. The archaeological excavations of 1978 showed that the southern passage of the crypt passed under the south wall of the nave, and it is therefore just possible that it emerged in a south-east *porticus*. Were that the case, then from the time of Alfred Westou until the mid-12th century translation of Eata's relics, a pilgrim would not only visit the relics of the patron, St Andrew, but his visit would continue with the veneration of a local saint, St Eata – the sort of multiplication of pilgrim sites within a single building that would later be found at Canterbury with its various *loci* for the veneration of Thomas Becket.

Thus, at the Conquest Hexham had three shrines of local saints: Acca and Ealhmund at the high altar, and Eata in a *porticus* south of the sanctuary. Other relics of pre-Conquest bishops were subsequently claimed in the church, but their cult was centred on relics of dubious authenticity, and they seem to have played a supporting role to the main cast of saints.

The documentary evidence for the movements of Hexham's relics in the immediate post-Conquest period is somewhat confused, and we are dependent on the testimony of Prior Richard and Ailred of Rievaulx, both writing long after the events, together with the interpolations in Symeon of Durham which may be more or less of the same date as the other two sources. Ailred is likely to be the best witness, given that he was related to some of the protagonists from whom he could have gleaned first-hand information. He tells us that the church was derelict as a result of 'Danish' invasions, but, at the time Durham cathedral became a monastery in 1083, his grandfather Eilav, one of the dispossessed canons, petitioned Archbishop Thomas of Bayeux to be allowed to restore the church of Hexham.[20] Eilav died before that project was completed, and the work was taken up by his son, Eilav II. This Eilav reroofed the church, and restored the high altar platform; and he discovered the relics of Acca and Ealhmund. Once again the *porticus* of St Peter proved a useful temporary store, where Eilav placed the holy bones on a linen sheet on top of the altar. Unwisely, as it turned out, he put his adolescent brother Aldred on guard. The boy tried to extract a relic for his personal use, in which attempt he was thwarted by saintly intervention. Finally, Eilav placed the relics together in a single reliquary shrine, supported on a stone slab. This sounds like a typical table shrine of the period, consisting of a slab raised on pillars. The shrine provided for St Cuthbert in 1104 at Durham cathedral was of this form, consisting of a stone slab behind the high altar, raised up on nine pillars.[21] This is significant: Eilav may well have been trying to emulate at Hexham the newly installed shrine at Durham, where his father had been a canon.

Not surprisingly, Ailred credited his father with the creation of more prestigious arrangements for the Hexham saints, but he then rather confusingly introduced what seems to be a variant tradition. He told how one of the first Augustinian canons to be installed in 1113 by Archbishop Thomas II of York, Edric, discovered two caskets beneath the high altar, containing bones and dust, identified by labels (*tituli*) as relics of Acca and Ealhmund.[22] Two miracles followed, but Ailred did not say what Edric did with the relics. The story was repeated with further variation by the author of the interpolated passages in Symeon's *Historia Regum*: Edric was investigating a 'heap of earth' within the church's chancel, near to the high altar, and unearthed just one small wooden chest, containing (as two labels proclaimed) relics of St Acca.[23] However, these relics were probably small additional relics previously separated from the principle shrine, and in this light the anecdotes are not incompatible with the notion that the main shrine was by 1113 located behind the high altar.

The next insight we have into the cult of saints at Hexham is in the mid-12th century. There seems at this time to have been a renewed interest in saints' cults throughout England. At Winchester in 1150, for example, 'relics were translated of the holy confessors Birinus, Swithun, Hæddi, Beornstan, and Ælfheah',[24] perhaps by Bishop Henry of Blois, though this is not made clear in the contemporary account. In the same year, the body of the ritually murdered child William of Norwich was translated into that cathedral. Then in 1154, Alexander, prior of Ely, translated into his cathedral priory church the bones of seven of his church's greatest benefactors, including Archbishop Wulfstan of York, Ealdorman Brihtnoth, and five pre-Conquest bishops.[25] The event may have encouraged Bishop Henry of Blois, just back from exile at Cluny, to bring the benefactors of his own church closer to the relics of St Swithun in 1158. He created within the choir apse a platform on which the altar of the saint with its reliquary was raised up, with a tunnel beneath, the 'Holy Hole', giving suppliants limited proximity to the relics, and he placed on walls around the apse the remains of the aforesaid benefactors, who were pre-Conquest king and bishops, so that they could benefit from the power of the saint.[26]

It is in this febrile atmosphere that we should consider the translation of the Hexham saints in 1155. The account of proceedings written by Ailred of Rievaulx is particularly valuable as one of the most complete surviving descriptions of a major translation in the mid-12th century.[27] He explains that the Augustinian canons of Hexham felt that their saints were no longer worthily enshrined; they were indignant that they were housed together in wooden boxes, scarcely a worthy or glorious sight for the common people who so often enjoyed the benefits that the saints could confer on them.[28] So, having discussed the matter and worked themselves up into a fine frenzy, they approached Prior Richard with a proposal to house the relics in a more becoming manner. Accordingly, three new reliquaries were prepared. The largest was 'of suitable size, covered with silver and gold', and adorned with jewels.[29] The two smaller reliquaries were equally finely decorated but more cheaply.[30] Prior Richard announced the date of the translation, and the brethren prepared themselves with psalms, prayers, and spiritual exercises.

The great day arrived, and at around nine in the morning the prior and brethren assembled in the church, prostrating themselves barefoot in front of the high altar. They chanted in a loud voice both the penitential psalms and suitable prayers for confessors. Then, dressed in albs and still barefoot, the brethren placed the main chest on the pavement west of the altar step, a suitably spacious and sacred working area. Having taken out the relics, they laid them out on cloths (*pallia*) on the pavement. They found that there were four sets, each wrapped in a most elegant cloth. As the canons began to unroll the bundles they were conscious of a marvellous fragrance, and at first they conjectured that the bodies had been buried with spices (*aromata*). Then they realized that they were smelling the sweet scent of Paradise, which God had conferred on the bishops as an act of grace.

On opening the first bundle, gleaming bones were revealed. Fortunately, it was possible to identify which saint they belonged to, thanks to a label (*cedula*) proclaiming that the relics were those of Bishop Acca, believed to have died in 740. This must have been added by Eilav II at the previous translation. The bones were wrapped again in clean cloths, and, in order that the information provided on the *cedula* should not be lost, it was copied out on parchment and inscribed on a lead plate: 'in membrana simul et plumbi lamina eadem scribentes et sculpentes, reliquiis apposuerunt'.

The bones of Ealhmund were also conveniently identified by a similar label (Ailred does not say whether the canons recopied the information, though this must be likely). The contents of the third bundle also bore a label proving them to be relics of St Frithubeorht. Both sets of bones were wrapped up again. But the fourth set of relics was unmarked. Ailred then recalled that during his childhood it had been common knowledge that the *loculus* also contained the bones of Bishop Tilbeorht, so everyone accepted that the unnamed relics must be his. All four sets of bones, having been individually wrapped in precious cloths, were placed in the large reliquary in order that they should remain together just as they had been found.

Next the *scrinium* containing the bones of St Eata was brought from the south *porticus* and opened. Again, his sanctity was manifested by a miraculous fragrance. Within the reliquary was a lead *uas* (perhaps a purse reliquary) containing a few particles from the body of St Frithubeorht. The brethren replaced these in one of the reliquaries that they had prepared, together with fragments claimed to come from the body of St Babylas (a 3rd-century bishop of Antioch), and particles from the bones of St Acca and Ealhmund.

Finally, the *feretra* were set in place. A board or shelf (*tabula*) had been erected 'alongside' (*secus*) the high altar. It was supported on three columns and was decorated with 'sculptures' (*sculpturis*, presumably bas-reliefs) and paintings. The largest reliquary, containing the remains of Acca, Ealhmund, Frithubeorht and Tilbeorht, was set in the middle, flanked by the two smaller reliquaries: St Eata on the south side, and the relics of Frithubeorht from Eata's previous *theca*, together with fragments of the bones of Babylas, Acca and Ealhmund, on the north.[31] According to

Prior Richard, many other unnamed relics which had subsequently been given to the church were placed nearby, no doubt in order to benefit from the *præsentia* of the major saints.[32]

What can we make of the description of the way the reliquaries were displayed? According to Ailred the *tabula* was 'behind and next to' the altar (*retro et iuxta altare*); his use of the vague preposition *secus* suggests that the slab stood north–south parallel to the altar, and this is confirmed by the fact that it could support three reliquaries (Ailred calls them *thecæ*), one in the centre, and others to north and south. Given that it was supported on just three columns, the *tabula* was probably a shelf rather than a wide slab.

This integration of high altar and saintly relics is rather unusual; normally the shrine was located behind the high altar and at some distance from it, often with its own shrine altar. But some parallels for the arrangement at Hexham may be adduced. At Bury St Edmunds the saint's body had been translated in 1095, and was placed just behind the high altar, to which it was linked by a wooden platform (*ligneus tabulatus*), with a space underneath which was used by the sacrists for storing wax, thread, and other paraphernalia.[33] In 1198 this vulnerable structure caught fire when one of the candles on top of it fell over, and a new translation of the relics ensued.

The valuable accounts of the 12th-century hagiographers were not continued by later generations, and the cult of Hexham's local saints appear by the Reformation to have passed into complete oblivion. When in 1536 Henry VIII's commissioners, Drs Layton and Leigh, visited the northern dioceses, they carefully noted all examples of 'superstition' in the places they visited, especially pilgrimage and saints' cults. At Hexham, however, the only comment they made was, 'Here they have a missal called the red mass book of Hexham'.[34] The only contemporary reference to the sainted bishops seems to occur in a letter from Archbishop Lee to Thomas Cromwell in 1536, in which he observed regarding Hexham that 'many holy men, sometime bishops, there be buried in that church'.[35] There is no hint here that they were still regarded as saints, a sad decline which, perhaps, echoes that of the once-great church in which the bishops' cults formerly flourished.

NOTES

1. The church has long been known as 'Hexham abbey', though it was in fact an Augustinian priory from 1113 until its Dissolution in 1537.

2. E. S. Savage, *A Record of All Works Connected with Hexham Abbey since January 1899 and Now in Progress* (Hexham 1907), 53–54. The 'Great Pulpit' was also moved *c.* 1910, from the east side of the wall formerly blocking the west tower arch. (For these furnishings, see Charles Tracy's paper in this volume.)

3. Sidney Savage thought it likely that 'the original series comprised all twelve bishops of Hexham and not merely the seven that were canonized'; ibid., 53.

4. For example, James Raine; see *The Priory of Hexham: Its Chroniclers, Endowments, and Annals*, ed. J. Raine, 2 vols, SS 44, 46 (Durham 1864–65), II, xxxiii–xli; also H. M. Taylor and J. Taylor, *Anglo-Saxon Architecture*, 3 vols (Cambridge 1965–78), I, 252–55; R. N. Bailey, 'The Anglo-Saxon Church at Hexham', *AA*, 5th ser. 4 (1976), 47–67; idem, 'St. Wilfrid. Ripon and Hexham', in *Studies in Insular Art and Archaeology*, ed. C. Karkov and R. Farrell (Oxford, Ohio 1991), 3–25.

5. P. Bidwell, 'A Survey of the Anglo-Saxon crypt at Hexham and its reused Roman stonework', *AA*, 5th ser. 39 (2010), 53–145.

6. *The Life of Bishop Wilfrid by Eddius Stephanus*, ed. B. Colgrave (Cambridge 1927; repr. 1965).

7. Wulfstan Cantor, *Epistola specialis ad Ælfegum episcopum*, lines 49–60, in *The Anglo-Saxon Minsters of Winchester. Part 2: The Cult of St Swithun*, ed. M. Lapidge (Oxford 2003), 374–77.

8. Cambridge University Library, MS Ff i.27, p. 194. This manuscript is discussed by David Rollason in his edition of *Symeon of Durham, Libellus de exordio atque procursu istius, hoc est Dunhelmensis, ecclesie* (Oxford 2000), xxiv–xxix. The relic list is printed in *Symeonis Monachi Opera Omnia*, ed. T. Arnold, 2 vols, Rolls series 75 (London 1882–85), I, 168–69.

9. Symeon, *Libellus* (as n. 8), 162–65.

10. Symeon of Durham, *Historia Regum*, in *Symeonis Opera* (as n. 8), II, 32–33.

11. *Priory of Hexham* (as n. 4), I, xxxiv and plate on facing page; more recently discussed by R. Cramp, *County Durham and Northumberland*, Corpus of Anglo-Saxon Stone Sculpture in England 1 (Oxford 1984), 176.

12. *Priory of Hexham* (as n. 4), I, 36.

13. Printed in J. Raine, *St Cuthbert: with an Account of the State in which his Remains were Found upon the Opening of his Tomb in Durham Cathedral in the year MDCCCXXVII* (Durham 1828), 126.

14. *Symeonis Opera* (as n. 8), II, 33.

15. Ibid., 47–50.

16. *Epistola Luciani ad omnem æclesiam de revelatione corporis Stephani martyris primi et aliorum*, in *PL*, XLI, cols 807–18.

17. *Priory of Hexham* (as n. 4), I, 49.

18. Ibid, loc. cit.: 'In quadam enim porticu iuxta secretarium eiusdem ecclesiæ, versus australem partem, decenter in una theca collocatæ, quiescebant'.

19. Ibid., 124.

20. Ibid., 191.

21. *Symeonis Opera* (as n. 8), II, 359–60.

22. *Priory of Hexham* (as n. 4), I, 187.

23. *Symeonis Opera* (as n. 8), II, 35–36.

24. *Annales Monastici*, ed. H. R. Luard, 5 vols, Rolls series 36 (London 1864–69), II (Winchester and Waverley), 54, *s.a.* 1150: 'Hoc anno translatæ sunt reliquiæ sanctorum confessorum Birini, Swithuni, Æddæ, Birstani, Elfegi'.

25. J. Crook, '*Vir Optimus Wlstanus*: The Post-Conquest Commemoration of Archbishop Wulfstan of York at Ely Cathedral', in *Wulfstan, Archbishop of York*, ed. M. Townend, Studies in the Early Middle Ages 10 (Turnhout 2004), 501–24.

26. J. Crook, *St Swithun, Patron Saint of Winchester Cathedral* (Winchester 2010), 14–16.

27. *Priory of Hexham* (as n. 4), I, 190–95, 199–203.

28. Ibid., 193: 'Indignabantur vili tectos ligno, nichil gloriæ et honoris plebis præferre conspectibus, quæ eius beneficiis sæpius iocundabatur'.

29. Ibid., 194: 'Paratur theca congruæ magnitudinis, argentoque et auro vestitur. Inseruntur locis convenientibus gemmæ, et pro artificis industria opus summo decore variatur'.

30. Ibid., loc. cit.: 'Compinguntur etiam duæ minores non parvi decoris, quamvis non eiusdem pretii'.

31. *Priory of Hexham* (as n. 4), I, 200.

32. *Priory of Hexham* (as n. 4), I, 49.

33. J. Crook, 'The Setting of the Cult of St Edmund at Bury St Edmunds, 1095–1538', in *Medieval Art, Architecture, Archaeology, and Economy at Bury St Edmunds*, ed. A. Gransden, *BAA Trans.*, XX (Leeds 1998), 34–44.

34. *Letters and Papers, Foreign and Domestic, of the Reign of Henry VIII*, ed. J. Gardiner, R. H. Brodie and J. S. Brewer, 21 vols (London 1862–1920), X, 142 (item 364).

35. Ibid., 301 (item 716).

The Pulpitum at Hexham Priory

CHARLES TRACY

The late medieval timber pulpita at the Augustinian priories at Hexham and Carlisle are the only remaining examples of their type in Britain. Although Hexham's was badly mauled in the early 20th century by the architects responsible for rebuilding the ruined choir, enough of it survives to demonstrate its former structure and appearance. Like so much of the remaining choir and presbytery furniture at the east end of the church, the pulpitum is charged with both colour and imagery. All of the sculpture on the west face is missing, but, even so, in tandem with evidence from the other furnishings within this remarkable monastic space, it is possible to suggest an iconographic programme relating to the institution's monastic history.

DESCRIPTION OF THE SCREEN AND RELATED FURNITURE

THE pulpitum at Hexham priory was erected during the period of Prior Thomas Smithson (1499–*c.* 1520) (Fig. 1 and Col. Pl. XXIII in print edn). Constructed in oak, it is located on the east side of the crossing. From the nave, the west side presents an open entrance arch, with two bays of solid appearance to north and south. The entrance is slightly wider than the flanking bays, and offers a partial view of the high altar some 24.5 m to the east.[1] The original stone plinth, on which the monument rested, was reduced by approximately half in the early 20th-century restoration by the architects, Temple Moore and C. C. Hodges (Fig. 2).[2] The dado zone consists of sixteen painted panels, with four to each bay. Originally, these probably contained the images of thirteen Anglo-Saxon bishops of Hexham, and, possibly, three bishops of Lindisfarne. In five instances, the bishop's name and period of rule are still legible (Fig. 3).[3] The four bays of the arcade zone 'windows' are filled with blind tracery, and the loft bressumer is supported by lierne vaulting. The latter is let into the stonework of the compound crossing piers at each end. In its cavetto there is a series of bosses, displaying the first letter of each word of the donor's inscription, namely: 'O[RATE] P[RO] A[NIMA] D[OMINI] T[HOMAE] S[MITHSON] P[RIORIS] H[UIUS] E[CCLESIE] Q[UI] F[ECIT] [H]OC O[PUS]'.[4] The small bosses within the modern upper cornice must have been salvaged from the coving beneath the lost uppermost beam, identified by Hodges from a scar on the adjacent pier.[5] Upon them the initials of Prior Smithson occur twice over, separately on two, and combined on another. As with the bressumer, the missing coving had been let into the piers of the eastern crossing. A portion of this was reported as extant in 1907.[6]

The loft front consists of twenty-one bays, with vaulted and canopied statue niches of two different designs. In the centre are five canopies with filigree-traceried fronts, probably emphasizing the greater importance of the images contained within them (Fig. 4).[7] On the evidence of five surviving examples, the other sixteen canopies had a less intricate gabled design. On the clustered buttresses between each image-housing

BAA Trans., vol. XXXVI (2013), 152–170

FIG. 1. Hexham abbey: pulpitum from west side
C. Tracy

there remains a considerable amount of red and green polychromy. This is probably original.

It should be pointed out that, in consequence of the major reordering of the east end *c.* 1740, the west side of the pulpitum was overloaded with refugee panels from the choir. The assemblage can be seen in an engraving by Thomas Allom, published in 1833.[8] A collection of painted panels was contained within two screens, the first placed immediately above the pulpitum loft, and the second divided into two sections by a window, and canted backwards. The third zone consisted of a massive tripartite arrangement of tracery, probably in wood, which reached up to a substantial, and also probably wooden, infill above the level of the eastern crossing arch capitals. Most of it had gone by 1856, although the first of the secondary screens, immediately above the loft, remained in position until the restoration of 1907/08. An early photograph of the west face of the pulpitum shows what was left of this Georgian confection,[9] and John Carter sketched it as early as 1795.[10] This screen had twenty-four bays, and the south end displayed an echelon of ten bishops, and/or abbots, nimbed and holding scrolls. This component is now displayed in the south transept (see below) (Fig. 5). In the centre were five painted panels of the Dance of Death, the remaining four of which are now incorporated in the panelling of the rostrum on the north side of the chancel (Fig. 6).[11] The tracery heads are identical to those on the bishop panels, suggesting that they were always part of an ensemble on this screen. The remaining nine panels on the north side consisted of a Passion of Christ series, which is now located in the north choir aisle. These were interpolations. Although their original tracery

Fig. 2. Hexham abbey: pulpitum from west side. Detail of north-side dado panels and abbreviated stone plinth
C. Tracy

Fig. 3. Hexham abbey: pulpitum from west side. Cluster of painted dado panels on north side of entrance, including images of SS. Eata and John of Beverley
C. Tracy

FIG. 4. Hexham abbey: south end of pulpitum loft, showing six lateral sculpture niches and, at left, one central one, with filigree canopy front. Note also five of the initials of the Smithson inscription (T S P H E)

C. Tracy

FIG. 5. Hexham abbey: south transept. Echelon of ten bishops carrying scrolls, formerly inscribed with their names and periods of office. The second figure from the left declares 'S Eata VII an'. The fourth figure carries a Greek cross (possibly for St Wilfrid)

C. Tracy

FIG. 6. Hexham abbey: view of Litany Desk, and flanking apostle screens, on north side of chancel. The four remaining painted images of the Dance of Death, and the seven Anglo-Saxon canonized bishops are above

Courtesy J. King

heads are lost, the ghosting on the paintwork above the images indicates that they were distinctively different, with eight tracery arches instead of six.

The second canted zone of the Georgian arrangement contained the monumental paintings of Hexham's 7th-century founder, St Wilfrid, and another six of the church's twelve Saxon bishops. In each case the identification is painted in black letter script on the underside of a projecting plinth.[12] These figures, probably executed in the mid-15th century, are now located on the composite furnishing on the north side of the chancel (Fig. 6). It has been suggested that parts of it may have constituted a 15th-century high altar reredos.[13] Each panel is 1.5 m high. From left to right, the figures represent bishops Ealhmund (767–81), Eata (678–81, 685–86), Wilfrid (705–09), John of Beverley (687–705), Acca (709–32), Frithubeorht (734–66), and Cuthbert (684–85). All of them are haloed. They have been framed into two groups, with three figures on the left side and four on the right. The arrangement suggests that, originally, there was another grouping of figures which is now lost. An assessment of the artistic quality and function of this monument must await a much-needed archaeological study. In the 18th-century reordering, these two unequal groupings of bishops were positioned on either side of the central window under the chancel arch.

On the east side of the pulpitum (Fig. 7), the 18th-century chancel reordering also made its mark. We are told that a large gallery 'had been appropriated to the singers' above the organ, 'the front of which is divided into compartments, each containing a full-length figure, representing Christ, his apostles and the Virgin Mary'.[14] The fourteen panels specified must have been placed above the pulpitum loft on this side, although its relationship to the organ is unclear. At that time the loft front had not yet been pushed forwards. The panels in question now occupy the north side of the chancel, and are jointed into both sides of a rostrum, with five apostles on the west side, but only four on the east (Fig. 6). Three more images are incorporated within the five-sided rostrum, including the figures of Christ and the Virgin and Child.[15] Most of the joinery in this ensemble appears to be authentic and is all of a piece.

The extant oriel of the pulpitum is strikingly out of scale with the lateral panels on the east loft front (Fig. 8). Perhaps a more commodious oriel suited the organist in 1856, when the loft was moved forwards to accommodate a new instrument. However, the two lateral groups of four painted prelate panels on each side look authentic. The panels on the oriel, depicting saints Andrew, Etheldreda (who donated the land on which the monastery was built), Oswald (d. 641/2: an important figure in the region), and John the Evangelist, were reconfigured at this time. Importantly, Carter's late 18th-century plan shows that the oriel originally had five sides.[16] The present double-width front face is thus inauthentic. Under the inscription, 'Paintings on the front and right side of the Rood of the foregoing screen', he noted that the seated, crowned and haloed male figure faced front, that is, towards the east, but that the haloed female was on his right, that is, it faced north-east.[17] Whereas his plan suggests that there should have been five images, he mentions only the two other extant ones, saints Andrew and John. Today, the irregular six-sided oriel includes these four images, but leaves blank the two lateral panels on the west side.

Attempts have been made to explain the origins of the rostrum and apostles screen on the north side of the chancel, a favourite speculation being that they were part of the furnishings of the former refectory. The suggestion that it was a litany desk, presumably for the canons' use, is more convincing, especially given the presence of the apostles.[18] In 1740, the wholesale dispersal of the choir and chancel furnishings, which, by the end of the 19th century, included the complete banishment of the early 15th-century choir-stalls from the body of the choir, seems to have had one overarching purpose, to insert as much raked and galleried congregational seating as possible into the east end, which had served as Hexham's parish church since the Reformation.

The blind tracery oak panels in the arcade bays of the pulpitum's west facade are in many ways the jewels of the monument. They were hinged by Temple Moore, to enable the occupants of his new nave to see through to the east end. One can understand the rationale for this, because, as already explained, the 'abbey' was no more than a parish church, and the congregation would have been eager to capitalize upon the restitution of their nave.

Aymer Vallance described the pulpitum as 'a close structure of parallel walls of timber both back and front'.[19] Unfortunately, the archaeology of the original east front has also been severely compromised, by the removal of the panels at the back of the return stalls when the congregational galleried seating was erected at the west end of the choir.[20] In 1856, these panels were reinstated, but only in deal. Concomitant with the erection of the large organ on the rood-loft at that time, pairs of substantial

FIG. 7. Hexham abbey: general view of east side of pulpitum
C. Tracy

FIG. 8. Hexham abbey: east side of pulpitum, with details of loft paintings. Note that the two arcade 'windows', flanking the entrance on the west side, are in the 'open' position; also the inserted strengthening arches inside at ground-floor level
Conway Library, Courtauld Institute of Art

oak relieving-arches were inserted inside the pulpitum at dado-rail level and between the middle posts at the mid-point on each side (Fig. 8). To provide greater stability for the loft floor, the pulpitum facade, including the projecting oriel, was moved eastwards by approximately 1.2 m. At ground level, the extension appears to have been supported at the east end of the passageway by an additional narrow bay of the width as the ancient passage door dividers, and also by the insertion on the east side of the doors of an original pair of columns scavenged from the east facade (Fig. 9). The style of the lierne vaulting of the bressumer beam on the east side is probably authentic, as it mimics that on the west side, which certainly is. How much of the bressumer vaulting on the west side had survived by 1856 is unknown, but, in any case, it was all replaced. At ceiling level the extent of all the new work can be easily read in the eastern part of the passageway vault (Fig. 10). Apart from the central bay above the doors, it is all a patently modern reproduction of poor quality.[21]

FIG. 9. Hexham abbey: pulpitum. North side of passageway from the west. Note the single bay extension on the east side, and the inserted ancient column, which replaced the larger restored one, which now supports the remodelled oriel and vaulting on the east side *C. Tracy*

The main interest on the east side is the painted panels. The two groups of five, displaying the images of bishops, have tracery heads, similar but not identical to those on the apostle and Dance of Death panels now located in the chancel. The tracery heads on the oriel feature dense webs of layered and elongated mouchettes, an elaboration of one of the designs on the pulpitum passageway doors, and also similar to some tracery heads on the Gondibour screen at Carlisle cathedral.

As already intimated, the 20th century heralded another 'restoration' of the already violated pulpitum, including the demolition of the original stone newel stair on the south side. It was replaced by a single cast-iron winding stair at the north-east end, which was duly execrated by Vallance. This insertion necessitated an adjustment to part of the original parapet. It has been assumed that the more recent of the two stone newel staircases on the north side, which afford access to the loft, was removed in 1856.[22] However, there is no trace of it on Carter's sketch plan of 1795.[23]

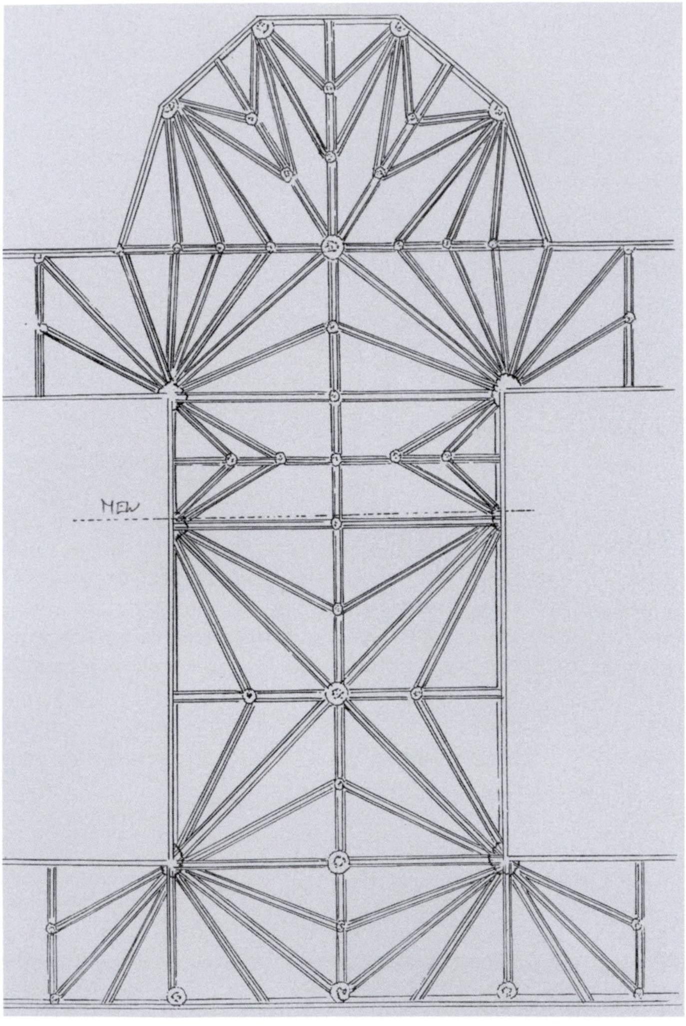

FIG. 10. Hexham abbey: pulpitum. Vaulting of central section
Courtesy J. Clark

The pulpitum passageway was closed off on both sides with a single panel on either side of a central door. As already mentioned, an extra bay was added on the east side in 1856 (Fig. 9). The tracery-heads of the doors are now missing. In the spandrels above are coeval paintings of the Annunciation (to the north) and the Visitation (to the south). The lierne vaulting of the 'central' bay is original, but, as mentioned above, was entirely renewed to the east, and throughout the length and breadth of the modern east elevation (Fig. 10).

Today the presentation of the west elevation is still as Vallance would have known it, with the traceried oak panels invariably open.[24] Although he never mentioned it, Vallance would have noticed the inauthentic finish of the arcade 'windows', which in 1811 were reported as being painted (Fig. 11).[25] The eastern elevation is quite as bad, with its brash newly painted vaults and illumination. But most shocking is the ruination of the pulpitum interior, nakedly advertising both the remnants of the lost newel staircases and the hubris of those who renovated it. Vallance's disapprobation of the early 20th-century reordering is the cry of a wounded antiquary. The fate of the west front's oak panels was lamented by him in the following terms:

> The beautiful traceried panels of the pulpitum front have been savagely treated, two of them severed from their framework by cutting all round, and hinged like shutters; while the other two, which, because of the presence of the piers at either end, could not be made to swing back in their entirety, were sawn down the middle vertically, one half being left a fixture, and one half hinged, to allow it to fold back, a shocking mutilation of the mediaeval work, and such that has caused no little breakage to the tracery [...] Those responsible for all these maltreatments actually claimed to have 'saved' the pulpitum. Saved it from what? [...] To what condition its self-styled saviours have reduced this unique monument is deplorable [Figs 2, 7, 8, 9, 11].[26]

One may assume that Vallance's anger was out of character, yet it was evidently sincere. The mutilated state of the monument is irreversible, and the lowering of the screen puts it out of kilter with the building's architecture. At arcade level, the traceried panels remain difficult to appreciate, as they are invariably open. The eastern elevation now seems to have little purpose other than supporting the huge organ which dwarfs it.

THE FUNCTION OF THE PULPITUM

PULPITUMS were raised pulpits, invariably required for the correct conduct of the offices in monastic and secular greater churches. They played an important role in the liturgical customs of medieval English secular and monastic institutions. Unfortunately, the only English Augustinian customary to have survived is that of Barnwell priory in Cambridgeshire: there is no such documentation for Hexham.[27] But something of the function of Hexham's pulpitum may perhaps be gleaned from the customary of the secular cathedral of Old Sarum, which reveals that (to quote W. H. St John Hope):

> [T]he pulpitum was intended for the singing of the lessons at matins, the reading of the Epistle, the singing of the gradual and the alleluya and the reading of the Gospel from an eagle desk, on Sunday and all great days. Also for the lesson at Mass, for certain functions, when a station was made before the cross or rood that stood above it, as in the Sunday and other processions, and for the singing of the genealogy at matins on Christmas Day. On the days when the Epistle was read from the pulpitum, which was done facing eastwards towards the quire, the gradual was also sung in the pulpitum by two boys in surplices, and not, as was usually the case, at the choir step. The pulpitum was, in many cases, furnished with a pair of organs.[28]

FIG. 11. Hexham abbey: west side of pulpitum. Detail of north end arcade 'window'. This one has been sawn down the centre and hinged on the south side only
C. Tracy

Hope further stated that 'as the customa[ries] and rubrics show, this use of the pulpitum at Salisbury was followed in almost exactly the same way at Lincoln, York, Exeter, Hereford and Lichfield'.[29]

An inventory of the contents of the treasury at Old Sarum mentions an eagle lectern (*letricum aquile*), and a cloth for it (*tuella*).[30] It is not clear whether this was for use in the presbytery or the pulpitum loft. However, in a fabric roll from Exeter cathedral there is a charge for ironwork 'circa aquilem in le Polpit'.[31] In 1400–01 there was a payment to a carpenter 'pro lectrino in pulpito', ordered by the precentor of the college of Windsor.[32] There was a wooden altar in the pulpitum in the 14th-century chapel of St George and St Edward at Windsor, *c.* 1382–83, and another, presumably also of wood, at King's College, Cambridge, 1503–04.[33] Although organs were often found in pulpitums, they were by no means universal.

In the greater English churches, oriels projecting out from the east side of a pulpitum are unusual. Just six examples can be cited besides that at Hexham, at Lincoln cathedral (*c.* 1370), Benedictine Chester abbey (*c.* 1390), Carlisle cathedral (*c.* 1410), St David's cathedral (1475–90), Ripon Minster (1488–94), and, formerly, Durham cathedral, 'where they had wont to singe the 9 lessons in the old time on principall dayes standinge with theire faces towards the high altar'.[34]

Originally, Hexham's pulpitum is unlikely to have been the only major transversal screen in the church. Although no written evidence for it survives, it is probable that, before the ruination of the nave, a separate rood-screen and loft had been set up within the western crossing of the transept. This arrangement was found at Durham, where there was a nave altar on the west side (Fig. 12), and many other monastic churches.[35] (It is unfortunate that we know nothing of the provision for the rood at Augustinian Carlisle, which also had a wooden pulpitum.) When, in 1296 and 1297, the priory was attacked and partially destroyed by the Scots, the canons decided to seal off the nave at the western crossing arch. After this, the rood must have been set up above the pulpitum.[36]

ICONOGRAPHY AND INSTITUTIONAL ANTIQUITY: THE COMMUNITY OF SAINTS

HEXHAM priory was founded *c.* 1113, on the site of the Saxon cathedral, which had ceased to exist by the middle of the 9th century, when the episcopal lands were divided

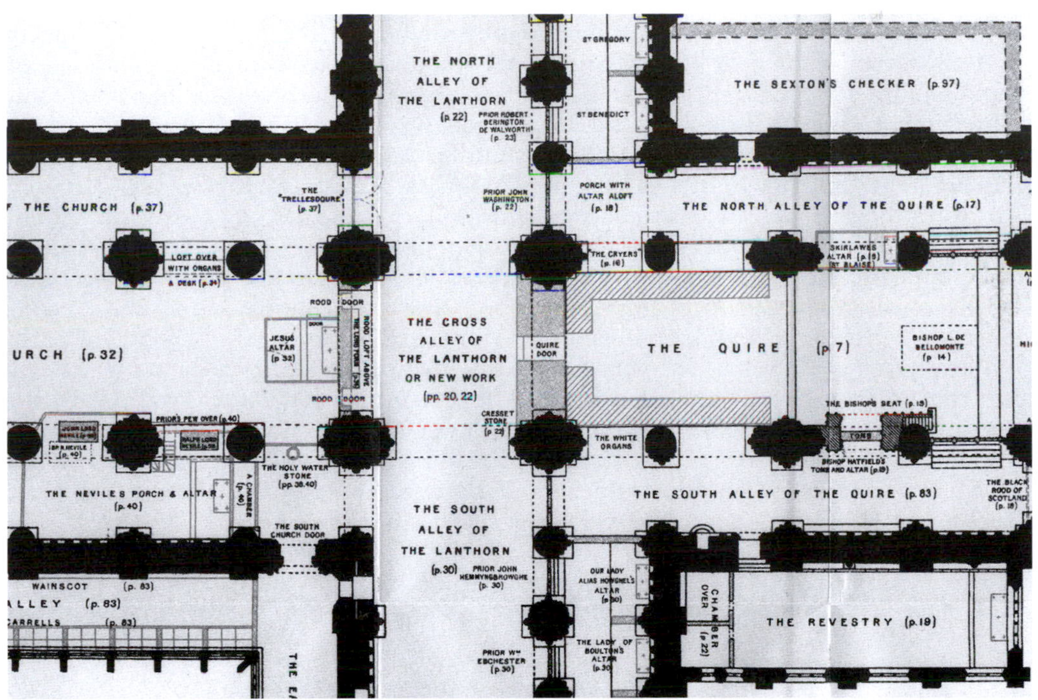

FIG. 12. Durham cathedral: detail of ground plan by W. H. St John Hope

between Lindisfarne and York.[37] The institution's antiquity and pre-Conquest status were evidently a source of great pride to the canons during the later middle ages, and influenced the iconography of the screen and (as noted) other furnishings. Moreover (as mentioned above), the iconographic programme on the west front of the pulpitum included thirteen Anglo-Saxon prelates, five of them still labelled, on the dado panels.[38] There are sixteen panels in total, and it has been suggested that the remaining three may have contained images of former bishops of Lindisfarne. In any case, the depiction of clergy on the face of a pulpitum, either painted or sculpted, is otherwise extremely rare in England.

The content of the dado panels reveals only part of the original scheme. Not accounted for is the imagery of the twenty-one empty canopy niches on the loft front. Ultimately, we cannot know what this was. Elsewhere in England, it was common to find kings of England represented on the west faces of pulpitums in both secular and monastic churches. By the time the Hexham pulpitum was erected, two such series existed at the most influential of all northern churches, Durham cathedral and York Minster. It is likely that the prior and some of the senior canons, at least, would have known these images. In light of this, we cannot discount the possibility that the niches on the loft once contained royal imagery.

However, the choice of images for the western facing dado of the pulpitum (of the pre-Conquest bishops) is more localized than one would usually encounter in a church of this size. This placed a heavy emphasis on the institution's pre-Conquest history, particularly when coupled with the twenty unidentified episcopal figures which must have been formerly displayed in the chancel.[39] In this respect it may be worth turning to Hexham's status as an Augustinian house, for one of the more notable aspects of Augustinian settlement in England is the number that were re-foundations of Anglo-Saxon monastic or collegiate churches — particularly those, like Hexham, created in the first half of the 12th century. By way of analogies one might cite a distinguished cluster of Augustinian houses in the upper Thames valley that inherited pre-Conquest traditions, and indeed pre-Conquest saints; Dorchester (St Birinus), Oxford (St Frideswide) and Bicester (St Edburga). None of these retains its individual pulpitum, but all retain evidence that their Anglo-Saxon origins and cults were valued in the later middle ages. The most obvious parallel for Hexham, in that it was also the site of an Anglo-Saxon bishopric, is Dorchester. It is impossible now to reconstruct the full extent to which allusions to Dorchester's past, and its roster of early bishops, may have proliferated within the later Augustinian church, but it is at least clear that the cult of St Birinus flourished. The 7th-century bishop was provided with a new shrine *c.* 1320, while antiquarian evidence suggests that the south chancel window was dedicated to scenes from his life.[40] Evidence for more extended visual considerations of pre-Conquest subjects is lacking at Bicester and Oxford, but that their principal Anglo-Saxon cults were celebrated is not in doubt.

As such, the surprise at Hexham is more the vehicle than the message. One catalyst for the display of Anglo-Saxon figures on the pulpitum may have been the memory of Hexham's 8th-century bishop Acca, who 'procured from all parts the relics of the blessed apostles and martyrs, erected altars in distinct chapels, and collected all the legends of the saints, their miracles and sufferings'.[41] In light of all this, it seems likely that imagery of particular significance to the canons was displayed on the loft. Given that the loft has five statue niches with special traceried canopies, a hierarchical arrangement seems to have been intended, probably involving the cult of St Augustine and/or those of saints buried at Hexham.

It can thus be proposed, albeit tentatively, that the echelon of canopied statues included at its centre the images of any five of the following saints: Ambrose, Augustine, Gregory the Great, and Jerome (the doctors of the Latin Church, who, if grouped together, would have represented Augustine in a highly prestigious light); Anthony of Egypt (abbot and patriarch of monks); Wilfrid (founder of the monastery and first bishop of Hexham) and Cuthbert (monk and sometime bishop of Hexham). Anthony, Cuthbert and Augustine were part of the painted scheme at Carlisle. At the same time, a case for inclusion in these prominent positions could also be made for saints Acca, Ealhmund and Frithubeorht, who were supposedly buried in the crypt, and whose relics, according to Ailred of Rievaux, were placed on a three-legged table near the high altar.[42]

But what of the seemingly less prestigious canopied niches on either side? Once again, these figures probably carried an overtly local or Augustinian message of historical as well as devotional importance to the canons. Historical retrospection may also have influenced the very unusual placement of painted images of the Annunciation and Visitation in the passageway of the pulpitum, which are redolent of the particularly strong devotion to the Virgin Mary in Anglo-Saxon Northumbria (memorably enunciated by the Venerable Bede's 'Beatissima Dei genitrix et perpetua virgo': Fig. 13). It is worth adding here that the composition of the Visitation is curious and, seemingly, rare. Mary meets her cousin Elizabeth outside the gates of a city. St Luke describes the latter as 'a town in the hill country of Judah' (Luke 1:39). On the hillside, three crucifixions are taking place. These details would have evoked Elizabeth's premonition of the sacrifice of Christ, as well his birth, at the moment of their meeting, when she sees that Mary is with child.[43]

Regarded as a whole — and regardless of whether the suggestions offered here are correct — such an edifice of images must have strongly evoked the doctrine of the community of saints (expressed in the second clause of the ninth article in the received text of the Apostles Creed), a subject touched on in some letters of the pseudo-Augustine, now credited to St Caesarius of Arles (*c.* 543).[44] According to John Lingard, people in Anglo-Saxon England developed the practice of venerating the saints together with the basic tenets of Christianity. The practice:

> [F]ormed an integral part of their public and private worship. In public they were frequently called upon to celebrate the anniversaries of individual saints, and yearly to keep the festival of All Hallows, as a solemnity of the first rank and importance. In private, at their morning and evening devotions, they were instructed [. . .] to worship God, and to pray first to St Mary, and the holy apostles, and the holy martyrs, and all God's saints in heaven with feelings of confidence and affection, to consider them as friends and protectors, and to implore their aid in the hour of distress, with the hope that God would grant to the prayer of the patron what he might otherwise refuse to the petition of the supplicant.[45]

The convocation of sacred figures presented by the pulpitum, each contained in its own niche (as though it occupied its unique heavenly mansion), must have made a strong impression on anyone who observed such instructions: this is no less true of the late middle ages than of the Anglo-Saxon period.

In addition to the imagery of the screen, the presence of the apostles on either side of the litany desk on the north side of the chancel (Fig. 6) would have provided an

FIG. 13. Hexham abbey: painting of the Visitation, with three crucifixions on the adjacent hill side, on the south side of the pulpitum passageway
C. Tracy

appropriate focus for the regular recitation of the Office in an Augustinian priory. Indeed, this imagery makes perfect sense in view of the Augustinian belief that:

> Christ Himself [had] instituted a perfect religious state, and that it was embraced by the apostles and many of their disciples from the very beginning of the Church. [Also that] from the time of the apostles there have always been in the Church clerics who, following the example of the primitive Christians, living 'secundum regulam sub sanctis Apostolis constitutam' [according to the rule established by the holy apostles], had all things in common. [Moreover] we read in the Life of St Augustine that when he was made a priest, he instituted a monastery within the church and began to live with the servants of God according to the manner and rules constituted by the holy apostles.[46]

Thus, the painted images of the apostles, which were never part of the pulpitum, would have provided an appropriate pedagogic and meditational focus for the canons' private and institutional use. They are, more or less, coterminous with the full-length figures of the twelve apostles at Carlisle, painted on the backs of the northern range of choir-stalls. Originally, the latter were components of a six-part cycle datable to the priorate of Thomas Gondibour (*c.* 1462–*c.* 1501).[47] The apostles at Carlisle, unlike those at Hexham, have been provided with scrolls, which articulate the section of the apostles creed for which each one of them was allegedly responsible.[48]

THE STYLE OF THE CARVED ORNAMENT

WHEREAS the architectural style of this monument is conventional enough, the tracery exhibited on the western arcade 'windows' (Fig. 11), as well on the oak screens in the Leschman Chantry on the north side of the high altar (Fig. 14), is only closely matched elsewhere on the Gondibour screen at Carlisle.[49] Some of the panel-head tracery on the pulpitum, and on the many coeval Hexham refugee choir fittings, also falls into this stylistic group.[50] At Carlisle, the tracery forms seen on Hexham's 'windows' was studied by Robert Billings in 1842, and it is clear that there must, at that time, have been a great deal more of it than is now extant. The more one studies this idiosyncratic ornament, the more outstanding its quality and technical detail is recognized to be. Large-scale examples of it, such as those on the west elevation of the pulpitum, would have presented a considerable challenge to the artists charged with executing it. The Hexham panels thus represent some of the most remarkable medieval decorative wood-carving in Britain.

It would have been Thomas Gondibour who first commissioned the talented and prolific workshop responsible for the woodwork in both places. Smithson himself probably took the initiative to employ them at Hexham, to make both the pulpitum and the screens for the chantry chapel of his predecessor Roland Leschman, who died in 1499. The style of the large-scale show tracery on the Hexham screen looks more Flemish than French. It is meticulously drawn, with up to three nests of loops displayed, and elaborate sub-tracery. Its size, expansive treatment and variations in scale seem to indicate a stylistic development from Carlisle. A Flemish example of smaller-scale sub-tracery can be seen in the choir-stalls at St Salvator, Bruges, of the second quarter of the 15th century, but this lacks the nests of loops present at Carlisle and Hexham.[51] It may be observed that the vocabulary is different from that of the French Flamboyant style, which inherited the organic tendencies of 14th-century English Decorated tracery. By contrast, a geometrical rigidity underlying the drawing of the tracery is noticeable at Hexham. The panel tracery-heads and running-ornament are broadly related to the same work, and are certainly not English in style.

The question now arises whence this style came. Ecclesiastical and trading links with Scotland certainly existed at the end of the 15th century, yet convincing comparisons have not been made between Carlisle or Hexham and Scottish churches. A traceried window on the west side of the south transept at St Michael, Linlithgow is a single convincing exception (Fig. 15).[52] Indeed, the border counties appear to have been much more exposed, directly or indirectly, in the years around 1500 to continental cultural influence via France and Flanders, than to that of metropolitan England. This is also, of course, the picture in Scotland, and the ornament of the Hexham pulpitum is to be more firmly identified with the visual culture of that country than with the culture of most of England.

ACKNOWLEDGEMENTS

I am grateful to Canon Graham Usher for allowing me to examine and photograph the furniture, to the Abbey's verger and administration for their cheerful cooperation. I am indebted for their wise advice to John Clark, Colin N. Dallison, Canon David Weston, Jane Cunningham, and Richard Fawcett.

FIG. 14. Hexham abbey: Prior Leschman chantry. Detail of parclose screen on south side. Note the evidence for Continental-style lamination technique
C. Tracy

FIG. 15. St Michael, Linlithgow: traceried window on west side of south transept
Courtesy R. Fawcett

NOTES

1. The width of the side bays is 1.4 m, while the entrance bay is 1.8 m.

2. The monument was lowered by some 508 mm. In view of the thoroughgoing nature of the early 20th-century restoration, present-day historians are heavily dependent on the meticulous analysis of Aymer Vallance, and also on C. C. Hodges's measured drawings. See A. Vallance, *Greater English Church Screens* (London 1947), 107–08; idem, 'The Pulpitum and Rood-Screen in Monastic and Cathedral Churches', *Transactions of the St Paul's Ecclesiological Society*, VI (1909), 199–200; C. C. Hodges, *The Abbey of St Andrew, Hexham* (London 1888); idem, with J. Gibson, *Guide to the Priory Church of St Andrew, Hexham*, 2nd edn (Hexham 1921), 55.

3. Hodges recorded what was legible of the inscriptions in the late 19th century as: Scs cuthbertus reg. viii. a, S. eata reg. vii a, Scs Wilfridus archiepus, S. Johannes reg. unum a., see Hodges, *Abbey* (as n. 2), 47. Another saint, alcmundus reg. xiii a., was added in Hodges and Gibson, *Priory Church* (as n. 2), 55. See below, n. 37, for a full list of Hexham's Anglo-Saxon bishops.

4. See W. A. Hutchinson, *A View of Northumberland*, 2 vols (Newcastle upon Tyne 1778), II, 91, and pl. 6. There were no other priors in the 15th or 16th centuries with a surname beginning with the letter S.

5. The original cornice must have been very similar to the one still *in situ* on the south side of the Leschman chantry screen.

6. E. S. Savage and C. C. Hodges, *A Record of All Works Connected with Hexham Abbey* (Hexham 1907), 50. See also Vallance, *Greater Screens* (as n. 2), 108.

7. This suggestion was first made in J. Clark, 'The Late Mediaeval Fittings in Hexham Abbey' (unpublished MA thesis, University of Leicester, 2005), 219.

Hodges and Gibson suggested that they 'were probably the remains of the tabernacle of the high altar', but this is unlikely. See Hodges and Gibson, *Guide* (as n. 2), 55.

8. A view across the transept from the north end, engraved by J. Sands, published by Fisher Son & Co., London.

9. Vallance, *Greater Screens* (as n. 2), pl. 7.

10. London, British Library, MS Additional 29933 (vol. 7), fol. 113.

11. To avoid confusion, the projection on the east side of the pulpitum will be referred to here as the oriel, and the pulpit on the north side of the chancel as the rostrum.

12. See J. Fairless, *A Guide to the Abbey Church at Hexham* (Hexham 1853), 11.

13. John Carter described the panels as 'Tables or niches containing seven perfect paintings of the ancient bishops of this church placed against the wall in the transept (as they apparently were at that time) removed of late years from the east ends of the aisles of the choir' (BL, MS Additional 29933 (vol. 7), fol. 139).

14. E. Mackenzie, *View of the County of Northumberland*, 2 vols (Newcastle upon Tyne 1825), I, 277. (This book is a prime source for details of the relocation of the choir furnishings.)

15. The rostrum itself must originally have been on the same level as the adjoining screen. It has been raised in modern times, and is higher still than it was in 1795, when Carter sketched it.

16. BL, MS Additional 29933 (vol. 7), fol. 122.

17. Carter made two large detailed sketches of both these figures, and assumed that they represented Christ and the Virgin Mary.

18. *The Priory of Hexham: Its Chroniclers, Endowments, and Annals*, ed. J. Raine, 2 vols, SS 44, 46 (Durham 1864–65), II, lxix.

19. Vallance, *Greater Screens* (as n. 2), 107; idem, 'Pulpitum' (as n. 2), 199.

20. The original plain screen behind the stalls survives to dado level.

21. John Clark made a brave attempt to interpret this work retrospectively, which cannot have been easy (Clark, 'The Late Medieval Fittings' (as n. 7), 221–22).

22. Hodges, *Abbey of St Andrew*, 46.

23. Carter, *Collection of Sketches*, fol. 122.

24. The pulpitum's presentation has not been improved by the set of angled yellow wooden choir-stalls imposed in the 1990s, which contrast unhappily with the blackened woodwork behind.

25. Mackenzie, *View* (as n. 14), 276.

26. Vallance, *Greater Screens* (as n. 2), 108.

27. J. W. Clark, *The Observances in Use at the Augustinian Priory of S. Giles and S. Andrew at Barnwell, Cambridgeshire* (Cambridge 1897).

28. W. H. St. John Hope, 'Quire Screens in English Churches with Special Reference to the Twelfth Century Quire Screen in the Cathedral Church of Ely', *Archaeologia*, 68 (1917), 46–48. At Old Sarum, 'On Sundays and festivals the Epistle was read by the subdeacon from the pulpitum or rood-loft at the western end of the quire. The Gospel was also read from the pulpitum, but with much more ceremony. First one of the taperers and one of the choristers went up to the loft to adorn the eagle desk there, probably with a hanging of some sort. Then a procession was formed, of the two taperers and the tribuler, the subdeacon

carrying the book, and the deacon, from the altar and through the middle of the quire to the rood-loft, where the deacon read the Gospel turned towards the north'. W. H. St John Hope, 'The Sarum Consuetudinary and Its Relation to the Cathedral Church of Old Sarum', *Archaeologia*, 68 (1917), 118.

29. Hope, 'Quire Screens' (as n. 28), 48.

30. Ibid., 48.

31. *The Accounts of the Fabric of Exeter Cathedral, 1279–1353, Part 2: 1328–1353*, ed. A. M. Erskine, Devon and Cornwall Record Society, ns 26 (Torquay 1983), 236.

32. Hope, 'Quire Screens' (as n. 28), 48.

33. Ibid., 50, n. 3.

34. *Rites of Durham*, ed. J. T. Fowler, SS 107 (Durham 1903), 16.

35. See Hope, 'Quire Screens' (as n. 28), fig. 9.

36. An attempt was made to reconstitute the nave in the 15th century: E. Cambridge, 'C. C. Hodges and the Nave of Hexham Abbey', *AA*, 5th ser. 7 (1979), 159–68; J. Cunningham, 'Buildings and Patrons: Early Gothic Architecture in the Diocese of Durham *c.* 1150–*c.* 1300' (PhD thesis, Birkbeck College, University of London, 1995), 244. The priory seems to have been well placed to commence this work, as well as the long-running renovation of the choir and chancel from the mid-15th century, given that its income from property during the 14th and 15th centuries has been estimated at between £400 and £500. See *HN*, III, 153. Moreover, in 1429, 'a debt of 400 marks was excused in the will of Roger Thornton on condition that the money was spent on the building of the church' (Cunningham, 'Buildings and Patrons' (as this note, above), 239).

37. Historical texts on Hexham Priory include *Priory of Hexham* (as n. 18), *HN*, III; J. V. C. Farquhar, *The Saxon Cathedral and Priory Church of Hexham* (Hexham 1935, 1940). There is a useful historical summary in D. Knowles and R. N. Hadcock, *Medieval Religious Houses. England and Wales*, 2nd edn (London 1971), 159–60. Texts on the building's fabric and furnishings include G. A. Cooke, *Topographical and Statistical Description of the County of Northumberland* (London s.d. [*c.* 1825]); W. T. Taylor, *Simple Guide to the Priory of Hexham* (Hexham 1929).

38. The complete list of Saxon bishops is as follows: Eata (678–81, 685–86); Tunbeorht (681–84); Cuthbert (684–85); John of Beverley (687–705); Wilfrid (705–09); Acca (709–32); Frithubeorht (734–66); Ealhmund (767–81); Tilbeorht (781–89); Æthelbeorht (789–97); Heardred (797–800); Eanbeorht (800–13); Tidfrith (813–21).

39. The ten now in the south transept, and a similar number mounted on the east side of the pulpitum.

40. T. Ayers, 'The Sanctuary of Dorchester Abbey, Oxfordshire: Its Design and Iconography' (unpublished MA thesis, Courtauld Institute of Art, University of London, 1991), 63. On Dorchester, see also W. Rodwell, *Dorchester Abbey Oxfordshire: The Archaeology and Architecture of a Cathedral, Monastery and Parish Church* (Oxford 2009).

41. A. B. Wright, *History of Hexham* (Alnwick 1823), 169.

42. Ailred of Rievaux, *De Sanctis Ecclesiae*, quoted in B. Nilson, *Cathedral Shrines of Medieval England* (Woodbridge 1998), 43.

43. Of course, such images were also theologically appropriate in a passageway, as they declared the advent of grace symbolized by the transition from crossing to chancel.

44. *PL*, XXXIX, cols 2189, 2191, 2194. In the high middle ages, the *civitas Dei* was understood to incorporate almost everyone interested in the Christian faith other than heretics, schismatics and apostates. See 'Communion of Saints', *Catholic Encyclopedia*, <http://www.newadvent.org/cathed/04171a.htm> [accessed 1 November 2012].

45. J. Lingard, *History and Antiquities of the Anglo-Saxon Church*, 2nd edn, 2 vols (London 1858), I, 75.

46. 'Canons and Canonesses Regular', *Catholic Encyclopedia* (as n. 44).

47. The representation of the apostles is situated in the second bay of the north choir aisle, between the life of St Anthony (north-west bay), and the life of St Cuthbert (north-east bay). The life of St Augustine is in the south-east bay. The first two bays on the south side were originally provided with paintings, but the evidence of them has disappeared. D. Park and S. Cather, 'Late Medieval Paintings at Carlisle', in *Carlisle and Cumbria*, 214–22.

48. For the panel paintings behind the choir-stalls at Carlisle cathedral, see also D. W. V. Weston, *Carlisle Cathedral History* (Carlisle 2000), 67–71. For a discussion of the iconography of the apostles creed, its theological significance and applications in England and Europe during the middle ages, see C. Tracy, 'The 14th-Century Canons' Stalls in the Collegiate Church of St Mary, Astley, Warwickshire', *JBAA*, 162 (2009), 103–20.

49. C. Tracy, 'The Stylistic Antecedents for the Gondibour Screen at Carlisle Cathedral', in *Carlisle and Cumbria*, 175–98 and figs 1, 2, 7, 8, 16, 19, 21.

50. Ibid., fig. 20.

51. Ibid., fig. 25.

52. I thank Richard Fawcett for discussing this subject with me.

The Architecture of Tynemouth Priory Church

RICHARD FAWCETT

The cliff promontory at Tynemouth is a site with a rich history, both as the home of a succession of religious communities and as a place of strength. The subject of this paper is the Benedictine priory church dedicated to the Virgin Mary and the martyred Saxon King Oswin, construction of which was started in the 1090s following the transfer of the house from the authority of Durham to that of St Albans. Little remains of the first Romanesque church, and the site's great architectural glory is what survives of the late 12th-century eastern arm, whose design illustrates the ferment of ideas taking place across northern England and southern Scotland in the decades on each side of 1200.

TYNEMOUTH priory, like Whitby abbey and Lindisfarne priory, is one of those intensely evocative northern sites that is both visually dramatic and deeply imbued with memories of the heroic early days of Christian missionary activity. The physical evidence for its proto-history as a religious site is seen in several carved stones found at various dates.[1] The Benedictine priory, which is the subject of this paper, was dedicated to the Virgin Mary and St Oswin, king of Deira, who was murdered by his cousin, Oswiu, in 651.[2] Legend says that Oswin appeared in a dream to the hermit priest Edmund in 1065, directing him to persuade Bishop Egelwine of Durham to search for the saint's body within the surviving ruins of the church at Tynemouth.[3] Formal religious life was revived in about 1074, when Earl Waltheof of Northumberland granted the church to Aldwin, a monk of Winchcombe abbey in Gloucestershire. Aldwin aspired to revive the northern centres of religious life recorded by Bede, and he was encouraged to settle at Jarrow by Bishop Walcher of Durham.[4] Tynemouth became a possession of Durham when Jarrow was transferred to the cathedral priory in 1083. As a result of a quarrel between Robert Mowbray, earl of Northumberland, and Durham's Bishop William of St Calais, however, Mowbray withdrew Tynemouth from Durham, granting it instead to St Albans, resulting in the continuing resentment of Durham.[5] This transfer is generally said to have taken place in about 1083, though that date is based on Durham charters now thought to be forgeries, and a date around 1090 is more likely.[6]

THE ROMANESQUE CHURCH

SINCE enough of the church's east end must have been complete for St Oswin to be translated into it in 1110,[7] it may be assumed that construction started immediately in the1090s.[8] Work must have continued after the translation: since 1111 it was said that a workman named as Arkill was spared death through Oswin's intervention

BAA Trans., vol. XXXVI (2013), 171–192

when he fell from the roof.[9] The chief remains of the Romanesque church are: lengths of the outer walls of the seven-bay aisled nave, part of the arcade and gallery stages of the north-east nave bay, varying amounts of the crossing piers, and the lower portions of the west and south sides of the south transept (Fig. 1 and Col. Pl. XXIV in print edn). The eastern limb was entirely replaced in the course of a campaign of the later 12th century, but its plan is known through excavation. There is said to have been some unrecorded investigation of the easternmost parts in 1887 by R. J. Johnson,[10] and full excavation of the eastern limb was carried out in 1904–05 by W. H. Knowles as part of the research for the Tynemouth volume of the *History of Northumberland* (Fig. 2).[11] Knowles exposed a relatively short east limb probably of two aisled bays, terminating in a semicircular ambulatory with three radiating apsidal chapels, the axial chapel having a straight section before the apse. There was also an apsidal chapel on the east side of each transept. This plan has English precedents as early as the 1070s, at the Conqueror's abbey at Battle, founded on the site where Harold fell, and at St Augustine's abbey in Canterbury.[12] No lead was taken from either Tynemouth's first mother house of Durham, where work started in 1093, or its new mother house at St Alban's, where building commenced soon after 1077: in both those cases an echelon plan was the choice.

The responds of the crossing piers towards the high arches below the tower had a pilaster faced with a leading half-shaft and flanked by three-quarter shafts; the surviving high capital on the north side of the west crossing arch was scalloped (see Fig. 5). The responds towards the nave arcades had the same profile, but the arches that led from the transepts into the nave and choir aisles had nothing more than a plain pilaster, supporting an unmoulded arch above a simple impost.

FIG. 1. Tynemouth priory: viewed from the north-west
Author

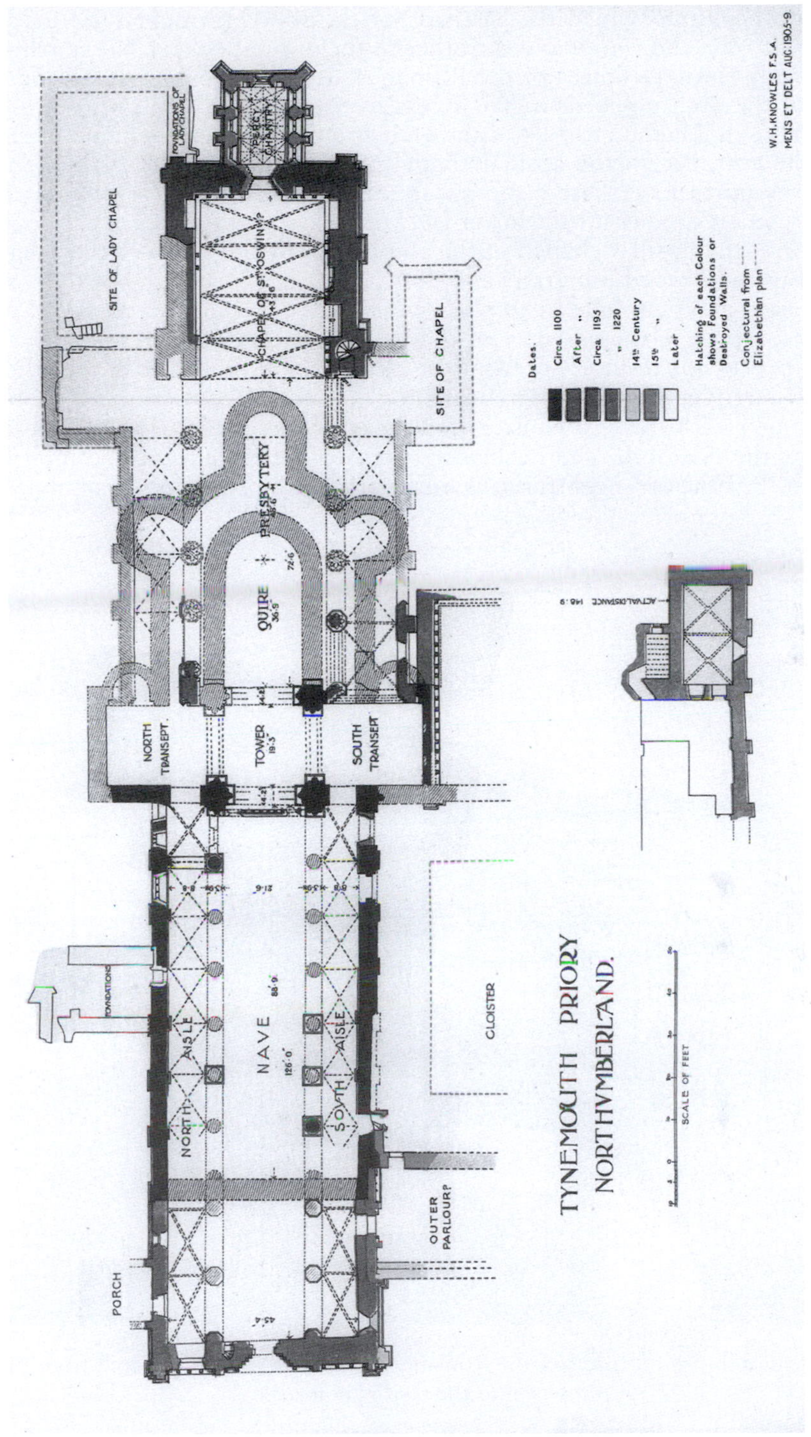

FIG. 2. Tynemouth priory: plan, after Knowles, *Archaeol. J.* (1910)

Of the two bays into which the east side of the south transept was divided, one corresponded to the choir aisle and the other to the apsidal chapel; the north transept was presumably similar. Traces of the Romanesque gallery openings can be seen on either side of the arch inserted to give access to the broader late 12th-century south choir aisle (Fig. 3). The outer order of the arch and the southern respond of the opening above the entrance to the apsidal chapel remain in evidence, as does the north respond of the north bay; these responds appear to have been of a similar profile as the crossing piers responds. At the lower level there are slight traces of the south jamb of the arch into the apsidal chapel. In the south wall of the transept there have been at least two round-headed blind arches.

The monastic choir probably extended westwards through the crossing, with the pulpitum and screen in the east bay of the nave, and this was presumably a reason for the east processional doorway from the cloister being initially in the second bay from the east (see Fig. 2). It was more usual for that doorway to be in the easternmost bay, and aligned with the east cloister walk, even if this meant that processions had to skirt round the side of the choir enclosure to reach the entrance to the choir through the pulpitum. But the arrangement at Tynemouth was not unique: a similar location

FIG. 3. Tynemouth priory: traces of the Romanesque gallery around the arch from the south transept into the south choir aisle
Author

for the east cloister doorway was adopted at the abbeys of Peterborough and Dunfermline, for example, while in churches with unaisled naves it was often necessary to locate the doorway either well down the nave or on the west side of the transept. The Tynemouth doorway's details are extremely weathered, though it was evidently of three orders, with a hood-mould embracing the arch.

The external walls of the Romanesque church are best preserved along the eastern bays of the nave. Along the north aisle the walls rise from a chamfered base course, with the bays articulated by shallow pilasters, and a double-chamfered string-course ran below the windows (Fig. 4). The only partly surviving window, in the easternmost bay, was a small round-headed opening with a narrow chamfered reveal and no hood-mould. It was replaced in the 14th century by a two-light window with a pair of cusped ogee arches when the eastern bay of the aisle was enclosed. The enclosure of that bay, and its likely continued use by the parish church in the nave after the Reformation, ensured its partial survival, and its arcade wall provides the fullest evidence for the design of the high elevations of the Romanesque nave (Fig. 5). The cylindrical pier has a heavily weathered cap decorated with an inversion of scalloping: a miniature arcade with imposts at the arch springings.[13] Within the bay are traces of a quadripartite ribbed vault. The only fragments of the upper storeys are the east respond and arch springing of the gallery. As in the south transept, the respond is a smaller version of the responds of the adjoining crossing piers, and this suggests parallels with the choir gallery at Durham cathedral; it is likely that the gallery openings were similarly subdivided. Such debts to Durham make it additionally unlikely that Tynemouth can have been started before the 1090s. Nothing is known of the clerestory, other than that there is no evidence of a mural passage in the north-west crossing pier.

THE EARLY GOTHIC FERETORY, PRESBYTERY AND CHOIR

THE rebuilt eastern limb was both considerably longer and taller than its Romanesque predecessor (Fig. 6). There is no firm dating evidence for its construction, though the architectural details point to commencement in the last decades of the 12th century, presumably during the priorate of Akarius, who had moved on from Tynemouth to become abbot of Peterborough by no later than 1200.[14] Major benefactions were received in 1189 from Richard I, effectively establishing the liberty of Tynemouth,[15] and perhaps suggesting the community was gathering fresh resources in advance of a major initiative.

A leading motive for rebuilding was presumably the wish for a clear architectural distinction between the more liturgically important parts and the nave. The new work consisted of an aisle-less feretory and presbytery of four narrow bays, and an aisled choir of five bays to its west; footings have been found of lateral projections at the junction of the two elements, though insufficient has survived to know if these were part of the initial design or later additions. The plan may have its ultimate source in the eastern limb of Southwell minster of *c.* 1100,[16] though variants were already being explored across northern England and southern Scotland in the second half of the 12th century. The most ambitious was at the Augustinian cathedral priory of St Andrews, started for Bishop Arnold (1160–62),[17] and on a smaller scale it is found at the Augustinian abbey of Jedburgh, started around 1138,[18] the Augustinian priory of Cartmel of after 1188[19] and the Premonstratensian abbey of Dryburgh, of the later 12th century.[20]

Fig. 4. Tynemouth priory: Romanesque masonry in the north nave wall
Author

Fig. 5. Tynemouth priory: the Romanesque north-east bay of the nave
Author

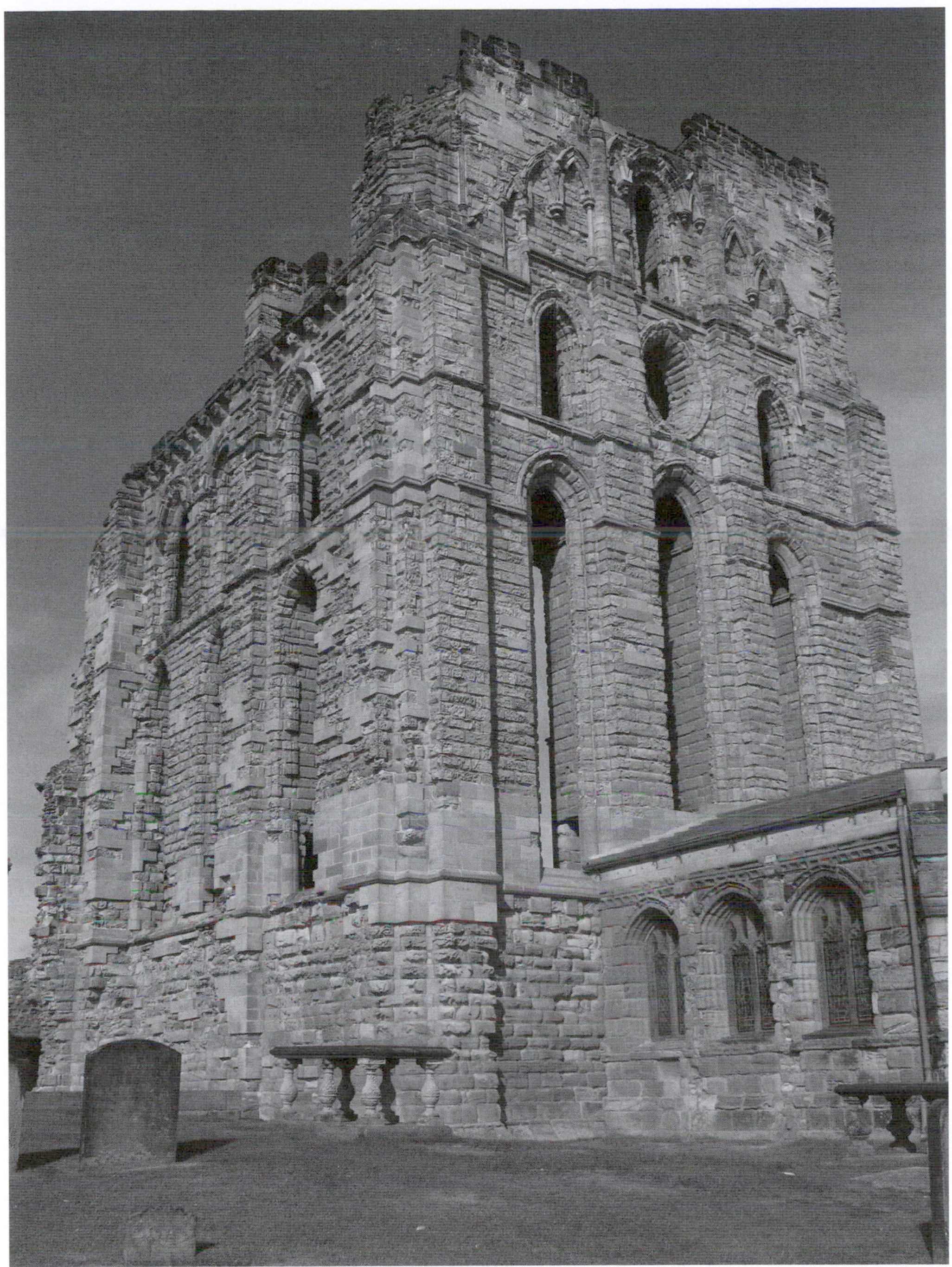

FIG. 6. Tynemouth priory: the feretory and presbytery viewed from the south-east
Author

Because of the greatly enlarged scale of the new eastern limb, much of it was outside the walls and arcades of the earlier building. This had the advantage that the central vessel of the Romanesque eastern limb could remain in use for the performance of the *opus dei* while the earlier stages of the rebuilding were taking place around it. Since the new aisled choir has been almost entirely lost, the building sequence of the eastern limb is uncertain. Minor differences in the heights of the bases of the two western responds of the choir arcades have been taken to suggest that the north arcade was built first, when there were also thoughts of replacing the nave,[21] with the implication that the choir was built before the presbytery. On balance, it appears more likely that work started at the east end, beyond the Romanesque eastern limb, and that differences between the two responds stemmed from difficulties of tying in with the Romanesque crossing piers while parts of the earlier building were still in place.

Externally, the verticality of the surviving east and south walls of the new feretory and presbytery present a wonderfully dramatic appearance, with the relative simplicity of detailing concentrating attention on the soaring window openings. The walls rise from a base course with a deep splay capped by a roll, and are articulated by shallow pilaster buttresses at the angles, between the windows of the east wall, and between the first and second windows from the east of the south flank. The provision of a pilaster on the south flank only between the second and third bays may reflect the internal division between feretory and presbytery. The two tiers of windows rest on string-courses, that below the upper level along the south flank extending round to the taller windows of the east face at arch springing level and continuing around the arches as hood-moulds. The detailing is more enriched at the higher levels: while the lower windows of the south flank have chamfered reveals, the upper windows have both an additional order carried on nook shafts and a hood-mould. In the east wall the central window at the main level rises higher than the others, with a vesica in the reduced space above. Any parapet along the south flank has been lost apart from the corbel table; the east wall has a complex gable, with ramping arcading flanking a central window, and with angle pinnacles that have an arch to each face. Groupings of soaring single-light windows as seen in Tynemouth's east front were to become more common in both northern England and southern Scotland, as in the west front of the Augustinian priory at Lanercost, the south transept gable of York Minster and the east gable of Glasgow cathedral. But amongst the few examples likely to be contemporary with Tynemouth are those in the south transept of the Tironensian abbey of Arbroath.[22]

Internally, there is considerable enrichment throughout (Fig. 7 and Col. Pl. XXV in print edn). At the lowest level is a blind-arcaded dado, which incorporates a recess within a depressed two-centred arch at the centre of the east wall and a number of liturgical fixtures along the south wall. Above that, both the east and the south wall have three bays of windows, each of two tiers, with mural passages at both levels, and with triplet wall shafts rising between the bays to the vaults. The tall windows of the lower tier have two orders of mouldings carried on *en délit* shafts with mid-height shaft rings, while the upper tier of south windows, within the vault wall arches, are also embraced by two orders of mouldings. Along the east wall the windows of the lower tier rise to greater height, with the upper windows — lancets in the side bays and a vesica at the centre — being less richly detailed. There were evidently difficulties in matching up the outer skin of the east wall to the inner skin, and at the lower level the southern window is misaligned with its inner arch. The north side of its inner arch was consequently shouldered, while the adjacent wall shaft cap appears to have been heightened.

FIG. 7. Tynemouth priory: the internal east and south walls of the feretory and presbytery
Author

The overall inter-relationship of parts seen in the aisle-less eastern parts of Tynemouth, with arcaded dado at the lowest level and two tiers of windows above, shows analogies with a number of contemporary buildings, including the west side of the south transept at the Augustinian priory of Hexham[23] and the presbytery of Dryburgh abbey,[24] though neither of those was vaulted. The ultimate consummation of this approach is seen in the Nine Altars chapel at Durham cathedral which, like the eastern parts of Tynemouth is covered by complex vaulting, the difficulties of whose construction may have been barely anticipated when work was initiated.[25]

At Tynemouth, the contrast between the closely spaced vaulting over the eastern parts and the timber ceilings or open-timber roofs over the rest of the church must have made very clear which were the liturgically more significant parts. A noteworthy feature must have been the tripartite treatment of the east end of the vault, with two intermediate vault springers between the upper tier of windows. It is difficult to find parallels for such an arrangement in the British Isles, though they are to be found in mainland Europe, with several in Normandy, including the north transept at Fécamp[26] and the chapter-house at Saint-Georges-de-Boscherville.[27] So far as any judgement can be reached on what remains at Tynemouth, however, there may have been uncertainty on how to handle the intermediate springers, which rise very steeply, barely leaving the security of the wall. Each of the two vault severies over the outer sections must consequently have been strikingly asymmetrical.

Dog-tooth is extensively deployed throughout the eastern parts, in the vault ribs, the hood-moulds of the lower windows of the east wall, the hood-moulds and jambs of the upper windows of the south wall, and the upper string-course of the east wall. Other than some capitals that are simply moulded, a majority have foliage decoration that is generally too weathered to permit precise comparisons (Fig. 8a). But in some cases it can be seen to have had thin layers of crisply detailed acanthus-like forms of a type also seen on the north transept doorway at Ripon minster (Fig. 8b).

The aisle-less eastern section of the church was almost certainly designed to contain both St Oswin's feretory and the presbytery, with the altar and shrine physically closely associated since, when the shrine was translated in the 1340s, it was said it had been united with the high altar.[28] Craster and Hadcock argued that the shrine was in the second bay from the east, with the high altar immediately adjoining it to the west,[29] but this leaves problems in understanding how the altar related to a number of fixtures. At the centre of the east wall is a recess with a depressed arch, which was later pierced to provide an entrance into an added axial east chapel. Along the south wall from east to west are: in the first bay what is probably a tomb recess of secondary construction; in the second bay a rectangular aumbry and a trifoliate-arched piscina; and in the third bay a pair of deep recesses capped by a pair of trifoliate arches. Hadcock and Craster suggested the recess in the east wall was the location of the Lady altar, and that the pair of recesses in the third bay was the location of the shrine of St Henry of Cocquet Island, but this would place the aumbry and piscina east of the altar. On balance, it appears more likely that the high altar was in the eastern part of the second bay from the east, meaning that the aumbry and piscina were immediately to its south, with the pair of deep recesses best understood as sedilia. The precise location of the shrine is uncertain, though the central recess in the east wall is a strong candidate, with the inserted tomb recess in the south wall being provided for a patron who was anxious to be buried as close as possible to the saint.

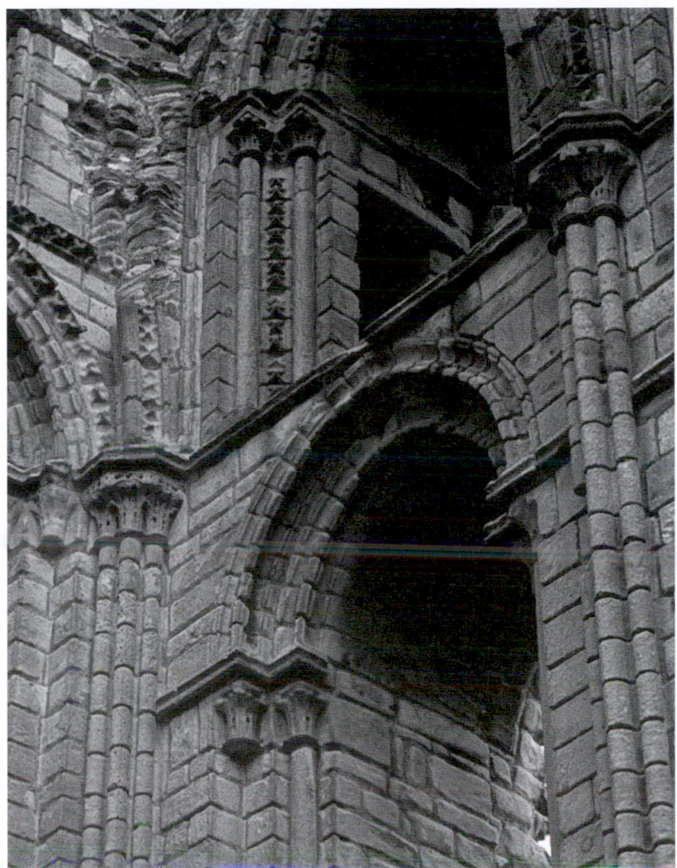

FIG. 8. a. Capitals in the south-east corner of the feretory; b. Ripon minster: the capitals of the west jamb of the north transept doorway
Author

Marking the transition between presbytery and choir is a narrow bay corresponding to the east wall of the choir aisles; there is a spiral stair at this point on the surviving south side. This bay continues some themes of the aisle-less eastern bays in its three arches of blind arcading to the dado and the vaulting at the uppermost level; the other levels, however, are more like those recorded for the choir (see Fig. 7 and Col. Pl. XXV in print edn). Above the dado there is first a blind arcade of two arches, and then, corresponding to the triforium in the adjacent choir, is a pair of pointed arches within a single round arch with a blind trefoil in the tympanum. The latter is essentially the same as the central pair of arches in the choir triforium, and the triforium passage continues behind it. At the level of the clerestory, within the arc of the vault, there is blank walling. This bay shows some relationship with the narrow second bay from the west in the nave of Ripon minster, which may initially have extended in an alternating pattern of wide and narrow bays down the nave there.[30]

Moving westwards into the choir, the chief survivor is part of its south-west aisle bay and the lowest part of the west respond of the north arcade (Fig. 9). On both sides the western choir arcade responds are slotted into the Romanesque arch from the transept into the choir aisle, against the flank of the tower pier, and the respond and springer of the arch into the previous choir aisle remains visible on the south side. The new arcade responds are treated differently on the two sides. On the south the new respond barely projects beyond the pared-back core of the crossing pier, whereas on the north a spur of wall was extended well beyond the crossing pier, with a three-quarter pier projecting off its east end. On both sides the new arch into the choir aisle from the transept was designed to be distinct from the arcade piers in the choir, with something of the appearance of a proscenium arch from the west. The responds of these arches have a stepped profile with engaged shafts carrying foliate capitals, whereas the choir piers were of octofoil clustered-shaft form, the cardinal shafts being filleted and the diagonal shafts keeled. The cap of the surviving arcade respond has an undecorated bell above each shaft, as have the triplet wall shafts along the outer aisle wall; the abaci of those wall shaft capitals continue into a string-course at mid-height of the single lancet in each bay. The aisle wall shafts are supported by corbels above a lower string-course at the sill level of the windows.

Despite the almost complete loss of the choir, a combination of the surviving fragments and of views of its south arcade wall before collapse give us a good idea of its design (Fig. 10).[31] Those views show a three-storeyed design. Each bay of the triforium had an arcade of four arches in front of a wall passage, the middle pair being grouped within an arch whose tympanum had a blind foiled figure. The clerestory was of slightly greater height that the triforium, with an arcade of three equal-height arches to each bay, the wider central arch corresponding to the window on the outer face of the passage. The bays were defined by wall shafts rising from the abaci of the arcade piers, and the storeys were marked by string-courses. Unlike the feretory and presbytery, the choir was unvaulted. Slight indications on Brand's view that the wall shafts continued a short distance above the wall head cornice would be consistent with the possibilities that they either connected with the principal rafters of an exposed roof structure, or that there was a boarded ceiling with ribs between the bays. Aesthetically, a boarded ceiling of polygonal section following the profile of the rafters and collars of the roof might have sat more comfortably than an open roof alongside the ciborium of vaulting over the eastern part of the building.

To an even greater extent than the transitional bay described above, the choir elevation showed strong similarities with a part of Ripon minster, in this case the choir before the insertion of vaults (Fig. 11),[32] though the use of pointed arches throughout

FIG. 9. Tynemouth priory: the south-west bay of the choir
Author

the clerestory, together with the filleting of the cardinal shafts of the arcade piers, suggests Tynemouth was the later of the two. But other buildings should also be taken into account in considering the context of Tynemouth's choir. The choir and transepts of the Cistercian abbey of Byland probably had a similar elevation on the evidence of the stump of the east arcade wall of its south transept,[33] albeit the piers in the presbytery and north transept there had twelve rather than eight shafts. Byland may be closer in date to Tynemouth than Ripon, depending on how much was built before the move to the present site in 1177. Another building with a related elevation, and that is possibly contemporary with Tynemouth, is the nave of the Gilbertine priory of Old Malton, where, although only the two lower storeys survived 18th-century truncation, the design of the clerestory is known from depictions made before its destruction.[34] Tynemouth's choir can thus be understood as one of a group of closely related buildings, with the majority being further south, in Yorkshire.

THE EXTENDED NAVE

WITH the presumed removal of the monastic choir out of the crossing, and the western limb perhaps becoming little more than a processional pathway to the choir

Fig. 10. Tynemouth priory in 1789. Brand, *History and Antiquities of Newcastle* (1789)

so far as the monks were concerned, more space was acquired by the layfolk who had the use of the nave as their parish church. The problems of monastic and parochial communities coexisting within the same building are well attested,[35] and it was frequently deemed expedient to provide alternative accommodation for the parish. There is no record that this possibility was considered at Tynemouth, however, where, indeed, the nave was now extended westwards by two additional bays that were rather longer than those of the Romanesque nave (see Fig. 2). On the architectural evidence, this was carried out soon after completion of the new eastern limb, perhaps around the second decade of the 13th century, and it resulted in a changed relationship between the church and the west claustral range. There is no evidence that a west range had been initially envisaged for the Romanesque priory, though one was eventually constructed, at some point in the later 12th century on the scant architectural evidence. This range must have projected beyond the line of the original west front, a situation that was by no means unusual, though it did perhaps detract from the prominence of the west front. An incidental advantage of the nave's westward extension was therefore that it again projected clear of the claustral ranges, and it was possible to give enhanced expression to the west front.

Despite the lesser height of the nave by comparison with the extended eastern limb, a valiant effort was made to give the new west front an imposing architectural presence (see Fig. 1 and Col. Pl. XXIV in print edn). Nevertheless, there appear to have been some difficulties in the planning, since the great doorway, with its continuous inner order framed by five orders carried on *en délit* shafts, is not quite central to the front: the blind arch flanking it to the north is consequently narrower than that to the south. The original form of the fenestration above the doorway is not known, though a shaft adjacent to the buttress to the south of the central bay must have been

FIG. 11. Ripon minster: reconstruction study of the choir before the insertion of vaults
W. S. Weatherley

associated with either a window or a blind arch. The treatment of the aisle ends survives best on the south side. At the lowest level is a blind arcade of three arches, with a pair of deep niches above; the half-gable to the aisle roof was decorated with a ramping arrangement of blind arches, perhaps intended as a smaller-scale reflection of the treatment of the east gable. The front has been modified several times. A small tower was built against the end of the south aisle, perhaps in the 14th century, of which only the footings survive.[36] Greater changes were made when a central seven-light window and a smaller one at the west end of the north aisle were inserted. This may have been done in the late 14th or early 15th century for Prior John Whethamstede, whose nephew, Abbot John Whethamstede of St Albans (1420–40 and 1451–65) wrote a poem praising his uncle's activities.[37]

Internally, the arcade walls of the western bays are lost, but the surviving base of the eastern octagonal pier of the south arcade suggests that the new work was built up against the Romanesque west front, and that the front was only dismantled once work was well advanced. At that stage the west bay of the Romanesque nave presumably had to be rebuilt to the new design. The responds built in with the later west front have bases of superimposed-roll type, and the simple bell caps supported arches of two chamfered orders. Brand's view suggests that the new work was designed to sit sympathetically with the existing nave, having a large round — and perhaps originally subdivided — arch to each bay at gallery level, and a single pointed window at clerestory level. The levels were demarcated by string-courses and the bays defined by wall shafts rising from the abaci of the arcade piers. The extended aisles were covered by quadripartite vaults with hollow-chamfered ribs rising from corbels. The outer walls were constructed of ashlar rising from a base course with a deep splay between two rolls, a form related to that below the choir, and there was a doorway covered by a porch on each side of the west bay.

Following on from the eastward relocation of the choir, a new processional door was formed in the east bay of the south nave aisle, and the original door in the second bay from the east was blocked. At the same time a choir screen was constructed below the west crossing arch, with a door on each side of the nave altar. The west side of this screen has been considerably altered, with the existing moulded arches of the doorways probably representing a later adaptation; between them is the ghosting of a decorative arcade of five pointed arches. The east side of the screen is better preserved, with dog-tooth to the segmental rear-arches of the doors, the cornice, and the arches of the blind arcade; the main loss has been the six shafts of that arcade (Fig. 12).

LATER WORKS

THE years between 1314 and 1318 were the most disturbed in the priory's history,[38] and the institution's recovery soon afterwards, under priors Richard of Tewing (1315–40) and Thomas de la Mare (1340–49), is all the more remarkable. In 1320 provision was made for a wayleave for carts from the slate quarries at West Backworth during the construction of the monks' dwellings.[39] The first major new work on the church was a Lady chapel, which a plan of 1582 indicates was the large rectangular structure on the north side of the presbytery, of which only excavated footings remain visible (see Fig. 2). The first reference to this chapel was in 1336, though work may have been started ten years earlier when an endowment of land was provided for its maintenance.[40] Lady chapels in such locations are often seen as particularly associated with the great Benedictine abbeys of the eastern counties, at Ely, Peterborough and (Cluniac) Thetford; however, taking account of similarly located Lady chapels at Augustinian Bristol and Oxford, and the likelihood that a large chapel which stood on the north side of Benedictine Dunfermline served this purpose, they were perhaps more widespread than now appears.

It has been argued that the Lady chapel was the destination of St Oswin's shrine when it was relocated by Abbot de la Mare between 1346 and 1349, at a cost of £70.[41] This suggestion is largely based on the assumption that the Lady chapel was the only recently built structure sufficiently spacious to accommodate the shrine of the priory's patron saint.[42] Although it might seem unlikely to combine the functions of feretory and Lady chapel, this would not be altogether exceptional. At Durham cathedral, for example, the shrine of Bede was relocated to the Lady chapel in the Galilee at the western end of the church,[43] while at Salisbury cathedral it is very likely that the shrine of St Osmund was in the Lady chapel known as the Trinity chapel.[44] Thus, while the possibility that Oswin's destination was the new Lady chapel cannot be confirmed, it should not be ruled out. It is thought that a number of carved spandrels found in this area, some of which are carved on both sides, could have been associated with the shrine, perhaps forming part of a base.[45] Whatever the case, however, it must be conceded that the carvings are more remarkable for their survival than for their quality.

One of the most inexplicable later additions to the church was an upper storey, which Brand's view shows extended the entire length of the eastern limb (see Fig. 10). A roof crease cut into the inner face of the east gable suggests that the roof over the eastern limb had already been reconstructed to a lower pitch behind the retained gable, and the rear-arch jambs of the window in that gable were given a widened splay to the part that would have been enclosed within the roof. But, in the later operation, the early Gothic east gable was heightened on each side by a triangle of masonry in which the pinnacles were retained at the angles, and behind which a shallow-pitched roof at a higher level could be accommodated (see Fig. 6). Along the flanks of the eastern limb, a wall of about the same height as the clerestory was added, with a single large traceried window in each bay (Fig. 13). The windows over the presbytery section were set at a slightly higher level than those over the choir, presumably because of the retention of the vault over this part, the residual traces of which are shown in views by both Brand and Waters. The lower position of the windows over the choir suggests that the ceiling over that part was reconstructed to a flattened form and that there was a division of some form between the two parts of the upper chamber. Each of the upper storey's windows was framed externally by a depressed two-centred arch, and internally by a rounded rear-arch, but nothing is known of their tracery, which deprives us of what would have been the principal diagnostic evidence for their date. Where it survives, the new upper wall is carried on the inner skin of the clerestory wall, leaving space for an external walkway with a low parapet on its outer edge, the walkway passing through apertures in the buttresses between the bays.

The function of this upper storey is unrecorded. Upper storeys above eastern limbs are found — or once existed — elsewhere, as at the Augustinian priory of Christchurch in Hampshire, where it served as a school for part of its later history. But they seem to be more common in the north, with examples at Brinkburn priory (also Augustinian)[46] and Benedictine Lindisfarne priory, which, like Tynemouth, are both in Northumberland. In the latter cases, it has been suggested the heightening was to fortify sites near the troubled border with Scotland that were at risk of attack, and the utilitarian character of the heightening would be consistent with such use. But the upper chamber at Tynemouth, like that at Christchurch, was designed with some architectural finesse, and its location at the least militarily vulnerable end of a promontory that was fortified along the line of approach renders a defensive role unlikely. It has been speculated that it could have been added at the behest of Abbot Whethamstede to accommodate more altars,[47] though it must be doubted if parts of the church accessed by a long ascent up narrow spiral stairways could be liturgically useful. While the argument of relative inaccessibility can be applied against any proposed use, is it perhaps more likely it was one of a number of adaptations of parts of the church to domestic uses? At some stage in its history, the space over the south choir aisle had a fireplace and oven inserted; that space was reached by the stair that continued up to the chambers over the eastern limb, and it also communicated with a chamber over the chapter-house into which a fireplace was inserted.[48] It is possible that the chambers over the eastern limb, together with those over the south choir aisle and chapter-house, provided more commodious accommodation for members of the community as the emphasis on communal living was increasingly relaxed in the later middle ages.

The last significant identifiable addition to the church was a small chapel projecting axially from the east gable, which is set so low that only a minor heightening of the sill of the presbytery's central window was required to accommodate it (see Figs 2 and 6). Heraldry and monograms on its vault link it with Prior John Langton (*c.* 1450–78) and the earls of Northumberland. Since the earldom was forfeited from 1461 to about 1469, a date from the 1470s seems most likely for its construction. The function of the chapel is not recorded. While its position has led to its being sometimes described as a Lady chapel, that role was served by a building north of the presbytery; beyond that, the way that the chapel is closed off from the church by a doorway suggests it was essentially a private space. Craster's identification of it as a chantry for the Percy family is therefore perhaps the most plausible interpretation.[49] Whatever the case, however, locating a private chapel in such a prominent location is extremely unusual for anyone other than a monarch.[50]

The chapel is of three narrow bays above a base course with a bottom chamfer and an ogee-curve capped by a roll. It is entered by a doorway cut through the recess at the centre of the east wall; towards the church that door has a depressed two-centred arch with continuous mouldings, while the rear-arch is segmental. The mechanically regular succession of filleted or plain rolls — four externally and six internally — is perhaps a reminder that Tynemouth is close to the border with Scotland, where such mouldings were more common than in England. Many of the chapel's details should be treated with caution, since it was restored by John Dobson in 1850–52 after uses that included a mortuary chapel and a powder magazine. The two-light rectilinear tracery in the windows of the side walls in particular has been heavily restored and, since views of the interior before restoration show the walls as blank, it is unclear if Dobson had full evidence on which to base his window designs. The chapel is covered by a complex vault of depressed profile, in which the tight pattern of over-scaled ribs combined with the close concentration of carved bosses leaves little of the vault web visible (Fig. 14). There are no precise parallels for the pattern of ribs, though the way in which the expression of the individual bays is sacrificed to the overall unity of the vault has parallels with the net vaults of the west country, as in the nave of Tewkesbury abbey of *c.* 1335–49.[51] As at Tewkesbury, there are three parallel longitudinal ribs, combined with two sets of diagonal ribs, one of which is confined to the

FIG. 12. Tynemouth priory: the east face of the choir screen
Author

FIG. 13. Tynemouth priory: the superstructure added to the eastern limb
Author

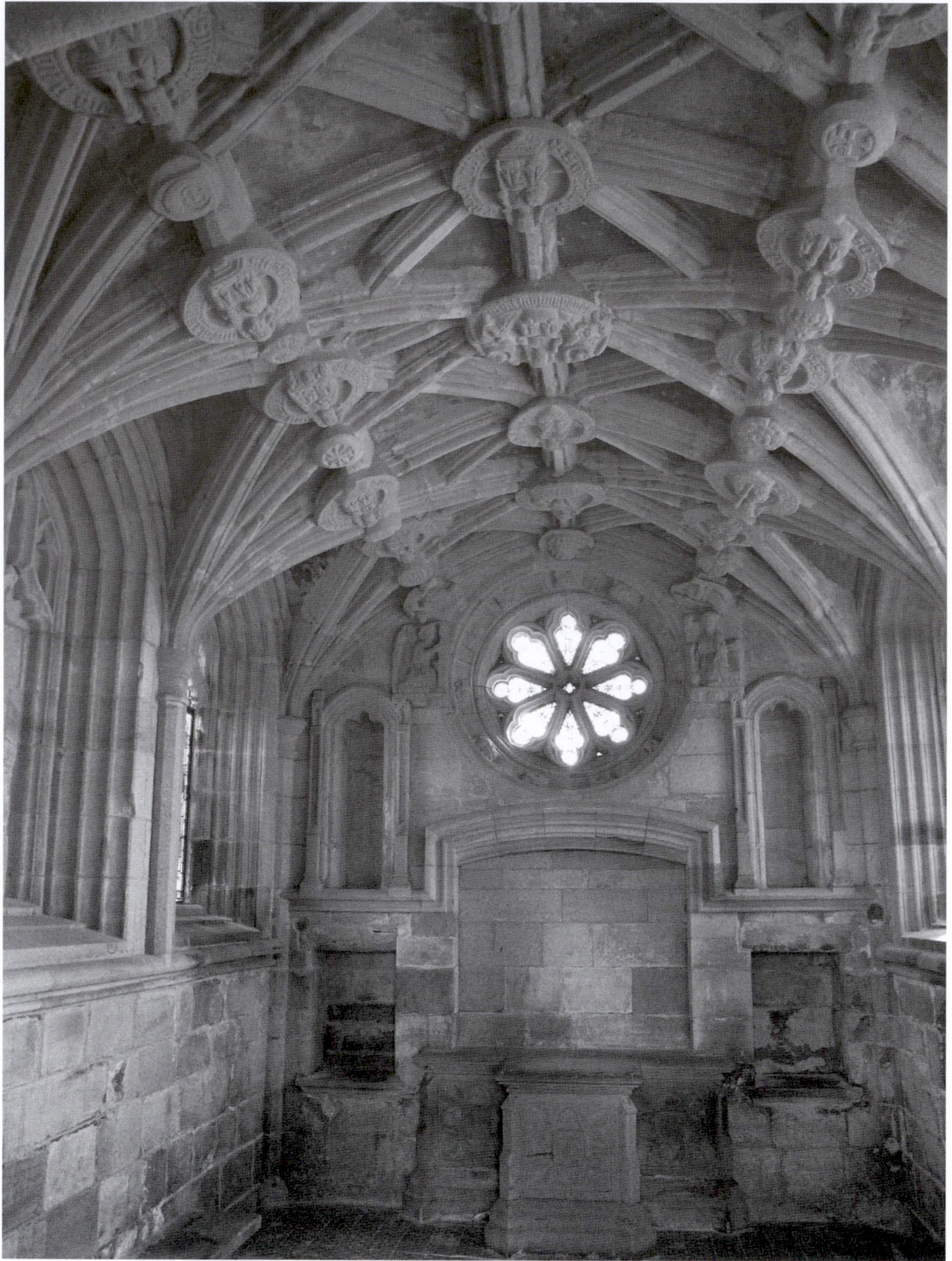

FIG. 14. Tynemouth priory: the interior of the Percy chapel
Author

individual bays, while the other crosses over into the adjacent bay. It seems unlikely, however, that there could have been any direct connection between two buildings so widely separated in time and place. An attractively subtle feature of the design is the way in which the diagonal ribs crossing into adjacent bays are subordinated to those within the individual bays.

THE END OF THE PRIORY

BY the early 16th century the priory was recorded as being in poor repair, with particular attention focused on the decayed state of the windows and roofs in 1527.[52] The end was foreshadowed in a visitation by the king's commissioners in 1536, which deemed the community to be in poor moral state. Dissolution came on 12 January 1539, when the prior, fifteen monks and three novices finally surrendered their house.[53] Parts of the nave continued in parochial use until 1668, when a new parish church was built in South Shields, at which point the last phase of religious life in the priory church came to an end.

NOTES

1. *HN*, VIII, 131–36; R. Cramp, *County Durham and Northumberland*, Corpus of Anglo-Saxon Stone Sculpture in England 1 (Oxford 1984), I, 226–29; II, pls 220–27.

2. On Oswin, see Bede, *EH*, 254–60.

3. *Matthæi Parisiensis, monachi Sancti Albani, Chronica majora*, ed. H. R. Luard, 7 vols, Rolls series 57 (London 1872–83), I, 531–32; 'Vita Oswini, regis deiorum', in *Miscellanea Biographica*, ed. J. Raine, SS 8 (Edinburgh and London 1838), 12.

4. *Symeonis monachi opera omnia*, ed. T. Arnold, 2 vols, Rolls series 75 (London 1882–85), II, 309; D. Knowles, *The Monastic Order in England*, 2nd edn (Cambridge 1963), 166–67.

5. An extended account of Tynemouth's relationships with Durham and St Albans is given in *HN*, VIII, 34–152 *passim*.

6. *Durham Episcopal Charters, 1071–1152*, ed. H. S. Offler, SS 179 (Gateshead 1968), 5; D. Bates, 'The Forged Charters of William the Conqueror and Bishop William of St Calais' and E. Cambridge, 'Early Romanesque Architecture in North-East England' (appendix, 'A Note on Tynemouth Priory'), in *Anglo-Norman Durham*, ed. D. Rollason, M. Harvey and M. Prestwich (Woodbridge 1994), 115–16, 159–60.

7. 'Vita Oswini' (as n. 3), 24–25.

8. The frequently repeated suggestion that the burial of the Scottish king Malcolm III in the church in 1093 demonstrates that work on the new church was well advanced can be discounted; that burial presumably took place in the old church.

9. 'Vita Oswini' (as n. 3), 28.

10. W. H. Knowles, 'The Priory Church of St Mary and St Oswin, Tynemouth, Northumberland', *Archaeol. J.*, 67 (1910), 8.

11. Ibid., 7–9; *HN*, VIII, 136–47.

12. E. Fernie, *The Architecture of Norman England* (Oxford 2000), 102–08.

13. There was evidently some variety of capitals types, because in the stone store at the priory is a respond capital of corinthianesque form.

14. *The Heads of Religious Houses in England and Wales, I. 940–1216*, ed. D. Knowles, C. N. L. Brooke and V. C. M. London, 2nd edn (Cambridge 2001), 96 and 61.

15. *Gesta Abbatum monasterii Sancti Albani*, ed. H. T. Riley, 3 vols (Rolls Series, XXVIII/, 1867–69), I, 265.

16. A. H. Thompson, 'The Cathedral Church of the Blessed Virgin Mary, Southwell', *Transactions of the Thoroton Society*, 15 (1911), 15–62.

17. *Chronicle of Melrose*, ed. A. O. Anderson and M. O. Anderson (London 1936), 78; E. Cambridge, 'The Early Building History of St Andrews Cathedral', *Antiq. J.*, 57 (1977), 277–88.

18. I. B. Cowan and D. E. Easson, *Medieval Religious Houses: Scotland*, 2nd edn (London and New York 1976), 92.

19. A. W. Clapham, *English Romanesque Architecture: After the Conquest* (Oxford 1934), 91–92.
20. R. Fawcett and R. Oram, *Dryburgh Abbey* (Stroud 2005), 56–63.
21. H. E. Craster and R. N. Hadcock, 'Tynemouth Priory', *AA*, 4th ser. 14 (1937), 207–08.
22. R. Fawcett, 'Arbroath Abbey: A Note on its Architecture and Early Conservation History', in *The Declaration of Arbroath*, ed. G. Barrow (Edinburgh 2003), 50–85.
23. C. C. Hodges, *The Abbey of St Andrew Hexham* (Hexham 1888), pl. 14.
24. Fawcett and Oram, *Dryburgh Abbey* (as n. 20), 56–63.
25. P. Draper, 'The Nine Altars at Durham and Fountains', in *Medieval Art and Architecture at Durham Cathedral*, ed. N. Coldstream and P. Draper, *BAA Trans.*, III (Leeds 1980), 74–86.
26. M. Baylé, *L'Architecture Normande au Moyen Age*, 2nd edn, 2 vols (Caen 2001), I, pl. facing 137; II, 152–55.
27. L. Grant, *Architecture and Society in Normandy 1120–1270* (New Haven and London 2005), 72 and fig. 41.
28. *HN*, VIII, 95.
29. Craster and Hadcock, 'Tynemouth Priory' (as n. 21), 213.
30. S. Harrison and P. Barker, 'Ripon Minster: An Archaeological Analysis and Reconstruction of the 12th-Century Church', *JBAA*, 152 (1999), 49–78.
31. The most valuable of those views of the choir is a pull-out engraving in J. Brand, *The History and Antiquities of the Town and County of the Town of Newcastle upon Tyne*, 2 vols (London 1789) (in vol. II). The information on that view is supplemented in a painting by Waters of 1783 reproduced as pl. IX in *HN*, VIII. R. N. Hadcock has published a reconstruction of the elevation in Craster and Hadcock, 'Tynemouth Priory' (as n. 21).
32. Harrison and Barker, 'Ripon Minster' (as n. 30).
33. P. Fergusson, *Architecture of Solitude* (Princeton 1984), 79–82, fig. 16; Harrison and Barker, 'Ripon Minster' (as n. 30), fig. 2.
34. Fergusson, *Architecture of Solitude* (as n. 33), 84–85.
35. N. J. G. Pounds, *A History of the English Parish* (Cambridge 2000), 56.
36. In a survey of 1577 it appears to be referred to as 'a litle towre used for a prison called the hy prison'. The survey is reprinted in Knowles, 'The Priory Church' (as n. 10), 42–50, with this entry at 46.
37. *Annales monasterii Sancti Albani*, ed. H. T. Riley, 2 vols (Rolls Series, XXVIII/5, 1870–71), I, 220–21.
38. *HN*, VIII, 85–88.
39. This information is contained in the Tynemouth cartulary (fol. 80v), in the collection of the duke of Northumberland.
40. *HN*, VIII, 91; Tynemouth Cartulary (as n. 39), fol. 172.
41. Knowles, 'The Priory Church' (as n. 10), 23.
42. Craster and Hadcock, 'Tynemouth Priory' (as n. 21), 212, for example, say, 'When the shrine of St Oswin was translated to another part of the church, it was to a position more quiet, less restricted and more spacious. The only more spacious position in the church would seem to be the new Lady chapel'.
43. *Rites of Durham*, ed. J. T. Fowler, SS 107 (Durham 1903), 44–45.
44. S. Brown, *Sumptuous and Richly Adorn'd: The Decoration of Salisbury Cathedral* (London 1999), 23.
45. Ibid., loc. cit.
46. The Brinkburn upper storey was removed in the course of a restoration in 1859, but is known from pre-restoration photographs.
47. Craster and Hadcock, 'Tynemouth Priory' (as n. 21), 216.
48. Ibid., 214–15 and fig. 3. Rather puzzlingly, the chamber over the south choir aisle, also appears to have been accessible from a small door on the east side of the arch from the south transept into the choir aisle, a door which had the retained north respond of the Romanesque gallery forming part of one jamb. There is now no way of knowing how that door was accessed, unless it was associated with a gallery, as suggested by Craster and Hadcock, 'Tynemouth Priory' (as n. 21), 214.
49. *HN*, VIII, 103–04.
50. Amongst the very few cases of an axially located chantry chapel to the east of a major church is Henry VII's chapel at Westminster Abbey of 1503–12, which superseded an earlier proposal by that king for an axial eastern chapel at Windsor. The chapel at Westminster of Henry V, which dates from 1437 and is the work of the mason John Thirsk, is also on the central axis, and to the east of the high altar and the shrine of St Edward the Confessor, though it is within the body of the building.
51. R. K. Morris, 'The Gothic Church: Vaulting and Carpentry', in *Tewkesbury Abbey: History, Art and Architecture*, ed. R. K. Morris and R. Shoesmith (Little Logaston 2003), 131–38.
52. *Letters and Papers, Foreign and Domestic, of the Reign of Henry VIII*, ed. J. Gardiner, R. H. Brodie and J. S. Brewer, 21 vols (London 1862–1920), IV, 1469.
53. *HN*, VIII, 108–09.

Manuscripts, History and Aesthetic Interests at Tynemouth Priory

JULIAN LUXFORD

This paper selectively reviews the surviving medieval books of Tynemouth priory for the evidence they contain about the historical and aesthetic interests of local monks. The material analysed begins with the testimony to the historical status of the monastery and character of St Oswin found in the oldest survivals, moves on to the attitudes represented by a letter describing the privations and consolations of the monastery, and extends to discussion of a description of Hagia Sophia and other churches in Constantinople contained in a composite manuscript now in the British Library. In the concluding section of the paper the embellishment of existing books is briefly reviewed, particularly the illumination of three psalters made elsewhere and adapted for use at Tynemouth and St Albans in the 15th century.

THE aim of the following discussion is to illuminate aspects of the cultural history of Tynemouth priory though selective study of the monastery's books.[1] It is not an analysis of book-provision at the priory, or an attempt to reconstruct the reading habits of its monks and novices. The evidence for these topics is in any case rather narrow: the twenty surviving manuscripts (or parts thereof) and four printed books commonly recognized to have a Tynemouth provenance, and the ten additional titles listed in the late 13th- or early 14th-century union catalogue known as the *Registrum Anglie de libris doctorum et auctorum veterum*, probably represent a modest fraction of the priory's original collection, and it is difficult in a number of cases to know when a surviving volume produced at St Albans or elsewhere made its way north.[2] The focus will instead be on indications of the art, architectural and broader aesthetic interests of the monks that have been ignored or insufficiently discussed in the past. Over and above the generic aspects of Benedictine life, three localized factors appear to have been particularly effective in shaping these interests: the extraordinary site and topography of the priory, its identification with St Oswin, and, through inevitable processes of supply and exchange, its relationship to the mother-house at St Albans. Surviving Tynemouth books have an important role in representing each of these, alongside written sources from St Albans and the architecture and archaeology of the site.

It is appropriate that the earliest surviving books from Tynemouth are those whose texts establish the antiquity of the monastery and the sanctity and character of Oswin, who rivalled the Virgin Mary in local affections and duly received a moiety of the priory's dedication. This individual, the last king of the Northumbrian province of Deira, was murdered in Yorkshire in 651 by order of his cousin Oswiu, but it was thought, from the 11th century at least, that he had been buried at Tynemouth. Bede's fulsome (and from a medieval perspective unquestionable) account of him in the

Ecclesiastical History was the basis of his reputation for sanctity: Oswin had been religious, physically attractive, 'marvellously' humble, a relative and friend of saints, and killed in a way that suggested martyrdom.[3] This testimony, and the text in which it was embedded, thus became a cornerstone of the priory's historical and spiritual status, and the monks sought it out as a matter of course. Cambridge, Pembroke College MS 82 contains a copy of the *Ecclesiastical History* that belonged to Tynemouth and was almost certainly made there in the second quarter of the 12th century.[4] Various additions to the manuscript show that, in addition to his intrinsic merits, Oswin's local importance derived from his position in a network of holy Northumbrian kinship, an idea supported by the emphasis placed on his descent in the first chapter of the hagiographical *Life of St Oswin* written at Tynemouth in the same period, and in sermons on the saint contained in Oxford, Corpus Christi College MS 134 (fols 21, 27v–28r).[5] The tone for this is set by a genealogical diagram on fol. 139v, displaying names in roundels connected by lines of descent in what is either a 12th-century hand or a later imitation of one (Fig. 1). It demonstrates at a glance both

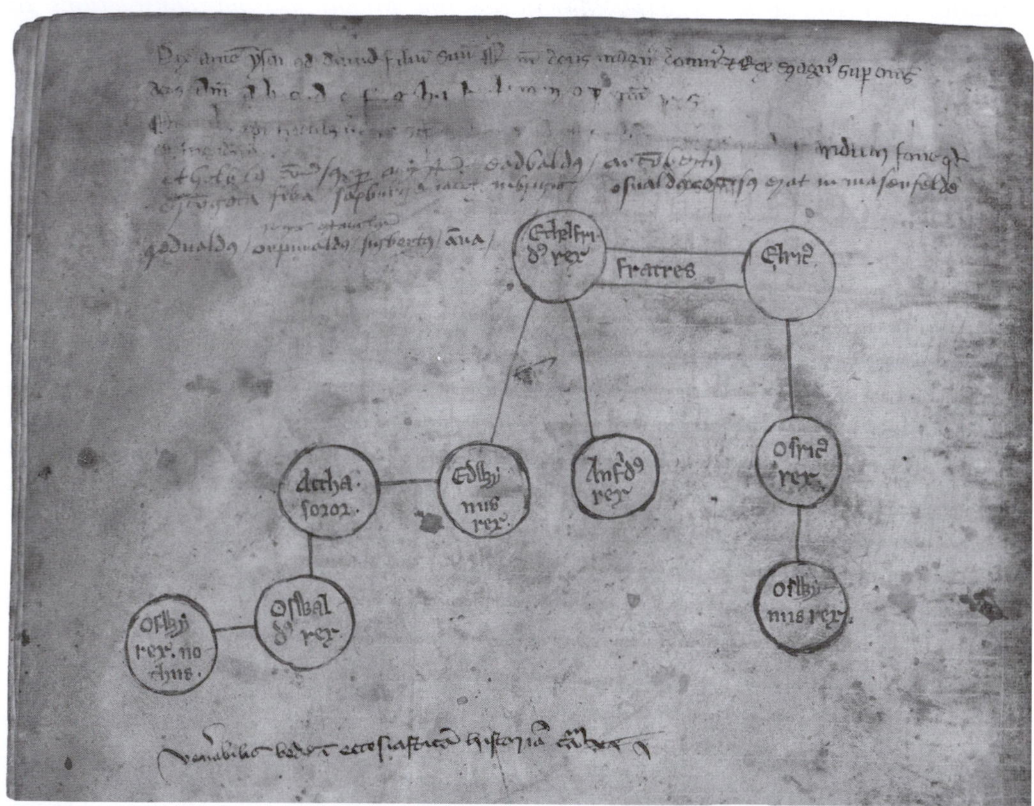

FIG. 1. Cambridge, Pembroke College MS 82, fol. 139v. Upper half of a page containing a genealogical diagram displaying Oswin's royal and saintly pedigree. At the top of the page are extracts from I Kings 17:17 and Psalm 94:3, an alphabet and historical/genealogical notes in a 15th-century hand (including 'Osualdus occisus erat in maserfelde')

Reproduced by permission of the Master and Fellows of Pembroke College, Cambridge

Oswin's royal pedigree and the fact that he numbered the sainted kings Edwin (d. 633) and Oswald (d. 642) as cousins. Interest in these figures is further indicated by marginalia on Bede's text. Following the example of an earlier reader, who had picked out references to Oswin on fols 45v and 54v, a 15th-century annotator wrote notes about incidents involving Edwin, Oswald and Oswin, including the carriage to Kent by St Paulinus of a golden cross and chalice that had belonged to Edwin (fol. 45r), the erection by Oswald of a miraculous cross at Heavenfield (fol. 47r), Bishop Aidan of Lindisfarne's exclamation 'may this hand never decay!' as he seized the charitable Oswald's right hand (fol. 49v: here the annotator was prompted to add a manicule), the death and miracles of Oswald (fols 51v–54r), his charity (53v), and the corresponding humility of Oswin (fol. 55r). Mistakenly, he also noted a letter 'sent by Pope Vitalian to King Oswin in Britain', and the holy relics 'sent to England to King Oswin and [his] queen',[6] where in fact King Oswiu (d. 670), the agent of Oswin's death, had received these presents. Here the annotator's zeal for his protector saint induced him to read 'Osuino' for 'Osuio', and to accept the otherwise undocumented fact that the chaste Oswin had a consort.[7]

Other monks wrote in the margins of Pembroke MS 82, including a late medieval reader interested in the antiquity of his house. As well as identifying a reference to Oswin not previously annotated (fol. 55r), he sought out Bede's mention of a 'monastery [...] by the mouth of the Tyne' ruled by an abbot named Herebald (d. 745), and flagged it by writing 'nota de herebaldo abbate de Tinemouth' in the margin alongside (fol. 100r). Evidently, he had no doubt that Bede was describing an early manifestation of his own house during a period of primitive independence under its own superior: the matter was presumably confirmed for him by the presence of 'saint' Herebald's tomb in the priory church.[8] The local bias that produced this note was perpetuated by reminding readers of their institution's roots in the heroic Bedan landscape from which Oswin himself had emerged. This concept, and the interest in Oswin's blood relationship to other saints, was more fully represented in a manuscript seen by the 16th-century antiquary John Leland, which stated that Edwin had built a wooden chapel at Tynemouth, which Oswald replaced with a small monastery of wood and stone.[9] Enthusiasm for local history had also influenced an earlier annotator of *c.* 1200 to supply an encomium of Siward, earl of Northumbria (d. 1055), which concludes with the statement that Tostig, Siward's successor, 'laid down the foundations of the church of Tynemouth' (fol. iiir).[10] This reflects a belief that the re-foundation of the monastery commenced before both the Norman Conquest and its annexation to St Albans. The idea surfaces again in the *Life of St Oswin*, where Tynemouth's re-foundation and rebuilding by Robert Mowbray (d. 1115/25) are qualified by the observation that Tostig was responsible for beginning the works ('as it is said').[11] One can easily understand its appeal. By positing the involvement of the last Anglo-Saxon earl, who had presided over the invention of Oswin's relics in 1065, the spiritual and physical regeneration of the site could be rolled into a single event, leaving no evident gaps in the history of monastic custodianship of Oswin's relics.[12]

The local legacy of Bede's *History* is found in a highly developed form in Oxford, Corpus Christi College MS 134, an Oswin *omnium gatherum* produced at Tynemouth during the mid- to late 12th century.[13] This compact volume expresses the temper of devotion to the saint more effectively than any other surviving object, and it remained in use into the later middle ages, when biblical quotations were added to fol. 92v.[14] Its texts were intended to exemplify the somatic and metaphysical qualities in which Oswin's reputation for holiness was grounded. The bedrock of Bede's description is embroidered with relish: for example, a sermon in the manuscript informs readers and hearers that the king had been 'handsome in appearance and pure in devotion; tall of stature but higher in contempt for the world; beautiful of face but more beautiful in faith; perfect in body, lively in mind, pleasant in speech, profound in perception, [and] courteous in manner; born of a ruler, of the race of a line of kings, and full of the glorious grace [of God]'.[15] Because its subject was one of beauty, the book itself was beautified by the addition of large coloured initials in red, blue and green, almost certainly copied from exemplars made elsewhere (Fig. 2). Their quality is low by professional standards, as is that of the manuscript as a whole: held alongside contemporary Tynemouth volumes like Durham Cathedral Library MS A.IV.6, a glossed copy of the books of Daniel and Esdras made *c.* 1125–50, and the slightly later BL, MS Harley 3847, containing Hugh of St Victor's *De Sacramentis*, Corpus Christi MS 134 looks decidedly local in execution as well as application. This may, however, have been important, if the evidence of local production conveyed to readers by its rough aesthetic suggested personal, unmediated experience of the virtues and wonders described in its texts.

Corpus Christi MS 134 opens with a calendar from Hexham priory adapted for use at Tynemouth by the insertion, among other things, of the feast (20 August, graded principal) and octave (27 August, graded in albs) of Oswin, 'regis et martiris precellentissimi' (fol. xi verso). The leaf containing March and April is missing, but the feast of Oswin's translation on 11 March must once also have been present. There follow short items that form a preface to the main texts: an explanation of the divisions of world history, a summary of the three continents and their constituent countries, a genealogy of the three Marys, a calculation of the number of years between the birth of Christ and the passion, invention and translation of Oswin, a detailed description of the physical appearance and dress of the Three Magi (no artist or meditator could have wanted a better guide), and a list of Tynemouth's relics. The longer items that follow are a copy of the *Life of St Oswin* (incomplete, but the earliest in existence), sermons on the character, passion and invention of the saint, accounts of his miracles, and a noted office of St Oswin whose text is mainly dependent on the *Life*.[16] Although the relationship of some of the short items to Oswin seems obscure, they were written out at the same time as the *Life* and sermons, meaning that the arrangement was a considered one. The fact that they deal in threes cannot be coincidental: it was perhaps thought that the Oswin-centric division of history would be better remembered through association with other tripartite accounts of a sacred nature. Even on its own, this division had the edifying effect of associating Oswin with Christ by repeatedly pairing their names: 'From the year of our Lord's birth until the passion of St Oswin, king and martyr, 651 years. From the passion of the same until the finding of his body, that is to say, the year of our Lord's birth 1065, there were 414 years. From the discovery to his translation, that is, the year of our Lord's birth 1110, forty-five years'.[17] This idea is developed in the sermons and *Life* through copious references to the saint's exemplary humility, his chastity and charity, and the passion and example of Christ. One of the sermons has as its mantra the idea that Oswin's very name meant 'richness of love'; another, likening his patience and modesty to that of King David, calls him 'principe humilitatis' and 'rex humilis'.[18] Ultimately, the association extended to patent Christomimesis in a claim that Oswin had been martyred by having a spear stabbed into his side. This belief is reflected in images of the saint holding a spear on Tynemouth's 14th-century common seal (Fig. 3), the sepulchral brass

FIG. 2. Oxford, Corpus Christi College MS 134, fol. 6r. The opening of the Life of St Oswin, decorated by a local artist. (The post-medieval ascription to 'Iohannes de Tinmouth' is wrong)

Reproduced by permission of the President and Fellows if Corpus Christi College, Oxford

FIG. 3. Impression of the 14th-century common seal of Tynemouth priory, representing The Virgin and Child (L.) and St Oswin holding a sceptre and the spear with which he was thought to have been martyred. This seal remained in use until the priory's dissolution in 1539

of Thomas de la Mare at St Albans, and elsewhere. It may also help to account for the interest in the holy lance demonstrated by the rubric 'lancea Christi' in another of the priory's books.[19]

While Oswin's virtues and miracles were naturally understood in subordinate relation to the personality and mission of Christ, his relics easily outshone even those objects in the priory's possession most intimately associated with sacred history. With the dubious exceptions of Henry of Coquet Island (d. 1127), and the Bedan abbot Herebald, neither of whose bodies is likely to have been elevated, Oswin's was the only 'whole relic' the monks owned, and thus the only relic to merit the acquisition and display of a large, prestigious feretory.[20] With a proper sense of decorum, the inventory on fol. 2r of Corpus Christi MS 134 presents the relics of Christ, the Virgin Mary, and other biblical figures first, but the entry 'the body of the most blessed OSWIN, king and martyr, and his vestments', which follows immediately after, was given its own decorated initial and must have represented the feature of greatest interest to any reader (Fig. 4).[21] Of course, Oswin's relics did a different job: while biblical artefacts such as those of Christ's nativity, crib, presentation, agony in the garden, cross, and tomb, or the vestments and tomb of the Virgin Mary, or the patriarchs

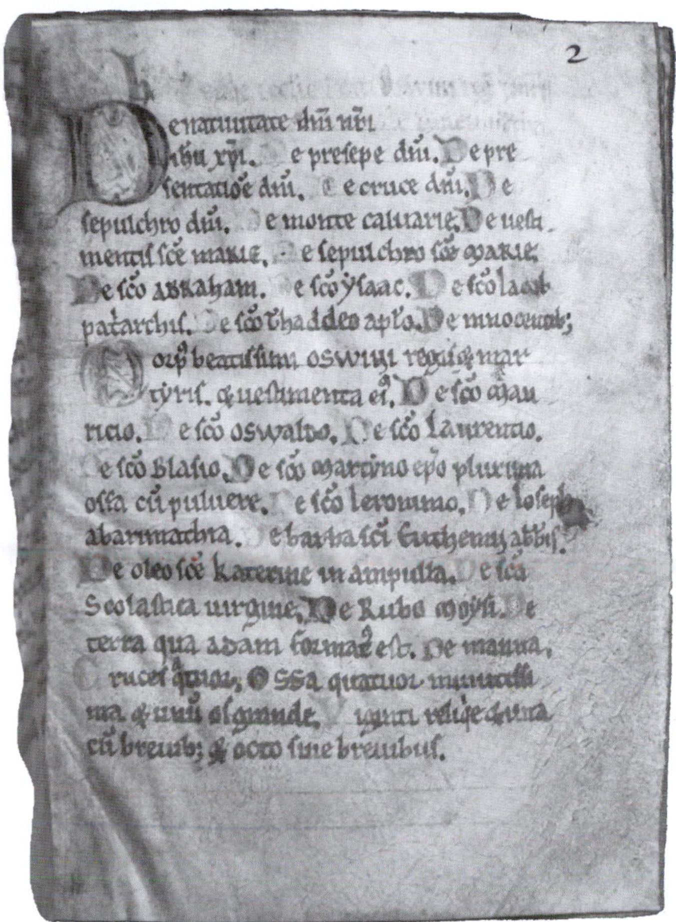

FIG. 4. Oxford, Corpus Christi College MS 134, fol. 2r. Tynemouth priory's 12th-century relic-list. The heading, in red, reads: 'He sunt reliquie ecclesie beati Oswini regis et martyris de Tynemutha'

Reproduced by permission of the President and Fellows if Corpus Christi College, Oxford

Abraham, Isaac and Jacob, were probably of most use in the devout re-imagining of sacred history and topography, Oswin's bones and vestments were potent miracle-workers, and thus enjoyed a popular and widespread prestige. Indeed, they may well have been the only 'active' relics the priory owned at the time the list was made.[22] Like those with which the list opens, the relics mentioned after Oswin's look to have been important primarily for symbolic and devotional purposes. Apart from a remnant of St Oswald, none belonged to an indigenous saint. The particles of martyrs (Maurice, Lawrence, Blaise, Martin, and Catherine) and confessors (Joseph of Arimathea, Jerome, Euthymius the Great, and Scholastica), pieces of the burning bush, manna, and earth from which Adam was made, and thirty-seven relics and relic-crosses whose identity the list's author did not trouble to record (though in at least twenty cases they appear to have been identified with *authentiques*), probably represent a foundational collection sent from the mother-house in the 1090s with the intention of supplying spiritual authorization equivalent to the temporal sanction contained in Robert Mowbray's charters. Certainly, most of the named items specified here are paralleled in the early 15th-century inventory of St Albans's relics.[23] As such, their collective function was to validate and augment an institutional reputation for sanctity rooted primarily in the relics and miracles of Oswin.

It is highly probable that more relics were acquired after the composition of this list. In 1536, Henry VIII's commissioners mentioned 'the chalice of St Cuthbert, the finger of St Bartholomew, and the girdle of St Margaret' in addition to 'the shrine or monument of St. Oswyn'; all objects likely to have been specified had the priory owned them when the list was made.[24] Apart from the mention of relic-crosses, and a deposition of 1539 that certain bones had been garnished with gold and silver, nothing is known about the embellishment or presentation of relics at Tynemouth except those of St Oswin.[25] For the patron saint, a gem-studded *theca* of gilded silver, remade in the late 12th century, is the only reliquary mentioned: there is no evidence that his head, miraculous hair, or vestments were displayed separately, and no claim is made on his crown, the spear with which he was supposed to have been martyred, or any other object associated with him.[26] (In fact, the monks of Durham claimed to possess Oswin's head.)[27] However, as no other house seems to have owned any of them, it is reasonable to think that such accessories did exist at Tynemouth. It has recently been suggested that one may survive in the form of a small psalter, now BL, MS Cotton Galba A.V (Fig. 5).[28] This book was originally prefaced by the inscription 'The book of Oswin, king of the Deirans', cut out or otherwise destroyed before the mid-17th century.[29] In fact, the manuscript was written and illuminated in Ireland, probably in the mid-12th century; but its script and decoration must have looked sufficiently archaic in later medieval Northumbria for it to be associated by the monks with their spiritual patron. (This link was still credited in the 19th century by the editor of the *Life of St Oswin*.)[30]

From the monastic perspective at least, the relationship between the beauty of Oswin and his miracles on the one hand and the locus of his cult on the other extended to both the church and the weathered stump of rock on which it stood.[31] Where the church is concerned the association must have been direct, and emphasized by the materials, iconography and workmanship of stained glass, wall paintings, textiles, and other fittings, particularly in the area of the feretory. The topography of the crag also complemented the cult in an obvious way, elevating and isolating it above its surrounds, as, in its own way, the site of the mother-house did for the cult of Alban. Perhaps inevitably, it also functioned to edify by contrast. A striking indication of this is provided by an anonymous, undated letter at the back of Thomas de la Mare's register, now Cambridge, University Library MS Ee.4.20, fol. 283r–v (Fig. 6).[32] This manuscript may never have belonged to Tynemouth: the only link is the name of Robert Blakeney on fol. 284r, which could have been added before he was elected prior of the northern cell in 1536. The letter, however, which was written by a monk at Tynemouth, or one who had spent time there, is richly descriptive of the place. If its composition was not simply a formulaic or rhetorical exercise (De la Mare's register is in part a formulary, and James Clark calls the letter 'florid' and 'full of classical allusions'), then its ostensible purpose was to warn monks at St Albans or one of its other cells to avoid being sent to the priory on account of the rigours of life there.[33] This is attempted by a pessimistic portrayal of the area, its weather, local inhabitants, and unpalatable diet. About three-quarters of the way through, however, the tone changes abruptly to one of high praise for the merits of Oswin, the convent and the church. It is as though the author suddenly perceived an insult to the saint in

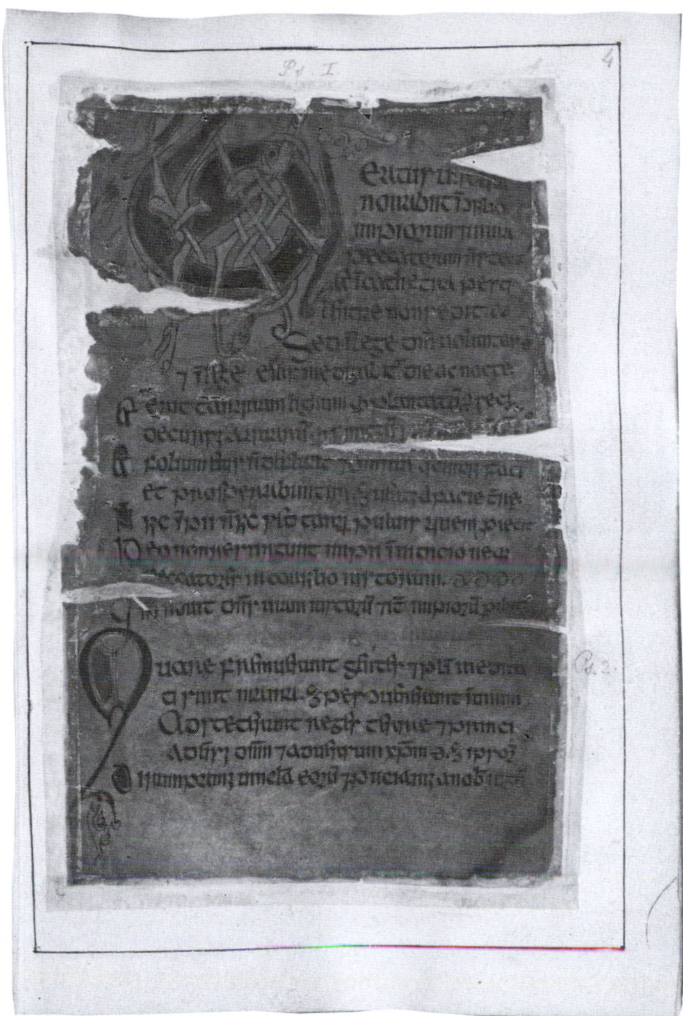

FIG. 5. BL, MS Cotton Galba A.V, fol. 4r (Psalm 1 and part of Psalm 2). The first surviving leaf of a 12th-century Irish psalter once prefaced by the inscription 'Liber Oswini Deirorum Regis'
Reproduced by permission of the British Library Board

his Jeremiad, and wished to put things to rights. Of course, this cannot be the case. Rather, the intention seems to have been the rhetorical one of accenting praise by contrasting its objects with their diametrical opposites. Thus, where the crag is high, cold and 'most wretched', the church it supports is 'newly and tastefully built [and] wonderfully beautiful'.[34] The laity who subsist on the shores are defiled by the climate and a diet of seaweed, to the extent that the men look like Moors ('mauri'), the women like Ethiopians, the girls are filthy ('squalide'), and the boys resemble black Hebrew children; but within the church rests 'the body of the blessed, glorious, merciful martyr Oswin, in a tomb embellished most beautifully with silver, gold and gems'.[35] Sailors drown as their ships strike the rocks below the crag, while above them 'the glorious martyr Oswin, best, most effective doctor of the sick', succours those whom neither practice nor physician can help: 'deaf, lame, blind and mute are made

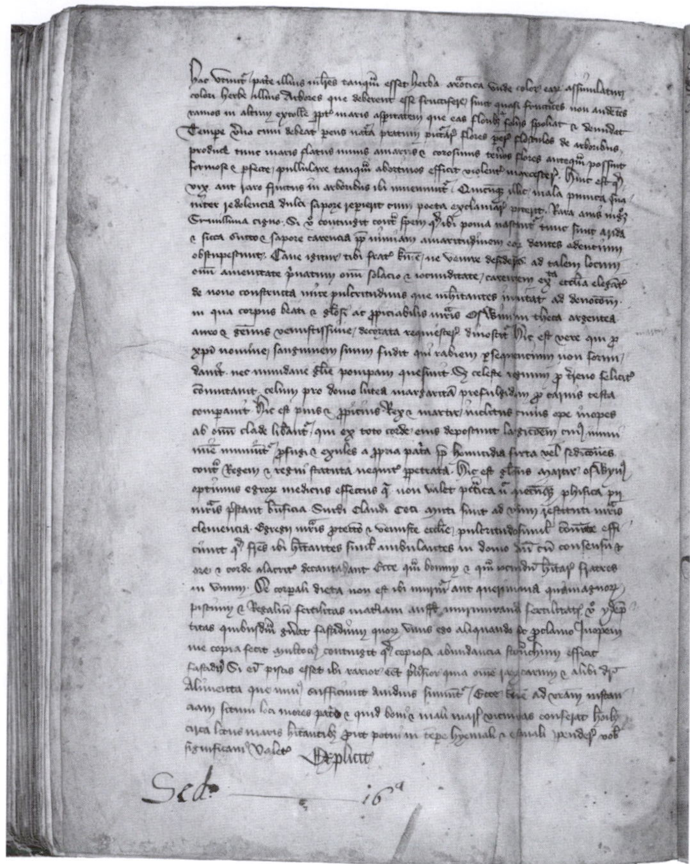

Fig. 6. Cambridge, University Library, MS Ee.4.20, fol. 283v. Part of a copy of a letter describing conditions and religious observance at Tynemouth. The copy dates from the 15th century, but the letter was probably written in the 12th or 13th century

Reproduced by permission of the Syndics of Cambridge University Library

whole by the martyr's mercy'.[36] While rain, snow and the north wind assail the site, 'the great martyr, and the beauty of the church' combine to protect the monks and consolidate *esprit de corps*.[37] Thus, as grey seabirds horribly announce the coming storm with hoarse cries ('rauca voce'), the convent sings the verse most redolent of monastic harmony: 'Behold how good and how pleasant it is for brethren to dwell in unity'.[38] In short, the church, with its shrine and relics, represents an oasis of sanctity and fraternal love in a hostile, quasi-pagan wilderness.

Knowledge of when this letter was written would assist in the imaginative reconstruction of medieval attitudes to Tynemouth and its cult. The information in the St Albans chronicles (chiefly the *Chronica majora* and *Gesta abbatum*) is of limited use here, although at least one indication survives from the early 15th century that the place was considered a sequestered backwater.[39] Various dates have been proposed, from the early 12th century to the early 15th. Because the letter suggests that the relics were highly active and popular, and the church is described as newly built, a date early in this range is likely. What is apparently Oswin's last recorded miracle occurred in 1384, suggesting a later medieval drop-off in activity at his shrine commensurate with that experienced elsewhere.[40] And although new works, including the Lady chapel and relocation of the shrine, were accomplished under priors Tewing and De la Mare, they can hardly be equated with 'ecclesia eleganter de novo constructa'.[41] The knowledge of classical literature displayed in the letter corresponds to the evidence for a literary 'renaissance' at St Albans during the 14th and 15th centuries, and chimes nicely with a quotation from Cato — 'Rumores fuge, ne incipias nouus auctor haberi' — written during this period in a blank space in Tynemouth's surviving register.[42] However, the learned rhetoric could as easily belong to an earlier age, and the letter as it survives be a copy of something older that was valued for its style and colour. Thus, while 'de novo constructa' need not be taken too literally, a date of composition for the letter in the early to mid-12th century or the early to mid-13th — that is, after the erection of either the Romanesque or the Gothic church — seems probable.

This document portrays the monastic church as a sort of *theca exterior* standing around the *theca interior* that held Oswin's bones, protecting its sacred contents against the hostilities of nature and ignorance. Part of the building's beauty was evidently thought to reside in this function, and that of accommodating the monks and their labour. There is more than a hint in this description of *terribilis est, locus iste* (Genesis 28:17); of the crag as the fearful place at the gate of heaven, where God is manifest through his beloved saint in a mansion that symbolized heaven itself.[43] But the church, or for that matter memories of even grander buildings like those at Durham and St Albans, were not the only available stimulants to meditation on the splendour of God's house. Across the sea that bounded the eastern horizon was another, more extraordinary structure, one famous in the middle ages as a consummation of architectural splendour and a yardstick of the ingenuity and ambition of builder and patron alike. Hagia Sophia in Constantinople was known at Tynemouth, at least from the 14th century, through a short account of it contained in a collection of chronicles and documents owned by the priory (Fig. 7). This volume, now BL, MS Cotton Vitellius A.XX, is made up of a number of separate booklets on historical subjects. *Sammelbände* of this sort certainly existed at Tynemouth — Oxford, Corpus Christi College MS 144 is another example — but in this case the collation may have occurred after the Dissolution.[44] (It occurred before Robert Cotton obtained it, however, because there is a pre-Cotton list of contents on fol. 1*v that includes the 'Descriptio Constantinopolis' discussed here.)[45] There is nevertheless very strong evidence that the various items in the manuscript, including the account of Constantinople in which Hagia Sophia is described (fol. 239r), belonged to the monastery in the middle ages.[46]

The language of this account is conditioned by the material nature of what is described. There is, accordingly, a strong emphasis on seeing, which is anticipated in the heading 'A view of Constantinople, that mighty city founded on miraculous and unutterably great work'.[47] In fact, what is offered is not panoramic, but divided between Hagia Sophia and the churches of the Pantocrator and the Holy Apostles. For the author (or redactor), the city's material glory is epitomized by the architecture of Hagia Sophia and the copiousness of its staff, the latter an important consideration for monastic readers, whose judgements about artistic and architectural magnificence were likely to be influenced by function and morality as well as appearance. To begin with, it is said, the building has cisterns underneath it, some containing sweet water, some salt water, others rainwater. The body of the church is supported at its lower level by 173 marble columns, while above there are 245 columns around the choir,

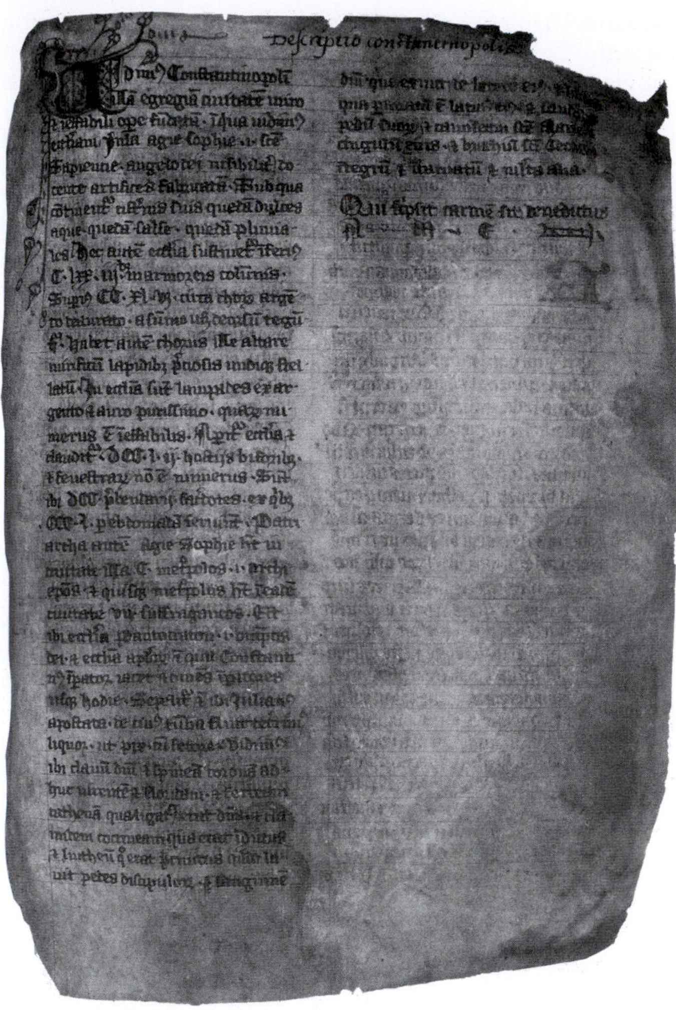

FIG. 7. BL, MS Cotton Vitellius A.XX, fol. 239r. The description of Hagia Sophia in Constantinople. The heading 'Descriptio Constantinopolis' is in the hand of the topographer and antiquary John Leland, who inspected Tynemouth's books sometime between 1536 and 1540

covered from top to bottom in silver and gold. In addition to this choir there is an altar marvellously sparkling all over with precious stones, and an uncountable number of lamps of the purest silver and gold. For opening and closing the building there are 752 doors, each with two leaves, and windows 'without number'. A total of 700 prebendal priests serve Hagia Sophia, of whom 350 celebrate each week. Moreover, the Patriarch of Hagia Sophia has in the city 100 archbishops to serve under him, and each of these has seven suffragans also based in Constantinople.[48] By contrast, the church of the Patocrator is merely named, and that of the Holy Apostles is noteworthy purely for its illustrious burials and relics. The burials recited are those of Constantine, 'all the emperors down to this day' ('et omnes imperatores usque hodie'), and Julian the Apostate, from whose tomb a liquid is said to flow. Among the relics are such *arma Christi* as one of the nails, the crown of thorns, the iron chain with which Christ was bound, the scarlet robe ('clamidem coccineam') in which he was clothed, some of the blood which flowed from his side, and — presumably of interest to Tynemouth's monks in the context of Oswin's passion — the spear whose thrust elicited this effusion. The bodies of the apostles themselves are not mentioned, although an arm of St George does appear.

While a copy of this description may originally have been sent north from St Albans, its textual source (if not its ancestry) is indistinct. It is not taken directly from Bede, Ralph de Diceto, Ralph Niger or the 'English pilgrim', other English writers to be mesmerized by the idea or reality of Hagia Sophia, and it is not excerpted from Procopius's *De aedificiis* or any of the other eastern accounts.[49] Obviously, it has its origins in such literature, and must relate at some remove to a text like Diceto's, which contains similarly egregious statistics — for example, 365 gates, 1000 priests divided into two weekly rotas — and describes the jewelled altar and other aspects of the building (but not the columns) as objects of wonder. By nature, this is a modern conundrum, but the question of authorship probably interested the document's readers to an extent, because it is invoked by the inclusion of the colophon (which embodies a request for prayer) 'Qui scripsit Carmen [/] sit benedictus Amen'.[50] The author's anonymity must have seemed an appropriate expression of humility in the shadow of his subject. Quite how the rest of the account, and particularly the description of Hagia Sophia, may have affected a reader at Tynemouth is a question whose interest is not entirely neutralized by its difficulties. Such a reader's psychological *accessus* to the forest of columns, jewel-starred altar and multiplicity of windows must have been through buildings with which he was acquainted by experience: his own 'wonderfully beautiful' church, and whatever other large monastic and collegiate churches he had encountered in the limited compass of his travels. In the absence of indications to the contrary, and unless by some means the reader knew better, the assumption must have been that Hagia Sophia, like English and Scottish churches, was of basilican form. It does not follow, of course, that the description induced a vision of a radically enlarged and embellished version of Tynemouth priory church, or any other building its readers had seen. The relationship between the conceptual edifice and its physical analogues is unlikely ever to have been so rigid. But the suggestion that an intimately familiar building was invoked as a means to imagining another of surpassing complexity and beauty does not seem misplaced: mental images, however colourful and detailed their development, had of course to be rooted in material likenesses.[51]

*

TO steer the subject of aesthetic interests towards the more tangible matter of manuscript decoration is to be led by nothing more logical than the nature of surviving evidence. The rewards are not stupendous. None of the remaining liturgical books attributable to Tynemouth contains important decoration. A late 13th-century diurnal, now Cambridge, University Library MS Kk.6.45, is the most handsome, having two full borders, each with a five-line, inhabited initial: Christ is represented on fol. 3r and a mitred figure on fol. 77r. In the Fitzwilliam Museum at Cambridge there is another diurnal of about a century later, now in two parts (MSS 274, 1-1973), which is plain except for red and blue initials and flourishing. The noted office of Oswin in Corpus Christi MS 134 has been handsomely embellished with coloured initials and red staves, but their execution, as previously indicated, is rough by the standards of the professionally made books that entered the priory during the 12th and 13th centuries. Besides

Durham Cathedral Library MS A.IV.6 and BL, MS Harley 3847, briefly mentioned above, these books included Oxford, Magdalene College MS lat. 171, a copy of Geoffrey of Monmouth's *Historia Regum Britannie* of similar date to Corpus Christi MS 134. This has an erased Tynemouth *ex libris* which looks to be of the later 12th or 13th century, a 15th-century *constat* inscription suggesting that it was in the possession of an individual monk for an extended period, and numerous marginalia, including two that demonstrate interest in Stonehenge (fol. 57r).[52] Again, its decoration — typically for the *Historia* — is of a minor character only, being restricted to initials in gold, red and green at the heads of the different books and chapters. Like monks elsewhere, Tynemouth readers sometimes added embellishments of their own to their monastery's books. These include crosiers drawn in Harley 3847 to flag up passages in *De Sacramentis* (fols 5r, 54r, 114v), a cryptic device (perhaps a *memento mori*: it includes the word *moriens*, 'dying') combining musical notation with snatches of verse and a motif of two interlocking hearts in Oxford, Bodleian Library MS Digby 20, fol. 167v, and a coat of arms (fol. 106v) and elaborate letters 'M' (fol. 80v) and 'A' (fol. 97r) in the margins of BL, MS Cotton Faustina B IX. An elaborate 'M' was commonly used to evoke the Virgin Mary, but may have been stimulated here by references of Simon de Montfort in the accompanying text. In Oxford, Corpus Christi College MS 144, there is a 14th-century copy of Richard of Wallingford's *Tractatus Albionis* (a treatise on the use of an astronomical instrument called Albion) with finely executed copies of the diagrams needed to make sense of the text, and some attractive red and blue pen-work initials in a southern English style.[53] More of the diagrams, also well drawn, exist in a copy of the same work in Oxford, Bodleian Library MS Laud misc. 657. In this case the manuscript seems to have been made at, and certainly for, Tynemouth, because it contains (fol. 1v) a record of donation to the priory and its monks in the same hand as the text.[54]

For extensive illumination one must turn to three small psalters, none of them originally made for Tynemouth but all of which contain evidence of adaptation for use at the priory in the period leading up to the Dissolution. In each case the book has been remodelled by the addition of quires containing liturgical and devotional material emphasizing the status of Oswin, and this is what its connection with the monastery rests on. It should be admitted that this is an uncertain basis. Oswin was considered an important saint at St Albans, where the feasts of his deposition (with its octave) and invention were kept as they were at the northern cell.[55] His invocation is also doubled, along with that of Alban, in a litany in Oxford, Bodleian Library MS Laud misc. 4 (fol. 135r), which appears to have been made for St Albans rather than Tynemouth. Thus, while it is considered a strong indication, double invocation of the saint is not a definite basis for attributing a litany to Tynemouth. A further complication is that some St Albans books may have been given features that would make them serviceable at Tynemouth were they ever to be required there: this, as Richard Pfaff has argued, seems to have been the case with Laud misc. 4.[56] A Tynemouth provenance for these psalters is thus assumed here with a note of caution, despite the confidence with which at least two of them have been attributed to the monastery in the past.[57]

The older sections of these manuscripts are small, and this has determined the size of the additions. All three must have been for personal, devotional use. In two cases the sections containing the psalms and canticles are of continental origin, while in the third it is English. The oldest of them, Cambridge, Trinity College MS R.10.5, was made in Ghent *c.* 1265–75, and has Flemish borders, initials and line-fillers throughout.[58] Folios 177r–193v were added in the early 15th century, and contain a litany, collects and office of the dead. The manuscript currently begins at Psalm 29, but the evidence of the other two psalters suggests that it once opened with an English calendar of 15th-century date. A Tynemouth provenance is indicated by the double invocation of Oswin, and, perhaps, the lack of such for Amphibalus and his companions (fol. 177v).[59] The decoration of this adventitious section, consisting of professionally executed gold initials on blue, pink and white grounds, with foliage sprays sometimes enclosing the text-block on two sides, is spread over fifteen consecutive pages in the office of the dead (fols 186v–193v). Illumination of similar type and quality is found in the other manuscript with a foreign component, Oxford, Bodleian Library, MS Lat. lit.g.8. Here the text of the psalms was written and decorated in northern France or Flanders in the early 14th century.[60] This section of the manuscript, now dispersed, contained elaborate, figured initials with the conventional iconography at the seven canonical divisions of the psalter, accompanied by full borders and marginal drolleries.[61] The remaining, English section, of eighty leaves, was added *c.* 1430.[62] It contains verses on the articles of faith, sacraments and confession, a series of tables for calculating Easter and various dates and events, a calendar, litany, office of the dead, and long series of private devotions. There are four gold initials on pink and blue grounds with grisaille embellishment and long foliate sprays, and a series of smaller champe ones distributed throughout.[63] This is, again, the work of a southern illuminator; and a verse formula for calculating Easter in Middle English on fol. viir exhibits no trace of a northern dialect. What links the manuscript to Tynemouth, over and above Oswin's double invocation in the litany and the occurrence of his feasts (the translation graded in copes) in the calendar, is a declaration of ownership by Robert Blakeney on the last leaf.[64] Blakeney was prior of Tynemouth during the last four years of the monastery's existence. As in Thomas de la Mare's register, his name here lacks the ascription 'prioris de Tynmouth' that was added to printed books he donated to his house.[65] On balance, however, the evidence suggests that he encountered this attractive book at Tynemouth sometime between 1536 and 1539 and adopted it for personal use.

Oxford, Bodleian Library MS Gough lit.18 is a slightly smaller volume, complete and entirely of English execution (Fig. 8 and Col. Pl. XXVI in print edn). It is the most handsomely illuminated of any book attributable to Tynemouth, and worth outlining in a little more detail, as it has apparently never been discussed in print.[66] Once again, an early 15th-century calendar, litany and office of the dead have been added to an older book, in this case one probably made in the first quarter of the 14th century. The contents of the calendar and litany are closely related to that in Bodleian MS Lat.lit.g.8, and have the same evidence for placing the manuscript at Tynemouth during the last century of the monastery's life.[67] As was probably the case with the other two psalters, the older, extraneous part of the book, shorn of its original ancillary texts, became the heart of a new manuscript, with a fresh calendar inserted before the psalms and a litany and office of the dead after them. Here, however, in addition to figured initials at the major divisions of the psalter (fols 1r, 41r, 55r, 69v, 87r, 103r, 118v), the manuscript contained a series of full-page prefatory miniatures. In the 15th-century rearrangement these were placed before the calendar, the order found in a number of luxury psalters and books of hours of the first half of the 14th century.[68] The miniatures are not of conspicuously high quality, but are nevertheless significant for their stylistic links with more ambitious illumination, and also, in the case of the full-page images, for their iconography. The artist was familiar with models represented in the best manuscripts of his day, and reproduced these with a workmanlike

FIG. 8. Oxford, Bodleian Library MS Gough lit.18, fol. xvir. This image of Christ in Majesty is one of four early 14th-century images which precede a Tynemouth/St Albans calendar added in the early 15th century

Reproduced by permission of the Bodleian Library, Oxford

confidence. An image of Christ in Majesty on fol. xvir, presented as a diptych with the Crucifixion (fol. xv verso), is the best of the four. Its richer relations include the Majesty in the Pabenham-Clifford / Grey-Fitzpayn Hours of *c.* 1308 (Cambridge, Fitzwilliam Museum MS 242, fol. 28v), the frontispiece of the Vaux-Bardolf Psalter of *c.* 1310–20 (London, Lambeth Palace Library MS 233, fol. 14v) and the Majesty in the Hours of Alice de Reydon of *c.* 1320 (Cambridge, University Library MS Dd.4.17, fol. 10r).[69] The other two full-page miniatures, of a beardless, haloed figure in a red robe holding a disk with the *Agnus Dei* (fol. xiv verso), which may be an unusual representation of either John the Baptist or John the Evangelist, and a seated Virgin and Child with a tonsured figure in a white habit kneeling before them and praying (fol. xviir), appear unlikely ever to have been juxtaposed, but may instead have been paired with other, lost images.[70] All of the miniatures display aspects of technique familiar in illumination of the period, such as a combination of broad, black outlines for large motifs and finer, wirier lines for hair and faces, a juxtaposition of tonal and linear modelling in the garments, and the use of burnished gold (here unpunched) wherever decorum required it. The dotted, chequer-work backgrounds overlain with a thin mesh of octagonal motifs connected by smaller squares, found in both the full-page miniatures and the psalm-initials, are another common feature.[71]

The supplicant in a white cowl represented on fol. xviir — who, if he is not simply a generic representative of his order, is likely to have commissioned the psalter — presumably wished to be recognized as a Cistercian.[72] He is certainly not a black monk, though his presence was acceptable to the manuscript's Benedictine owners, for whom he probably represented an exemplar of pious devotion. Simple deductions of this kind represent the limit of what can be said about the awareness and use of both this and the other two psalters discussed here. No obits or other indications of personal interests have been added to the calendars or litanies, and none of the texts or images shows signs of heavy use. The survival of three small, illuminated psalters, each adapted for local use, would be exceptional anywhere, and may represent a particular interest in the form and use of this type of manuscript at Tynemouth rather than a fortunate accident of preservation.

However, while one would like to think that these manuscripts were seen often enough by a sufficient number of monks to demonstrate a common thread of aesthetic experience, there is no warrant for doing so. This observation points directly to an overarching problem for any attempt to illustrate the nature of collective experience through books for which broadly based circulation cannot be established. For this reason, most of what has been said here about the aesthetic interests of Tynemouth's monks has been supportable with reference to other sources, textual and material. The exceptions — these psalters and the description of churches in Constantinople — were perhaps accessible, like the copies of the *Tractatus Albionis*, to relatively few. Yet, unlike the *Tractatus*, they are demonstrably the products and representatives of enthusiasms that transcended Tynemouth priory; enthusiasms from which even the tyranny of distance could not entirely isolate.[73]

ACKNOWLEDGEMENTS

I wish to thank James Carley, Nigel Morgan, Lucy Freeman Sandler, and Rod Thomson for help and advice relating to points contained in this paper, and Julian Reid for allowing access to manuscripts and supplying images.

NOTES

1. The surviving books are listed in *Medieval Libraries of Great Britain*, ed. N. Ker, 2nd edn (London 1964), 191; *Medieval Libraries of Great Britain: Supplement to the Second Edition*, ed. A. G. Watson (London 1987), 66; *Medieval Cartularies of Great Britain*, ed. G. R. C. Davis, rev. C. Breay, J. Harrison and D. M. Smith (London 2010), 199 (no. 982). All have been consulted in research for this paper, along with Durham, University Library MS Cosin V.v.15, which Ian Doyle and Alan Piper suggest (in an unpublished draft catalogue entry) 'may have connections with Tynemouth and St Albans abbey' (the Tynemouth 'evidence' (fol. 16v) is, however, extremely thin). Oxford, Bodleian Library MS Laud misc. 4 has been discounted on the authority of R. W. Pfaff, *The Liturgy in Medieval England* (Cambridge 2009), 167 and n. 31.

2. *Registrum Anglie de libris doctorum et auctorum veterum*, ed. R. H. and M. A. Rouse, Corpus of British Medieval Library Catalogues 2 (London 1991), 310–11.

3. Bede, *EH*, 209 (quotation), 256–59.

4. On the manuscript and its contents, see R. M. Thomson, *Manuscripts from St Albans Abbey 1066–1235*, 2 vols (Woodbridge 1982), I, 38, 116–17; N. R. Ker, *Catalogue of Manuscripts Containing Anglo-Saxon* (Oxford 1957), 124. Binding fragments from this manuscript, now Cambridge, University Library MS 313-82, are textually very interesting. They contain a fragment of a treatise on the Trinity composed in 1245 and a later 14th- or early 15th-century copy of a Middle English version of the Virgin Mary's song of the Nativity, beginning 'As I welk thorow a garthyn grene'. (The dialect is northern English, and the carol was thus presumably written at Tynemouth.) For two other copies of the carol, see C. Brown and R. H. Robbins, *The Index of Middle English Verse* (New York 1943), 62 (no. 378).

5. 'Vita Oswini, regis deiorum', in *Miscellanea Biographica*, ed. J. Raine, SS 8 (Edinburgh and London 1838), 2–5. The sermons are mentioned further below.

6. 'Forma epistole a papa vitabano missa in britania regi oswyno' (fol. 69r); 'Nota de [...] reliquijs sanctorum missis in angliam regi oswyno et regine' (fol. 69v).

7. The 'Vita Oswini' (as n. 5), 17, calls Oswin 'a shrine of chastity' ('castitatis sacrarium'). No queen or offspring were imagined by its author (and Bede mentions none).

8. [*Joannis Lelandi antiquarii de rebus Britannicis*] *Collectanea*, ed. T. Hearne, 2nd edn, 6 vols (London 1770), III, 408 (listing 'S. Herebaldus abbas ejusdem loci' as the only illustrious burial at Tynemouth besides Oswin; but others are mentioned at ibid., IV, 42–43).

9. Ibid., IV, 43 ('Edwinus [...] sacellum erexit Tinemutæ ex ligno' and 'S. Oswaldus monasteriolum de Tinemuthe ex ligneo lapideum fecit'). According to Durham tradition, Oswin himself founded at least twelve monasteries in Northumbria: *Rites of Durham*, ed. J. Fowler, SS 107 (Durham 1903), 138.

10. '[Siuuardus] successit Tosti, qui fundamenta ecclesie Tinmue iecit': printed in Thomson, *Manuscripts* (as n. 4), I, 116.

11. 'Vita Oswini' (as n. 5), 15.

12. Although not necessarily custodianship at Tynemouth: the relics are said to have been sent there from St Albans in 1107 in *Chronica Johannis de Oxenedes*, ed. H. Ellis, Rolls series 13 (London 1859), 43. This information must have come from St Albans itself.

13. The leaves of the manuscript measure on average 105 × 70 mm. For a description, see R. M. Thomson, *A Descriptive Catalogue of the Medieval Manuscripts of Corpus Christi College Oxford* (Cambridge 2011), 66–67.

14. Including 'Domus meus domus orationis uocabitur dicit Deus' (Matthew 21:13; Mark 11.17; Luke 19:46): the other is from Psalm 100:5. Whether the manuscript remained at Tynemouth until 1539 is uncertain. It carries late 15th- or early 16th-century *ex libris* inscriptions (fols 3r, 62v, 85v) which are apparently not monastic (compare Thomson, *Descriptive Catalogue* (as n. 13), 67).

15. 'Uenustus aspectu que sincerus affectu. Statura sublimis, sed contemptu mundi sublimior. Pulcher facie sed fide pulchrior. Corpore integer, mente alacer, affatu iocundus, sensu profundus, moribus ciuilis, natalibus herilis; regum successione generosus, que gratuarum plenitudine gloriosus' (fols 20v–21r). Compare Bede, *EH*, 256.

16. The office is briefly discussed by A. Hughes, 'The Monarch as the Object of Liturgical Veneration', in *Kings and Kingship in Medieval Europe*, ed. A. J. Duggan (London 1993), 387, 395–96.

17. 'Ab incarnacione domini usque ad passionem sancti Oswini regis et martyris anni DCLI. A passionem eiusdem usque ad sui corporis inuentionem fuerunt anni ccccxiiij., uidelicet anno incarnationis dominice millesimo sexagesimo quinto. Ab inuentione eius usque ad translationem anni xlv id est anno incarnatione domini millesimo centesimo decimo' (fol. 1r–v).

18. See fols 22r–26v ('rex humilis' etc at 24r–v; he is also likened to Job at 22v), 27r–v ('Oswin uero fortitudo amici, uel latitudo caritatis intelligitur': this is reiterated); 'Vita Oswini' (as n. 5), 1–5, 6, 16, 17.

19. See Leland, *Collectanea* (as n. 8), IV, 114: 'Oswinus a latere perfossus lancea obiit anno [...] 651'. For the reference to the holy lance, see BL, MS Cotton Vitellius A.XX, fol. 143r (this rubric emphasizes Roger

of Howden's account of the lance's translation). On the seal, see (briefly) W. de Gray Birch, *Catalogue of Seals in the Department of Manuscripts in the British Museum: Volume I* (London 1887), 783.

20. On whole relics, see M. Spurrell, 'The Promotion and Demotion of Whole Relics', *Antiq. J.*, 80 (2000), 67–85. The brief *Life* of Henry mentions no shrine, but does say that he was buried in a wall-arch south of St Oswin's tomb (*Nova Legenda Anglie*, ed. C. Horstman, 2 vols (Oxford 1901), II, 25), making it likely, as others have suggested, that the double-arched recess in the presbytery is a Gothic version of his original monument. (On this hypothesis, see also Richard Fawcett's paper in this volume.)

21. 'Corpus beatissimi OSWINI, regis et martyris, que uestimentis eius.' The Latin list has been accurately transcribed but never published: see I. G. Thomas, 'The Cult of Saints' Relics in Medieval England' (unpublished Ph.D. thesis, University of London 1974), 528–29. For an English translation of it, see W. S. Gibson, *The History of the Monastery Founded at Tynemouth in the Diocese of Durham*, 2 vols (London 1846–47), I, 201–02.

22. A composition-date pre-1127 (i.e. earlier than the date of this copy) might be claimed on the basis of Henry of Coquet's absence. But no relics are mentioned in Henry's *Life*, and neither is his tomb represented as a site of miracles. His 'feast' (16 January) is not in the manuscript's calendar.

23. Printed in *Gesta abbatum monasterii Sancti Albani*, ed. H. T. Riley, 3 vols, Rolls series 28 (London 1867–69), III, 539–45.

24. *Letters and Papers, Foreign and Domestic, of the Reign of Henry VIII*, ed. J. Gardiner, R. H. Brodie and J. S. Brewer, 21 vols (London 1862–1920), X, 142.

25. Ibid., XIV/2, 277, 281; also J. Crook, *English Medieval Shrines* (Woodbridge 2011), 304–05.

26. For Oswin's hair (impervious to fire) and *theca*, see 'Vita Oswini' (as n. 5), 19, 59; for the shrine see also *HN*, VIII, 66, and Cambridge, University Library MS Ee.4.20, fol. 283v (discussed further below). 'Vita Oswini' (as n. 5), 33, indicates that the shrine incorporated an image of the saint, while ibid., 36, mentions a particular stone (either a gem or a canopy of some sort) that was placed on or over ('superposita') the *theca*. On Oswin's shrine, see also Crook, *Shrines* (as n. 25), 274–75.

27. Leland, *Collectanea* (as n. 8), III, 408: 'Godricus Anachoreta Dunolmi, & capita Oswini & Oswaldi regum & martyrum'.

28. D. J. Craig, 'Oswin', in *ODNB*, XLII, 93–94; G. McCombie, *Tynemouth Priory and Castle* (London 2008), 25. The manuscript measures approximately 130 × 90 mm. For other houses with Oswin-relics, see Thomas, 'Cult' (as n. 21), 443.

29. Recorded in a 17th-century catalogue in Oxford, Bodleian Library MS Additional A.91, fol. 72v: 'Psalterium [. . .] cui praefixa fuerant haec verba: "Liber Oswini Deirorum Regis"'.

30. On the manuscript generally, see F. Henry and G. L. Marsh-Micheli, 'A Century of Irish Illumination', *Proceedings of the Royal Irish Academy*, 62 (1961–63), 111, 141–43, pl. 22. The inscription was sufficient for Ker, in his *Medieval Libraries* (as n. 1), to associate the book with Tynemouth. For the credulity of the editor (Raine), see *Miscellanea Biographica* (as n. 5), viii.

31. Direct evidence for an aesthetic understanding of miracles is found in the margin of Pembroke MS 82, fol. 55v, where a 15th-century reader has written, 'Nota pulchrum miraculum sancti Aidane[:] quomodo tempestas maris sedata per infusionem olei sanctificati'. The idea is very strongly marked in the miracle-accounts of the *Life*.

32. Published *in extensio*, with a partial, loose translation, in *HN*, VIII, 71–73.

33. J. Clark, *A Monastic Renaissance at St Albans: Thomas Walsingham and His Circle* c.*1350–1440* (Oxford 2004), 234. The classical material includes two borrowings from Juvenal's *Satires* and quotations from Ovid's *Metamorphoses* and *Epistulæ ex Ponto*.

34. '[E]cclesia eleganter de novo constructa mire pulchritudinis'. The crag, however, is called 'hunc artissimum locum'.

35. '[C]orpus beati et gloriosi ac propiciabilis martiris Oswini in theca argentea auro et gemmis venustissime decorata requiescere'.

36. 'Hic est gloriosus martir Oswynus optimus egrorum medicus effectus; qui non valet practica nec precumque phisica, pii martiris prestant beneficia. Surdi, claudi, ceci, muti sunt ad usum restituti martiris clemencia.' See also 'Vita Oswini' (as n. 5), 33.

37. 'Egregii martiris protectio et venuste ecclesie pulcritudo'.

38. 'Ecce quam bonum et quam jocundum habitare fratres in unum' (Psalm 132:1).

39. Clark, *Monastic Renaissance* (as n. 33), 233–34.

40. *HN*, VIII, 98 (last miracle). On decline in some (but not all) important cults in the later middle ages, see B. Nilson, *Cathedral Shrines of Medieval England* (Woodbridge 1998), 168–90, 210–42.

41. *Gesta abbatum* (as n. 23), II, 379–80; *HN*, VIII, 91.

42. 'Flee from rumours, and do not be the author of new ones': Brentford, Syon House Muniments D.xi.1, fol. 158v. (I have consulted this manuscript, with the necessary permission, using BL, microfilm M 402.)

43. For the monastery as Oswin's 'mansione', see 'Vita Oswini' (as n. 5), 31.

44. For the likelihood that Corpus Christi MS 144 was assembled in the 15th century, see J. North, *Richard of Wallingford: An Edition of His Writings with Introductions, English Translations and Commentary*, 3 vols (Oxford 1976), II, 127; Clark, *Monastic Renaissance* (as n. 33), 111, 145.

45. On the volume's early modern ownership, see C. G. C. Tite, *The Early Records of Sir Robert Cotton's Library: Formation, Cataloguing, Use* (London 2003), 160. The name of the book-collector John Richardson occurs on the last leaf, suggesting that the volume was still in the north of England in the early 17th century. Compare A. I. Doyle, 'William Claxton and the Durham Chronicles', in *Books and Collectors 1200–1700: Essays Presented to Andrew Watson*, ed. J. P. Carley and C. G. C. Tite (London 1997), 350.

46. It is necessary to rehearse this evidence. The account of Constantinople (item 15 in the manuscript) containing the description of Hagia Sophia is one of a series of parts (items 13–16) which share a commonly ruled text-block of 37 lines to the page and a consistent style of rubrication. Item 13, a brief compendium of world history (fols 109v–132r), must be from either Tynemouth or St Albans, because — apart from a note about the Virgin Mary's birth — its scribe added only two marginal rubrics, 'Albanus' (fol. 112v) and 'Oswynus' (fol. 114v). Item 14 is a series of extracts from Roger of Howden's chronicle (fols 133r–238v) that contains numerous rubrics and annotations relating to Northumbrian history (e.g. fols 134r, 137r, 177r, 214r). It is written in the same hand as item 15, on Constantinople. On the verso of the same leaf (i.e. fol. 239v) there begins an account of the miracles of the saints of Hexham, a proximate house in which Tynemouth's monks naturally had a developed interest, and from whom they obtained such items as the calendar in Oxford, Corpus Christi MS 134. This ends on fol. 242r; on fol. 242v there is a note about the foundation of Tynemouth priory in a 16th-century (but post-dissolution) hand. Items 1, 4, 9–11 and 16 of Vitellius A.XX have Tynemouth or Tynemouth-related content. The evidence in favour of a Tynemouth provenance is thus compelling, and presumably explains why Neil Ker (*Medieval Libraries* (as n. 1), 191) attributed the whole volume to the priory without query.

47. 'Vidimus Constantinopolitanus, illam egregiam ciuitatem miro et ineffabili opere fundatam.' The incipit can also be read as 'We have seen Constantinople', etc.

48. '[I]n qua [i.e. Constantinopolis] uidimus ecclesiam prima agie sophie id est sancta Sapiencie, angelo dei uisibiliter docente artificies fabricatam. Sub qua continentur cisternis suis quedam dulcea aque, quedam salse, quedam pluuiales. Hec autem ecclesia sustinetur inferius C.lxx.iijbus marmoreis columnis [et] superius CC.xlvbus circa chorum argenteo deaurato a summo usque deorsum teguntur. Habet autem chorus ille usque mirificis lapidibus preciosis undique stellatum. In ecclesia sunt lampades ex argento et auro purissimo quarum numerus est ineffabilis. Aperitur ecclesia et clauditur D.CC.lij hostijs biforibus, et fenestratrum non est numerus. Sunt ibi DCC prebendarij sacerdotes, ex quibus CCCl per ebdomadam seruiunt. Patriarcha autem agie sophie habet in ciuitate illa C. metropolis, id est archiepiscopos, et quisque metropolis habet in eadem ciuitate vij suffraganeos.'

49. *Itineraria et alia geographica*, ed. P. Geyer et al., 2 vols, Corpus Christianorum Series Latina 175–76 (Turnhout 1965), I, 279 (description in Bede's *De locis sanctis*); *The Historical Works of Master Ralph de Diceto*, ed. W. Stubbs, 2 vols, Rolls series 68 (London 1876), I, 91–94; *The Chronicles of Ralph Niger*, ed. R. Anstruther (London 1851), 189–91; K. N. Ciggaar, 'Une description de Constantinople traduite par un pèlerin anglais', *Revue des études Byzantines*, 33 (1975), 250–55; C. Mango, *The Art of the Byzantine Empire 312–1453: Sources and Documents* (Englewood Cliffs, NJ 1972), 72–103.

50. This colophon is commonplace is medieval texts.

51. Compare M. Carruthers, *The Craft of Thought: Meditation, Rhetoric and the Making of Images, 400–1200* (Cambridge 1998), 14–15.

52. An early note 'de stanhenge', alongside Geoffrey's mention of this edifice, has later been embellished with a decorative motif and the word 'nota'. The inscriptions *ex libris* and 'Iste liber constat [...]' (the rest cut off) are on the front pastedown.

53. The initials are at fols 44r (inhabited by a dragon and vine-scroll), 54r and 71r. This manuscript was given to Tynemouth by John Bamburgh, a monk and sometime sub-prior of the house active in the mid-15th century. See Thomson, *Catalogue* (as n. 13), 72–73.

54. North, *Wallingford* (as n. 44), II, 130.

55. P. Wormald, *English Benedictine Kalendars after* A.D. *1100*, 2 vols, Henry Bradshaw Society 77, 81 (Cambridge, 1939–46), I, 36, 41.

56. Pfaff, *Liturgy* (as n. 1), 167 n. 31.

57. E.g. Ker, *Medieval Libraries* (as n. 1), 191; see also *HN*, VIII, xiii; [s.a.], 'Notable Accessions', *Bodleian Library Record*, 7 (1962–67), 165.

58. N. J. Morgan and S. Panayotova, *A Catalogue of Western Book Illumination in the Fitzwilliam Museum and the Cambridge Colleges. Part One, Volume Two: The Meuse Region, The Southern Netherlands* (London and Turnhout 2009), 38–39 (no. 155). The page dimensions are 90 × 55 mm (very slightly

lower and wider in the added section). Some initials have been excised.

59. Amphibalus and his companions were, however, invoked twice in other litanies from Tynemouth: see Fitzwilliam MS 274, fol. 18v; Oxford, Bodleian Library MS Lat.lit.g.8, fol. 1v.

60. It is vaguely possible that the Franco-Flemish and English parts of the manuscript were brought together after the middle ages. The manuscript's leaves measure 107 × 70 mm.

61. A packet of black-and-white photographs showing the pages with illuminated initials is kept with the manuscript. The first in the sequence (Psalm 1) is missing.

62. I owe this estimated dating to Nigel Morgan.

63. The large initials, each five lines high, are on fols 12v ('Dlacebo' – the 'D' an error for 'P'), 25v (Fifteen Oes), 36v (the prayer 'Domine deus omnipotens'), and 41v (prayer of St Anselm before the mass).

64. 'Dompnus Robertus Blakeney huius libri est pocessar' (fol. 63v).

65. I.e. Cambridge, Christ's College D 10 24 (*recte* D 9 24), fol. 15r; D 9 25, fol. 1r; D 9 26, fol. 13r; York Minster Library Inc. XIV K 3, fol. 1r. In all cases the inscription is 'Ex dono Domini Roberti Blakeney prioris de Tynmouth'. These acquisitions for the priory, one a work of history in three volumes (Antoninus Florentinus's *Chronicon*: pr. Basel 1502), the other of theology (Petrus de Aquila, *In quatuor libros Sententiarum* and *Quaestiones super libros Sententiarum*: pr. Speyer 1840), show Blakeney up in rather a good light. All the volumes have been annotated and otherwise marked up by readers. The section on England in Christ's College D 9 25 (from fol. 211v) has attracted particular attention.

66. Its illumination is noted in O. Pächt and J. J. G. Alexander, *Illuminated Manuscripts in the Bodleian Library, Oxford, 3: British, Irish and Icelandic Schools* (Oxford 1973), 51 (no. 553). The leaves of the manuscript measure on average 88 × 57 mm.

67. Only Alban, Oswin and All Saints have double invocations (fols 166r, 169r) in the litany. The calendar includes the dedication of the church of St Alban on 29 December (fol. xxviii verso) and the abbey's feast of relics on 14 July (fol. xxivr).

68. See, for example, L. F. Sandler, *Gothic Manuscripts 1285–1385*, A Survey of Manuscripts Illuminated in the British Isles 5, 2 vols (London 1986), II, 13–14 (no. 1), 41–42 (no. 36), 47–48 (no. 41), 58–60 (no. 51), 64–66 (no. 56), 75–76 (no. 67).

69. For these images, see E. Duffy, *Marking the Hours: English People and their Prayers, 1240–1570* (New Haven and London, 2006), 18; *Lambeth Palace Library: Treasures from the Collection of the Archbishops of Canterbury*, ed. R. Palmer and M. Brown (London 2010), 52; P. Binski and P. Zutshi, *Western Illuminated Manuscripts: A Catalogue of the Collection in Cambridge University Library* (Cambridge 2011), pl. 47.

70. The figure does not point to the *Agnus Dei*, which, along with its beardlessness and lack of a rough garment tend to suggest it is not the Baptist. But to my knowledge there is no image in English art of John the Evangelist holding this attribute. A fuller discussion of this image must await a different context.

71. Compare, for example, Sandler, *Gothic Manuscripts* (as n. 68), I, ills 12, 67, 79, 194, 218, 300, 304.

72. A Carthusian is unlikely due to the absence of a scapular, as well as that order's habitual rejection of this sort of personalization; and a Premonstratensian is less likely than a Cistercian. Of course, the artist may not have felt bound to represent the habit accurately.

73. For interest in architectural gigantism of the sort represented in the description of Constantinople, see, for example, P. Binski, 'Reflections on the 'Wonderful Height and Size' of Gothic Great Churches and the Medieval Sublime', in *Magnificence and the Sublime in Medieval Aesthetics*, ed. C. S. Jaeger (New York 2010), 129–56; D. Keene, 'Tall Buildings in Medieval London: Precipitation, Aspiration and Thrills', *The London Journal*, 33 (2008), 201–15. It cannot reasonably be doubted that Tynemouth owned more impressive examples of illumination that the three surviving psalters.

'. . . he went round the holy places praying and offering': Evidence for Cuthbertine Pilgrimage to Lindisfarne and Farne in the Late Medieval Period

EMMA J. WELLS

Little detailed research has been done into whether pilgrims visited St Cuthbert's original tomb-site and the complement of associated structures at Lindisfarne and Inner Farne throughout the late medieval period. Suggestions that the two northern cells became insular monastic institutions rather than general pilgrimage centres after the foundation at Durham in 996 would seem to be contradicted by evidence for continued existence of pilgrimage to the Northumbrian area, particularly during the 14th century. The extent to which pilgrims sought to make the long, often hazardous journey to Northumbria, as their counterparts had before the translation of Cuthbert's relics to Durham, is thus an open question. This paper cannot pretend to supply a conclusive answer, but will attempt to outline the archaeological and historical framework within which it may be considered.

INTRODUCTION

THE account of the opening of St Cuthbert's tomb at Lindisfarne in 698 was crucial to the saint's cult. Effectively, the incorruptibility of his body strengthened the image of the saint himself, proclaiming his miraculous qualities as displayed by his triumph over mortality. Accordingly, the corporeal aspect of the cult was centrally important: it supported the convent of Durham's 'claim to trace its origins back to Lindisfarne',[1] signified the earliest days of Northumbrian Christianity and acted as a symbol of the ownership of lands granted to Cuthbert in life and death.[2] Not only his body but any objects that had been in contact with the saint, before death or posthumously, were turned into relics and promoted for their thaumaturgical properties. Numerous sites associated with the saint, primarily the various structures adorning the landscapes of Lindisfarne and Inner Farne but also the churches and chapels visited by the convent during the journey of Cuthbert's incorrupt body between *c.* 875 and 882, 'were [. . .] promoted as sanctified locations with miraculous abilities'.[3] The 'wanderings' of the body made the places he rested at holy, the stones and landscapes absorbing his sanctity for pilgrims to experience in the future. As such, his cult should be understood in terms of a series of stations on a wider pilgrimage 'route', rather than an individual site.

To this day, visitors still flock to Lindisfarne priory to see the original resting place of St Cuthbert and the islands he inhabited during his lifetime located along this

BAA Trans., vol. XXXVI (2013), 214–231

stretch of Northumbrian coastline. But was this true in the medieval period? This paper will present evidence for a continuation of pilgrimage to Lindisfarne and Inner Farne — where Cuthbert spent the later part of his life until his death on 20 March 687 — after the saint's body was translated to Durham in 996. The reasons why pilgrims continued to visit the Northumbrian sites is beyond the realms of this paper, but the situation — a saint's original burial, site located a considerable distance from his main shrine — is sufficiently unusual (and therefore significant to the archaeology of the cults of saints) to render an examination of the assemblage of documentary, archaeological and material evidence for the Cuthbertine-pilgrimage phenomenon worthwhile.[4]

DOCUMENTARY EVIDENCE FOR THE CULT

THE documentary evidence for Cuthbert's cult is rich. There are three accounts by Bede, the *Life of St Cuthbert* written by an anonymous monk of Lindisfarne in the early 8th century, and a further corpus of source-material comprising an additional set of *miracula*.[5] Written between 1104 and 1109, Symeon of Durham authored the *Historia Dunelmensis ecclesiae*, while the *Monachi Dunelmensis Libellus de admirandis beati Cuthberti virtutibus*, dated to between 1165 and 1174, was written by Reginald of Durham.[6] What is striking about these collections is the extent of the diffusion of St Cuthbert's cult in the north of England. The large list of places and topographical details mentioned is remarkable, with less than half of the 12th-century stories in Reginald's *Libellus* actually occurring in Durham and an equal amount taking place elsewhere, mainly in Northumbria.[7] In fact, before 1170, only two healing miracles take place at Durham cathedral, whereas a third of them occur on the island of Inner Farne, with a great emphasis placed on Lindisfarne.[8] Furthermore, in the *Libellus*, visitors primarily travel from Northumbria and Lothian,[9] and those involved in miracles at the parish churches and chapels dedicated to the saint originate from the immediate region.[10]

The evidence implies that in the late 12th century the cult was firmly secure in the north-east. Nevertheless, in *c.* 1199 the *Miracles of St Cuthbert at Farne* was compiled, to coincide with the official canonization of the saint. Interestingly, nearly all of the miraculous locations in this text are within a ten-mile radius of Farne.[11] They also share the characteristics of, and occurred at the same time as, a series of miracles recorded by Reginald ascribed to the years following 1170; the year in which both Thomas Becket and Godric of Finchale died.[12] Over two-thirds of the miracles accounted for by Reginald are cures and over half occurred within the immediate environs of Durham cathedral priory itself, implying the instability in the popularity of Durham as a cult centre in the documentary accounts.[13] Due to the proximity of Finchale to Durham, it can be supposed that the death of Godric would have had some effect on Cuthbert's cult, as both saints would have attracted the same pilgrim crowd from the surrounding areas.[14] Still, regardless of where the cures were performed, the miracle collections encourage pilgrimage to locations associated with the cult of St Cuthbert.

It would appear that the Durham convent waged a two-pronged campaign to attract pilgrims to both Durham and Lindisfarne-Farne through reports of curative miracles, thus authenticating its own heritage and establishing the sanctity of the Cuthbertine cult. Perhaps Victoria Tudor's assertion that Lindisfarne and Farne were the main foci for those who lived north of the Tyne, while Durham served the spiritual needs of the population south of the river, was the case for the majority of the 12th century; but the competition posed by Becket and Godric meant that the Durham convent had to garner additional support for its own cult. It did this in part by promoting the Northumbrian locations in addition to Durham.[15]

The perceived need to refocus attention on Northumbria is seen in the continued occurrence of miracles further north, promoting the dissemination of Cuthbert's thaumaturgical power and affirming his right to be regarded as a saint. It has been suggested that, in the early 12th century, Lindisfarne actually re-emerged as an alternative centre for the cult.[16] My contention is that the Northumbrian locations remained as foci throughout the period, but that in the late 12th century they were secondary sources of attention, whose main value lay in authenticating the origins of the cult. Hence the prominence of Lindisfarne and Farne in the *miracula*.

ARCHAEOLOGICAL EVIDENCE FOR PILGRIMAGE ACTIVITY

The creation of relics

THERE was an expectation that a cult would involve relics in order to be considered authentic. For the cult of St Cuthbert, these appear to have been architectural and spatial in nature. The priority of the Durham convent in the creation of the architectural environment of the cult is clear: to encourage the physical experience of the pilgrim in establishing the memory of the saint.[17] This was particularly important during the later medieval period, when Lindisfarne and Farne did not possess any primary, corporeal relics, but only the original resting place of the saint within the priory-church.[18] As such, the cult centred around the tomb itself and its complement of dependant sacred sites embodied in the various retreats once used by the saint.[19] Rather than bones, hair or other bodily parts, places were marshalled as witnesses to Cuthbert's sanctity. For example, the timber church at Lindisfarne where Cuthbert was buried in 687, dismantled and re-erected at Norham and used by the Cuthbertine community under Bishop Ecgred (830–45), was regarded as a sacred relic in itself. At Chester-le-Street during the period between 883 and 995, the original timber church was replicated in stone by Æthelric of Durham, providing the temporary resting place of Cuthbert's body with a more permanent setting. Finally, the original sepulchre and the water trench and site where his body was prepared for burial at Lindisfarne were revered in the Anglo-Saxon period, while miracles were accomplished by a drink infused with dust gathered from such sites.[20]

What becomes apparent is a desire to promote where Cuthbert spent his life and where miracles he had accomplished had taken place. Indeed, Alan Piper ascribed the significance of Farne to the special opportunity it afforded to the cult as it 'focused on the saint's life rather than his relics'.[21] Evoking such memories was therefore crucial to retaining the sanctity of Lindisfarne and Inner Farne. The archaeological consequence of this was the siting of several holy places in close proximity to one another, the majority of which date from the medieval period.

Pilgrimage on the islands associated with St Cuthbert

THE documentary accounts recall how Cuthbert made a place to dwell on Inner Farne in 676. He constructed two buildings: an oratory and a round dwelling with an accompanying enclosure of roughly 18 m in diameter, along with a cross (Fig. 1).[22] In addition, the surviving chapel of St Cuthbert was completed in 1371–72 for use by the inhabitants of the monastic cell, and in *c.* 1500 Thomas Castell, prior of Durham (1494–1519) 'buildid the toure in Farne island for defence of the grounde'.[23] The self-contained tower provided a view over the whole island and simultaneously accommodated the island's few inhabitants, replacing the earlier domestic range thought to be the structure known as the 'chapel of St Mary' (remains of which are incorporated

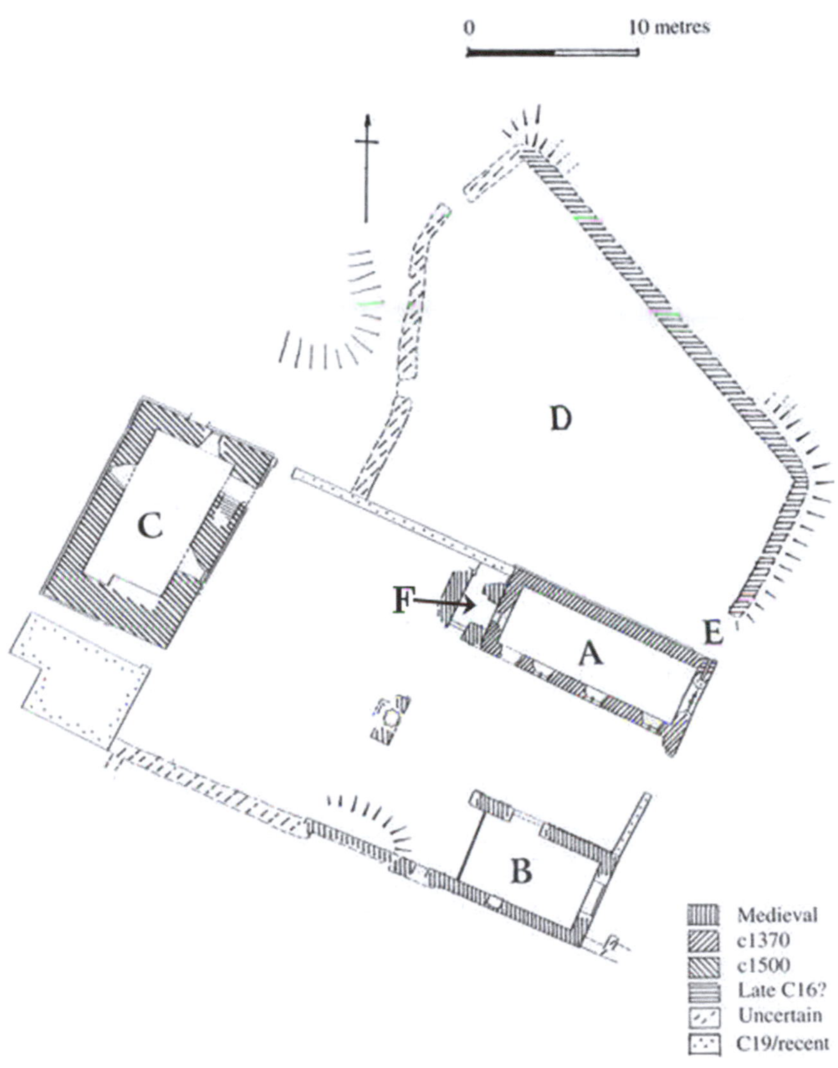

FIG. 1. Inner Farne/Farne Island: monastic cell ground plan with provisional phasing. A) St Cuthbert's chapel; B) remains of St Mary's chapel (now visitor centre); C) Prior Castell's tower; D) outer court; E) gateway to outer court; F) remains of 'Galilee'
After a survey by P. F. and M. G. Ryder 1996 (modified by author)

into the present visitor centre).[24] John Speed's 1611 map of Inner Farne suggests that Castell's tower covered Cuthbert's original dwelling house at the west as it contains a spring (as did Cuthbert's cell). Rosemary Cramp has suggested that the 14th-century chapel of St Cuthbert was built over his oratory.[25]

Before moving to Farne, Cuthbert retreated to an island some 180 m south-west of Holy Island, later to be used by Æadberht as a retreat around the time of Cuthbert's death.[26] Surviving remains include a T-shaped chapel consisting of a room divided into two compartments creating a possible cell and oratory, and a north-west circular mound which is associated with Cuthbert's original circular cell, although there are no identifiable architectural features (Fig. 2).[27] Cramp considered the chapel foundations to be primarily medieval, and more recent studies date the oratory to the 13th century, with Crossman's 19th-century excavation concluding that it lay on top of an earlier structure within an older enclosure.[28] Indeed, the ruins of the oratory do appear to date from the medieval period — as evidenced by the precision and consistency of the masonry coursing of the walls — indicating the structure was rebuilt at some point before the Dissolution (Fig. 3). The purpose of this, at least where the chapel was concerned, was not liturgical. After Æadberht there were no known inhabitants,

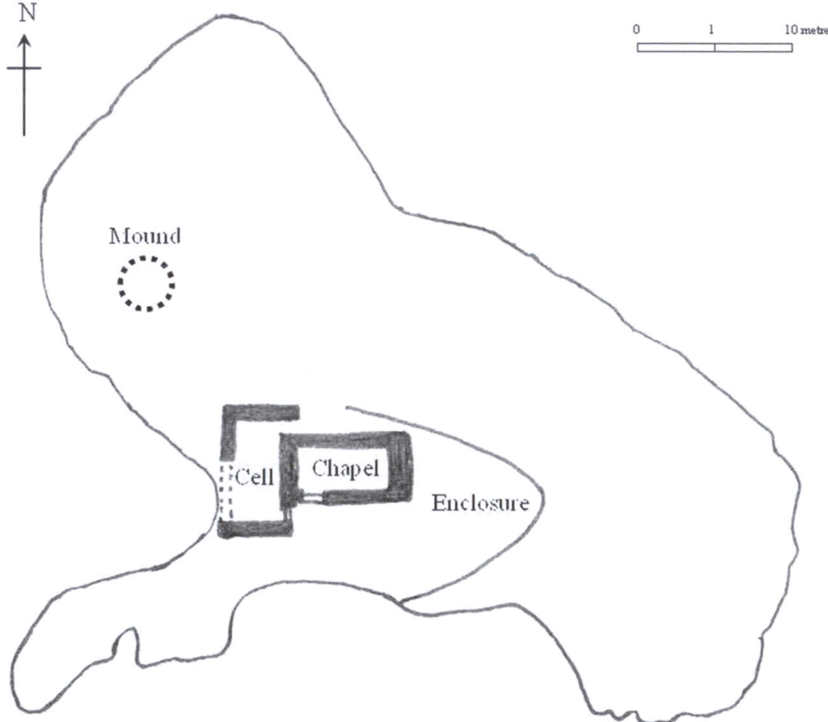

Fig. 2. Inner Farne/Farne Island: i) Possible site of 14th-century *hospitium* and 7th-century guesthouse; ii) 14th-century chapel and possible site of early oratory; iii) Prior Castel's tower and possible site of early cell; iv) Remains of 'chapel of St Mary' and current visitor centre

Drawn by author after Speed 1611

which suggests that the crumbling structure was restored to maintain its association as a sanctified Cuthbertine site: a 'tourist attraction' for pilgrims to visit and observe where the saint had lived and worshipped.

The cell at Farne was also reused after Cuthbert. Bishop Æathilwald was the first occupant who turned the hermitage into what could be described as an early pilgrimage centre by inhabiting the structure himself.[29] He was followed by Felgild in the 8th century who restored the now-ruined oratory and turned the calf's skin that Æathilwald had used for shelter into a relic by cutting it up and distributing it, claiming that it possessed the sanctity of Cuthbert.[30] The hermitage was sporadically inhabited by a succession of monks until the late 12th century, when a formal Benedictine cell of Durham was founded on the island and staffed by two monks, one a *magister*, the other a *socius*. The names of the masters are known from 1255 until the Dissolution.[31]

There are various contemporary references categorically supported by the archaeological evidence for medieval pilgrimage to the island of Farne. First, during this period the account rolls document many visitors, and, as such, the 7th-century guest-house built by St Cuthbert for visiting monks (located near the landing place), which existed until at least the 12th century, was often in use.[32] This assumption is supported by a comment in Reginald's *Libellus* about how visitors were shown the lower, huge stones of the guesthouse wall in the belief that the saint had put them in place himself.[33] Following this, the buildings of the monastic cell on Farne were erected. Extensive refurbishments and new buildings were erected in the 14th century. As will be shown, some of these structures were erected on the site of, and with the stones from, the early cell and enclosure.[34]

Of this monastic establishment, a small amount of evidence for a second guesthouse remains.[35] In the account rolls of 1360–61, a small *hospitium* is described as the 'Hall of St Cuthbert' built for visiting pilgrims.[36] This is most likely to have been the 'Fishe House' identified on Speed's map (Fig. 4).[37] What remains is an assemblage of rubble masonry close to the water's edge, measuring approximately 4.7 × 3.8 m with a doorway at the east end (Fig. 5). Three courses of dressed stone are visible in the north-east corner.[38] The evidence alludes to an originally large structure, needed to accommodate pilgrims visiting the remote island two miles from the coast. Located near the present landing place, we may infer that it was built on the site of Cuthbert's guesthouse described by Reginald (and in the same area), thus replacing the earlier structure, either because it was ruinous or because a larger structure was needed to accommodate an increase in visitors to the island. Perhaps, then, as the island continued to attract pilgrims throughout the 12th and 13th centuries, this led to the need for a new *hospitium* in the 14th century.

Further evidence for pilgrimage to the island lies in the foundations of a small room adjoining the west end of St Cuthbert's chapel (Fig. 6). Measuring 2 × 1.5 m internally, it stands up to 1.2 m high with an entranceway of two steps in the south wall.[39] In the mid 19th-century George Tate described it as a once-vaulted chamber 8 ft high, connected to the main building by a now-blocked recess.[40] He referred to it as a 'dead house' used for rites of burial after three coffins were discovered in the adjacent ground (a similar practice is found at the west narthex of Fountains Abbey church).[41] More recently, however, Peter Ryder's extensive study proposed that the structure functioned as a 'Galilee' annexe to the two-storey tower that once stood at the west end of the chapel, which he relates to arranging limited access for pilgrim visitors.[42] This feature was typical of churches dedicated to St Cuthbert. It is similar (if on a

FIG. 3. Holy Island: St Cuthbert's Isle, remains of chapel and cell
Photo by author

smaller scale) to the Galilee chapels found at numerous northern cathedrals and abbey churches.[43]

The tower-chamber arrangement although small, rose above the chapel roof, as Samuel Grimm's late 18th-century drawings illustrate. At first-floor level a doorway opened from the chapel into the adjacent chamber (Fig. 7).[44] The location of this doorway implies presence of a stair, and possibly a gallery, within the chapel for the purposes of limited viewing of the interior, again supporting the idea that it served visiting pilgrims.[45]

Moreover, the inclusion of the ground-floor recess may account for Ryder's 'pilgrim chamber' theory. From its placement in the south side of the west wall, the once two-light ogee-arched window was most likely used to view the church's interior. This buttresses Ryder's suggestion that the porch was a space reserved for the devotion of penitents (or at least female visitors, due to the misogyny attributed to the saint by this time), restricting access to the main chapel, yet allowing direct sight to the high altar without disturbance to the monastic practices occurring within.[46]

Evidence of two discrete spaces alludes to devotional segregation by sex or class. Agreeing with the idea that the lower recess was used for view, perhaps for the confinement of females, Ryder proposed that male visitors, or those of some particular

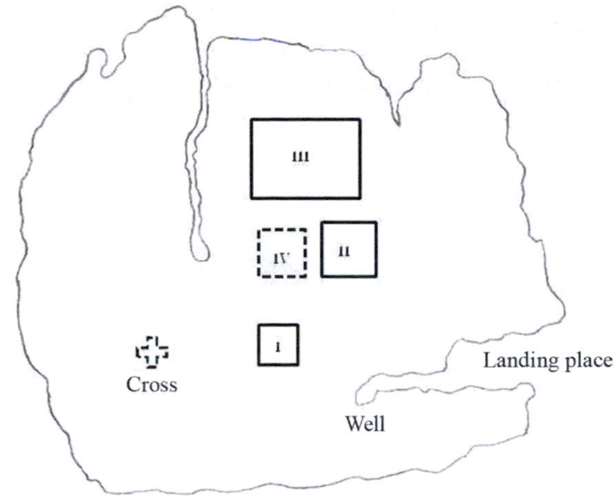

FIG. 4. St Cuthbert's Isle, as seen from the south-west of Holy Island: plan of excavated and surveyed remains
Drawn by author after Crossman, Watt and McBarron

FIG. 5. Inner Farne/Farne Island: View of structural remains from north-east
Photo by P. F. Ryder

FIG. 6. Inner Farne/Farne Island: South-west view of St Cuthbert's chapel showing 'Galilee' remains
Photo by P. F. Ryder

status, ascended into the first-floor space of the tower and then into the western gallery which commanded sight of the chapel interior.[47] Similar two-storey annexes occur nearby, for example at St Henry's chapel (or hermitage) on Coquet Island, in the Prior's chapel at Finchale priory, and in a number of secular manorial chapels including Warkworth castle; all sites of pilgrimage during the later medieval period.[48]

Farne had acted as a focus for the cult since before the arrival of the monks due to Cuthbert's eremitical life there, but it certainly seems that an increase in hospitality attracted far more visitors to the island. Frequent visitation by pilgrims is further suggested by the heavy use made of the Farne boat in the 14th century and the purchase of ale in 1421–22 for visiting guests.[49] Moreover, offerings were still being made at Farne in the later 14th century, if only in small numbers. Receipts range from 3s. 8d. made in the church in 1361–62 to 5s. received 'from the shrine' in 1417.[50] Although the financial affairs of Lindisfarne and Farne were tightly controlled by Durham, the priory was expected to be financially independent of the mother-house. Therefore, the latter receipt most likely implies money received from Lindisfarne priory and made up of offerings at the cenotaph there, as no evidence survives for a shrine on Farne Island itself. Nevertheless, according to the Farne accounts, 10s. was yielded from the 'box of St Cuthbert' in 1486–87, 6d. was left in 1508–09, and, finally, 4d. was offered in 1536–37.[51] Although continual references to offerings do not exist, the accounts provide important information to show that the island was the object of a significant number of pilgrims throughout the later medieval period. It certainly appears as though there were numerous sites at which offerings could be made.

OTHER EVIDENCE FOR PILGRIM ACTIVITY

IN the large repertoire of materials consulted in research for this paper, not one medieval find can definitively be attributed to the cult of St Cuthbert, and only a handful of finds actually survives from the entire north-east.[68] At Lindisfarne itself, there has been only one pilgrim-badge discovery (Fig. 10). Unfortunately, the motto is indecipherable, and looks simply like a patterned design. (There may thus be some doubt about whether it is a pilgrim-badge at all.) However, four ampullae have been discovered at Spennymoor, Morpeth, Warkworth and Berwick. These are more significant to this analysis as they may be related to a Cuthbertine pilgrimage route, given the dedicated wells at Farne, Lindisfarne and Bellingham, to name the most notable, and the 14th-century hermitage and nearby bridge of the same period at Warkworth.[69] The low rate of finds may at first suggest that there is in fact a true absence of the Cuthbertine cult in Northumberland.[70] Yet the remains of cults are often so ephemeral that it is difficult to argue that a cult did not exist due to the absence of finds. Methodological problems may account for the paucity of evidence. The majority of these finds derive from urban contexts near riverine or coastal locations.[71] It remains to be seen whether this can be attributed to the good conditions of survival in such locations, whether they are ritual deposits, or whether badges were sold on quaysides.[72] Still, Brian Spencer argued that in England ampullae were the souvenir of choice until overtaken (in many places at least) by badges in the 14th century: this corresponds, perhaps, to the lack of finds.[73] Assuming that this was the case in the north-east, very few badges may ever have been produced. It may be ventured that the lack of pilgrimage-related material is attributable rather to the fact that the objects, perhaps made of perishable materials, either did not survive or simply have not been found yet. If so, future work in the rivers and fords of the Northumbrian landscape may prove fruitful.

CONCLUSION

ALTHOUGH the evidence for pilgrimage to the Lindisfarne area is limited, my contention is that around the time of the construction of Ædward's church, and soon after the translation, pilgrimage existed at the priory. When the population of Lindisfarne waned as the centuries drew on, the primary focus moved to Inner Farne, though a small number of pilgrims continued to visit the hermitage and the buildings

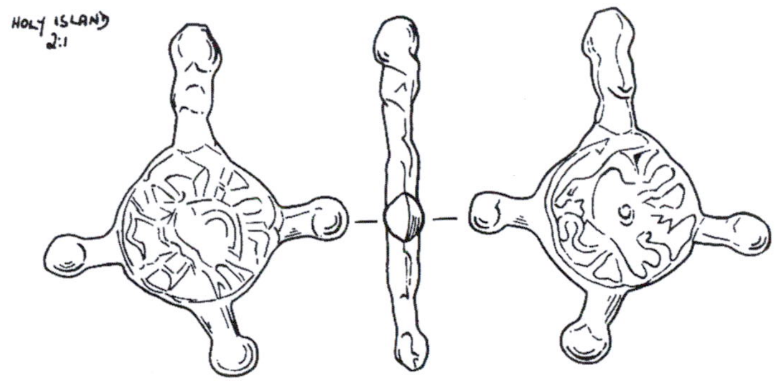

FIG. 10. Possible pilgrim badge found on Lindisfarne. Pewter, 33 mm, motto indecipherable
Copyright and courtesy of Newcastle University

on the Heugh. A larger survey of the length of veneration of burial sites after translations of saintly relics is needed to indicate the length of time that a site without a body remained attractive to medieval pilgrims. Nonetheless, from the evidence presented, Lindisfarne and Farne acted as the 'lifetime' pilgrimage stations of the north-eastern route. Where Cuthbert spent his exemplary life, his sanctity remained within the fabric of the buildings. That throughout the medieval period original burial sites were still revered after relics had been removed (e.g. Thomas Becket) illustrates the strength and in some cases endurance of saintly associations. Nevertheless, it must be noted that Lindisfarne is a rather unusual case as most burial sites are located within the immediate vicinity of the translation site. More research is needed to understand this important issue of medieval Cuthbertine pilgrimage: it is hoped that this paper will help to induce it.

ACKNOWLEDGEMENTS

My gracious thanks must be extended to the following individuals: Pam Graves, Richard Plant, Peter Ryder, Sarah Blick, Linda Rollason, Derek Craig and David Harrison, without whose help and advice this paper could not have been written. I must also thank the committee members of the British Archaeological Association who awarded me a full scholarship to participate and attend the conference. Finally, to Julian Luxford — firstly for his comments on this paper — and Jeremy Ashbee, for giving me the greatest of opportunities by allowing me to present at a British Archaeological Association annual conference as a PhD student, and for subsequently inviting me to contribute to this volume.

NOTES

1. The monks of Lindisfarne priory and the cell at Farne did not constitute a convent proper during the later middle ages. No monk permanently resided at either location: monks were sent out from Durham priory to work at one cell before being moved on to the next or back to the mother-house. The two cells were dependencies of the cathedral priory at Durham. See *The Durham Liber vitae: London, British Library, MS Cotton Domitian A.VII: Edition and Digital Facsimile with Introduction, Codicological, Prosopographical and Linguistic Commentary, and Indexes*, ed. D. and L. Rollason and A. J. Piper, 3 vols (London 2007). See also A. J. Piper, 'The Names of the Durham Monks', in *The Durham Liber vitae and its Context*, ed. D. W. Rollason, A. J. Piper, M. Harvey and L. Rollason (Woodbridge 2004), 117–26.

2. D. W. Rollason, 'The Wanderings of St Cuthbert', in *Cuthbert: Saint and Patron*, ed. D. W. Rollason (Durham 1987), 57.

3. For a detailed discussion of the corporeal aspects of the early cult, see A. Thacker, 'Lindisfarne and the Origins of the Cult of St Cuthbert', in *St Cuthbert, His Cult and His Community to AD 1200*, ed. G. Bonner, D. W. Rollason and C. Stancliffe (Woodbridge 1989).

4. Most burial sites are located close to the translation site (i.e. within the same building): see, for example, Beverley (St John), Canterbury (Becket), Kentigern (Glasgow), Swithun (Winchester), and William (York). The distance between Cuthbert's burial site at Lindisfarne and his reliquary-shrine at Durham is approximately 86 miles by (modern) road and 69 miles as the crow flies. Either distance is possible for medieval travel based on evidence for medieval route-ways, many of which follow a similar path to today's roads. For a lengthy discussion of this subject, see G. Hutton, 'Roads and Routeways in County Durham: 1530–1730' (unpublished PhD thesis, University of Durham, 2011).

5. *Two Lives of Saint Cuthbert: A Life by an Anonymous Monk of Lindisfarne and Bede's Prose Life*, ed. and trans. B. Colgrave (Cambridge 1985) (this includes the anonymous *Life of St Cuthbert*: 'Vita sancti Cuthberti auctore anonymo', and Bede's metrical *Life of St Cuthbert*: 'Bedas metrische Vita sancti Cuthberti'); Bede, *EH*; *Historia de Sancto Cuthberto: A History of St Cuthbert and a Record of His Patrimony*, ed. T. Johnson Smith (Woodbridge 2002).

6. Symeon of Durham, *Libellus de exordio atque procursu istius, hoc est Dunhelmensis, ecclesie. Tract on the Origins and Progress of this the Church of Durham*, ed. and trans. D. W. Rollason (Oxford 1998); Reginald of Durham, *Reginaldi Monarchi Dunelmensis Libellus de admirandis beati Cuthberti virtutibus*, trans. J. Raine, SS (1835) (a portion of the material alludes to the 1150s). See also V. Tudor, 'The Cult of St Cuthbert in the Twelfth century: The Evidence of Reginald of Durham', in *St Cuthbert, His Cult* (as n. 3), 447–67.

7. W. M. Aird, 'The Making of a Medieval Miracle Collection: The *Liber de Translationibus et Miraculis Sancti Cuthberti*', *Northern History*, 28 (1992), 23. See also Tudor, 'The Cult' (as n. 6), 449, for an analysis of the context of the *miracula*.

8. It must be noted that all but one of the individuals concerned in the miracle accounts that take place on Lindisfarne are of monastic status: Tudor, 'The Cult' (as n. 6), 455, 461–62.

9. Ibid., 465.

10. Ibid., loc. cit.

11. Ibid., 466. See also (particularly) E. Craster, 'The Miracles of St. Cuthbert at Farne', *AA*, 4th ser. 29 (1951), 93–107 (for the 10-mile radius, see 95).

12. Aird, 'The Making' (as n. 7), 24.

13. Ibid., 9; Tudor, 'The Cult' (as n. 6), 455, 456.

14. For an examination of the geographical dispersion of both cults, see R. C. Finucane, *Miracles and Pilgrims: Popular Beliefs in Medieval England* (London 1995), 166–69.

15. Tudor, 'The Cult' (as n. 6), 465.

16. Aird, 'The Making' (as n. 7), 12.

17. A. F. Harris, 'Pilgrimage, Performance and Stained Glass at Canterbury Cathedral', in *Art and Architecture of Late Medieval Pilgrimage In Northern Europe and the British Isles*, ed. S. Blick and R. Tekippe, 2 vols (Leiden and Boston 2004), I, 272.

18. This was commemorated by a cenotaph after the relics had been removed.

19. Thacker, 'Lindisfarne and the Origins' (as n. 3), 107; E. Cambridge, 'Why Did the Community of St Cuthbert Settle at Chester-le-Street?', in *St Cuthbert, His Cult* (as n. 3), 371.

20. The numerous wells dedicated to St Cuthbert including one at Lindisfarne and two on Farne also suggest that holy water was used to promote the cult. See D. O'Sullivan and R. Young, *Book of Lindisfarne: Holy Island* (London 1995), 108–09.

21. A. Piper, 'The First Generations of Durham Monks and the Cult of St Cuthbert', in *St Cuthbert, His Cult* (as n. 3), 445.

22. Ibid., loc. cit.; also I. A. Richmond, 'Saint Cuthbert's Dwelling on Farne', *Antiquity*, 15 (1941), 88–89. See further Thacker, 'Lindisfarne and the Origins' (as n. 3), 112, and C. J. Brooke, *Safe Sanctuaries: Security and Defence in Anglo-Scottish Border Churches, 1296–1603* (Edinburgh 2000), 79–81.

23. Masonry of the 12th and 13th centuries is visibly incorporated into the chapel, suggesting it was built on top of an earlier structure. J. Raine, *The History and Antiquities of North Durham* (London 1852), 345. Castell's rebuilding was recorded by John Leland a few years after the cell was dissolved in 1536: P. F. Ryder, 'Prior Castell's Tower, Inner Farne — Archaeological Recording & Structural Interpretation' (unpublished report, National Trust 1998), 1. See also R. Cramp, *The Hermitage and the Offshore Island* (Basildon 1981), 19.

24. Ryder, 'Prior Castell's Tower' (as n. 23), 12.

25. Cramp, *Hermitage* (as n. 23), 19. The present chapel was completed in 1371–72, according to information given in the account rolls: Raine, *North Durham* (as n. 23), 346.

26. *Two Lives* (as n. 5), 342.

27. We know from Bede that Cuthbert built a circular enclosure of turf and local stone, which this mound may represent: see O'Sullivan and Young, *Book of Lindisfarne* (as n. 20), 42–43.

28. See W. Crossman, 'Chapel of St-Cuthbert-in-the-Sea', *History of the Berwickshire Naturalists Club*, 13 (1890), 241–42; Cramp, *The Hermitage* (as n. 23), 7.

29. Thacker, 'Lindisfarne and the Origins' (as n. 3), 105.

30. Ibid., 106; D. W. Rollason, *Saints and Relics in Anglo-Saxon England* (Oxford 1989), 105.

31. Raine, *North Durham* (as n. 23), 340–42.

32. V. Tudor, 'Durham Priory and its Hermits in the Twelfth Century', in *Anglo-Norman Durham 1093–1193*, ed. D. W. Rollason, M. Harvey and M. Prestwich (Woodbridge 1994), 69. See also Cramp, *The Hermitage* (as n. 23), 19.

33. Reginald, *Libellus* (as n. 6), 228.

34. Piper, 'The First Generations (as n. 21), 445.

35. *B/E Northumberland*, 277.

36. Raine, *North Durham* (as n. 23), 345.

37. G. Watt, *The Farne Islands: Their History and Wildlife* (London 1951), 28-9.
38. Northumberland County Council Conservation Team, *Monastic Settlement on Farne Island*: <http://archaeologydataservice.ac.uk/archsearch/record.jsf?titleId=959856> [accessed 1 November 2012].
39. Ibid.
40. The upper parts were removed *c.* 1842: see G. Tate, 'The Farne Islands', *History of the Berwickshire Naturalists Club*, 3 (1850–56), 226.
41. Tate, 'Farne Islands' (as n. 40), 226. Galilees and funerary functions are often far from separate. See K. Kruger, 'Architecture and Liturgical Practice: The Cluniac Galilaea', in *The White Mantle of Churches: Architecture, Liturgy, and Art around the Millennium*, ed. N. Hiscock (Turnhout 2003), 139–59.
42. There is a documentary reference to a 'campanile' in the 1360–61 account rolls: see P. Ryder, 'St Cuthbert's Chapel, Inner Farne — Archaeological Recording & Structural Interpretation' (unpublished report, National Trust 1999), 1.
43. Examples can be found at Durham cathedral and the abbeys of Fountains, Rievaulx and Byland (to name a few). On the topic, see S. A. Harrison, 'Observations on the Architecture of the Galilee Chapel', in *Anglo-Norman Durham* (as n. 35), 213–34; G. Coppack, 'Some Descriptions of Reivaulx Abbey in 1538–9: The Disposition of a Major Cistercian Precinct in the Early Sixteenth Century, *JBAA*, 139 (1986), 100–33; S. A. Harrison and P. Barker, 'Byland Abbey, North Yorkshire: The West Front and Rose Window Reconstructed', *JBAA*, 140 (1987), 134–51; R. Halsey, 'The Galilee Chapel', *Medieval Art and Architecture at Durham Cathedral*, ed. N. Coldstream and P. Draper, *BAA Trans.*, III (Leeds 1980), 59–73.
44. Ryder, 'St Cuthbert's Chapel' (as n. 42), 16.
45. Ibid., loc. cit.
46. See V. Tudor, 'The Misogyny of Saint Cuthbert', *AA*, 5th ser. 12 (1984), 157–67.
47. Or perhaps in some lost structure further to the west. Ryder, 'St Cuthbert's Chapel' (as n. 42), 17.
48. As well as Warkworth (Peter Ryder, personal communication), Bolton castle chapel also had a private gallery for the use of the Scrope family, accessed via a stairway from the solar in the south-west tower: A. Pettifer, *English Castles: A Guide by Counties* (Woodbridge 1995), 287–88; M. E. Wood, *The English Mediaeval House* (London 1965), 236; Ryder, 'St Cuthbert's Chapel' (as n. 42), 26. (See also Frank Woodman's paper in this volume.)
49. For the boat, see Durham Cathedral Muniments (hereafter DCM), 'Medieval Accounting Material, Master of Farne', GB-0033-DCD-Farn. acs, 1362–63. For the purchase of ale see Raine, *North Durham* (as n. 23), 350.
50. Raine, *North Durham* (as n. 23), 350.
51. See Ibid., 345, 349, 356–58.
52. E. Cambridge, 'The Priory', in O'Sullivan and Young, *Book of Lindisfarne* (as n. 20), 71–72.
53. This practice of creating a cult 'theme park' is comparable to the 13th-century reconstructions of the two corresponding chapels of St Michael on Looe Island off the Cornish coast and the Lammana chapel directly opposite on the mainland: *Looe Cornwall — Archaeological Evaluation and Assessment of Results* (report by Wessex Archaeology 2009): <http://www.wessexarch.co.uk/files/68734_Looe%20Cornwall.pdf> [accessed 1 November 2012].
54. Recorded in Bede's version of the *Two Lives* (as n. 5), 299–300. The same account occurs in very similar form in the anonymous *Life* (as n. 5) (137–39), yet the boy is quoted as visiting 'the places of the sacred martyrs, giving thanks to the Lord'. See also M. Herity, 'Early Irish Hermitages in the Light of the Lives of Cuthbert', in *St Cuthbert, His Cult* (as n. 3), 53–54.
55. This area was also surveyed by the Lindisfarne Research Project in 1984–85: see O'Sullivan and Young, *Book of Lindisfarne* (as n. 20), 46.
56. Ibid., 47.
57. O'Sullivan and Young, *Book of Lindisfarne* (as n. 20), 47–48.
58. We may assume that this structure is the present Romanesque church: Cambridge, 'The Priory' (as n. 52), 67.
59. The outgoing master of Farne Island, Ralph Blakeston, recorded the portable belongings of the cell in 1520, including six pounds of wax, to be found 'super tumbam sancti Cuthberti in Insula Sacra': DCM, GB-0033-DCD-Farn. acs, 1519–20(A). Leland's description of the cenotaph was as follows: 'yn the body of the chirch is a tumbe with the image of a bisshop yn the token that S. Cuthberth ons was buried or remained in his feretre there': *Leland's Itinerary in England and Wales*, ed. L. T. Smith, 5 vols (London 1964), I, 74.
60. Reginald, *Libellus* (as n. 6), 46. See also Cambridge, 'Community' (as n. 19), 368. For the account rolls see Raine, *North Durham* (as n. 23), 125. However, a cenotaph was most likely erected directly from after his death in 687 until around the time the body was moved to Norham in order to mark the original burial site, as Bede's account of this time recalls the elevation of the body in 698 directly above this site.
61. *Two Lives* (as n. 5), 313 and Symeon, *Libellus* (as n. 6), 640.

62. Richard Plant, personal communication. Similar practices occurred as early as the 9th century in the crypt of St Wystan's church at Repton, Derbyshire, and later at Ely, Canterbury and Rochester. See P. Draper, 'The Late Twelfth-Century East End of Rochester Cathedral', *Medieval Art, Architecture and Archaeology at Rochester*, ed. T. Ayers and T. Tatton-Brown, *BAA Trans.*, XXVIII (Leeds 2006), 97–113.

63. All we know of the cenotaph is that it was located inside the church from Reginald's statement 'infra ecclasiam' (Reginald, *Libellus* (as n. 6), 46). Furthermore, the Farne Island accounts make reference to the structure being on Holy Island 'super tumbam sancti Cuthberti in Insula Sacra': DCM, GB-0033-DCD-Farn. acs, 1519–20(A). See also Cambridge, 'The Priory' (as n. 52), 67, 69; Cambridge, 'Community' (as n. 19), 368.

64. Raine, *North Durham* (as n. 23), 104.

65. There is a long pause until offerings reappear in 1501.

66. A priory document from 1365 refers to the churchyard of St Columb, Lindisfarne. This suggests the existence of another chapel on the island, although the exact location of the building is unknown. Although still unclear, O'Sullivan and Young proposed that the origins of the chapel may stem from the site of an early burial ground. The location of the chapel was possibly the north side of the village. A number of burials were discovered east of this presumed site, suggesting that there were early graveyards with distinctions between secular and monastic interments (O'Sullivan and Young, *Book of Lindisfarne* (as n. 20), 45–46). Additional evidence which may support the existence of this chapel lies in receipts made to the 'box of St Columb'. Image shrines were often accompanied by an offerings box, or pyx, for pilgrims to make their oblations. Such boxes and their accompanying images were often located in their own separate chapels. These could reside either in cathedrals, parish churches or in dedicated freestanding buildings. Examples for which accounts of offerings survive include Our Lady of the Undercroft in the crypt of Canterbury cathedral, Red Mount (or 'Our Lady of the Mount') chapel in King's Lynn and Our Lady of Bolton, the latter a separate chapel within the southern transept of Durham cathedral. See R. Marks, *Image and Devotion in Late Medieval England* (Stroud, 2004), 190–205. However, perhaps, the box at Lindisfarne could simply have served as a depository for co-devotion to both Columba and Cuthbert. The practice of keeping separate accounts of monies brought in from different pilgrim stations, even when they were in close proximity, was recurrent throughout the medieval period. See B. Nilson, *Cathedral Shrines of Medieval England* (Woodbridge 1998), 105–10.

67. Raine, *North Durham* (as n. 23), 82 (account rolls for Holy Island).

68. This included an unpublished assemblage of over 3000 objects removed from the River Wear by Gary Bankhead.

69. David Harrison, personal communication.

70. Sarah Blick, personal communication.

71. B. Spencer, *Medieval Pilgrim Badges: Some General Observations Illustrated Mainly from English Sources*, Rotterdam Papers I (Rotterdam 1968), 139. See also J. Stopford, 'Some Approaches to the Archaeology of Christian Pilgrimage', *World Archaeology*, 26 (1994), 69.

72. Jim Bugslag asserted that the 'negative evidence' regarding pilgrim badges is methodologically unsound as 'there are substantial areas of Europe in which no medieval pilgrims' badges have been found, for lack of propitious conditions': J. Bugslag, 'Pilgrimage to Chartres: The Visual Evidence', in Blick and Tekippe, *Art and Architecture* (as n. 17), I, 170. See also Stopford, 'Some Approaches' (as n. 71), 69.

73. B. Spencer, *Pilgrim Souvenirs and Secular Badges* (Woodbridge 2010), 3. Although this was predominantly the case for many shrine-sites, the 15th century also brought about a large increase in the use of ampullae. See Spencer, 'A Scallop-Shell Ampulla from Caistor and Comparable Pilgrim Souvenirs', *Lincolnshire History of Archaeology*, 6 (1971), 59–66, and also W. Anderson, 'Blessing the Fields? A Study of Late-Medieval Ampullae from England and Wales', *Medieval Archaeology*, 54 (2010), 182–203.

The Early Development of Alnwick Castle, *c.* 1100–1400

JOHN GOODALL

Alnwick castle is one of the most important historic monuments in Northumberland; a building continuously maintained and ambitiously developed as a nobleman's seat since the middle ages. The aim of this article is to unravel the principle stages of its architectural development from the foundation of the castle around 1100 until about 1400, when the bones of the present buildings were completed. It will also consider the parallels for the architecture at Alnwick and explain the significance of the castle in a national context.

THERE has probably been a castle at Alnwick, a strategically important settlement on the Great North Road to Scotland, since around 1100 (Fig. 1 and Col. Pl. XXVII in print edn).[1] The early history of the barony is obscure, but it is thought to have been founded by the Vescys (or Vescis), a family with extensive property in Yorkshire.[2] Whatever the precise circumstances of its establishment, the castle itself is first securely documented in 1136. That year it was treacherously rendered to David I of Scotland and was of sufficient scale to be described as a 'powerful castle' or 'munitissimum castellum'.[3]

All the evidence suggests that the castle was indeed exceptionally large and important by the standards of the region. It occupies a natural spur enclosed on three sides by the valleys of the river Aln and its tributary Bow Burn. On the fourth side — to the west — the castle is bounded by Bailiffgate, a settlement apparently distinct from the medieval town and occupied by those performing castleguard or otherwise connected with the castle administration.[4] Sandwiched between Bailiffgate and the west wall of the castle was the Great North Road, which rose up from the adjacent medieval bridge over the River Aln.

The logic of the castle plan in relation to the natural topography and its coherent relationship with the town and Bailiffgate implies that the building was laid out from the first on roughly its present plan.[5] The survival within the outer curtain of stretches of 12th-century masonry further suggests that the line of the castle fortifications has been constant in some places since then. That said, there is good evidence that the castle has twice been expanded northwards: first by the addition of the present inner bailey (known today as the Keep) in the 14th century and again with a new terrace — the Gun Terrace — a product of 18th- and 19th-century changes. The latter change is well documented, but the details of the former expansion have not been commented upon before and will be discussed below. Of the early internal layout of the castle, nothing is securely known and it might have comprised one or two baileys.

This early castle was probably fortified in stone from the first. As well as the surviving fragments of early walls mentioned above, the gate to the present inner bailey (or Keep) cannibalizes the remains of a large Romanesque gate tower. This building was

BAA Trans., vol. XXXVI (2013), 232–247

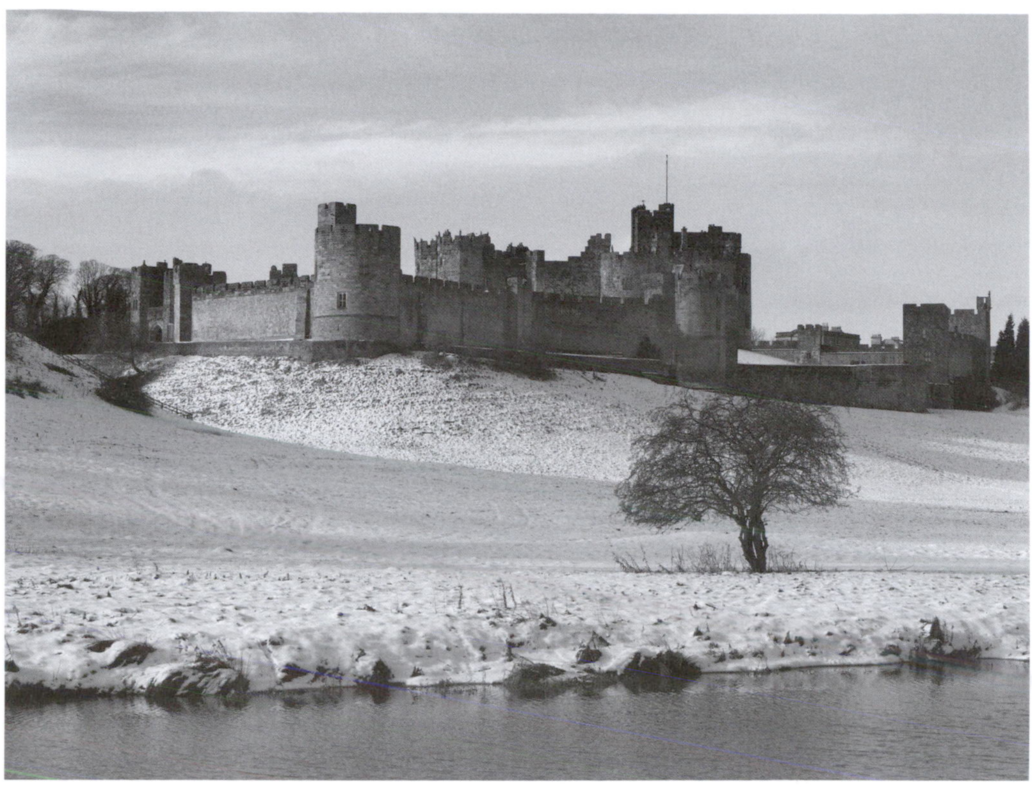

FIG. 1. View of Alnwick castle from the north-east
Paul Barker / Country Life Picture Library

evidently laid out on a rectangular plan with walls of different thicknesses to the front and rear. There are several northern parallels for stone-built castles of the 12th century with a walled perimeter entered through a large gatehouse, as for example at Prudhoe (Northumberland) and Egremont (Cumbria). As with the former of these examples, it is likely that Alnwick never possessed a motte.

The gatehouse at Alnwick was evidently a building of unusually high architectural quality. This is shown by the surviving Romanesque gatepassage arches, which are richly ornamented with chevron and other carving (Fig. 2). Although restored and with some sculpture seemingly pieced in or reset, this detailing seems authentic. It is important to note that the disposition of the sculpture on these arches and the different thickness of the gatehouse walls suggest the 14th-century remodelling reversed the building: the arch facing into the inner bailey courtyard is both more massively constructed and more richly ornamented than its counterpart within the gatepassage. Both details would suggest that the former was originally the entrance arch of the gate. By extension, that the present inner bailey was an addition to the original castle.

It is rare to find such a quantity of decorative carving on a castle gatehouse of the 12th century. The only obvious northern comparison for such treatment is the great

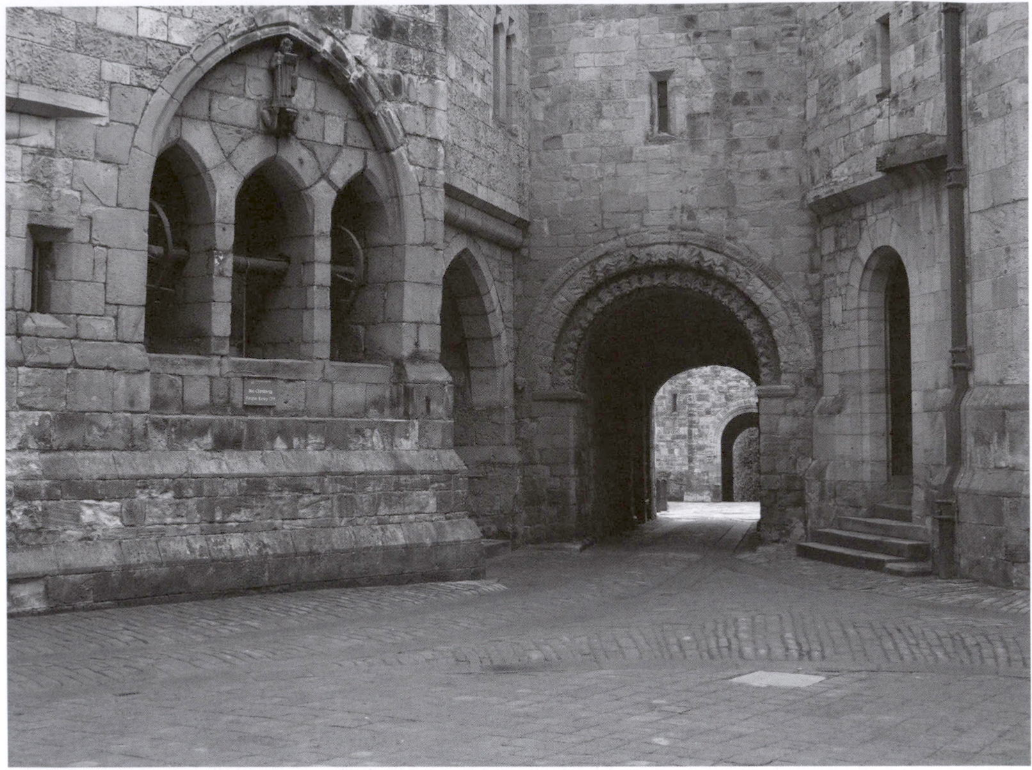

FIG. 2. The inside facade of the inner bailey gatehouse. The Romanesque arch incorporated in the present gate was probably the principal entrance to the 12th-century castle. The wellhead is visible to the left

Paul Barker / Country Life Picture Library

gate of Durham castle, which was probably built by Ralph Flambard, bishop of Durham from 1099 to 1128.[6] The Durham gateway has also been much adapted and restored, but the Romanesque detailing of its entrance passage is relatively well preserved (Fig. 3). Its chevron is not dissimilar in form and detail to that found at Alnwick. On the basis of this parallel, it is not implausible to suggest that Alnwick gatehouse was erected prior to the first mention of the castle in 1136.

Little is securely known of the 13th-century development of Alnwick castle and the present buildings preserve no clearly identifiable fabric from this period. A royal command to slight it, along with the other Vescy castle at Malton (Yorkshire), was issued in May 1213.[7] If the order was followed, the building nevertheless appears to have been reoccupied almost immediately afterwards. The last Vescy lord of Alnwick died in 1297 and the castle passed into the possession the bishop of Durham. It was not long before a powerful and ambitious new owner presented himself.[8]

By a charter dated 19 November 1309, the soldier and captain Henry, Lord Percy, purchased the barony of Alnwick with its castle from the bishop of Durham.[9] Lord Percy's family interests had hitherto been focussed in Sussex and Yorkshire, and his

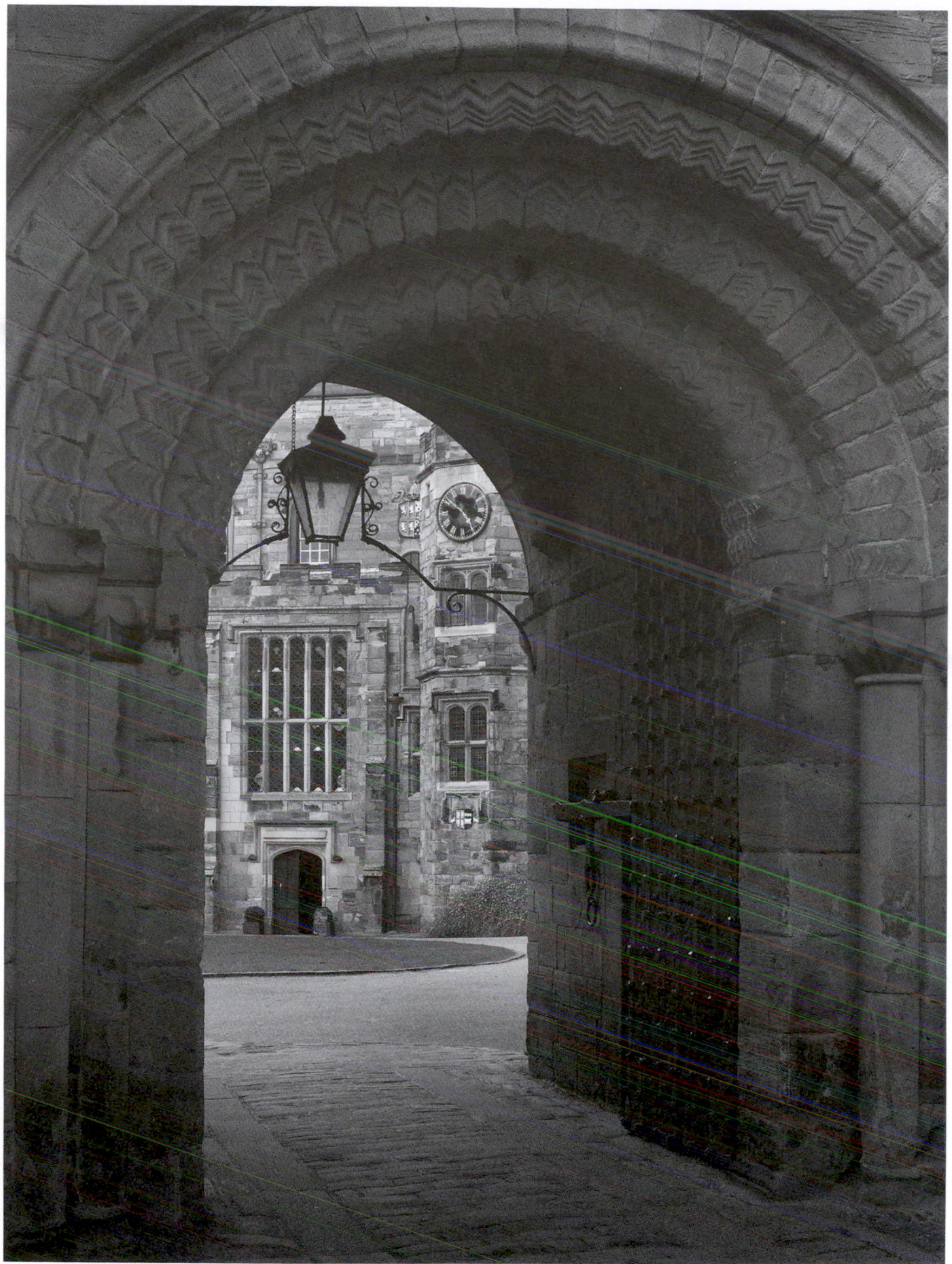

FIG. 3. The outer arch of the great gate of Durham castle
Paul Barker / Country Life Picture Library

interest in this northern possession was the direct product of Edward I's celebrated attempt to assert his feudal authority over Scotland from 1296. In 1306, as a reward for support in his Scottish campaigns, Edward I granted Lord Percy the forfeited Lowland earldom of Carrick.[10] This was one of several Scottish grants the king made to his leading followers in order to elicit their support.

Such gifts, however, were of limited value unless Scottish resistance could be overcome. It is no surprise, therefore, that Lord Percy joined the army assembled by Edward I in 1307 to deliver what was intended to be a final and crushing blow in this long-running war. The army, however, never achieved its purpose. Edward I died on the journey north at Burgh-on-Sands on 7 July 1307 and the Anglo-Scottish War stalled. Rather than take up his father's command, Edward II became embroiled in a bitter domestic dispute over his favouritism towards the Gascon knight Piers Gaveston.

It is against this political backdrop that the purchase of Alnwick should be viewed. Lord Percy's intention was doubtless to create a springboard from which to secure his potential possessions north of the border when hostilities resumed. There may also have been royal backing for the purchase as Edward II attempted to stiffen the defences of the Scottish frontier while his attention was turned elsewhere. Other figures acted in a similar way. Roger Clifford, for example, another of Edward I's outstanding commanders, built up considerable property across the northern march over the first decade of the 14th century. Then, in 1310, he also received the valuable honour and castle of Skipton in Yorkshire by royal grant.[11] Both men had predatory interests north of the border, and a marriage alliance was later struck between two of their children: Roger Clifford's daughter, Idonea, married Lord Percy's son, Henry Percy, 2nd Lord Percy (1301–52).

It must have been immediately after this purchase of Alnwick in 1309 that Henry Percy began to redevelop Alnwick. There is no documentary record for what he did, but a sequence of works can be reasonably inferred from the architectural evidence. His principal undertaking was probably to initiate a new inner bailey (the Keep) comprising a complete suit of domestic apartments enclosed by a corona of drum towers. This was laid out at the mouth of the former gatehouse to the castle, possibly on the site of a former barbican.

The case for asserting that Henry Percy began the inner bailey is essentially circumstantial. It rests principally upon the clear stylistic contrast that exists between its architecture and that of the buildings undertaken by his son in the 1340s (more of which below). It also deserves mention that, by the 14th century, a major castle with only a gatehouse along its perimeter wall would have looked both antiquated and modest. This grand new project made the building a more appropriate seat for a prospective Scottish earl. By expanding the castle outside the walls, moreover, the existing defences were not compromised by the operation.

Henry Percy had less than five years to work on the inner bailey, and the likelihood must be that it was finished after his death. As we shall see, his son certainly built the present entrance gate to the inner bailey in the 1340s, and it may be that much else besides was completed at this time. Whatever the case, sweeping changes in the 18th and 19th centuries have obscured virtually all the internal medieval fabric of the corona of towers and its associated domestic buildings. Probably the only fitting that relates to the first phase of work is the handsome wellhead that stands adjacent to the entrance (see Fig. 2).[12] There is, however, an impressive body of material that records the late medieval form of the buildings within it. It can be no more than educated guesswork as to whether the details of this reflect the original early 14th-century design.

A survey of the castle in 1567 describes the seven towers of the corona and explains that they were set within a dry ditch. The internal court was enclosed by residential buildings including a series of withdrawing apartments, a hall and a kitchen block. Above the whole composition — rising 14 yards (12.8 m) above the leads of the roof — was a tall lookout tower with space for a watchman to lie and a place for a beacon to be fixed.[13] The principal castles in this area are all intervisible, so this tower was presumably intended to facilitate communication between them. It is no coincidence that a similar tower of the 1370s survives at the nearby Percy castle of Warkworth (Northumberland).

This textual description of 1567 can be set against a visual record of the entire castle drawn up by Ralph Treswell the younger in 1608. Treswell's remarkable survey comprises five floor plans and a bird's-eye view of the castle. Engravings of part of this survey and black-and-white photographs of the whole have been published.[14] The household accounts record both Treswell's payment of £7 10s. for the work and the costs of the necessary vellum as £1 7s. 6d.[15]

The idea of an inner bailey in the form of a corona of towers had a long history in English castle architecture. Precedents for the building at Alnwick with drum towers and integrally planned domestic buildings can be found nearly a century earlier at sites such as Clifford (Herefordshire), probably begun in the 1220s. Possibly connected directly with the works at Alnwick, however, is the inner bailey at Skipton, begun by Roger Clifford around 1310. Badly damaged in the Civil War and reconstructed in its aftermath, the original details of the inner bailey at Skipton are also problematic to reconstruct. Nevertheless, what both coronas clearly share is an unusual and impressive scale.

One effect of creating the new inner bailey at Alnwick across the former entrance to the castle was that it re-orientated the building westwards and southwards. It is likely to have been in connection with this work, therefore, that two new gatehouses were added to the castle. That to the south was aligned with inner bailey gatehouse and is known from Treswell's survey and early views of the castle. It was square in plan with buttresses flanking the main entrance. By the 17th century its gatepassage had been blocked. Little more can be said with security about its form because the whole structure was reordered as the Garden Gate in the course of 19th-century rebuilding work.

To the west, meanwhile, a cross wall dividing the castle enclosure into two baileys was erected (or possibly rebuilt) and a new gate — the Middle Gate — constructed at the point it intersected with the south curtain. This takes the form of a rectangular block with a single tower commanding the gatepassage (Fig. 4). Buildings of this design are a rarity in England, but parallels can be found from the early 13th century, as for example the remodelled Peverell Gate at Dover castle (Kent). One surviving detail of this gate, moreover, is likewise very unusual: the tower rises from a spur plinth. This detail of spurs — a means of linking the rectangular foundation of the tower with its semicircular superstructure — has a complex history and its appearance at Alnwick is highly significant.

Probably developed from Roman precedents in France in the late 12th century, castle towers with spurs appear in several large-scale royal building projects in the south-east of England around 1200.[16] From there the idea of spurs was exported to

FIG. 4. The Middle Gate viewed from the west
Author

South Wales in the later 13th century, perhaps through the medium of royal masons working at Hereford cathedral. Given how unusual this detail is, the likelihood must be that the mason involved at Alnwick had experience of English castle building in south Wales. One possible explanation for his presence in Northumberland is that he was amongst the masons drafted by Edward I to serve in Scotland. Certainly, the only northern precedent for the form appears in miniature on the towers of the gatehouse erected by Edward I at Knaresborough castle in Yorkshire from 1304.[17]

Before leaving the subject of spur bases, it is worth pointing out that this detail became a leitmotif of the Alnwick castle works. While no other northern castle ever incorporated the form, the later 14th-century gate towers both employ it. So, too, does the Bondgate or Hotspur Gate to the town completed in 1450.[18] This long-term survival of the detail as an element of a distinctive and local architectural vocabulary is precisely paralleled in South Wales, where the spur continued to appear in castles such as Newport and Llawhaden into the mid-15th century.

The political background to Henry Percy's redevelopment of the castle from 1309 was tumultuous. As Edward II's favouritism distracted attention from the northern border and dragged the kingdom into civil war, Robert Bruce began to consolidate his own claim to the Scottish throne. Only when English interests in Scotland came to the point of complete collapse in 1314 did Edward II finally march north at the head of an army. The result was the humiliating English catastrophe of Bannockburn, fought near Stirling on 24 June 1314. Edward II narrowly escaped capture and the theatre of the Anglo-Scottish conflict moved decisively south of the border. There is no evidence that Lord Percy was involved in the Bannockburn campaign. Possibly he was unwell, for he died in October the same year. His young heir, also called Henry, was a minor at his father's death and only inherited the barony 1318 (very unusually, he received control of his inheritance before he was properly of age, a mark of the desperate political situation at the time).[19] The likelihood is, therefore, that the castle works at Alnwick stopped for at least four years.

Throughout the 1320s those on the border were compelled to look to their own defence in the face of Scottish raiding and extortion. Significantly, however, the king did subsidise their efforts with cash payments. These payments, combined with freedom from royal intervention, gave the principal barons of the border the means to build. Further encouragement came, moreover, with the revival of English fortunes in the on-going war from 1330. Having established his political independence after the death of his father, Edward III focussed his energies on Scotland and began to support a rival to the Scottish throne, Edward Balliol.

Henry Percy, 2nd Lord Percy, was foremost amongst the active followers of Balliol, through whom he aimed to revive his claims to a grand Scottish inheritance. And in 1333, following the Scottish defeat of Halidon Hill, he briefly realized his territorial ambitions. It was probably against the background of these events that work to the architectural redevelopment of Alnwick initiated by his father revived. The buildings begun in this period seem relatively consistent in such details as the use of ribbed barrel vaults, simplified window tracery patterns, shouldered doorway shapes and cross-loop forms, though slight modulations in design may suggest a rolling programme of construction. All these details appear to be in contrast to those used in the works attributed here to his father.

One major component of the new operation was the reconstruction of the outer circuit of the castle walls. A series of towers on rectangular and circular plans were erected along the line of the wall (Fig. 5). At the same time the wall was restored and strengthened with new battlements and a number of rectangular turrets. Where the 14th-century battlements survive there remain sockets for fitting swinging shutters between each merlon. This arrangement gave the defenders on the parapets additional protection in the event of an attack.

The combination of rectangular and circular tower forms used on the curtain walls at Alnwick is very unusual. Over the course of the 13th century the polygonal and rectangular towers popular in Romanesque castle architecture in England fell from fashion. In their place circular or semicircular forms became universally popular. From the early 14th century, however, towers on a rectangular plan began to appear again, as for example in the 1320s at Dunstanburgh (Northumberland) and the royal castle at Pickering (Yorkshire). And it was the rectangular tower that was to become the staple of early Perpendicular design at buildings such as Edward III's Windsor (which are, in fact, remodelled 12th-century structures). The combination of forms at

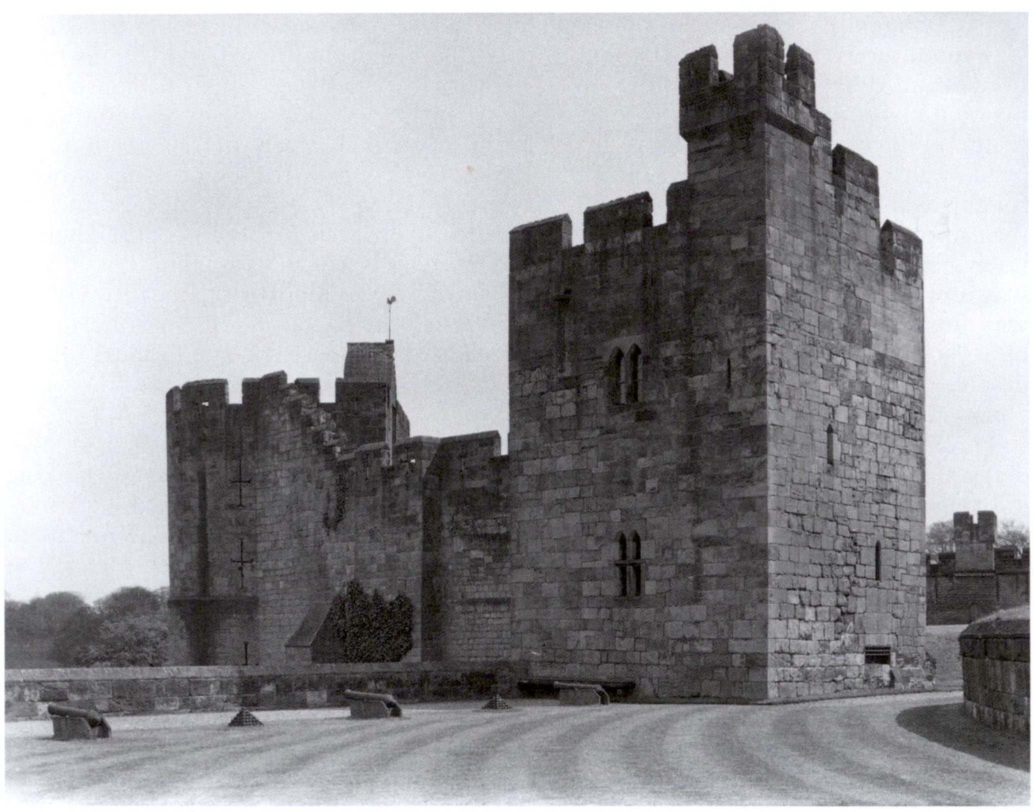

FIG. 5. The Postern Tower (right) and Constable Tower (left) are respectively designed on square and circular plan. They incorporate windows with simplified tracery
Country Life Picture Library

Alnwick, therefore, implies a sophisticated understanding of architectural fashions on the part of the designer.[20]

No less remarkable was the treatment of the new west facade to the castle. This was symmetrically planned around a central twin-towered gatehouse with an integral barbican (Fig. 6). Barbican gatehouses of this kind can be found in England from the 1220s onwards, as at the east gate of Lincoln, but the form enjoyed particular popularity in the middle decades of the 14th century, when they were created at castles including Warwick (*c.* 1340) and Arundel in Sussex (*c.* 1380). Excavations of the Alnwick gatehouse in 1902 revealed evidence for the original drawbridge arrangements within it.[21] The fine panel carved with a Percy lion above the barbican gate can be dated by its heraldry and emblems as an addition of the 4th earl of Northumberland between his restoration to the title in 1471 and 1489. It was perhaps in the same period that the wall to the south of the gatehouse was given a new parapet with false gun barrels projecting from its string-course (Fig. 7). Curiously, a painting by Peter Hartover (fl. 1674–90) in the duke of Northumberland's collection also shows similar decorative gun barrels on other buildings in the castle, including the inner bailey towers and the lost south gate.[22]

FIG. 6. The west gatehouse and barbican
Country Life Picture Library

The west gatehouse and barbican forms the centrepiece of a regular facade composition with pairs of turrets and angle towers. This particular treatment is a commonplace of English castle design from the mid-15th century onwards, as at Herstmonceux (Sussex). Its origins, however, also stretch back to the late 13th century in buildings such as Caernarfon castle.[23] This facade composition at Alnwick may suggest a connection of the designer with royal building works, as would another feature of the gatehouse design: in the battlements is a sculpted garrison of fighting men brandishing cross-bows and swords or hurling stones.

These battlement figures today appear throughout the castle, their ranks having been greatly augmented for dramatic effect in the 18th century and then thinned out in the 19th century. Some originals do survive and the figures appear in some antiquarian views, including that by Peter Hartover. This view, however, does not seem entirely reliable as an indicator of their medieval disposition: it omits them, for example, on the western gate, where they certainly existed in the middle ages.

The first English examples of inhabited battlements of this kind appear in the 1270s at St Thomas' Tower at the Tower of London and the chapter-house of York Minster. In the early 14th century they appeared in several castle buildings connected with

FIG. 7. A section of the parapet of the western castle wall. Its cornice is studded with gun barrels
Author

royal or London masons, including the Eagle Tower at Caernarfon, the Martin Tower at Chepstow and the great tower of Knaresborough. So the inhabited battlements are yet another piece of evidence that the mason at Alnwick had experience of London or royal building operations.[24]

Henry, 2nd Lord Percy also erected the gatehouse to the inner bailey or Keep. This is identical in form to the outer gatehouse, though constructed without an integral barbican (Fig. 8). As already described, the inner gate cannibalized the main Romanesque gate to the castle and effectively turned it around by the addition of two polygonal towers to what had previously been the rear facade. This gate offers the only evidence for dating Henry Percy's work at Alnwick: carved below the parapets is an array of thirteen shields. The complete sequence was recorded in the 17th century by William Dugdale, though the loss of tinctures even by that date renders four of the identifications uncertain.[25] The remaining eight, however, offer a close dating for the tower.

In the centre are the ancient arms of England and France quarterly, which were assumed by Edward III in 1342. This demonstrates that the sequence was created after that date. There also appear the arms of de Warenne. Because this line was extinguished with the death of John de Warenne, earl of Surrey, in 1347 it seems very likely that the sequence also predates that year. In other words, the heraldry, and therefore the gate, was realized between 1342 and 1347. There does appear to be a

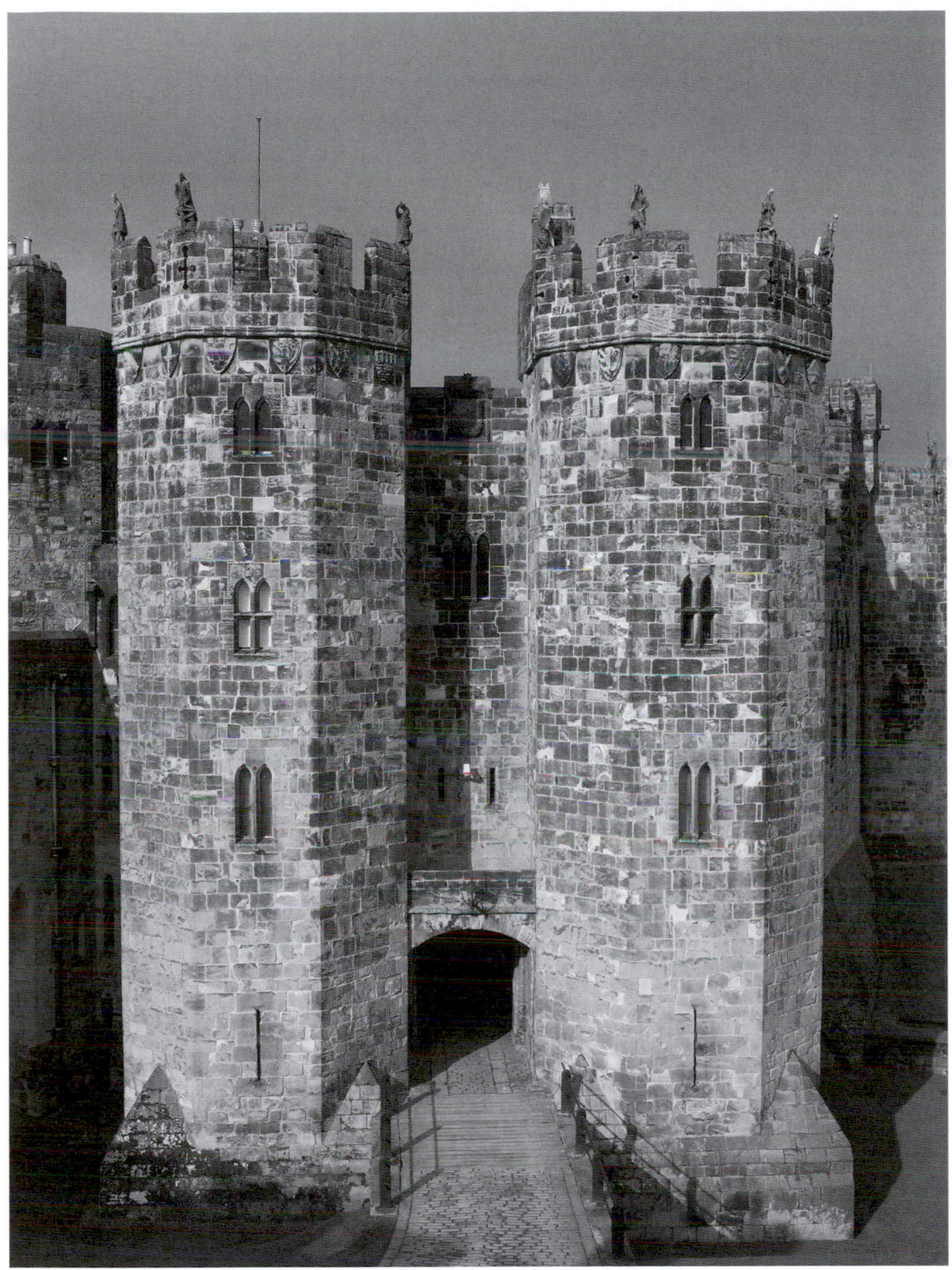

FIG. 8. The exterior facade of the inner bailey gatehouse, erected in the 1340s
Paul Barker / Country Life Picture Library

further logic behind the sequence of shields shown here and, though it cannot be conclusively proved, this is worth exploring briefly.

Assuming this time bracket is correct, the remaining securely identifiable arms refer to Robert, Lord Clifford (d. 1344), William Bohun, earl of Northampton (d. 1360), Henry Grosmont (d. 1361), Gilbert Umfraville (d. 1381), Ralph, Lord Neville (d. 1367), and John, Lord Fitzwalter (d. 1361). Aside from the king, five of these figures were definitely present in the Halidon Hill campaign of 1333: William Bohun, Henry Grosmont, John de Warenne, Gilbert Umfraville and Ralph Neville. Since there are no good administrative records of those fighting in this campaign, it is perfectly possible that the only two outstanding individuals — John, Lord Fitzwalter and Robert Clifford — were also present.

It is further significant that three of the figures listed above — William Bohun, Henry Grosmont and John de Warenne — were certainly not present at Neville's Cross in 1346, another battle that this display might reasonably be supposed to celebrate. Although their identification is less certain, two of the remaining arms charged with a lion rampant might reasonably be associated with Lord Percy himself and John Lord Mowbray, who were both also involved in 1333. The outstanding arms are a lion rampant differenced with a crown, a fess and a cross. Various identifications have been offered for these arms, but without evidence of tincture it must remain an open question as to whom they represent.

If the connection with Halidon Hill is correct, the gatehouse heraldry could be understood to celebrate in retrospect a highpoint in Henry Percy's territorial claims. Whatever the case, the dating of the Alnwick works to the 1340s is corroborated by the architectural evidence of two other nearby castles. The gatehouse of Bothal castle is thought to have been erected by Sir Robert Bertram under a licence issued in 1343.[26] Not only is it designed in identical fashion to its counterpart at Alnwick with two polygonal towers (without spurs), but it displays its own collection of heraldry and preserves the remains of battlement figures.[27] This building was presumably designed by the Alnwick master mason, or by someone intimately familiar with the Alnwick works.

Meanwhile, Prudhoe castle preserves a circuit of towers that are a very close match for those at Alnwick. They are similarly constructed on both rectangular and circular plans and incorporate an identical vocabulary of arrow loops and vaulting forms (Fig. 9). Likewise, the main gatehouse, a 12th-century structure, was also reordered with an integral barbican in the same period.[28] Prudhoe was probably remodelled by Gilbert Umfraville, 9th earl of Angus, during the 1340s.[29] At that time he acted in close alliance with Henry, 2nd Lord Percy. Again, therefore, the likelihood is that there was some very direct connection between the building operations at Prudhoe and Alnwick.

Of the 14th-century internal arrangements of the outer baileys of Alnwick castle, little can now be said with certainty. The 1567 survey and Treswell's drawings record the late 16th-century arrangement of buildings within them in detail.[30] Only one, however, is unambiguously medieval: the chapel that formerly stood in the east bailey. It was four bays long and without aisles. The relatively steep pitch of its roof might argue for a date in the 14th century or earlier.

By the time of his death in 1352, Henry, 2nd Lord Percy must have largely completed his transformation of Alnwick. It is very significant that he chose burial, not in his native Yorkshire, but at Alnwick priory.[31] For the future, his family became

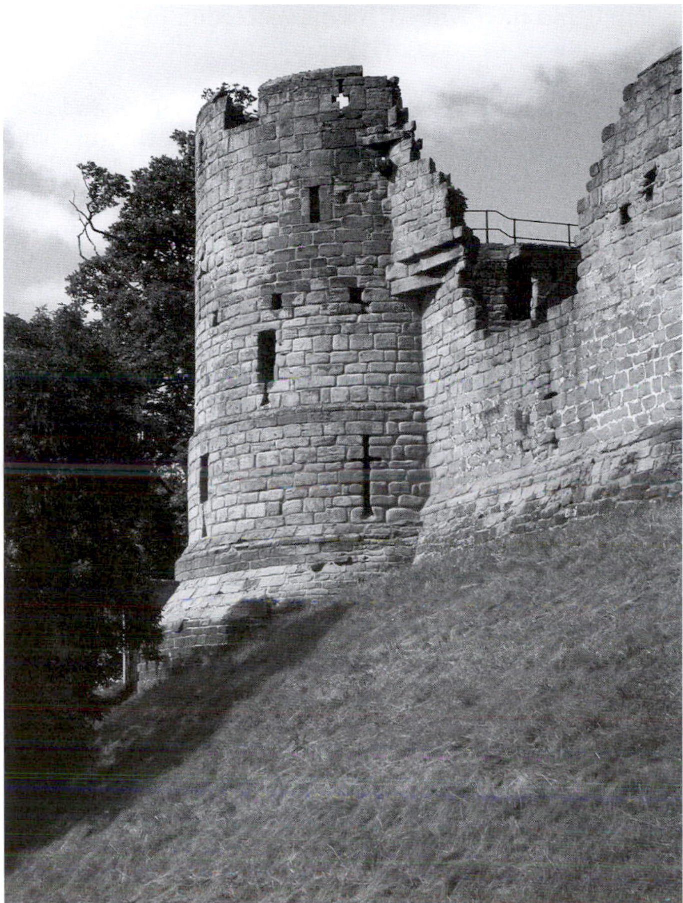

FIG. 9. The western tower of Prudhoe castle. One of several towers in the castle with architectural details resembling those found in the 1340s works at Alnwick
Author

established as one in a small and exclusive circle who conducted the affairs of the March. The pre-eminence of Alnwick as the Percy family seat, however, did not last long. Henry's grandson, yet another Henry, was elevated to the earldom of Northumberland — a title defunct since the 12th century — on the accession of Richard II in 1377. Rather than develop Alnwick, the new earl remodelled the nearby castle of Warkworth with a great tower, one of the masterpieces of secular medieval architecture in England. For the remainder of the middle ages this castle, now a ruin, was arguably the favoured residence of the family.[32]

Though Alnwick continued to be maintained and augmented, it was not substantially altered for another four centuries. Today, its medieval fabric must be viewed through the prism of two hugely important remodelling programmes that are of independent interest but outside the scope of this present analysis. The first of these followed the inheritance of the Northumberland estates by Sir Hugh Smithson through his wife in 1750. He assumed the name Percy that year and, following his first visit to the castle, determined to remodel it as his seat. This operation, which came to incorporate major changes to the landscape, was probably initiated by Henry Keene and was underway by 1752. James Paine and then Robert Adam succeeded to the project, which reputedly absorbed the vast sum of £10,000 by 1768, nearly a decade before it was completed.[33]

The 18th-century interiors of the castle are largely known from drawings and documentary evidence, though some sense of their elegance is conveyed by the surviving interior of the residential tower at Hulne priory, a hunting lodge in the Little Park. Nearly all trace of them was otherwise swept away a century later by the 4th duke, who succeeded to the title in 1847. He thought the castle inconvenient for modern living and in 1849 commissioned Anthony Salvin to restore what might be described as the baronial character of the building. Salvin was already experienced in medieval castle restoration and drew up designs in a convincing antiquarian idiom.

Meanwhile, the duke travelled to Italy where he met the archaeologist and classicist Luigi Canina. Along with an assistant, Giovanni Montiroli, Canina produced drawings for the interior apartments in the style of a 16th-century Roman palace. It was in accordance with these two contrasting idioms of architecture — a medieval baronial exterior by Salvin and a Roman Renaissance interior by Canina and Montiroli — that the castle familiar to the modern visitor was created between 1854 and 1865.[34]

NOTES

1. For a full listing of the standard bibliography on the castle, see D. J. C. King, *Castellarium Anglicanum: An Index and Bibliography of the Castles in England, Wales and the Islands*, II (New York 1983), 325; and J. R. Kenyon, *Castle, Town Defences and Artillery Fortifications in the United Kingdom and Ireland. A Bibliography 1945–2006* (Donington 2008), 245. The most important antiquarian study is G. Tate, *The History of the Borough, Castle, and Barony of Alnwick*, 2 vols (Alnwick 1866–69).

2. P. Dalton, 'Eustace Fitz John and the Politics of Anglo-Norman England: The Rise and Survival of a Twelfth-Century Royal Servant', *Speculum*, 71 (1996), 358–83.

3. '*Eustachius quoque filius Johannis, unus de baronibus Regis Angliae, quoddam munitissimum castellum, quod Alnewic dicitur, in Northumbria habens* . . .'. Richard of Hexham, *De Gestis Regis Stephani et de Bello Standardii*, in *Chronicles of the Reigns of Stephen, Henry II and Richard I*, ed. R. Howlett, 4 vols, Rolls series 82 (London 1884–90), III, 158.

4. M. R. G. Conzen, 'Alnwick, Northumberland: A Study in Town-Plan Analysis', *Transactions and Papers of the Institute of British Geographers*, 27 (1960), 21–23.

5. Ibid., 20–27.

6. J. Goodall, *The English Castle* (London and New Haven 2011), 106.

7. C. Coulson, *Castles in Medieval Society. Fortresses in England, France and Ireland in the Central Middle Ages* (Oxford 2003), 159.

8. J. M. W. Bean, 'The Percys' Acquisition of Alnwick', *AA*, 4th ser. 32 (1954), 309–19.

9. The original charter is still in the muniments at Alnwick castle.

10. J. M. W. Bean, 'Percy, Henry, first Lord Percy (1273–1314)', *ODNB*, 60 vols (Oxford University Press 2004), XLIII, 690–91 (at 691).

11. H. Summerson, 'Clifford, Robert, first Lord Clifford (1274–1314)', *ODNB*, XII, 107–09 (at 108).

12. P. Brears, *Cooking and Dining in Medieval England* (Totnes 2007), 74–75.

13. W. A. Hutchinson, *A View of Northumberland*, 2 vols (Newcastle upon Tyne 1778), I, 197–203.

14. The engravings in C. H. Hartshorne, *Illustrations of Alnwick, Prudhoe and Warkworth* (London 1857), and the photographs of the plans in G. R. Batho, 'The State of Alnwick Castle, 1557–1632', *AA*, 4th ser. 36 (1948), 129–46, pls XIII–XVII.

15. Batho, 'The State' (as n. 14), 144.

16. Goodall, *English Castle* (as n. 6), 173–78.

17. R. A. Brown, H. M. Colvin and A. J. Taylor, *The History of the King's Works: The Middle Ages*, 2 vols + plans (London 1963), II, 688–89.

18. J. H. Harvey, *English Medieval Architects: A Biographical Dictionary down to 1550*, rev. edn (Gloucester 1984), 201.
19. Coulson, *Castles in Medieval Society* (as n. 7), 312–13.
20. Goodall, *English Castle* (as n. 6), 154 and 246–47.
21. W. H. Knowles, 'The Gatehouse and Barbican at Alnwick Castle with an Account of the Recent Discoveries', *AA*, 3rd ser. 5 (1909), 286–303.
22. Reproduced in C. Shrimpton, *Alnwick Castle* (Derby 1999), 45.
23. Goodall, *English Castle* (as n. 6), 362–63.
24. Ibid., 205–06.
25. W. Dugdale, *Northumbrian Monuments: or the Shields of Arms, Effigies and Inscriptions in the Churches, Castles and Halls of Northumberland*, Newcastle upon Tyne Record Committee Publications 4 (Newcastle upon Tyne 1924), 11–14.
26. *Calendar of Patent Rolls, Edward III vol. 6 (1343–1345)* (London 1902), 30.
27. C. J. Bates, *The Border Holds of Northumberland* (Newcastle 1891), 283–96.
28. S. West, *Prudhoe Castle* (London 2006), 8–11.
29. F. Watson, 'Umfraville, Gilbert de, Seventh Earl of Angus (1244? –1307)', *ODNB*, LV, 880–82 (at 881–82).
30. Batho, 'The State' (as n. 14), *passim*.
31. '*Cronica monasterii de Alnewyke*', ed. W. Dickson, *AA*, 1st ser. 3 (1844), 40 (where the old style year of 1351 is given).
32. For a recent account of this building, see J. Goodall, *Warkworth Castle and Hermitage* (London 2006).
33. G. Worsely, 'Alnwick Castle, Northumberland II', *Country Life*, 182 (issue 48), 8 December 1989, 74–78.
34. G. Worsely, 'Alnwick Castle, Northumberland I', *Country Life*, 182 (issue 47), 1 December 1989, 174–78. A description of the castle soon after its transformation by Salvin appears in G. T. Clark, *Medieval Military Architecture in England* (London 1884), 175–84.

Border Towers: A Cartographic Approach

PHILIP DIXON

The towers of the Anglo-Scottish border have been a familiar topic since the days of Sir Walter Scott, and the society which created them has been the subject of essays, books and plays. And yet remarkably little analysis has been done about the changing patterns of building, variations in building types, social structure of the uplands, and the fluctuating fortunes of the wars in this troubled region. This paper seeks to outline these issues by considering the implications of a series of maps, which analyse data on these topics, and present the background for understanding the growth and decline of the Border Towers.

THE area which is the subject of the present paper lies on both sides of the Anglo-Scottish border, an area of uplands about 60 miles broad, extending from the Lammermuirs and the head of Eskdale in Scotland to the Weardale uplands and the Lake District in England. Apart from the Solway plain and the lowlands to the north of Newcastle, it is a landscape of high moors cut by river valleys, a topography which has tended to isolation in the communities on both sides of the border.

At the beginning of the Norman period the border line itself was of relatively recent formation, being the result of the contraction southwards of the Anglo-Saxon kingdom from Lothian, probably after the battle of Carham on the Tweed, in 1016 or 1018.[1] From then onwards the line was reasonably stable with only minor adjustments, sorted out by agreement in 1247 and after. This stability did not, however, mean peace, and the history of the region for nearly five hundred years is interspersed with wars and destruction. In this paper I shall attempt to discuss the development of crown and private fortification in the Borders by displaying a series of maps, together with some explanatory diagrams.

The area in question is shown in Figure 1: it forms a triangle between the towns of Berwick, Newcastle and Carlisle, and their hinterlands. In the upland central area of the region the various dales are indicated. In the following maps, evidence for the sequence of fortification is plotted in chronological sequence to show the changing patterns of border history and society. Figure 2 shows the distribution of fortifications in the two centuries before the beginning of Edward I's wars with Scotland in 1296. It shows that at this early period the frequency of castle building was not great, in comparison, for example, with the much greater density around Oxford, Northampton or in East Anglia. Major castles are to be found only at Bamburgh, Newcastle, Carlisle, Berwick and Roxburgh, with other significant fortifications at Norham or Mitford: considering the size of the area, this is not a great number. What is worth pointing out is the considerable number of mottes. At least forty-five have been recorded in the area. Some few form the core of major castles, converted to stone in the course of the 12th and 13th centuries, such as Warkworth or Alnwick, but the majority have remained earthworks, and it is likely that many lasted only a few years,

BAA Trans., vol. XXXVI (2013), 248–265

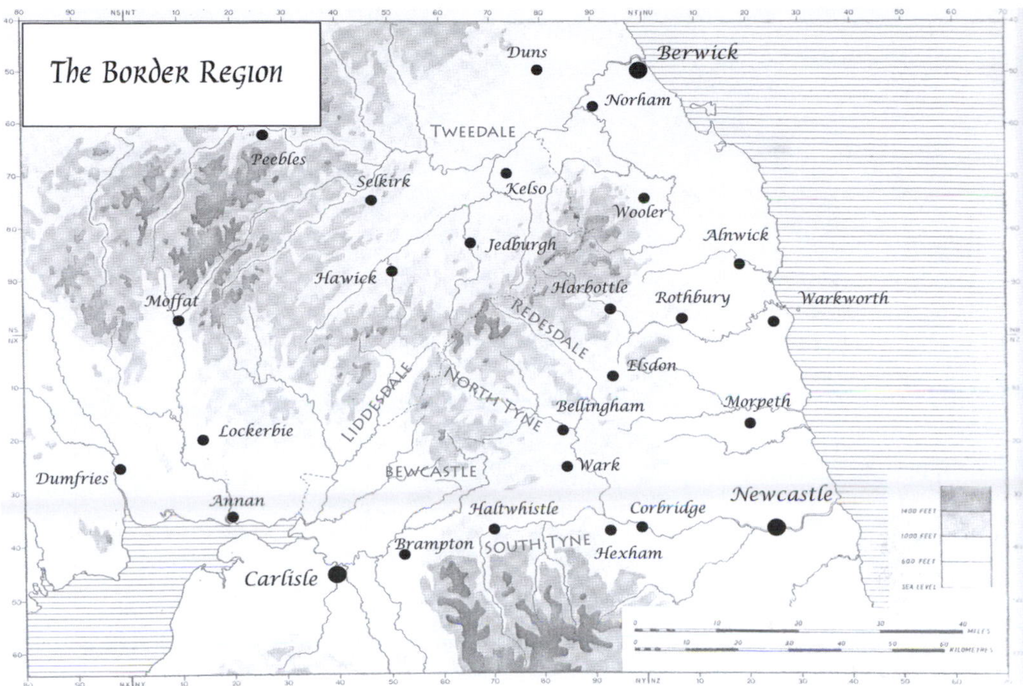

FIG. 1. The Border region, showing towns and the principal upland valleys

for example the motte of Wooler castle, described as early as 1255 as 'mota vasta'.[2] Within England, the greatest density of these mottes is along the Tyne-Solway gap, where many of the sites of these earthworks were numbered among the dependent vills of the new settlement of Carlisle, founded by Rufus in the 1090s, and presumably form part of the colonizing of the area. A similar origin underlies the cluster of mottes in the valleys of the Esk and the Nith in the west marches: these are the result of the early 12th-century expansion of the new lords into Scotland in the years around 1100, and their imitation by the surviving native lords in the area.[3] The map, therefore, indicates the novelties introduced by a comparatively short period of change from the 1080s to the second quarter of the 12th century. It demonstrates, furthermore, the subsequent development of the housing in the area, the creation of unfortified, or only lightly protected ground- and first-floor stone halls, which have been usually called 'hall houses'.[4]

The earliest surviving examples of these buildings belong to the 13th century, with ground-floor halls at Drumburgh near Carlisle probably of *c.* 1220 or 1230 and Featherstone on the South Tyne of about 1260, and a similar date for the first-floor hall at Haughton in the North Tyne. Some of these buildings are virtually complete, such as Aydon Hall or Morton in Nithsdale, and others are reduced to their ground floor, such as the hall houses at Dally or Tarset in North Tynedale. After thirty years of fieldwork about twenty of these buildings are now known, and they demonstrate the results of a period of relative tranquillity in the Border region after the invasions

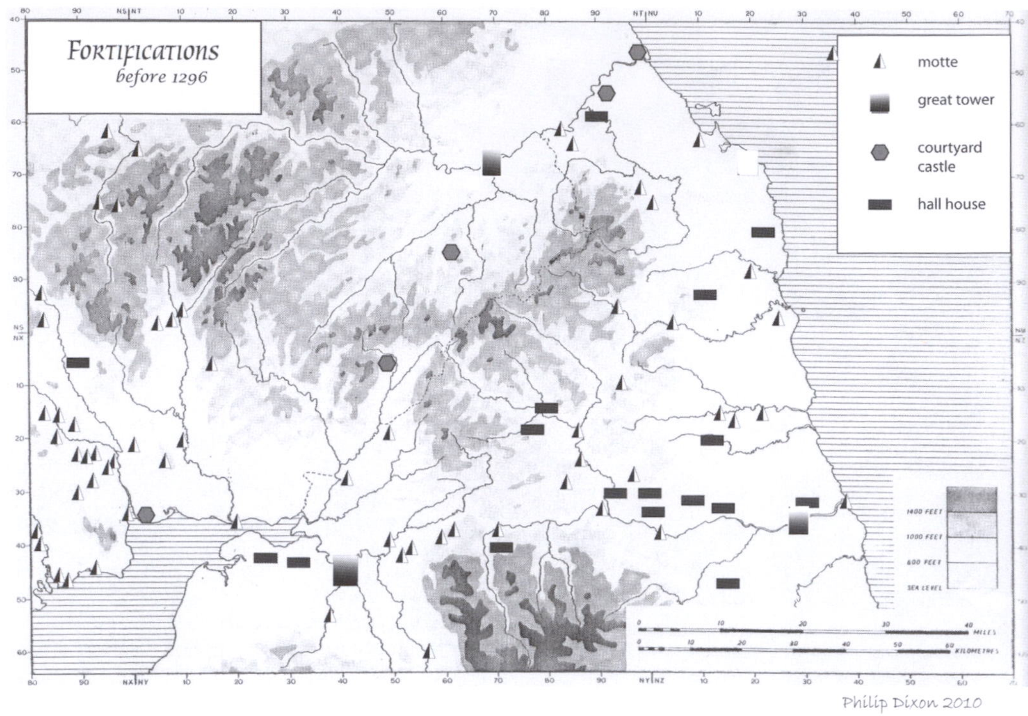

FIG. 2. Castles, towers, and halls before the outbreak of the Wars of Independence

of 1174, until the Scottish wars began under Edward I.[5] Periods of strife, such as the threatened invasion of 1246–47, were short and had little lasting influence on the building of the area.[6] The majority of these houses were certainly of manorial status, and their builders were the owners who in subsequent generations built towers.[7]

The changing situation after Edward's intervention in Scotland is shown in Figure 3 (and Col. Pl. XXVIII in print edn), which does not show these hall houses unless they were now rebuilt as fortified buildings, such as Haughton or Edlingham in Northumberland. Apart from these rebuilt examples, no more than twenty of the earlier castles seem by now to have been in use, reinforcing the point about the peaceful intermission in the region between the initial colonizing and the increase of warfare in the 14th century. A few of the largest of these new castles were built in the first half of the 14th century, the earliest perhaps being Dunstanburgh, from 1313 onwards, but this major work was only marginally linked to the developing crises on the Border.[8] Others were built, as their licenses indicate, during the period of relative peace after the treaty of Northampton of 1328 and the English victory at Halidon Hill in 1333.[9] These include the substantial castles at Ford (1338) and Etal (1341).

After 1346 almost no licenses to crenellate have been found for the English borders,[10] and dating the buildings becomes problematic, as few have chronologically distinctive architectural features. This is particularly true of the major class of buildings in this period, the towers, of which over seventy are shown on Figure 3. The key point here is 1415, the date of a survey of Northumbrian fortifications prepared for

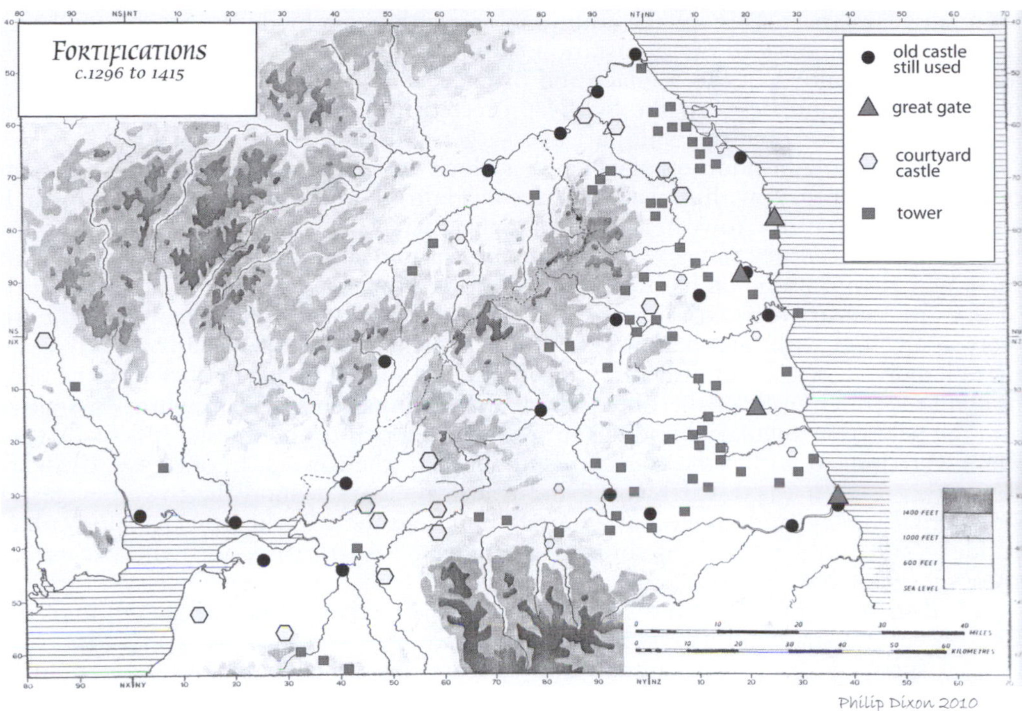

FIG. 3. Fortifications in the region in the first stage of the Wars of Independence

Henry V before the Agincourt campaign, and the resultant list provides a terminus for the eastern part of our region.[11] Many towers and castles are referred to in charters and similar documents, but none so far of the unlicensed buildings occurs in a documentary source before 1365 (Langley castle). It is thus possible that most of the towers shown on the map belong to the period from *c.* 1346 to 1415.

The date of the earliest surviving towers is even more problematic. Unconvincingly, Cruden claimed dates in the 13th century for several Scottish towers,[12] and dates such as '*c.* 1300' for the small priest's tower at Corbridge are mistaken.[13] The earliest certain date is 1305 for Shortflatt tower.[14] This is a particularly interesting building since it was clearly built against a first-floor hall, and provided a suite of chambers in a solar tower: this is described in an inquisition in 1450, when the manor contained a hall, three chambers (in the tower), three cellars (one in the tower and two under the hall), one kitchen and various other houses for husbandry (presumed to be detached buildings).[15] Shortflatt, in brief, represents a solar tower and adjacent hall, very similar to Aydon Hall nearby, which was built originally as a unfortified stone solar of two-and-a-half storeys attached to an earlier timber hall, which was soon afterwards replaced by the present first-floor stone hall and was then enclosed by curtain walls and battlements after 1305. The first unfortified phase of Aydon belongs to a period after 1280, perhaps as late as 1296, and it was fortified in 1305 in the same licence to crenellate as Shortflatt, since both were built by the same owner little more than ten years apart. Perhaps the additional strength given by de Reymes to the latter tower was a response to the devastation of the area by the Scots in 1297 and 1298,[16] and if so the context of the Wallace and Bruce invasions reveals the transition taking place in the region between the lightly protected hall houses and the much greater security of a tower, but one still part of a larger complex.

Fortification by the addition of a chamber block with thick walls continued throughout the 14th century, with dated examples at Halton (13th-century ground-floor hall and late 14th-century tower), Welton and Featherstone (13th-century ground-floor halls and 15th-century towers).[17] It remains uncertain how much even the largest of these new towers stood on its own. Examination of the two largest and best preserved of the 14th-century towers, Chipchase (*c.* 1350) and Belsay (*c.* 1380) suggests that both were associated with, and perhaps were even attached to adjacent halls. In any case, these massive towers contain halls, chapel, kitchen and chambers sufficient to accommodate the inner circle of their households, but lack bakehouses, brewhouses, stables and the necessary ancillary buildings for the wider servants and guests. It is likely that these were lodged within the courtyards attached to the towers. In one case, Crawley tower (licensed in 1343), earthworks and wall fragments around the tower suggest a substantial bailey and ranges of internal buildings beside the tower, appropriate enough for a builder who was son of the builder of Ford castle, and who became in 1361 sheriff of Northumberland.[18]

The distribution of these new fortifications is distinctive: almost all lie in the fertile English coastal strip and its hinterland, almost entirely avoiding the river valleys and central spine of the border. Equally, there are almost no examples of these 14th-century buildings in Scotland. In part, this may reflect the shortage of documents on the Scottish side of the Border, but none of the surviving buildings north of the Border displays architectural detail which proves its building before the 15th century. One may therefore conclude that the period after the middle of the 14th century saw considerable investment in building by many of the English landowners, but that few in Scotland followed suit.[19]

In contrast to the pattern of the initial fortification of the area, almost all the new castles and towers remained in use into the next century and beyond. Figure 4 shows the building during this period. Here the old towers and castles, mostly of the 14th century, are indicated by black dots, and the comparatively few (probably no more than thirty-four) new 15th-century buildings are shown by squares and, in one case, a hexagon. The distribution replicates that of the old pattern, simply making the pattern of English building denser, and only half a dozen new towers in Scotland, though these include the massive tower houses of Cessford and Comlongon, which were comparable in scale to the largest of the English towers, and were built by barons of national importance.[20]

At the end of this period, changes can be seen in the distribution across the region. Figure 5 shows the pattern of tower building during the century and a half between *c.* 1485 and 1625. Two results are clear: in the first place this map now distinguishes between towers of which some parts now remain, and towers known only from documentary sources. This is due to the greatly increased numbers of surviving documents during this period, but at least the 1415 survey allows direct comparison with the 14th-century situation in Northumberland. It is however possible that at least a few of the Scottish towers known only from archival sources belong in fact to the 15th century. In the second place the map shows that the building of towers in Northumberland and Cumberland on the whole did no more than thicken up the

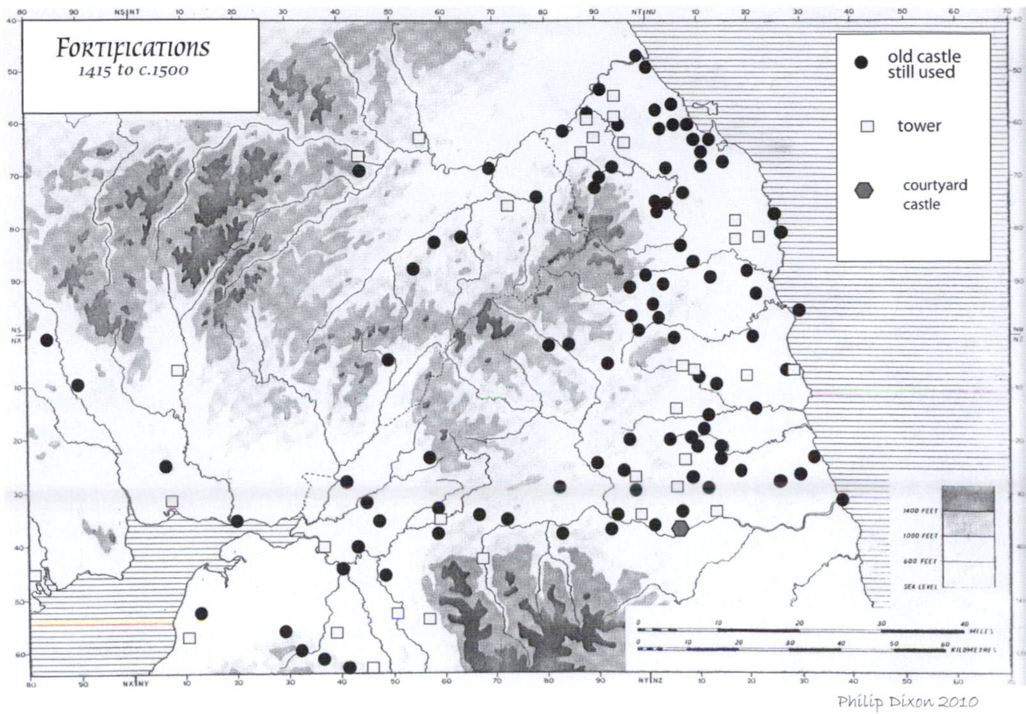

FIG. 4. Fortifications added during the 15th century

distribution already seen in those areas, with the addition of a number of buildings in the North Tyne and the edge of Cheviot, areas previously not represented. In Scotland, however, the pattern is completely changed, with nearly a hundred new towers in the immediate vicinity of the Border, and another hundred further inland in Dumfriesshire and Selkirk. The construction along the western Border dales of Liddesdale and Eskdale is particularly striking, and equalled in numbers the total built in England during this period.

The dates for this construction can be refined. Almost all the documentary sources relate to building during the second half of the 16th century, and the date-stones and architectural detail of the surviving towers fall into a similar pattern. This is not decisive, since documents increase exponentially during the second half of the century, and the increasing use of Renaissance details and the habit of including armorials and date-stones on the buildings make it easier to date buildings after 1560.[21] We know of a few structures which belong to the early 16th century, such as the rebuilding of the 13th-century hall at Drumburgh into a sort of defended barracks block, by Thomas, 1st Lord Dacre, but the number is small, and it seems likely that this burst of building fell into the period after the middle of the 16th century. This coincides perhaps by chance with a 'long pause' in the building of towers elsewhere in Scotland, identified by Cruden as a period from *c.* 1480 to *c.* 1560.[22] For the dating of some Liddesdale and Eskdale towers we have the contemporary evidence of Lord Herries, who stated in 1578 that in the previous thirty years the Grahams had built eight or nine towers

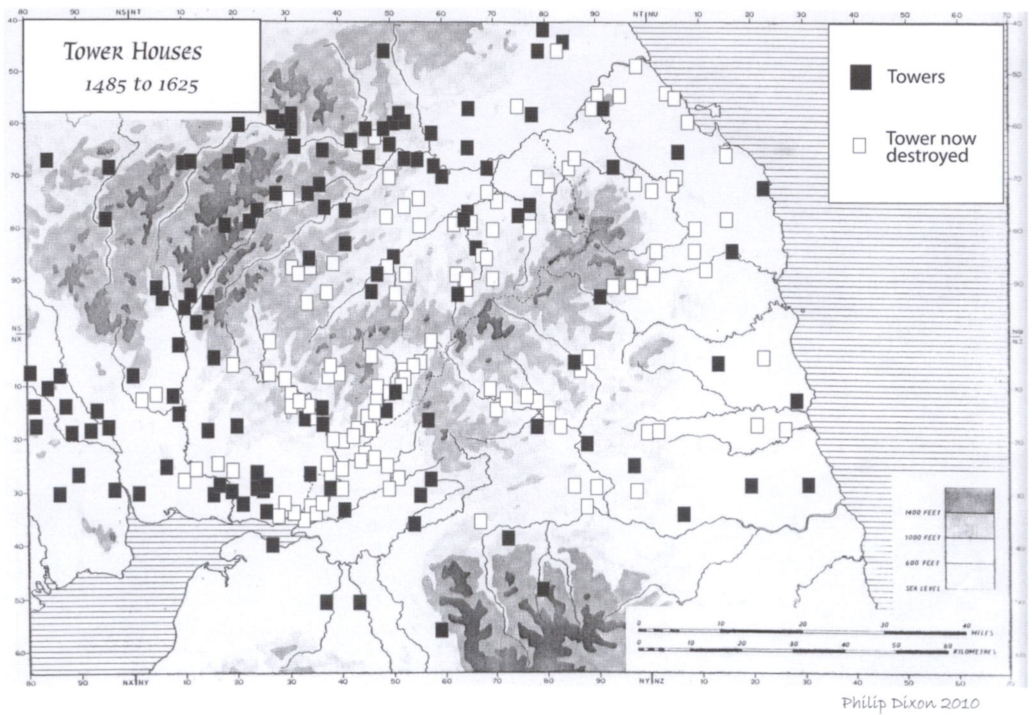

FIG. 5. Towers built during the final stage of the Wars

from the profits of theft amounting to a hundred thousand marks.[23] He linked this with the collapse of authority after the death of James V in the wake of the battle of Solway Moss.

This paper reviews the development of towers, but it would be incomplete without consideration of two types of fortified houses on the Border smaller than the tower. These are shown in Figures 6 and 7, which plot the distribution of pelehouses and bastles. There is confusion about the terminology, thanks to the erroneous definitions provided by the Royal Commission's publication, Shielings and Bastles, which limited the term 'bastle' to the smallest fortified farmhouses, ignoring the sub-manor houses smaller than towers and larger than the farmhouses, larger houses which were in fact actually called bastles by their contemporaries.[24] Though it is likely that by now the term has been appropriated solely for the farmhouses, in Figures 6 and 7 I have distinguished between the larger houses ('bastles') and the smaller houses ('pelehouses'). The maps make clear that this is not simply a terminological distinction: the bastles, like the towers in the earlier maps, lie in the fertile lowlands of the coastal plain and the Tweed basin, and Figure 6 includes buildings which rely only on documentary sources, but which, in fact, correspond in their distribution to the surviving bastles. It is clear that these sub-manorial houses represent the lower ranges of the tower-building classes, continuing the process of towerhouse building into the 16th century. As with the earlier maps, the area within the distribution, the Border valleys of Bewcastledale, Tyndale, Redesdale and Coquetdale, are almost empty of fortified

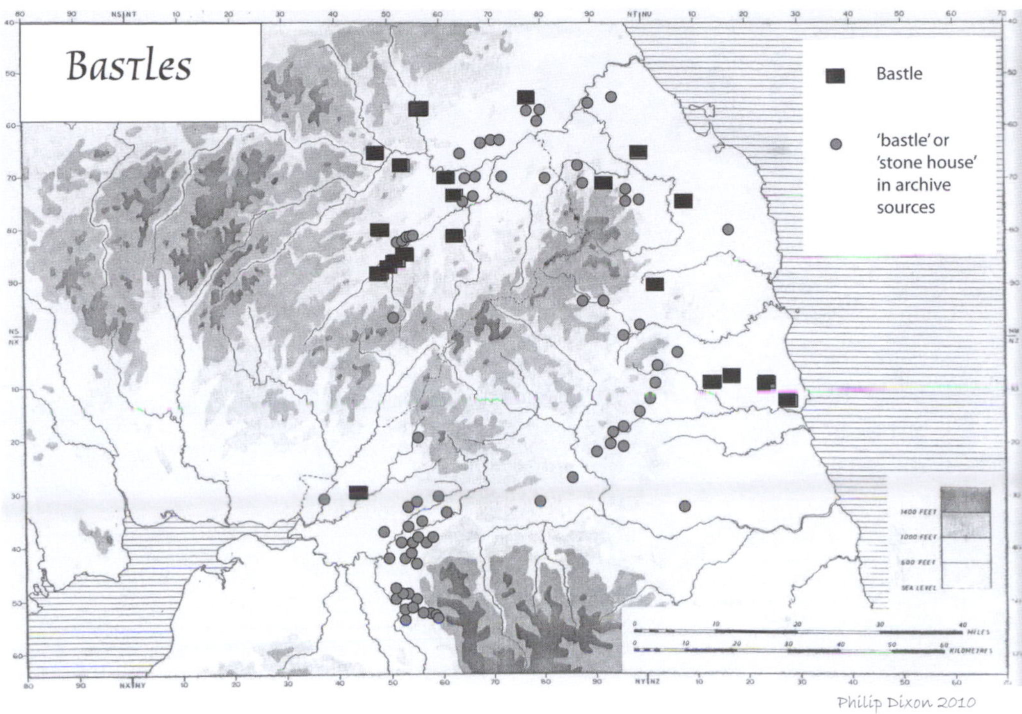

FIG. 6. Bastles belonging to the 16th and early 17th century

buildings. In part we may suspect that these regions were not entirely without fortification. In a partial survey of the region carried out in 1541 the houses of the 'heddesmen' of the North Tyne were described as strong wooden houses built of great squared oak, covered in earth and turf, and similar buildings were attacked and destroyed by axes and fire in Scotland.[25] After this period it is clear that the wooden houses of the upland valleys were replaced, rarely by towers, mostly by the building of pelehouses.[26] These are shown in Figure 7, which also includes as green dots those buildings described in documentary sources as 'stonehouse'; these sites are also included in the previous figure of bastles, and their distribution has been repeated here since the actual classification of each building is uncertain: the distribution suggests that many of them in the North of the region are more likely to belong to the class of bastles. Apart from those in the Tweed basin, however, many of the 'stonehouse' owners are similar in wealth and in the location of their houses to those in the upland dales, and it is possible that they are further examples of pelehouses in these areas.

The financial implications of this social structure is shown in Figure 8, which identifies the wealth held by builders and occupants of the various fortified buildings in the area, from £200 and above for castles, over £100 for tower builders — a similar sum for at least the most prosperous of the bastle builders — and about £40 or a little less for pelehouse owners and builders: this at a time when a milk cow might be valued at about 13s. 4d.

The reason for the burst of fortification can be seen in a diagram and some maps. Figure 9 shows the recorded incidence of raiding between *c.* 1500 and 1610. The chart

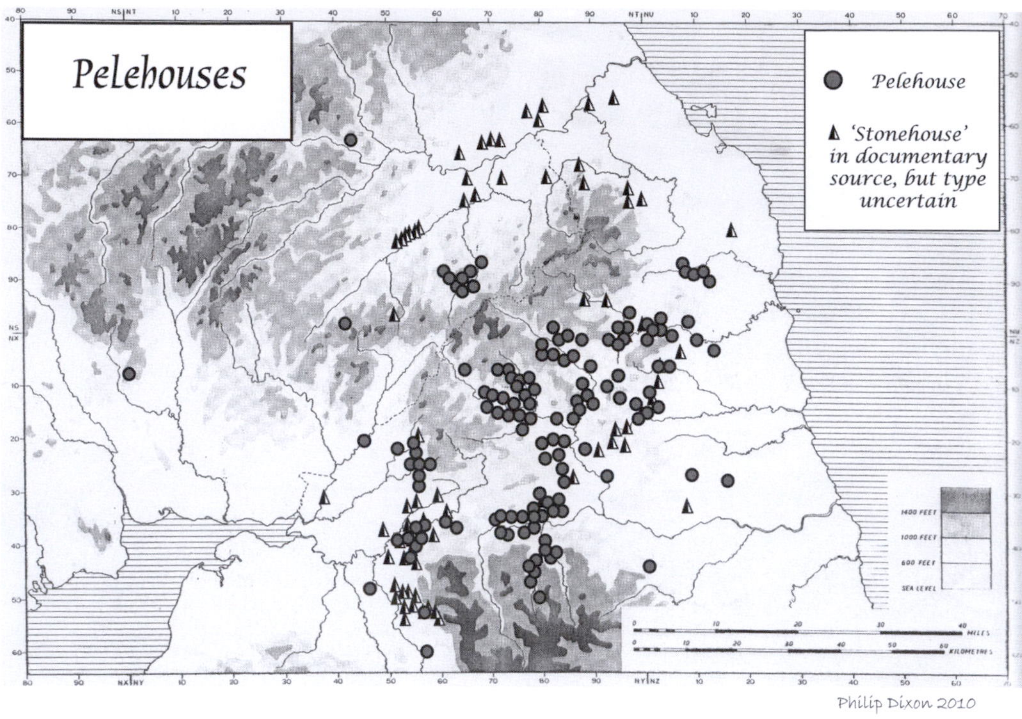

FIG. 7. Stonehouses and pelehouses of the 16th and early 17th century

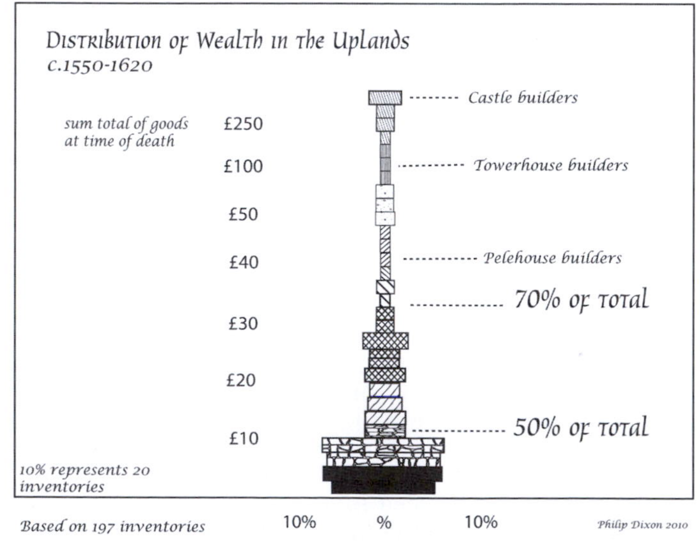

FIG. 8. The distribution of wealth in the uplands from 1550 to 1620, based on surviving inventories

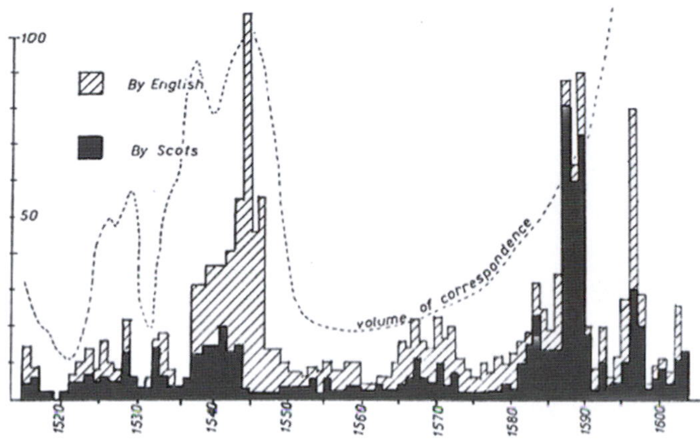

FIG. 9. The annual frequency of raiding during the 16th century

sets out the raiding year by year and distinguishes between Scottish and English raiders. It is cumulative. The Scottish totals are set out first and the contemporary English are set above them, beginning from the highest Scottish block: thus, for example, in 1512 there were fourteen recorded raids, four by Scots on England, and ten by English on Scotland, and in 1587 there were eighty-eight recorded raids, eighty-three by Scots and only five by English on Scotland. As a dotted line above these totals is set an estimate of the volume of preserved letters and reports, since clearly the numbers of recorded raids will depend to a degree on the survival of records themselves. Thus the 1540s show a great increase in English raiding, as an element in the War of the Rough Wooing, and equally a massive increase in archives, since the attention of both governments was directed to the Borders. Conversely, the unrest around the time of Mary Stuart's flight, and the rising of the Earls in the later 1560s is not matched by increased survival of the archives, and the same is true of the upsurge of raiding from Scotland coinciding with the execution of Mary. These are thus clearly genuine changes in the frequency of raiding, as is the decline in raiding after 1590 (with the exception of 1596, coinciding with the outrage of the capture of Kinmont Willie, and the anger at his subsequent rescue from Carlisle castle).[27] Overall, the pattern shows two interesting periods: in the first place the comparative tranquillity of the years after the abandonment of the English invasions of the Border, a period of about twenty-five years during which the Scottish lairds, many of whom had been assured to the English party, built great towers on the Western Marches;[28] in the second place the period after the 1590s when the previous high levels of raiding rapidly declined.

This is made clear in a series of maps. Figure 10 (and Col. Pl. XXIX in print edn) shows the raids recorded in detail during the period, and here and in subsequent raiding maps each spot on the map represents a hamlet or village raided and burnt. The map distinguishes between the places of origin of the raiders, and it is clear that the English of all three Marches were involved in raiding in the main the fertile lowlands of the Solway and the Tweed valley, with very few reprisal raids into England. Notable is the burst of raiding from Scottish Liddesdale into Scotland, the result of the temporary transfer of allegiance by the Armstrongs and others to the English party during the worst of the war. Profits from this activity presumably were the 'spulzie' which permitted the construction of towers in Liddesdale and the Debateable

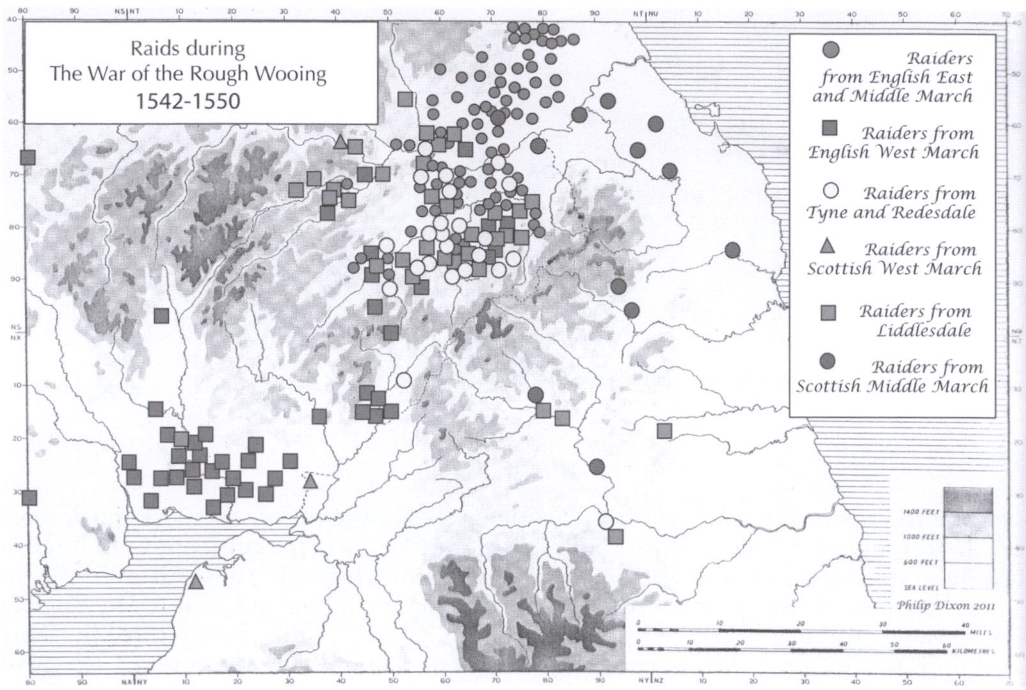

FIG. 10. The location of the recorded raids from 1542 to 1550

Land. The Armstrongs and the Grahams continued to profit, as is shown in Figure 11 (and Col. Pl. XXX in print edn), which concentrates on the period of collapse of the borders during the years after the execution of Mary Queen of Scots. Recorded English raiding was very small, less than a couple of dozen raids, mostly by the garrison of Carlisle and its adherents. Scottish raids were devastating, and involved the pillaging of Bewcastledale, the Tyne gap, and central Northumberland, including most of Redesdale. North Tynedale escaped, perhaps by some arrangement with the Armstrongs and Elliotts. A final map in this series, Figure 12 (and Col. Pl. XXXI in print edn), shows the final years of the border, with a continuation of the pattern of raiding from Liddesdale, but a general quieting elsewhere, and few raids from England into Scotland. The map demonstrates the vulnerability of Bewcastledale, and emphasizes the description at the time that the inhabitants were 'every man's prey'.[29]

The results of increasing stability towards the end of the 16th century, which these records imply, is likely, ironically, to have been a growth in the building of fortifications, since it is a general principle that it is in times of truce and peace that those who desire defensive works are able to afford to build them.[30] The period from *c.* 1550 to *c.* 1580 is likely to have been a critical period for the building of towers and probably many of the bastles, by members of the wealthier classes in Border society. Since they were profiting in the main by theft and rentals from the less wealthy farmers in the region, it is harder in these terms to explain the great outburst of pelehouse building in the English uplands, and so the changes in ownership and the consequent changes in financial liability are set out in a further series of maps. Figure 13 shows

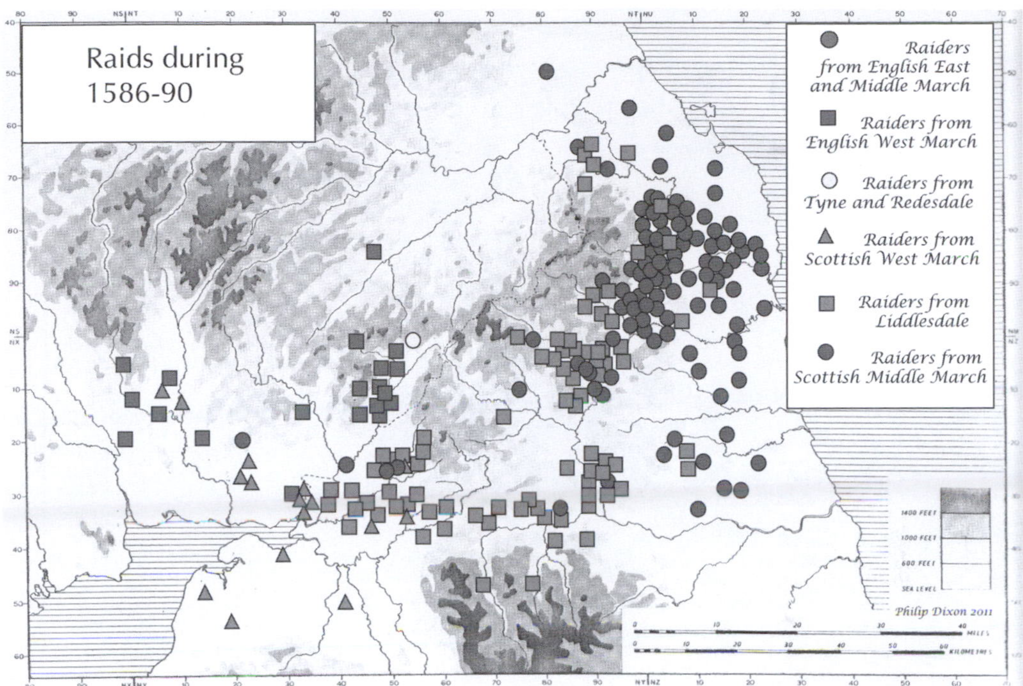

FIG. 11. The location of the recorded raids from 1586 to 1590

the distribution of crown estates on the English Borders at the beginning of the Tudor period. Only the baronies of Embleton and Liddell were ancient royal lands. The acquisition of the manor of Bewcastle and the resumption of the lordship of Tynedale (which had been alienated to absentees during almost the whole period since 1311) was due to the interest of Richard III, formerly warden and sheriff of Cumberland for life.[31] Much of the rest of the Border was in the hands of the Church, and of the great feudal lords, the Percies and the Dacres of Cumberland. Figure 14 shows the situation after the Dissolution of the monasteries, and other changes in land ownership during the middle of the 16th century. The date chosen is 1568 since by then the seized church lands had largely been alienated in other parts of the country. A number of these properties remained in royal hands, despite applications to the Augmentation Office by prospective purchasers,[32] and Henry's officials had agreed to the additional purchase of Redesdale from the Tailboys family (by exchange with lands in Warwickshire), and Hexhamshire (exchanged for Yorkshire lands with the archbishop of York, who had held the estate since the 7th century). All these lands remained in crown hands until the end of the Borders.

A final map in this series is Figure 15. Here we see the result of the Rising of the Earls in 1569, the disgrace of the Percies and the Nevilles, and the failure of the main line of the Dacres. All this happened in the 1570s, and there were untainted heirs to all the lands in question, but Elizabeth's officers chose to ignore their rights, and retained those parts of the lands which bordered the existing crown estates, the barony of Gilsland (claimed by Lord William Howard by right of his wife), Langley

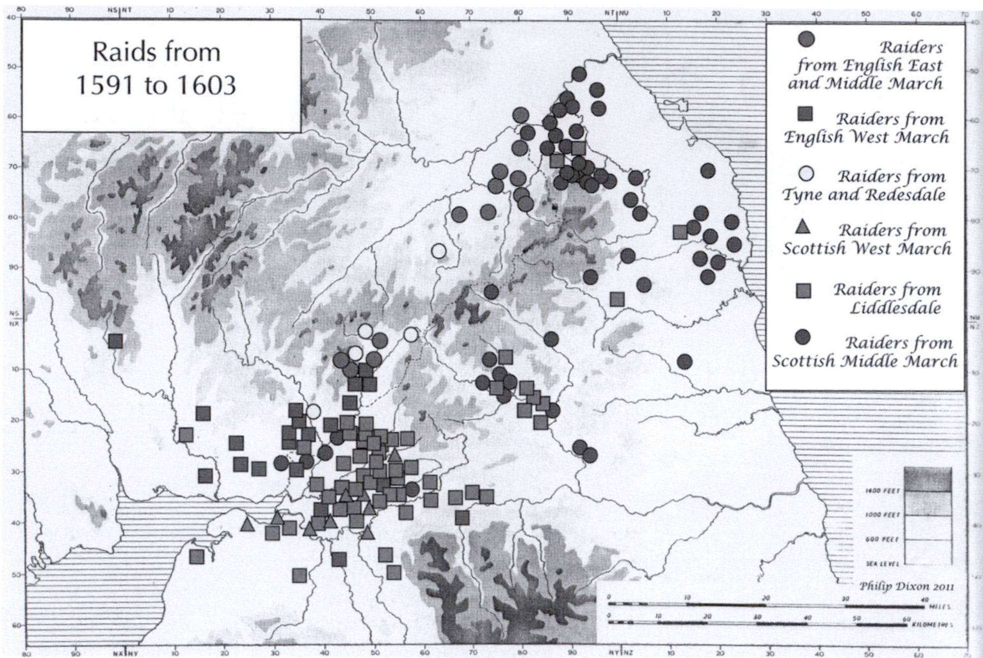

FIG. 12. The location of the recorded raids from 1591 to 1603

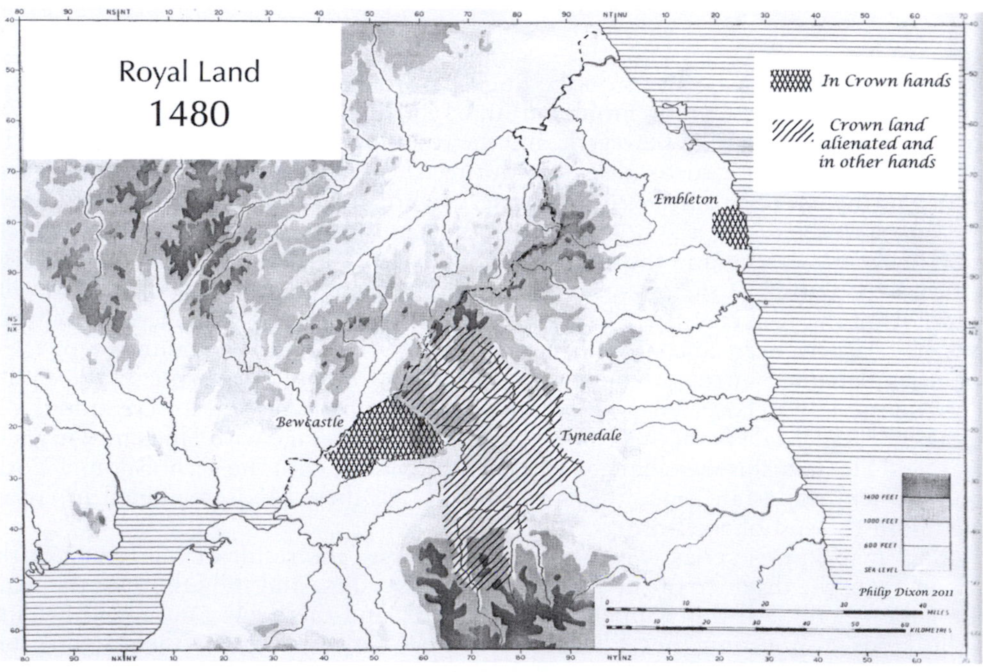

FIG. 13. The royal estates in the region at the beginning of the Tudor period

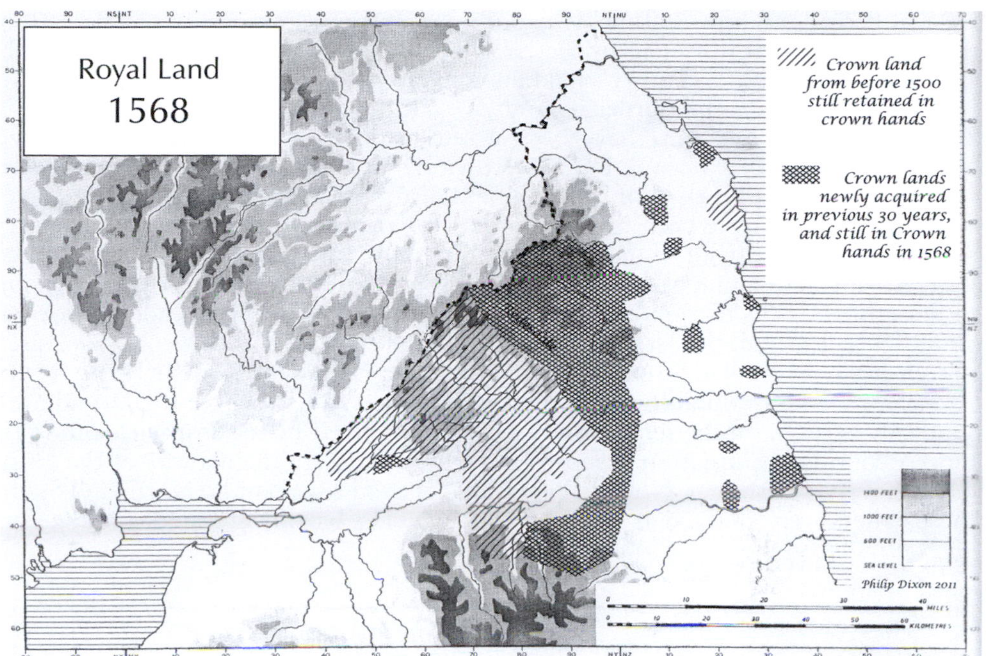

FIG. 14. The royal estates in the region before the Rising of the Earls

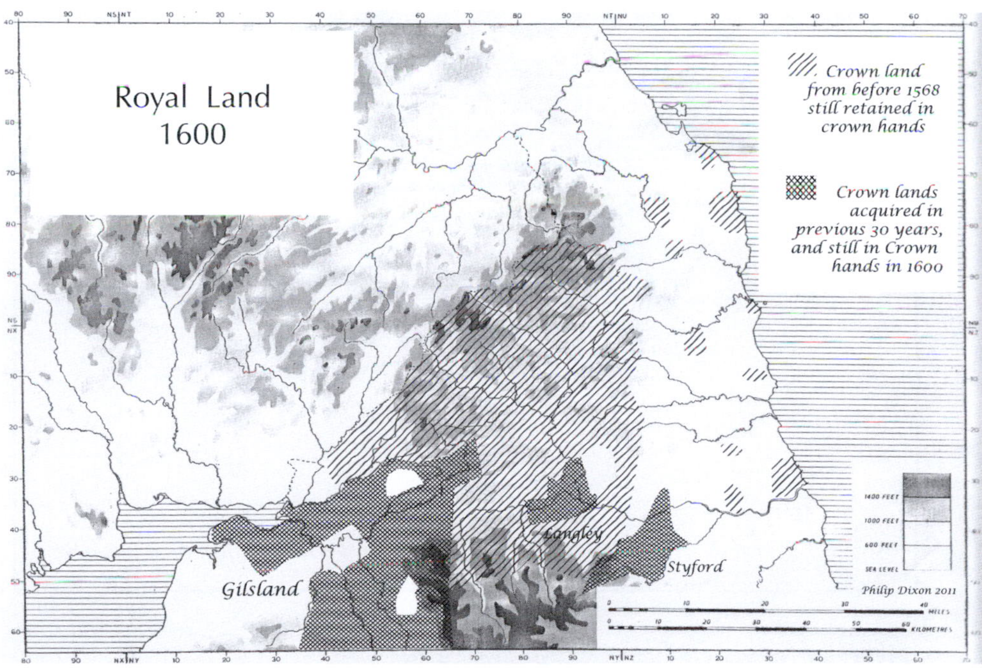

FIG. 15. The Royal estates in the region at the end of the Tudor period

(ancestral Percy land now retained when other estates were returned) and the barony of Styford and Bywell (forfeited by the Neville, 6th earl of Westmorland on his rebellion). Thus the result of a century's land market had been the acquisition by the crown of almost the whole of the Border uplands.

The reason for what must have been a settled policy is nowhere stated. It was probably to ensure that no one but the crown had the authority over the turbulent uplands, to prevent a renewal of rebellion and disturbance by the feudal overlords. It cannot, at any rate, have been to make profits for the crown from the new tenantry. Figure 16, based on early 17th-century rentals,[33] shows the farms on four large Dacre manors in Northern Cumberland. Each spot in the chart represents a single farm, and the scales allow a calculation of the rental per acre for each farmstead. The overall median figure is 6s. 2d. per (statute) acre, but as the chart shows this conceals a great variation between similar farms, from a median of 3s. 5d. for Westlinton to 9s. 5d. for adjacent Denton. Notable is the high rental of 13s. 4d. per acre for Drumburgh, though this barony, on the fertile Solway coast, produced better crop yields than the others. A contrasting situation is shown in Figure 17, where the manors of the North and South Tyne are shown. Notable here is that the old royal lands (North and South) in these valleys were charged at about 3d. per acre. The barony of Langley in the same

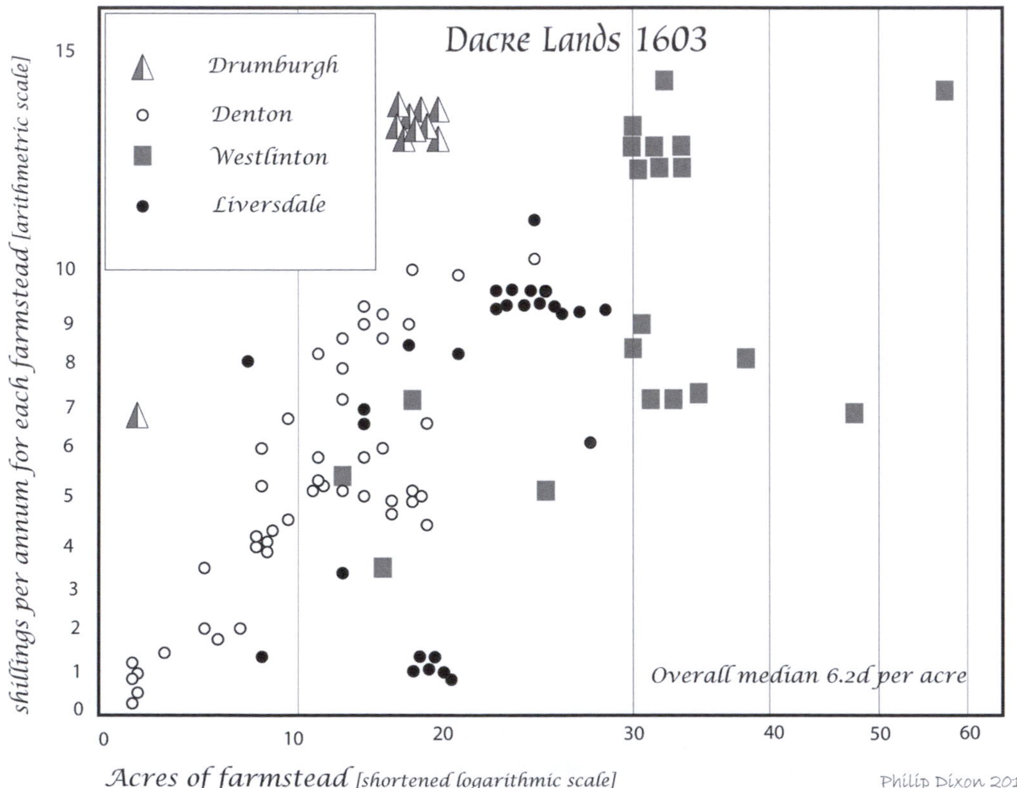

FIG. 16. The rentals for individual farms on the estates of the Dacres in 1603

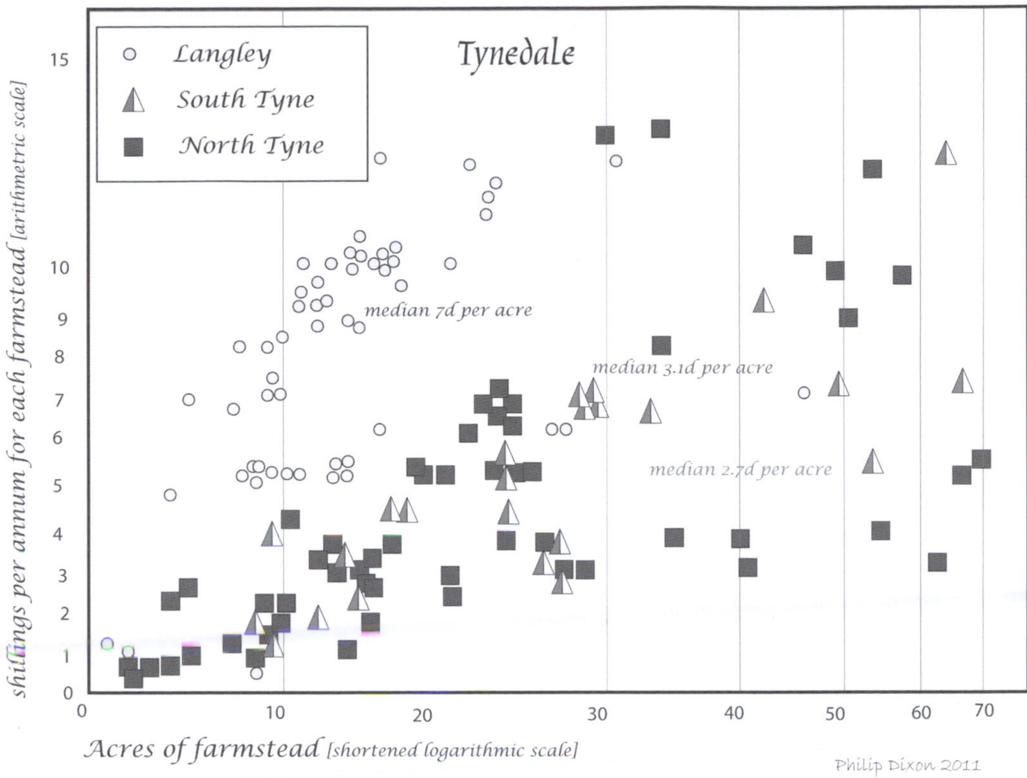

FIG. 17. The rentals for individual farms on some estates of the crown and the Percies in 1604

valleys, on the other hand, had by 1608 been in royal hands for no more than thirty years, and the median value of the farms was twice that of the adjacent royal manors. A final chart, Figure 18, emphasizes this point. It shows the royal manor of Bewcastledale, in crown hands since 1480; here more than half the tenants paid no rent at all, and the value of the median rental was no more than half a penny an acre. This is the more striking in that some of the same farms were included in a rental of 1295/6, when the median rental was greatly higher, at 7d. an acre, an even more striking difference when one considers the extreme inflation during these centuries. Profit through rentals was thus clearly not the crown's objective in this land transfer.

The examination of these maps and the charts demonstrates that the central uplands, where the bulk of the pelehouses and stonehouses were built, were suffering considerable disruption through uncontrolled raiding during the last quarter of a century before the Union. To a degree this was ameliorated by the failure of the crown to exact rents at what would be thought reasonable rates at the time. But the advantages of this situation would not be felt until the reivers of the Scottish Marches ceased removing the stock from the upland farms. In consequence I would suggest that the small fortified farms of the area belonged not to the time of raiding, but to the generation after the ending of the Border troubles in the first decade of the 17th century.

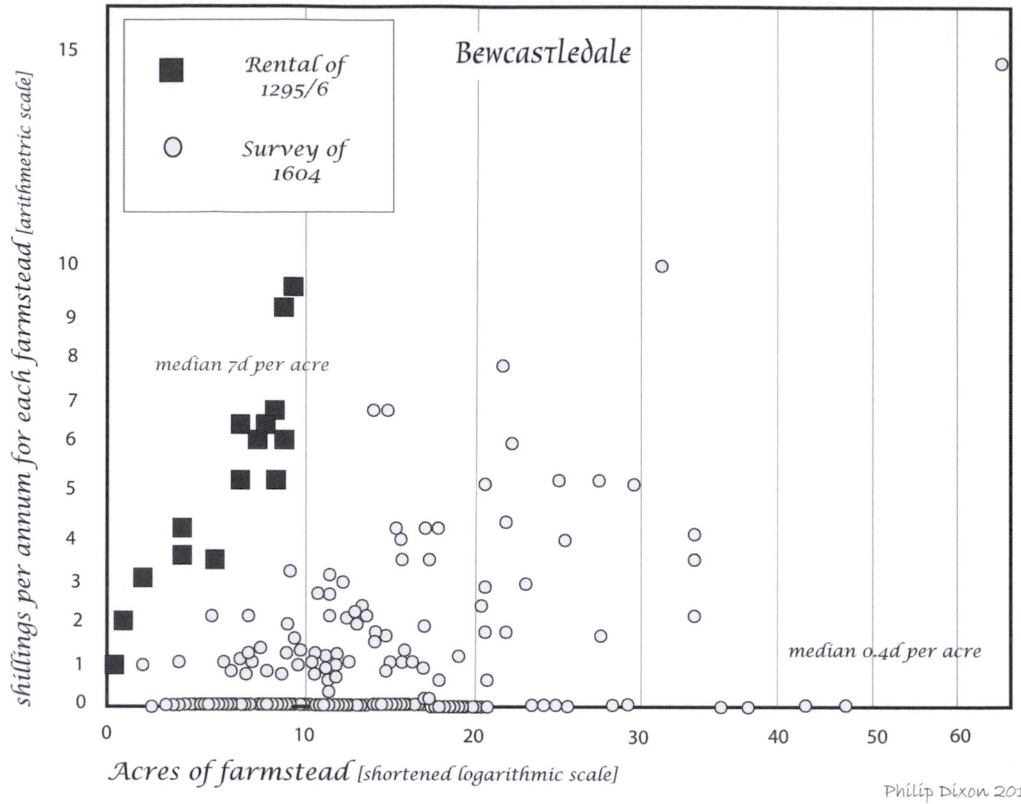

FIG. 18. The rentals for individual farms on the royal manor of Bewcastle in 1295 and 1604

NOTES

1. A. M. Duncan, 'The Battle of Carham, 1018', *Scottish Historical Review*, 55 (1976), 20–28; M. O. Anderson, 'Lothian and the Early Scottish Kings', *Scottish Historical Review*, 30 (1960), 98–112. For discussion of date, see W. Kapelle, *The Norman Conquest of the North: The Region and Its Transformation, 1000–1135* (London 1979), 21, 243 n. 48.

2. Inquisition of Isabel Ford (Inquisition Post Mortem, 39 Henry III, no. 40): see *Calendar of Documents Relating to Scotland Preserved in Her Majesty's Public Record Office, London*, ed. J. Bain et al., 5 vols (London 1881–1987), I, 374–75.

3. G. G. Simpson and B. Webster, 'Charter Evidence and the Distribution of Mottes in Scotland', *Chateau Gaillard*, 5 (1970), 175–92.

4. The term, used regularly by Stewart Cruden in *The Scottish Castle* (Edinburgh 1963), and common subsequently, is not entirely satisfactory since halls of one sort or another form part of all high status buildings.

5. *Anglo-Scottish Relations, 1174–1328: Some Selected Documents*, ed. and trans. E. L. G. Stones (London 1965), xv–viii; E. Miller, *War in the North* (Hull 1960), 5–18.

6. The building of the new gatehouse, the Black Gate, at Newcastle was probably Henry III's response to this threat. (On the Black Gate, see also Steven Brindle's paper in the volume.)

7. For discussion of the houses and the context, see P. W. Dixon, 'From Hall to Tower: The Change in Seigneurial Buildings after c.1250', *Thirteenth Century England IV*, ed. P. Coss and S. D. Lloyd (Woodbridge 1992), 85–109.

8. It was a refuge and political statement by the king's chief opponent, Thomas, earl of Lancaster.

9. R. Nicholson, 'The Siege of Berwick in 1333', *Scottish Historical Review*, 40 (1961), 19; J Sadler, *Border Fury: England and Scotland at War, 1296–1568* (Harlow 2005), especially 173–78.

10. C. J. Bates, *The Border Holds of Northumberland* (Newcastle upon Tyne 1891), 11, suggests that this was crown policy to encourage Border fortification. However this may be, it is part of a more general phenomenon: see C. Coulson, 'Freedom to Crenellate by Licence — An Historiographical Revision', *Nottingham Medieval Studies* 38 (1994), 86–137, and P. Davis, 'English Licences to Crenellate: 1199–1567', *Castle Studies Group Journal*, 20 (2007), 226–45: see also http://www.gatehouse-gazetteer.info/Indexs/Locindex.html.

11. The list (from BL, MS Harley 309) is reproduced in Bates, *Border Holds* (as n. 10), 15–20. The context is discussed by A. King, 'Fortress and Fashion Statements: Gentry Castles in Fourteenth-Century Northumberland', *Journal of Medieval History*, 33 (2007), 372–97.

12. Cruden, *Scottish Castle* (as n. 4), 110–11.

13. *HN*, X, 209 (suggesting *c.* 1390); M. Wood, *The English Mediaeval House* (London 1965), 168.

14. A. L. Raimes and H. L. Honeyman, 'Shortflatt Tower and Its Owners', *AA*, 4th ser. 32 (1954), 152–55.

15. Ibid., 152.

16. Ibid., 130–31.

17. References to individual sites and general discussion can be found in P. W. Dixon, '*Mota, Aula et Turris*: The Manor House of the Anglo-Scottish Border', in *Manorial Domestic Buildings in England and France*, ed. G. Meirion Jones, Society of Antiquaries Occasional Papers 15 (London 1993), 22–48.

18. *HN*, XIV, 408.

19. This building pattern reflects that found in southern England: see, for example, A. Emery, *Dartington Hall, Devonshire* (London 1970).

20. Cruden, *Scottish Castle* (as n. 4), 138; *The Royal Commission on Ancient and Historical Monuments and Constructions of Scotland ... County of Dumfries* (Edinburgh 1920), no. 537; Royal Commission, County of Dumfries (1920), no. 537; An Inventory of the Ancient and Historical Monuments of Roxburghshire (Edinburgh 1956), no. 207.

21. All but one of the thirty-four date-stones which have survived from the Border belong to the period after 1550; all but three after 1567.

22. Cruden, *Scottish Castle* (as n. 4), 144, 150–51.

23. *The Register of the Privy Council of Scotland*, ed. J. H. Burton and D. Masson, 14 vols (Edinburgh 1877–98), III, 78.

24. See H. G. Ramm, R. W. McDowell and E. Mercer, *Shielings and Bastles* (London 1970). For a review discussing these points, see P. W. Dixon, 'Shielings and Bastles: A Reconsideration of Some Problems', *AA*, 4th ser. 50 (1972), 249–58.

25. Bates, *Border Holds* (as n. 10), 49: the strong 'pele' of Ill Will Armstrong was cut down with axes in 1528 (BL, MS Cotton Caligula B VII, fol. 28r). For 'pyramidales turres ex sola terra' termed pailes and glossed 'four nuiked [nooked]', see *The Historie of Scotland, wrytten first in Latin by Jhone Leslie; and translated in Scottish by Father James Dalrymple*, ed. E. G. Cody and W. Murrison, 2 vols (Edinburgh 1888–95), I, 98.

26. For the social gradation of the builders, compare P. W. Dixon, 'Towerhouses, Pelehouses, and Border Society', *Archaeol. J.*, 136 (1979), 239–52.

27. On which, see T. Moss, *Deadlock and Deliverance: The Capture and Rescue of Kinmont Willie Armstrong* (Walton, 2007).

28. Report of 1578 in *Register of the Privy Council* (as n. 23), III, 78.

29. I.e. in 1583: see *Calendar of Letters and Papers Relating to the Affairs of the Borders of England and Scotland*, ed. J. Bain, 2 vols (Edinburgh 1894–96), I, 123.

30. Dixon, 'Towerhouses, Pelehouses' (as n. 26), 249–52.

31. J. F. Curwen, *The Castles and Fortified Towers of Cumberland, Westmorland, and Lancashire North-of-the-Sands* (Kendal 1913), 337.

32. For example, application to purchase Redesdale by Oliver Leader of London: TNA, Augmentations, particulars for grants: E 318, no. 697.

33. One has been published: *Survey of the Debateable and Border Lands Adjoining the Realm of Scotland and Belonging to the Crown of England, taken* A.D. *1604*, ed. R. P. Sanderson (Alnwick 1891). With this, contrast the 1294/5 survey of Bewcastle: TNA, SC 11, no. 154. Dacre lands were surveyed in 1589: see TNA, Exchequer E164/42. The barony of Langley was surveyed in 1608: see TNA, LR2 /224. Redesdale and adjacent lands were resurveyed in 1618: this was transcribed in the middle of the 19th century, but the original is now lost: see R. W. Hodgson and J. Hodgson, 'A Rental of the Ancient Principality of Redesdale, Copied from an Original Roll in the Possession of William John Charleton, of Hesleyside, Esq.', *AA*, 1st ser. 2 (1832), 326–38.

Women Behaving Badly. Warkworth Castle: Protection or Paranoia?

FRANK WOODMAN

Castles are great symbols of both feudal and military power. By the late middle ages, they were also residences, first and foremost. The combination of a military presence, from lowly knights to unwilling peasants, posed particular problems for families with unmarried daughters and often, young, rich widows. From c. *1300, a surprising number of highborn women fell victim to seduction, sometimes even dressed up as abduction. The carefully laid plans of the new, up-and-coming aristocracy of 14th-century England seemed especially vulnerable, and the aristocracy lost both daughters and widows. Did they take steps to 'protect' their womenfolk? It will be argued here that, in the inflexibly planned new castles of the later middle ages, it is sometimes possible to 'spot' the precautions taken by sensible parents.*

WARKWORTH castle is one of the most significant buildings of its type and date in Britain. It is also remarkably well preserved. By the 'castle', we here mean the great 1380s tower-house that so dominates the surrounding landscape, the actual castle having a full set of walls, towers and gates, plus the ruins in the lower bailey of a sprawling residence, all of many periods (Fig. 1 and Col. Pl. XXXII in print edn).[1] The tower-house unashamedly takes the form of an Anglo-Norman keep, even to the point of raising it upon a 'motte'. Built by Henry Percy (1341–1408), newly created earl of Northumberland, it is often cited as one of the first 'trophy houses'; appropriately so for a family whose rise to greatness and power was little short of meteoric. The Percy family was of minor consequence in 1300, but a century later it counted among the greatest in the land. Its rapid rise was a combination of military prowess, political skill, shrewd marriages, and a lot of luck. Typical of their type, the Percys quickly realized the importance of daughters as assets rather than burdens, their accumulation of cash-wealth courtesy of the French war offering tempting marriage settlements to the older land-rich but often cash-strapped established aristocracy.[2]

'HEIRESS HUNTING'

THE period around 1300 saw two important developments in the situation of 'women in society', at least those of noble and royal blood. The system of jointure, which gradually replaced the more traditional marriage dowry, benefited women as widows but would soon turn against men in a way quite unexpected and unwelcome. The dowry had proved unsatisfactory for generations. Land and other property passed from the bride's father to son-in-law transferred legal ownership between the two men, the bride acting merely as conduit. On widowhood, it was up to the bride's family, or sometimes the widow, to regain the original dowry, to be passed on to a

BAA Trans., vol. XXXVI (2013), 266–278

FIG. 1. Warkworth castle: tower keep

second or further marriage. Because of this, widows were given legal status for the only time in their lives, enabling them if necessary to pursue claims in court and other legal action to protect the interests of a possible son and heir if still under age. A widow's legal status was instantly surrendered upon remarriage. Where the dowry process invariably failed was the loss of the dower lands or property during the original marriage, sometimes stolen, confiscated or even gambled away.[3]

The jointure was intended to simplify the marriage settlement and to provide a speedier route for a widow's remarriage, making her far more attractive (financially at least) to a potential suitor. A jointure placed much, if not all, the land, property and cash from both sides in a marriage 'pot', to be 'enjoyed' by whichever party survived. As many aristocratic and royal women were married off at the age of twelve to husbands commonly much older (on the last marriage of Jean, duc de Berri, the heiress bride was twelve, he was about seventy-two!), it was envisaged that the young bride would be widowed soon, and was thus able to carry the whole of the combined estate to a further marriage under the terms agreed in the jointure (which could vary). Sons and heirs, even of legal age, might have to wait until their mother's death to inherit more than just a title, as happened to Aymer de Valance, earl of Pembroke, whose mother lived in widowhood for decades.[4] Quite suddenly, the early 14th century saw an outbreak of both rich widows and of 'heiress hunting'.

It is the intention of this paper to propose that the security of women, both as under-age or 'of age' daughters and young widows with jointures, became an urgent issue in the greater households of England, even to the extent that many newly built castle-residences of the period show potential evidence of physical segregation of sexes to the point of virtual imprisonment. Warkworth castle, it will be argued, presents one of the best surviving examples of the period not just for its state of preservation but also the 'reading' of the domestic quarters that is plain to see.

Some examples of the problem need to be mentioned, if only in brief. We may begin with Joan of Acre (1272–1307).[5] Daughter and one of the nineteen children of Edward I, Joan dutifully married Gilbert of Clare, earl of Gloucester, providing him with an heir and three daughters. That the marriage had a jointure cannot be doubted, given what happened immediately upon Gilbert's death in 1295. Joan ran off. She eloped with a lowly knight (they would always be 'lowly' knights), one Ralph de Monthermer, a widower. The marriage was quickly consummated and thus put beyond the reach of annulment, both parties being free and of age. The king fumed, but to no avail. He had a new son-in-law whether he wanted it or not (and he clearly did not!). Ralph did not help matters by parading in Westminster arrayed as the earl of Gloucester by right of his wife, the Gloucester heir being as yet under age.

Joan's actions should have been a warning shot for all the great families of England, but worse was to come, and from the same source, in the activities of Elizabeth of Clare (1295–1360).[6] Elizabeth, Joan's second daughter by Gloucester, formed part of a classic 'brother-sister' swap between Gloucester and the children of the earl of Ulster, John de Burgh. Elizabeth duly gave her husband an heir, though soon after, de Burgh died, leaving Elizabeth a young widow of substantial means. She ran off. Another 'lowly knight', Theobald of Verdun, justiciar of Ireland, carried away his prize, consummated the marriage and awaited the storm. It came quickly. King Edward II, Elizabeth's cousin, demanded her return, but bride and groom stood firm. Elizabeth became pregnant and the union was thus put beyond dissolution. She would give Theobald several children. Worse still, at least for the king, the Gloucester heir died childless and the entire Gloucester estate, the largest in England, had to be divided equally between the three sisters. Theobald had hit the jackpot. But then he died, leaving Elizabeth the richest woman of her day. The king had to act, and he did, kidnapping and imprisoning her until she agreed to his terms for a remarriage. Elizabeth had been victim of both seduction and abduction. But England was fast descending into chaos and, for both the king and the warring queen, Elizabeth's wealth was sorely needed for their battle chests. The widow was repeatedly 'rescued' by either side, only to be kidnapped again until finally she agreed to marry the king's candidate, Roger Damory. Elizabeth's story and her attempts at personal freedom could be duplicated several times, but space will not allow. Two at the highest royal level are, however, noteworthy for the background to Warkworth.

Such bids for female independence reached to the very top in the reign of Edward III. His cousin Joan, countess of Kent (1328–85), was unwisely kept unmarried, though of age.[7] The king undoubtedly hoped to use her Anglo-French royal lineage and vast inherited wealth to seal an advantageous overseas marriage alliance and thus advance the English war effort. Unfortunately for the king, Joan spotted Thomas Holland (a lowly knight), and even after eleven years of efforts to keep them apart Edward was forced to accept their union and Holland became earl of Kent.

A further affair that impacted upon the court at the time of the building of Warkworth involved Elizabeth Plantagenet (1364–1426), a daughter of John of Gaunt.[8] Gaunt arranged spectacular overseas royal marriages for most of his daughters, all in the hope of gaining a crown. With Portugal it worked. His daughter Elizabeth seems to have been kept in reserve until 1380, by which time she was sixteen or seventeen. Curiously, Gaunt finally gave her in marriage to John Hastings, 3rd earl of Pembroke. The oddest thing was that he was only eight. The marriage would never be consummated and was annulled in 1386. However, on the eve of Gaunt's departure for a campaign in Iberia, his last and now available daughter appeared before her father, very pregnant, and pointed to the child's father —John Holland, duke of Exeter, younger son of the earl of Kent mentioned above. Holland had a fearsome reputation for violence, and, though Gaunt disliked him, his prowess was mightily useful on the battlefield. However, the drastic family situation, revealed in full view of Gaunt's entourage, needed immediate action. A shotgun wedding took place on the spot. The child could not be born a bastard. Gaunt's fury can only be imagined.

THE PERCY FAMILY AND WARKWORTH CASTLE

HOW did the 'recently arrived' aristocratic families react and indeed deal with this potential torpedoing of their carefully laid marital planning? Much depended on compliant daughters and young widows marrying as they were told to and when. 'Behaving badly' could wreck not only the script but, worse still, a reputation won at great effort and usually expense.

Fortunately, the domestic arrangements of the Warkworth tower-house are remarkably intact and relatively easy to read (Fig. 2). Interpretation here is the key. Warkworth is a classic example of the period in that it is strictly geometrical and furthermore comes under the category of 'inflexibly planned'.[9] Once built, the rigid room arrangement, fitted in many layers like a Chinese box, is almost impossible to alter, offering no scope for the odd extension or even significant internal change.

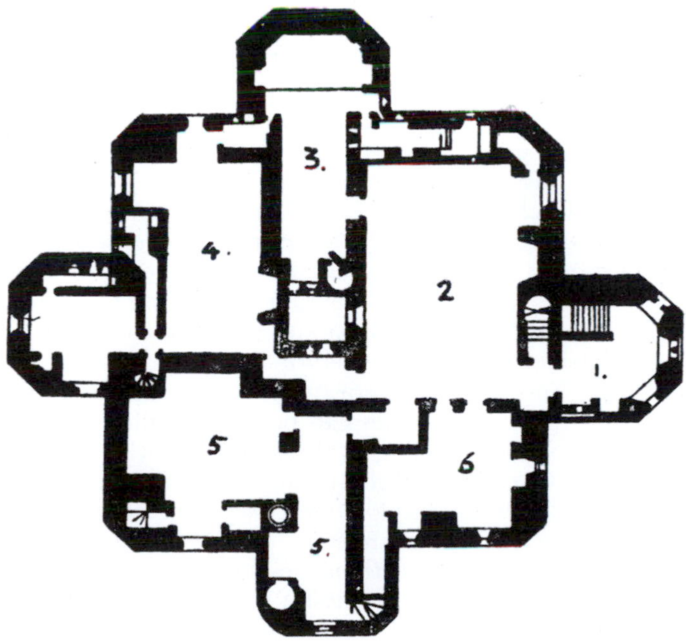

FIG. 2. Plan of Warkworth castle, first floor (after J. A. Gotch, *The Growth of the English House* (London 1909))

The 'living' accommodation is on the two upper floors, the semi-basement serving as storage space. The first thing that strikes the visitor is the grand internal stair, fitted neatly within one of the mid-point towers (Fig. 2, no. 1). This is a well-lit proper stair, making a strong statement about rising up to the lord's domain. Once on the main level, everything is remarkably small, not to say tight. The hall, chapel and great chamber (Fig. 2, nos 2, 3, 4) make it clear that few people accompanied the Percy clan into this inner sanctum. It has the feeling of an exclusive hideaway, distant from the hustle and bustle of the great house below. The hall would seat relatively few diners, less still as the original heating seems to have been by a central open fire. The access door from the 'high table' end to the chapel (Fig. 2, nos 3, 4) makes it clear that Percy and his entourage could depart or arrive to and from the chapel at the same floor level, and that Percy and the important 'high table' men of the family entered the chapel close to the altar. This is emphasized by another door virtually from the altar-space into the great chamber, the rest of the retinue presumably using the more public route.

Using the general rule that rooms with fireplaces and 'en-suite' latrines were living areas, Percy had the usual suite: great chamber, parlour and privy chamber. The north projecting mid-tower has anterooms at this level and another above, presumably for attendant members of the household. One feature of Warkworth is the setting of access doors to the upper levels within the reveals of the through doors, such that when a through door is opened it conceals a further turret door until someone enters the room and closes the through door. Only then can anyone access the second door and proceed upwards (Fig. 3). Furthermore, the upper levels of the private apartments are entered only via Percy's great chamber (Fig. 2, no. 4). Once above, a different through door leads out onto the chapel 'loft'.

This is perhaps the most tantalizing space in the whole castle. The 'loft' floor extended almost to the altar area of the chapel below, leaving only the apse with its tall windows rising from floor to ceiling (Fig. 4). The extent of the 'loft' floor may easily be gauged from the surviving corbels that carried it and from the setting of the upper-level fireplace and other access doors, including one leading through a rather torturous wall passage to a distant latrine (Fig. 5). One common view is that it was here that the Percy family attended mass, another, that it was for the 'private devotion' of Percy himself. Both ideas raise several questions.[10]

Why does the chapel at main-floor level have a direct access to the high table end of the hall? Why is there a 'private' access route from the altar area into Percy's great chamber? Was it possible for the family to 'attend' mass in any meaningful way suspended high above the altar with only a view of the celebrant's pate, and then only if they hung out over a railing? And, finally, why does a space for attending mass require a fireplace and an en suite latrine? If the 'loft' was for Percy's private use as an oratory, he already had his private 'en suite' next door, much nearer than the distant 'loft' latrine. Furthermore, where private oratories can be proved, they tend to have direct visual access with the altar whilst kneeling to assist the power of prayer. Such oratories occur in St Benet's and Christ's College in Cambridge and in Denny abbey. The Warkworth 'oratory' would have no visual contact with the altar unless praying was conducted in a highly unconventional manner.

The intimate scale of the tower-house at Warkworth suggests that only a limited number of the household could have used it, larger domestic operations being well catered for in the main house below. A great regional lord would surely take, or give

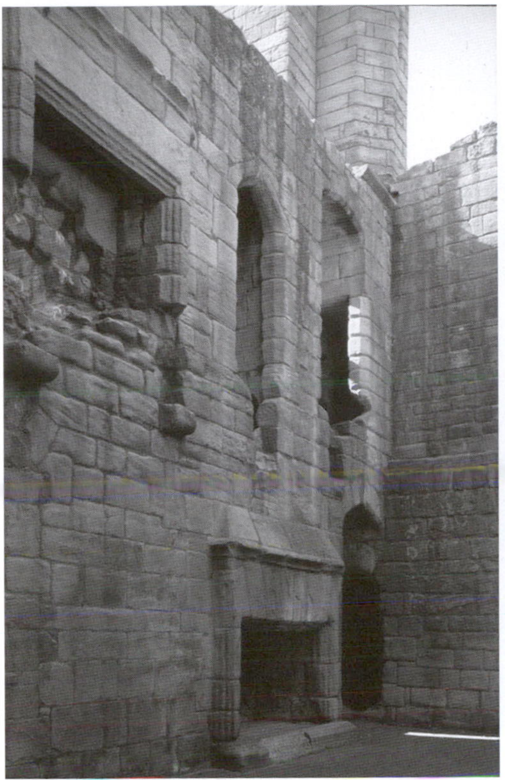

FIG. 3. Warkworth castle: the Great chamber

FIG. 4. Warkworth castle: the chapel, looking east

himself, a vital and visible role in the mass and other religious events, not withdraw to some lofty aerie. What would make more sense of the whole arrangement of private rooms including the 'loft' is that it was all conceived (by men) for the 'protection and security' of women. In this period, women were not expected to 'attend' mass in the same way as men. Indeed, in contemporary illustrations they are often depicted sitting on the floor, sometimes even with their backs to the altar, reciting the rosary or reading 'approved' texts from, for example, a book of hours. Lydgate produced such a book for Alice, duchess of Suffolk, to enable her to follow mass whilst reading from her hours.[11] Thus women 'heard' mass, a phrase still commonly used in Catholic communities. If they could do this without quitting their own private and secure quarters, so much the better. They had no view of the men below and equally, the men could not see them (Fig. 6).

Castle residences must have presented real headaches for anxious parents with unmarried daughters, granddaughters or young widows. At any one time there would be the lord's household retainers, knights (some of them undoubtedly 'lowly') on castle guard and their servants, plus common soldiers and other hangers on. It was in such settings that Joan, countess of Kent, and Elizabeth Plantagenet fell victim to seduction. Of course, it could also provide a perfect setting for the manipulation of

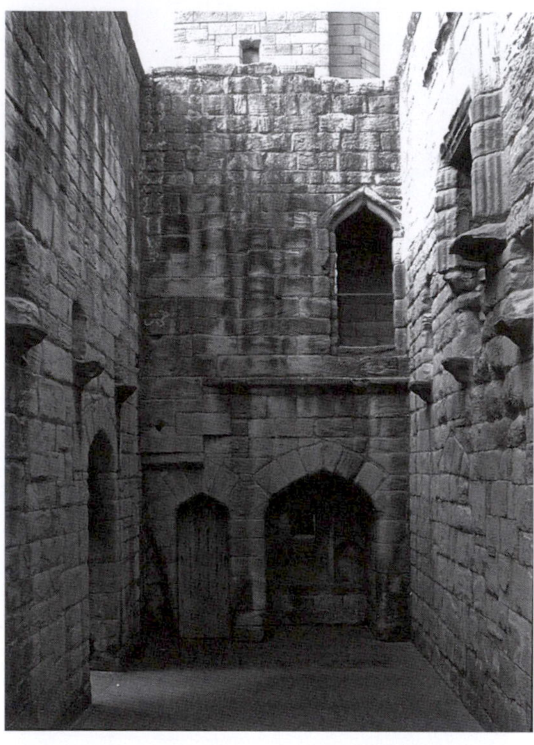

FIG. 5. Warkworth castle: the chapel, looking west, showing the 'loft' floor corbels

couples by well- (or not so well-)meaning parents. The Suffolks took the opportunity of compromising the position of the seven-year-old heiress Margaret Beaufort left in their care with their own six-year-old son John de la Pole. It took the king, lawyers, emissaries, the pope and a lot of money to sort the situation out.[12] On the other hand, the enclosed nature of the private apartments of Windsor castle allowed Margaret Beaufort's grandparents to throw their daughter Jane into the path of the young, unmarried James I of Scotland. They duly fell in love and married. By such manipulation, the Beauforts, born illegitimate, would see one of their next generation become queen of Scotland and so begin the long line of Anglo-Scottish Stuart monarchs.

Of course, such proposed segregated architectural arrangements for women to 'hear' mass would not be possible for less exalted parents who were forced to accompany their daughters and other female members of the family, often it seems divided by sex within the nave. Instructions for the behaviour of girls at mass are not unknown, such as that from John Barbour (d. 1395) to his daughter:

> And in the kirk kepe our all thing
> Fra smirking, keking [cackling], and bakluking.[13]

Mass was often the only opportunity for the young (and not so young) of the parish to flirt (hence no 'back looking'). Fatherly concern for such flirtatious behaviour at mass extends well into modern times — in Verdi's *Rigoletto*, the jester's daughter Gilda falls into disgrace and tragic death due to her catching the eye of her young 'student' at mass, the only time she is allowed out of the house; and in Wagner's

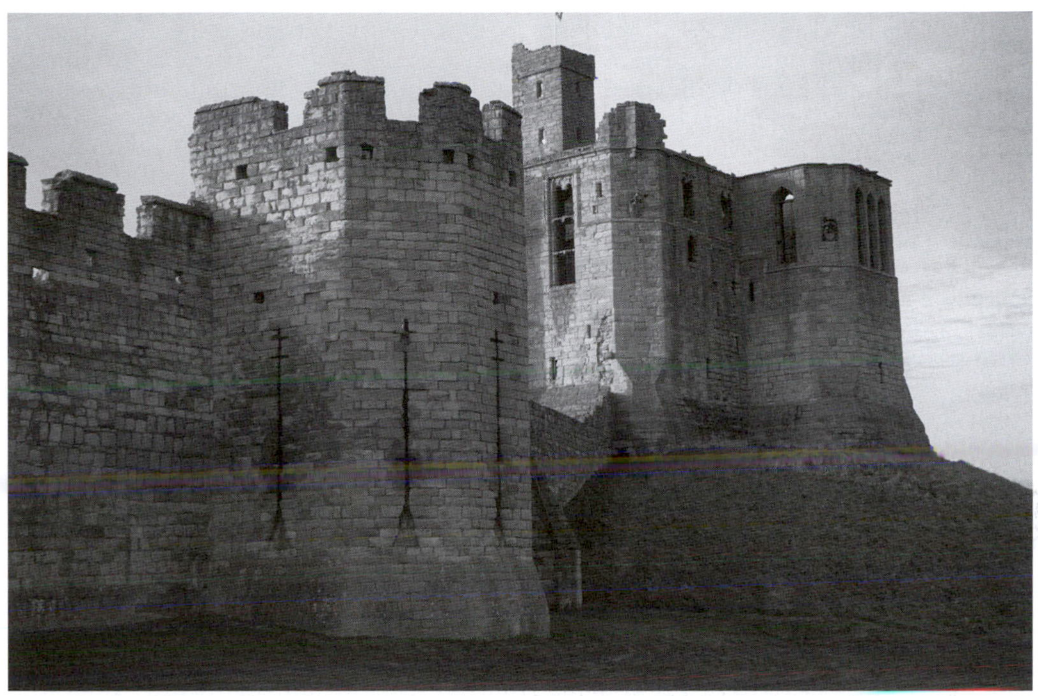

FIG. 6. Warkworth castle: tower keep from the south-east, with chapel windows at far right

contemporary *Meistersinger von Nürnberg* (set, like *Rigoletto*, in the 16th century) Pogner's daughter Eva captures the heart of the knight Walter by eye contact across the nave during mass.

Men also faced the anxiety of the restrictions upon 'lying with their wives' imposed by the Church. While marital love was both rare and considered ill advised, men slept with their wives as much to ensure the legitimacy of their children as for the security of knowing where their spouses were. Warfare, affairs of state and simply estate management would force the separation of couples for long periods, sometimes years, but there were also periods of abstinence required by the Church. Intercourse with one's spouse was prohibited during menstruation, pregnancy or nursing. As childbirth was the whole point of medieval marriage, those activities alone could occupy much of a young wife's time. Sex was also to be avoided on feast days, fast days, Sundays, Wednesdays, Fridays and Saturdays and any other times during daylight. Marital relations were also to be avoided during Lent, Advent, Whitsun week and Easter week, and at any time if naked.[14]

These draconian rules applied to married couples. The trouble for husbands was that it was difficult to apply them to unmarried people such as their offspring and to their wives and other men. Of course, the opposite — sex between married men and other women, married or otherwise — was taken for granted, but husbands had the additional anxiety of keeping other men off their wives. The legends of Tristan and Isolde and Arthur and Guinevere may have been popular, but they also acted as a warning.

At Warkworth, and at the other Percy castles, Henry Percy, the 1st earl, had to consider his aunt Margaret Percy, who had married William Ferrers, 3rd Baron Ferrers of Groby, after the death of her first husband, Sir Robert d'Umfraville, son and heir apparent of Gilbert, earl of Angus. She had brought with her a considerable slice of the Umfraville inheritance in her own right, which she kept as the dowager Lady Ferrers after her second husband died in 1370. Only when she died in 1375 did Henry Percy lay hands on this great inheritance.[15] Percy also had the care of three granddaughters: Elizabeth, daughter of Hotspur, and Elizabeth and Margaret, daughters of Sir Thomas. His own first wife, Margaret Neville, lived until 1372, but, following that, Percy's greatest concern was probably his new, young second wife Matilda (d. 1398), the immensely rich heiress of Gilbert de Umfraville, earl of Angus, who was also heiress to all the lands of Lucy.

Does this proposed segregation occur elsewhere in the period? Castle Bolton, similar in date (and other ways) to Warkworth, is another inflexibly planned structure, allowing little or no subsequent development. The main quarters occupy the first floor of the quadrangle structure, the hall and services to the north, and the double-height chapel opposite.[16] Lord Scrope's chambers and private rooms lead off from the high table end, and eventually out into the chapel at the main-floor level. Above his set, there is a second near identically planned set of rooms, entered only from within the lord's apartments beneath, with its own chapel access. Here, however, by dint of the double-story chapel, the last and therefore most private upper-floor room led onto a raised gallery, the extent of which may no longer be determined. It would certainly have 'protected' any womenfolk above from the gaze of anyone below. Bolton is especially interesting as, unlike Warkworth, it was the main family residence. Easter duty, the need for all to receive the Sacrament over the Easter period, would therefore be a consideration. What evidence survives from the outer wall and sacristy strongly suggests the former presence of a stair from the altar area up to the raised loft, thus enabling the priest to take communion up to this level and return via the sacristy to complete the mass. Significantly, a similar provision for a 'communion' stair was built into the rooms designed for Lady Margaret Beaufort at Christ's College in Cambridge. Margaret, a serial communicant, was unable to enter the chapel as it was against her own college rules and would in any case be considered inappropriate (Fig. 7).[17] Similar upper, secure women's lodgings might be argued within the ruined domestic range of Bodiam castle, another inflexibly planned building, as well as in domestic arrangements in houses of less exalted families such as West Bromwich manor house (Staffordshire).[18]

There is, of course, an alternative to the interpretation of such quarters as the result of male paranoia. There is evidence to suggest that women themselves favoured such segregated protection and, when given a choice, chose similar living conditions for themselves. In the mid-14th century, Marie St Pol, the hugely rich and childless widow of the earl of Pembroke, fought a long battle with Edward III to remain unmarried but stay in society.[19] Eventually, having won the support of the pope, she spent her remaining (long) life travelling around and doing good deeds. The one residence we know she designed for herself that can still be clearly read is at Denny (Cambridgeshire) where she attached a Poor Clare convent to the crossing and nave of a former religious house. Her private rooms occupy the upper level of the crossing, including the space beneath the former central tower. Here she contrived a room with a 'viewing opening' enabling her to look down to the ground-floor level of the nuns' choir. Hence

FIG. 7. Chamber built for Lady Margaret Beaufort, giving access to the chapel altar of Christ's College Cambridge

she could 'hear' mass without entering either the church or necessarily being observed. Of course, other than the celebrating priest, the only others present were women, but the parallel with Warkworth is obvious. A similar arrangement seems to have existed in the 14th-century Poor Clare house at Santa Maria Donna Regina in Naples, founded by the dowager queen Mary of Hungary. She lived from time to time within the convent, but not as a nun, her rooms apparently running alongside the south wall of the church. A number of internal 'window' openings survive in that wall that would have allowed a view of the mass, but sadly the adjoining room arrangement is lost. The nuns themselves were allocated space in a loft over the nave, as apparently the public were admitted at main-floor level for mass. The nuns could only 'hear' mass from their stalls, the altar being only visible if they stood against the railing and leaned over, which was probably not encouraged (Fig. 8).[20]

These arrangements speak of appropriateness and decorum. They may also reflect the fear of abduction, particularly in the case of Marie St Pol. The 1320s saw unrest and revolt in England, leading to the murder of Edward II. Lawlessness was rife, and unmarried or young rich widows had every reason to fear for their security. We have already mentioned Elizabeth of Clare, who was repeatedly kidnapped by warring factions. Her sister, Eleanor, co-heiress of Clare and rich widow of the executed Hugh Despenser, earl of Gloucester, enjoyed her freedom and money only briefly before being abducted and imprisoned in 1326, freed but abducted again the following year

FIG. 8. Elevated chamber in the church of Sta Maria in Donna Regina, Naples

by William de la Zouche, and threatened with death unless she married her captor. (She did.)[21]

The 15th century saw one of the most sensational examples of a woman taking her future in her own hands. Catherine de Valois, widowed queen of Henry V, made off with Owen Tudor, much to the fury of both the English and French courts and to the general hilarity of almost everyone else. Their union could not be undone. Lady Margaret Beaufort, widowed in her teens with a vast fortune and a son and potential heir to the throne, was very vulnerable to Yorkist abduction (not to mention murder). She had to be (twice) gathered safely into the remaining kin, and spent long periods locked up in various castles for her own protection.[22] While her accommodation in Cambridge, designed when she was in her sixties, was a matter more of appropriateness than any residual fear of abduction (let alone seduction), her female descendants were to have an unfortunate record, at least in the latter department. Her eldest granddaughter Margaret, widowed queen of James IV of Scotland, carried on so unashamedly and publically with a succession of lovers that the pope eventually had to intervene.[23] Her younger sister Mary (Rose), having reluctantly married Louis XII of France, ran off with the very man her brother Henry VIII trusted to bring her back. Henry lost a great 'trophy bride' while Charles Brandon gained a queen. (Brandon was not only 'lowly', but also not even from a knightly class.)[24] Their daughter

Frances, having seen her husband and daughter (lady Jane Grey) executed, had an affair with her stable boy and went on to make him duke of Suffolk. She was in her forties, he was twenty-five.[25] The last of the Beaufort females to take matters into her hands in this way — Mary Stuart — came, to say the least, to a bad end.

Of course, by the mid-16th century the position of women at the top of society had changed fundamentally. Queens ruled in their own right. Daughters and sisters acted as regents. While Mary Stuart may have let the side down, others were a considerable success. Interestingly enough, one of the 'inflexibly planned' buildings from the late 14th century cited above, Bolton castle, provided a perfect and ready-made set of secure rooms into which Elizabeth I could safely lock her cousin away.

NOTES

1. Warkworth castle has not received as much attention as it surely deserves. The new edition of the official guide is J. Goodall, *Warkworth Castle* (London 2006). See also A. Emery, *Greater Medieval Houses of England and Wales*, 3 vols (Cambridge 2000–06), I, 144–51. The complex geometry has been exposed in L. Milner, 'Warkworth Keep, Northumberland: A Reassessment of its Plan and Date', in *Medieval Architecture and Its Intellectual Context: Studies in Honour of Peter Kidson*, ed. E. C. Fernie and P. Crossley (London 1990), 219–28.

2. M. W. Bean, *The Estates of the Percy Family, 1415–1537* (Oxford 1958), 4, 8–9.

3. The best, most prolific and reliable source of medieval marriage arrangements can be found in the work of J. Ward, *Women of the English Nobility and Gentry, 1066–1500* (Manchester 1996). See also eadem, *Women in England in the Middle Ages* (London 2006) and eadem, *Women in Medieval Europe, 1200–1500* (London 2002).

4. On Valence, see J. R. S. Phillips, *Aymer de Valence, Earl of Pembroke 1307–1324* (Oxford, 1972); idem, 'Valence, Aymer de, Eleventh Earl of Pembroke (d. 1324)', *ODNB*, LVI, 41–45.

5. J. C. Ward, 'Joan [Joan of Acre], Countess of Hertford and Gloucester (1272–1307)', *ODNB*, XXX, 136.

6. F. A. Underhill, *For Her Good Estate: The Life of Elizabeth de Burgh* (New York 1999).

7. R. Barber, 'Joan, *suo jure* Countess of Kent, and Princess of Wales and of Aquitaine [called the Fair Maid of Kent] (c.1328–1385)', *ODNB*, XXX, 137–39; K. P. Wentersdorf, 'The Clandestine Marriages of the Fair Maid of Kent', *Journal of Medieval History*, 5 (1979), 203–31.

8. A. Weir, *Katherine Swynford: The Story of John of Gaunt and His Scandalous Duchess* (London 2008), 163–200.

9. J. A. Gotch, *The Growth of the English House* (London 1909): see his 'plan of the keep of Warkworth castle', 83.

10. J. Goodhall, *Warkworth Castle and Hermitage* (London 2006), 22.

11. M. Rubin, *Corpus Christi: The Eucharist in Late Medieval Culture* (Cambridge 1992), 158.

12. M. Jones and M. Underwood, *The King's Mother: Lady Margaret Beaufort, Countess of Richmond and Derby* (Cambridge 1992), 35–38.

The most recent research into this matter was downloaded onto the website <www.royalancestry.net> by Douglas Richardson of Salt Lake City, Utah, citing *John Benet's Chronicle for the years 1400 to 1462*, ed. G. L. Harriss, Camden Miscellany 24 (London 1972), 151–233.

[. . .] Under the year, 1452[/53], the chronicle records the divorce of Margaret Beaufort (future mother of King Henry VII of England) and John de la Pole: 'Et post Purificacionem habuerunt clerici convocacionem London in qua concesse sunt regi due decime, et circa idem tempus equitavit rex et cum eo justiciarii cum heyr determiner in Estsexiam et in Suschfolchiam et Norfolchiam. Et fecit rex divorcium fieri inter Johannem filium ducis Suffolchie et filiam et heredum ducis Somersecie pro causa [ ] Et vj die Marcii incepit parliamentum apud Redynge in qua concessum est regi una quintadecima et viginta milia hominum bellatorum cum arcubus.' The editors add the following information in [. . .] footnotes [. . .] [that] the convocation met on 7 February 1453[;] [that] this commission of oyer and terminer for East Anglia was issued on 8 January 1453 [. . .] [that] the divorce of John de la Pole and Margaret Beaufort at about this time has been assumed from evidence on the patent rolls. [. . .] The marriage had taken place between 28 January and 7 February 1450 when, in their attack on the duke of Suffolk, the Commons complained that 'sith the tyme of his areste, he hath doo the seid Margarete to be maried to his said sone.' [. . .] Both were beneath the age of 14 and, since they were within the prohibited degrees, a papal dispensation was obtained in August 1450 [...] [The] *Complete Peerage*, 14 (1998): 602 (*sub* Suffolk) states that the divorce took place before 6 March 1452/3 [...] Actually, it would be more specific to say that the divorce took place between 7 Feb. 1452/3 and 6 March 1452/3 [...]. There is no equivalent mention of Benet's Chronicle in the Richmond account in *The Complete Peerage vol. XIV: Addenda and Corrigenda*, ed. P. W. Hammond (Stroud 1998), 545. Margaret Beaufort's 2nd husband, Edmund Tudor, was Earl of Richmond.

13. Rubin, *Corpus Christi* (as n. 11), 153–54.

14. There are, not surprisingly, many works of reference, amongst the most recent being E. Amt, *Women's Lives In Medieval Europe* (New York, 1993) and S. McSheffrey, *Marriage, Sex, and Civic Culture in Late Medieval London* (University Park, PA 2006).

15. Bean, *Estates of the Percy Family* (as n. 2), 4, 8–9.

16. Emery, *Greater Medieval Houses* (as n. 1), I, 303–12.

17. Jones and Underwood, *King's Mother* (as n. 12), 202–31 (ch. 7).

18. For Bodiam, see Emery, *Greater Medieval Houses*(as n. 1), III, 317–19; and for West Bromwich manor house, ibid., II, 447–49.

19. F. Woodman, 'Pembroke, Countess of [Marie de St Pol]', in *The Dictionary of Art*, ed. J. Turner, 34 vols (London 1998), XXIV, 348; also Phillips, *Aymer de Valence* (as n. 4).

20. For Santa Maria Donna Regina, see S. Casiello, *Santa Maria di Donnaregina a Napoli* (Naples 1975); *The Church of Santa Maria Donna Regina, Art, Iconography, and Patronage in Fourteenth-Century Naples*, ed. J. Elliot and C. Warr (Farnham 2004).

21. Underhill, *For Her Good Estate* (as n. 6), 20. There is a strong suggestion that the sixteen-year-old daughter of the third Clare heiress Margaret Audley was also abducted, possibly with the collusion of her aunt Elizabeth. Information from Brad Verity: see <http://archiver.rootsweb.ancestry.com/th/read/GEN-MEDIEVAL/2003-10/1066250276> [accessed 1 November 2012].

22. Jones and Underwood, *King's Mother* (as n. 12), 35–65 (ch. 2).

23. H. Chapman, *The Sisters of Henry VIII* (Bath 1969), 65–140.

24. Ibid., 176–86.

25. For Frances Brandon, duchess of Suffolk, see E. Ives, *Lady Jane Grey: A Tudor Mystery* (Chichester 2009).

Previous Volumes in the Series

I. *Medieval Art and Architecture at Worcester Cathedral* (1978), ed. G. Popper
II. *Medieval Art and Architecture at Ely Cathedral* (1979), ed. N. Coldstream and P. Draper
III. *Medieval Art and Architecture at Durham Cathedral* (1980), ed. N. Coldstream and P. Draper
IV. *Medieval Art and Architecture at Wells and Glastonbury* (1981), ed. N. Coldstream and P. Draper
V. *Medieval Art and Architecture at Canterbury before 1220* (1982), ed. N. Coldstream and P. Draper
VI. *Medieval Art and Architecture at Winchester Cathedral* (1983), ed. T. A. Heslop and V. Sekules
VII. *Medieval Art and Architecture at Gloucester and Tewkesbury* (1985), ed. T. A. Heslop and V. Sekules
VIII. *Medieval Art and Architecture at Lincoln Cathedral* (1986), ed. T. A. Heslop and V. Sekules
IX. *Medieval Art and Architecture in the East Riding of Yorkshire* (1989), ed. C. Wilson
X. *Medieval Art, Architecture and Archaeology in London* (1990), ed. L. Grant
XI. *Medieval Art and Architecture at Exeter Cathedral* (1991), ed. F. Kelly
XII. *Medieval Art, Architecture and Archaeology at Rouen* (1993), ed. J. Stratford
XIII. *Medieval Art and Architecture at Lichfield* (1993), ed. J. Maddison
XIV. *Medieval Art and Architecture in the Diocese of St Andrews* (1994), ed. J. Higgitt
XV. *Medieval Art, Architecture and Archaeology at Hereford* (1995), ed. D. Whitehead
XVI. *Yorkshire Monasticism: Archaeology, Art and Architecture* (1995), ed. L. R. Hoey
XVII. *Medieval Art and Architecture at Salisbury Cathedral* (1996), ed. L. Keen and T. Cocke
XVIII. *Utrecht, Britain and the Continent: Archaeology, Art and Architecture* (1996), ed. E. de Bièvre
XIX. *'Almost the Richest City': Bristol in the Middle Ages* (1997), ed. L. Keen
XX. *Medieval Art, Architecture, Archaeology and Economy at Bury St Edmunds* (1998), ed. A. Gransden
XXI. *Southwell and Nottinghamshire: Medieval Art, Architecture, and Industry* (1998), ed. J. S. Alexander
XXII. *Medieval Archaeology, Art and Architecture at Chester* (2000), ed. A. Thacker
XXIII. *Medieval Art and Architecture in the Diocese of Glasgow* (1999), ed. R. Fawcett
XXIV. *Alban and St Albans: Roman and Medieval Architecture, Art and Archaeology* (2001), ed. M. Henig and P. Lindley
XXV. *Windsor: Medieval Archaeology, Art and Architecture of the Thames Valley* (2002), ed. L. Keen and E. Scarff
XXVI. *Anjou: Medieval Art, Architecture and Archaeology* (2003), ed. J. McNeill and D. Prigent
XXVII. *Carlisle and Cumbria: Roman and Medieval Architecture, Art and Archaeology* (2004), ed. M. McCarthy and D. Weston
XXVIII. *Medieval Art, Architecture and Archaeology at Rochester* (2006), ed. T. Ayers and T. Tatton-Brown
XXIX. *Cardiff: Architecture and Archaeology in the Medieval Diocese of Llandaff* (2006), ed. John R. Kenyon and Diane M. Williams
XXX. *Mainz and the Middle Rhine Valley: Medieval Art, Architecture and Archaeology* (2007), ed. Ute Engel and Alexandra Gajewski
XXXI. *King's Lynn and the Fens: Medieval Art, Architecture and Archaeology* (2008), ed. John McNeill
XXXII. *Prague and Bohemia: Medieval Art, Architecture and Cultural Exchange in Central Europe* (2009), ed. Zoë Opacic
XXXIII. *Coventry: Medieval Art, Architecture and Archaeology in the City and its Vicinity* (2011), ed. Linda Monckton and Richard K. Morris
XXXIV. *Limerick and South-West Ireland: Medieval Art and Architecture* (2011), ed. Roger Stalley

Copies of these may be obtained from Maney Publishing,
Joseph's Well, Hanover Walk, Leeds LS3 1AB, *UK*
www.maneypublishing.com